TAKING SIDES

Clashing Views on Controversial

Moral Issues

NINTH EDITION

TAKING SIDES

Clashing Views on Controversial

Moral Issues

NINTH EDITION

Selected, Edited, and with Introductions by

Stephen Satris
Clemson University

McGraw-Hill/Dushkin
A Division of The McGraw-Hill Companies

To my father and the memory of my mother.

Photo Acknowledgment
Cover image: © 2004 by PhotoDisc, Inc.

Cover Art Acknowledgment
Charles Vitelli

Manufactured in the United States of America

Ninth Edition

123456789BAHBAH7654

Library of Congress Cataloging-in-Publication Data
Main entry under title:
Taking sides: clashing views on controversial moral issues/selected, edited, and with introductions
by Stephen Satris.—9th ed.
Includes bibliographical references and index.
1. Ethics. 2. Social Ethics. I. Satris, Stephen, *comp.*
170'.22
0-07-284511-2
ISSN: 1094-7604

Preface

This text contains 38 essays, arranged in pro and con pairs, that address 19 controversial issues in morality and moral philosophy. Each of the issues is expressed in terms of a single question in order to draw the lines of debate more clearly.

Some of the questions that are included here have been in the mainstream of moral philosophy for hundreds of years and are central to the discipline. I have not shied away from abstract questions about moral knowledge, relativism, and the relationship between morality and religion. Other questions relate to specific topics of contemporary concern, such as human cloning, abortion, affirmative action, and drug legalization.

The authors of the selections included here take a strong stand on a given issue and provide their own best defenses of a pro or con position. The selections were chosen for their usefulness in defending a position and for their accessibility to students. The authors are philosophers, scientists, and social critics from a wide variety of backgrounds. Each presents us with a determinant answer on an issue—even if we ultimately cannot accept the answer as our own.

Each issue is accompanied by an *introduction,* which sets the stage for the debate, and each issue concludes with a *postscript* that summarizes the debate, considers other views on the issue, and suggests additional readings. The introductions and postscripts do not preempt what is the reader's own task: to achieve a critical and informed view of the issue at stake. I have also provided relevant Internet site addresses (URLs) on the *On the Internet* page that accompanies each part opener. And at the back of the book is a list of all the *contributors to this volume,* which provides information on the philosophers and social commentators whose views are debated here.

Taking Sides: Clashing Views on Controversial Moral Issues is a tool to encourage critical thought on important moral issues. Readers should not feel confined to the views expressed in the selections. Some readers may see important points on both sides of an issue and may construct for themselves a new and creative approach, which may incorporate the best of both sides or provide an entirely new vantage point for understanding.

Changes to this edition This new edition is significantly different from the eighth edition. There are seven completely new issues: *Should Congress Stay the Course on Education for Sexual Abstinence Until Marriage?* (Issue 7); *Should the Government Support Faith-Based Charities?* (Issue 9); *Should There Be Payment for Body Parts?* (Issue 10); *Is It Morally Permissible to Eat Meat?* (Issue 12); *Should the Supreme Court Prohibit Racial Preferences in College Admissions?* (Issue 14); *Are African Americans Owed Reparations for Slavery?* (Issue 15); *Should Hate-Crime Laws Explicitly Protect Sexual Orientation?* (Issue 16). In addition, the issue question for Issue 4, *Does Pornography Violate Women's Rights?* has been modified, and the NO selection has been replaced. In all, there are 15 new readings in this edition.

A word to the instructor   An *Instructor's Manual With Test Questions* (multiple-choice and essay) is available through the publisher for the instructor using *Taking Sides* in the classroom. A general guidebook, *Using Taking Sides in the Classroom,* which discusses methods and techniques for using the pro-con approach in any classroom setting, is also available. An online version of *Using Taking Sides in the Classroom* and a correspondence service for *Taking Sides* adopters can be found at http://www.dushkin.com/usingts/.

Taking Sides: Clashing Views on Controversial Moral Issues is only one title in the Taking Sides series. If you are interested in seeing the table of contents for any of the other titles, please visit the Taking Sides Web site at http://www. dushkin.com/takingsides/.

Acknowledgments   I would like to thank Theodore Knight, list manager for the Taking Sides series at McGraw-Hill/Dushkin, and Juliana Gribbins, developmental editor at McGraw-Hill/Dushkin, for their valuable editorial assistance and sound advice. A special thank-you goes to Pam Draper, librarian at Clemson University, for her cheerful help and cooperation in extensive resource-searching.
    Finally, a unique debt of thanks is owed to those who tolerated my strange hours and the time spent away from them as this book was being prepared and revised: Kim, Angela, and Michelle.

Stephen Satris
Clemson University

Contents In Brief

Contents

American anthropologist Melville J. Herskovits (1895–1963) takes the position that morality has no absolute identity and that it is a social and cultural phenomenon that varies according to the customs and beliefs of different cultural groups. In his view, the great enemy of relativism is ethnocentrism, especially as expressed by European colonialism. Professor of philosophy Louis P. Pojman holds that ethnocentrism is a prejudice like racism or sexism. He agrees that moral beliefs and practices vary greatly across cultures and from one person to another, but he finds very serious problems in the contention that moral principles derive their validity from dependence on society or individual choice.

Philosopher C. Stephen Layman argues that morality makes the most sense from a theistic perspective and that a purely secular perspective is insufficient. The secular perspective, Layman asserts, does not adequately deal with secret violations, and it does not allow for the possibility of fulfillment of people's deepest needs in an afterlife. Philosopher John Arthur counters that morality is logically independent of religion, although there are historical connections. Religion, he believes, is not necessary for moral guidance or moral answers; morality is social.

Author and social scientist Ruth Sidel contends that although feminism has made some progress, it holds the promise of even greater progress in the future toward a more caring society. Author and educator Elizabeth Powers argues that feminism naturally leads to strong governmental enforcement of feminist demands; a devaluing of housework, childrearing, and the family; and a struggle against the biology that links women with childbirth.

Issue 4.   Does Pornography Violate Women's Rights?   72

Philosopher Rae Langton argues that an analysis of the concept of *speech acts* shows that pornography subordinates women and silences their voice. Therefore, pornography destroys political liberty and equality and should not be allowed. Nadine Strossen, president of the American Civil Liberties Union, asserts that pornography itself is a manifestation of free speech, and its presence must be accepted as part of the affirmation of the values of liberty that support all rights, including women's rights.

Issue 5.   Is Abortion Immoral?   102

Professor of philosophy Don Marquis argues that abortion is generally wrong for the same reason that killing an innocent adult human being is generally wrong: it deprives the individual of a future that he or she would otherwise have. Philosopher Jane English (1947–1978) asserts that there is no well-defined line dividing persons from nonpersons. She maintains that both the conservative and the liberal positions are too extreme and that some abortions are morally justifiable and some are not.

Issue 6.   Must Sex Involve Commitment?   122

Philosopher Vincent C. Punzo maintains that the special intimacy of sex requires a serious commitment that is for the most part not required in other human activities. Philosopher Alan H. Goldman argues for a view of sex that is completely separate from any cultural or moral ideology that might be attached to it.

Joe S. McIlhaney, president of the Medical Institute for Sexual Health, argues that the idea of "safe sex" is a dangerous myth that has led to an epidemic of sexually transmitted diseases (STDs) among young people. He states that condoms are not effective on certain common but incurable STDs. James Wagoner, president of Advocates for Youth, maintains that abstinence-only sex education programs are unrealistic and ineffective. Young people, he asserts, must also know about contraception in order to help prevent unwanted pregnancies, STDs, and HIV/AIDS.

Law professor George J. Annas argues that human cloning devalues people by depriving them of their uniqueness and that it would radically alter the idea of what it is to be human. Law professor John A. Robertson maintains that there should not be a complete ban on human cloning but that regulatory policy should be focused on ensuring that it is performed in a responsible manner.

PART 3   LAW AND SOCIETY   167

Ronald J. Sider, president of Evangelicals for Social Action, and Heidi Rolland Unruh, project analyst for Evangelicals for Social Action, argue that the First Amendment, which prohibits the establishment of religion, should not stand in the way of the equal treatment of all religious sects. In particular, religious charities that refrain from proselytizing should be included among those charities that receive government assistance. Melissa Rogers, general counsel at the Baptist Joint Committee on Public Affairs, contends that entanglements between government and religious entities are dangerous and should not be encouraged. Government support of faith-based charities, in her opinion, will bring government oversight and regulation to the religious entity and will open the door to numerous abuses.

Assistant professor Michael B. Gill and professor of surgery Robert M. Sade maintain that healthy people should be allowed to sell one of their kidneys while they are still alive. They contend that it is not intrinsically wrong for a healthy person to sell a kidney, nor does selling body parts have the potential to exploit the poor. Professor of history David J. Rothman counters that payment for organs exploits the poor and benefits the wealthy. He asserts that it is doubtful that the sellers of the organs give their informed consent. Therefore, argues Rothman, body parts are turned into mere commodities, and this is degrading to people.

Political analyst David Boaz argues that in a free country, people have the right to ingest whatever substances they choose without governmental interference. Moreover, as our national experience with Prohibition shows, attempts at restricting substances create more problems than they solve. Professor of history David T. Courtwright maintains that the complete legalization of drugs is morally irresponsible. Moreover, controlled legalization will not work. Easy access to drugs through complete legalization will lead to more drug abuse and more drug addiction, and legally controlled access will result in a new black market.

Environmental thinker Holmes Rolston III maintains that meat eating by humans is a natural part of the ecosystem. He states that it is important that animals do not suffer needlessly, but it would be a mistake to think that animals, like humans, are members of a culture. Rolston concludes that people too readily project human nature on animal nature. Philosopher John Mizzoni counters that eating meat is not a nutritional requirement for humans and that by eating meat we are following a cultural practice—one that causes unnecessary suffering. Mizzoni agrees with Rolston that there is an important distinction between culture and nature but asserts that Rolston misapplies this distinction.

Professor of philosophy Albert G. Mosley argues that affirmative action is a continuation of the history of black progress since the *Brown v. Board of Education* desegregation decision of 1954 and the Civil Rights Act of 1964. He defends affirmative action as a "benign use of race." Professor of philosophy Louis P. Pojman contends that affirmative action violates the moral principle that maintains that each person is to be treated as an individual, not as representative of a group. He stresses that individual merit needs to be appreciated and that respect should be given to each person on an individual basis.

Columnist Deroy Murdock contends that programs of preferential treatment that award special bonus points to applicants of certain racial or ethnic backgrounds are no more than academic racial profiling. These programs assume that certain people need the bonus points. Murdock reasons that this shows that people from certain racial or ethnic groups are thought to be intellectually inferior. Professor of constitutional law and local-government law Jamin B. Raskin states that programs of affirmative action in college admissions do not violate the Constitution. If equality of opportunity is the goal, then there are many steps—not immediately involving the abolition of affirmative action—that could be taken in order to work toward that goal in a meaningful way.

Distinguished Leadership Scholar Ronald Walters states that much of the wealth of America was created with unpaid slave labor, while many of the social problems that plague African Americans today are grounded in the "pauperization" of African Americans as they were systematically deprived of the wealth they helped to create. Paying reparations is paying an unpaid bill, concludes Walters. Jay Parker, president of the Lincoln Institute for Research and Education, argues that African Americans have made great strides in recent years and that to support the idea of reparations is to perpetuate racial division and strife. He maintains that this is not good for African Americans, and it is not good for American society.

Issue 16. Should Hate-Crime Laws Explicitly Protect Sexual Orientation? 298

Elizabeth Birch, executive director of the Human Rights Campaign, reviews data on the prevalence and seriousness of hate crimes, including crimes against gay males and lesbians. She favors a federal law that addresses these matters because the federal government is traditionally responsible for the prosecution of civil rights violations and because the federal government can aid state and local police in law enforcement efforts. Paul M. Weyrich, president of the Free Congress Foundation, argues that the inclusion of sexual orientation as a protected category is part of a gay agenda that seeks the mainstreaming of homosexuality.

Issue 17. Should Handguns Be Banned? 310

Philosopher Nicholas Dixon examines the contrast between gun ownership and murders in foreign countries and gun ownership and murders in the United States. He argues that there is a causal relationship between gun ownership and murder and that a ban on handguns would bring more benefit than harm. Professor of law Daniel D. Polsby asserts that gun control legislation is misguided. He maintains that if there was a ban on handguns, criminals would still arm themselves, but law-abiding citizens would not, resulting in more crime and more innocent victims.

Issue 18. Should the Death Penalty Be Retained? 332

Professor of law Ernest van den Haag argues that the death penalty is entirely in line with the U.S. Constitution and that although studies of its deterrent effect are inconclusive, the death penalty is morally justified and should be retained. Psychologist Mark Costanzo denies that the death penalty has the positive practical effects that retentionists often attribute to it and states that religious and moral arguments go against the death penalty.

Faye Girsh, executive director of the Hemlock Society, maintains that patients have a right to physician-assisted suicide, that physicians themselves should not be regarded as criminals since they are complying with their patients' wishes, and that a public policy of physician-assisted suicide will not have the dire consequences that some opponents anticipate. Attorney Rita L. Marker argues that a policy that would permit physician-assisted suicide is best examined in the real-world context in which it would be implemented. Here, there is cost-consciousness in medical care, which brings about strong constraints on the amount of time physicians can spend with patients and encourages physicians to seek lower-priced alternatives whenever possible. Therefore, the relatively lower monetary cost of physician-assisted suicide makes it a desirable alternative for the wrong reasons.

Introduction

Thinking About Moral Issues

Stephen Satris

Getting Started

If you were asked in your biology class to give the exact number of bones in the average human foot, you could consult your textbook, or you could go to the library and have the librarian track down the answer, or you could search the Internet, or you could ask your friend who always gets *A*'s in biology. Most likely you have not previously had any reason to consider this question, but you do know for certain that it has one right answer, which you will be expected to provide for the final exam.

What do you do, however, when faced with a moral question like one of the ones raised in this text? Whereas it is a relatively straightforward matter to find out how many bones there are in the human foot, in addressing moral issues, understanding cannot be acquired as easily. Someone cannot report back to you on the right answer. You will have to discuss the ideas raised by these moral questions and determine the answers for yourself. And you will have to arrive at an answer through reason and careful thought; you cannot just rely on your *feelings* to answer these questions. Keep in mind, too, that these are questions you will be facing your entire life—understanding will not end with the final exam.

In approaching the issues in this book, you should maintain an open mind toward both sides of the question. Many readers will already have positions on many of the issues raised in this book. But if you are committed to one side of an issue, it will be more difficult for you to see, appreciate, and, most important, learn from the opposing position. Therefore, you first ought to ask yourself what your own assumptions about an issue are and become aware of any preconceived notions you may have. And then, after such reflection, you ought to assume the posture of an impartial judge. If you have a strong prior attachment to one side, that should not prevent you from giving a sympathetic ear to the opposing side.

Once the arguments have been laid out and you have given them careful consideration, you do not want to remain suspended in the middle. *Now* is the time for informed judgment.

A natural dramatic sequence is played out for each of the 19 issues discussed in *Taking Sides: Clashing Views on Controversial Moral Issues*. A question is posed, and you must open yourself to hear each author's arguments, reasons, and examples, which are meant to persuade you to take the author's viewpoint.

But then comes the second part of the drama. Having heard and considered both sides of an issue, what will *you* say? What understanding of the issue can *you* achieve?

You can choose aspects of the "yes" answer and aspects of the "no" answer and weave them together to construct a coherent whole. You can accept one answer and build some qualifications or limitations into it. Or you might be stimulated to think of a completely new angle on the issue.

Be aware of three dangers. The first is a premature judgment or fixed opinion that rules out a fair hearing of the opposing side. The second danger is in many ways like the first, but is somewhat more insidious. It is an unconscious assumption (or set of assumptions) that makes it impossible to hear the other side correctly. (The best antidote for this is to be able to give a fair and accurate account of the issue as it appears to someone on the opposing side.) Finally, the third danger is to lack a judgment after having considered the issue. In this case, two contrary positions simply cannot both be right, and it is up to the reader to make an effort to distinguish what is acceptable from what is unacceptable in the arguments and positions that have been defended.

Fundamental Questions

The 19 issues in this book are divided into three sections, or parts. The first section deals with fundamental questions about morality considered as a whole. It is in this context that it might be said that "morality is a religious matter" or perhaps, that "it's all relative." The issues in the first part do not directly confront specific moral problems; they question the nature of morality itself.

Already in Part 1 we see something that is a recurring feature of moral thought and of this book: moral issues are interrelated. Suppose, for example, that you answer the question, Is morality relative to culture? in the affirmative and also answer the question, Does morality need religion? in the affirmative. How can these two answers fit together? A positive answer to the second question is generally thought to involve a source for morality that is supernatural, beyond the customs and traditions of any one particular social group. But an affirmative answer to the first question suggests that morality is grounded in what is cultural and *not* supernatural. (It may be possible to maintain affirmative answers to both of these questions, but a person who does so owes us an explanation as to how these two ideas fit together.) Many other issues that at first sight might seem distinct have connections between one another.

A further point, and one that applies not only to the issues in Part 1 but to controversial issues in general, is this: In evaluating any position, you should do so on the merits (or lack of merit) of the specific case that is made. Do not accept or reject a position on the basis of what the position (supposedly) tells you about the author, and do not criticize or defend a position by reducing it to simplistic slogans. The loss of articulation and sophistication that occurs when a complex position is reduced to a simple slogan is significant and real. For example, a no answer to the question, Does morality need religion? might be superficially labeled as "antireligion" and a yes answer as "proreligion." Yet Saint

Thomas Aquinas, who has always been regarded as the foremost theologian of the Christian tradition, would respond with a no to that question. Moral questions are complex, and the reduction of answers to simple reactions or superficial slogans will not be helpful. The questions and issues that are raised here require careful analysis, examination, and argumentation.

Gender, Sex, and Reproduction

Part 2 includes several questions that have to do with ways of looking at society especially sex roles, sexual relationships, and reproduction. In many ways the issues in this section are basic to an understanding of our own place in society, our relation to others, and what we expect of men and women. Issues considered in Part 2 are: Does feminism provide a positive direction for society? Does pornography violate women's rights? Is abortion immoral? Must sex involve commitment? Should Congress stay the course on education for sexual abstinence until marriage? and, Should human cloning be banned?

The question of whether or not feminism provides a positive direction for society is one that relates to contemporary society. That is, even if we can agree that in the past feminism has provided much-needed benefit in addressing problems of second-class citizenship for women, does feminism also contain some disagreeable elements that are now coming to light? Has feminism already run its course, so that continued reliance upon it would be unhelpful? Or is there a positive view of society—some future ideal that we can aspire to—that feminism can enable us to envision and pursue?

The question, Does pornography violate women's rights? might also be considered a matter of society's liberalized sexual attitudes. But recent feminist scholarship has made this into a question that is not a simple matter of liberal versus conservative. The modern feminist contention does not focus on the sexual explicitness of pornography (as traditionalists and conservatives do) but rather on pornography as a form of sexual subordination of women, or a manifestation of male social dominance. To ask about *rights* and pornography is the correct question, then, for the contention here is that pornography may seriously interfere with the rights of women.

The question, Is abortion immoral? is not at all a new one. It threatens to polarize people into pro-life and pro-choice camps, but it is best to leave such labels and superficial slogans behind. Whenever an issue seems to demand answers very quickly, as this one might, it is better to go slowly and to first consider the arguments, examples, and rationale of each position before making up your mind.

The question, Must sex involve commitment? has traditionally been answered in the positive. The conservative answer certainly tends to be positive. But after the social changes that have liberalized society's sexual attitudes, does the traditional answer still stand? What, exactly, has changed in people's attitudes? Is it that people have come to see premarital sex as morally permissible (where they once thought it was immoral)? Or is it that they are no longer shocked by its widespread occurrence in real life, films, etc.? The word *must* in

"Must sex involve commitment?" is moral. The contention that sex must involve commitment is not intended to be a contention about how things actually are. In fact, those who answer this question positively would probably think that how things actually are is not at all how they should be.

The question, Should Congress stay the course on education for sexual abstinence until marriage? is complex. In addition to empirical questions about how effective this teaching is, there are also moral questions to consider. Indeed, many would say that the moral questions are the more important questions. Some may contend that even if the educational programs are not supported by empirical data demonstrating their effectiveness, the programs should still be kept in place, perhaps because they are sending the correct message. Yet many others would counter that it is not very realistic to expect that all young people will remain sexually abstinent until marriage. Moreover, it can be argued that it is positively wrong to leave young people uneducated about means of prevention of serious—and sometimes fatal—diseases.

The question, Should human cloning be banned? has arisen because technology now indicates that it could become possible to clone human beings. Some people think that science would be going too far here and that cloning people would be akin to "playing God." They also feel that not everything that technology makes possible should actually be done. Others see no problem with proceeding with experimentation toward human cloning. Is cloning just a case of using science to manipulate natural facts and achieve some desired results, or are the results here not to be desired?

Law and Society

Part 3 focuses on questions that involve our social nature. We ask what particular arrangements will (or will not) be tolerated in society. We also ask what laws we should have (or not have). This section considers the questions, Should the government support faith-based charities? Should there be payment for body parts? Should drugs be legalized? Is it morally permissible to eat meat? Is affirmative action fair? Should the Supreme Court prohibit racial preferences in college admissions? Are African Americans owed reparations for slavery? Should hate-crime laws explicitly protect sexual orientation? Should handguns be banned? Should the death penalty be retained? and, Should physician-assisted suicide be legalized by the states?

The first question in this section is, Should the government support faith-based charities? Government support of church organizations and activities is a sensitive subject for Americans, whose country has at its root a strict separation of church and state. And yet, many people would agree that there are great social problems and that the government, operating independently of the church, seems unable to solve them. Since there are problems such as homelessness, poverty, substance abuse, etc., and the charities that would address these problems are already a part of faith communities, then to many it seems natural to look to faith-based organizations—and perhaps to support them—in dealing with these problems.

The question, Should there be payment for body parts? is one that might initially sound quite gruesome. But the fact of the matter is that there are many more cases of people needing body parts—such as kidneys—than there are organs available for transplant. Part of the problem with the shortage of organs—again, we focus specifically on kidneys here—is that there is no financial incentive for donors to provide kidneys. Doctors and hospitals are compensated for their parts in the organ transplant process, but the donor—by law—cannot be compensated. There cannot be payment for body parts. Yet there is a shortage of body parts for those in need. Would compensation help? Is compensation something we should even be thinking about?

Asking whether or not drugs should be legalized raises a number of points that require consideration. Here we are asking about the future and about what kind of society we think is worth aiming for. Should we strive for a society in which certain substances are available on the open market to consumers who choose them, or should we aim rather to eliminate certain substances and to bring legal punishment to drug dealers and users? As the authors of the readings on this issue indicate, whatever the legal status of drugs, there will always be social costs.

The question, Is it morally permissible to eat meat? is one that probably would not have been taken seriously in earlier times. However, today there are people and organizations that promote vegetarianism on moral grounds. The simplest idea here is that animals are beings that can *suffer*, and they generally do suffer when they are raised for the commercial sale of meat. Most people can live without eating meat, so meat-eating seems to be a cultural practice that we have in our power to change. Of course, many people *like* meat-eating and are very reluctant to change. From their point of view, it might be pointed out that animals are part of nature, human beings are part of nature, and meat-eating—where one species eats another—is also part of nature.

The question, Is affirmative action fair? confronts a policy that is intended to address problems arising from the history and the current state of race relations in the United States. Most arguments in favor of affirmative action can be seen as either backward-looking or forward-looking. Arguments that regard affirmative action as a form of compensation or as a response to previous injustices are backward-looking because they focus on prior events. Arguments that regard affirmative action as a means of achieving integration or diversity or as a means of providing minority role models are forward-looking because they point to the future. Critics of programs of affirmative action, however, have charged that such programs lead to reverse discrimination and unfairly focus on "group rights," whereas the only actual rights are rights of individuals.

The question of whether or not the Supreme Court should prohibit racial preferences in college admissions is naturally connected with the question about affirmative action, but the two are not quite the same. Someone could be a proponent of racial preferences in early life and early schooling, for example, but not in college admissions. On the other hand, opponents of programs of affirmative action are generally opposed to racial preferences across the board—including in college admissions. One ironic aspect of this is that opponents often stress that *qualifications* should be of the utmost importance in society. Yet, if this is true, and if college is one place where people earn their qualifications, then it seems that a racially diverse society could very well make use of racial preferences. On the other hand, racial preferences, if routinely and automatically administered, could serve to further alienate racial groups that are often already antagonistic to each other. Racial preferences might seem more appropriate when they are used as an answer or a response to a problem, rather than simply as a matter of course.

The question, Are African Americans owed reparations for slavery? is an odd one in many ways. One thought is that living African Americans have never been slaves. But a second thought is that the history and legacy of slavery have a great impact on the status of African Americans today. (And, of course, *that* is the slavery that the reparations argument addresses.) Whereas most other American minorities came to this country in order to take advantage of opportunities not available in their home countries, the African American minority is the only one that was forced to come and forced into slavery. Now we realize that African Americans have been done a great injustice. But the question remains, what can we do now? What *should* we do now? Part of the oddness of the question is that the injustice that was done to the African American minority seems to be not measurable in dollars. Yet the wrongfulness and the evilness of slavery seem real enough. In some ways, slavery is a chapter of American history that many would like to put behind them. But is this simply ignoring a historical reality? And what of the reparations themselves? Will they help to put the chapter behind us, or will they perhaps bring it to center stage?

The question, Should hate-crime laws explicitly protect sexual orientation? has several aspects. First, there are broad questions about hate-crime laws themselves. The general idea is that crimes such as a neo-Nazi attacking a Jewish center or a couple of white supremacists dragging a black man tied to their pickup truck, are not exactly like most crimes of violence or murder. In the usual hate-crime cases, the perpetrator picks his victims out from a special victimized class, and the actual identity of the victim may be of almost no concern. The neo-Nazi may prey upon *any* Jewish people; he may not even know or care who in particular is in the Jewish center when he attacks. The crime serves to express hate for a certain group. Most of us—who are not neo-Nazis, white supremacists, etc.—would probably agree that the categories of those who should be protected from hate-crimes should include racial, ethnic, and religious categories. However, one should also consider the category of sexual orientation. Some people seek victims precisely because of the victims' (perceived) sexual orientation. Is this a case where hate-crime law should apply, or is this different?

The question of whether or not handguns should be banned is raised largely in response to the very high number of murders that are committed with handguns in the United States. According to an affirmative answer, the crime problem could be largely solved, while shotguns would still be allowed for hunting and other legal purposes. But some people who give a negative answer to this question see the strong arm of the government coming into play and fear that individual rights may be at stake. Others argue that banning handguns would not stop criminals from committing crimes; in fact, they assert, it may encourage them since they could count on law-abiding citizens as being without handguns.

Many subsidiary questions enter into the issue about the death penalty. Does the death penalty deter crime? Is it the only way to give some criminals what they deserve? Does it fall unfairly on minorities and the poor? Is there a worldwide contemporary movement away from capital punishment? And, finally, even if we had the answers to all these questions, is there a way of using those answers to address the overarching question of whether or not the death penalty should be retained?

The question of whether physician-assisted suicide should be legal or not is another question about life or death, but this time the person who would die would not be regarded as a criminal. Such a person, who may be dying or may be in great pain, requests the physician's assistance in killing himself. The question is whether this request should be fulfilled. If so, the end comes quickly. If not, the end will come, but not so quickly. But is helping to bring the situation to a quick end something that physicians should do?

The Internet Encyclopedia of Philosophy

This site is a very useful reference tool for the serious philosophy student. It contains an excellent collection of readings from classic philosophy texts and original contributions by professional philosophers around the Internet.

http://www.utm.edu/research/iep/

Ethics Updates

Ethics Updates is an online journal edited by Lawrence M. Hinman, a well-respected ethicist at the University of San Diego. The site includes definitions of basic ideas, online articles, audio files, video files, discussion boards, and sophisticated search engines. There is a wide variety of subject matter, running from ethical theory to applied ethics, and the site offers frequent opportunities for user input.

http://ethics.acusd.edu/index.html

Internet Philosophical Resources on Moral Relativism

This *Ethics Updates* site contains discussion questions and Internet resources devoted to moral, cultural, and ethical relativism.

http://ethics.acusd.edu/relativism.html

PART 1

Fundamental Issues in Morality

*E*ven before confronting particular moral issues, we find that there are several conflicting assertions that have been made about morality considered as a whole. Some people state that there is no such thing as moral knowledge and that morality can provide no answers. Among them, subjectivists contend that all moral talk is simply the expression of subjective feelings, which vary from person to person. Cultural relativists, on the other hand, argue that morality is different for different cultural groups: one culture determines what is right or wrong for that culture, and another culture determines what is right or wrong for itself. Still other people maintain that morality does not have a source in purely human experience and interaction. Religion, they say, is the ground of morality. These and other ideas are discussed in this section.

- Is Morality Relative to Culture?

- Does Morality Need Religion?

ISSUE 1

Is Morality Relative to Culture?

YES: Melville J. Herskovits, from "Cultural Relativism and Cultural Values," in Frances Herskovits, ed., *Cultural Relativism: Perspectives in Cultural Pluralism* (Random House, 1972)

NO: Louis P. Pojman, from *Ethics: Discovering Right and Wrong,* 2d ed. (Wadsworth, 1995)

ISSUE SUMMARY

YES: American anthropologist Melville J. Herskovits (1895–1963) takes the position that morality has no absolute identity and that it is a social and cultural phenomenon that varies according to the customs and beliefs of different cultural groups. In his view, the great enemy of relativism is ethnocentrism, especially as expressed by European colonialism.

NO: Professor of philosophy Louis P. Pojman holds that ethnocentrism is a prejudice like racism or sexism. He agrees that moral beliefs and practices vary greatly across cultures and from one person to another, but he finds very serious problems in the contention that moral principles derive their validity from dependence on society or individual choice.

As the social sciences began to be recognized in the nineteenth century, many thinkers developed a particular interest in the customs and morals of other groups of people. In 1865 (six years after naturalist Charles Darwin's *Origin of Species* and six years before his *Descent of Man*), Sir Edward Tylor (1832–1917), one of the great leaders in the scientific study of human beings, published his *Researches Into the Early History of Mankind.* Tylor believed that the study of ancient pagans and the study of uncivilized people and various heathen groups that lived outside the scope of civilized Victorian culture would throw light on English culture itself. It was Tylor's view that all people shared the same human capacities and mental potentialities and that there had been a progression, or positive development, from ignorant savagery to civilized culture. This was a daring view at the time. Many people (especially defenders of religious orthodoxy) believed both that Darwin was seriously wrong to affirm a development or evolution of human beings from animals and that Tylor was seriously wrong to affirm a development or evolution of intelligent civilized Christians from ignorant uncivilized pagan savages. The conventional view held by many was that God had created human beings in his image as rational and moral beings; any savages who existed in the nineteenth century must have fallen into that state through a neglect of reason, a lack of morality, and an absence of faith. Surely, this view continued, human beings were not initially created as ignorant savages who wore beads (if anything at all) and followed a pagan life of promiscuity and superstition.

Sir James Frazer (1854–1941) was greatly stimulated by his reading of Tylor. He too wrote extensively about the customs of primitive people, and he believed that such people exhibited "the rudimentary phases, the infancy and childhood, of human society." To the question of whether or not he had actually seen any of the savages that he had written so much about, Frazer is said to have replied, "God forbid!" Frazer and most social scientists of the late nineteenth century studied books, read the diaries of travelers, and corresponded with those in distant lands. Field study had not yet established itself as a necessary social scientific technique. The armchair studies of Frazer are by no means manifestations of laziness or lack of commitment; Frazer devoted his life to the scientific study of humankind and is said to have spent 12 hours a day for over 50 years reading, taking notes, and writing.

Presently, several well-known social scientists have endorsed a sophisticated type of cultural relativism. The armchair studies have been replaced by years of field studies that include a sympathetic involvement with the lives of the people one is studying. Gone is the view that so-called primitive people are standing on the lower rungs of the same ladder that leads to modern Western culture. There is no separation of the "civilized" and the "uncivilized." There are *various* civilizations and *various* cultures, and our own culture is only one of many.

Melville J. Herskovits was a champion of cultural relativism, which he saw as an antidote to European colonial attitudes and the ethnocentrism that they express. Herskovits was, in particular, a student of African societies and of the experience of blacks in the New World. He regarded it as a great mistake and a great tragedy that Europeans thought that they were the civilized ones and that the Africans were not. It was by force, not by civilization, that Europeans imposed themselves upon African cultures. According to cultural relativism, it is false to think that, in matters of morality, our own Western culture is uniquely in a position to make absolute moral judgments. The fact is that different cultures simply have different moralities. The moral precepts of a given culture might appear as absolute to the individual who is enculturated in that culture, but this is a common error. Such is the view that Herskovits expresses in the following selection.

Louis P. Pojman responds critically to cultural relativism. He agrees with Herskovits on the wrongfulness of ethnocentrism, but he argues that cultural relativism, at least with respect to morality, has several highly implausible consequences. And these consequences, when understood, should lead to the rejection of moral relativism.

Cultural Relativism and Cultural Values

All peoples form judgments about ways of life different from their own. Where systematic study is undertaken, comparison gives rise to classification, and scholars have devised many schemes for classifying ways of life. Moral judgments have been drawn regarding the ethical principles that guide the behavior and mold the value systems of different peoples. Their economic and political structures and their religious beliefs have been ranked in order of complexity, efficiency, desirability. Their art, music, and literary forms have been weighed.

It has become increasingly evident, however, that evaluations of this kind stand or fall with the acceptance of the premises from which they derive. In addition, many of the criteria on which judgment is based are in conflict, so that conclusions drawn from one definition of what is desirable will not agree with those based on another formulation.

A simple example will illustrate this. There are not many ways in which the primary family can be constituted. One man may live with one woman, one woman may have a number of husbands, one man may have a number of wives. But if we evaluate these forms according to their function of perpetuating the group, it is clear that they perform their essential tasks. Otherwise, the societies wherein they exist would not survive.

Such an answer will, however, not satisfy all those who have undertaken to study cultural evaluation. What of the moral questions inherent in the practice of monogamy as against polygamy, the adjustment of children raised in households where, for example, the mothers must compete on behalf of their offspring for the favors of a common husband? If monogamy is held to be the desired form of marriage, the responses to these questions are predetermined. But when we consider these questions from the point of view of those who live in polygamous societies, alternative answers, based on different conceptions of what is desirable, may be given.

Let us consider, for example, the life of a plural family in the West African culture of Dahomey.[1] Here, within a compound, live a man and his wives. The man has his own house, as has each of the women and her children, after the basic African principle that two wives cannot successfully inhabit the same quarters. Each wife in turn spends a native week of four days with the common husband, cooking his food, washing his clothes, sleeping in his house, and then making way for the next. Her children, however, remain in their mother's hut. With pregnancy, she drops out of this routine, and ideally, in the interest of her child's health and her own, does not again visit her husband until the child has been born and weaned. This means a period of from three to four years, since infants are nursed two years and longer.

The compound, made up of these households, is a cooperative unit. The women who sell goods in the market, or make pottery, or have their gardens, contribute to its support. This aspect, though of great economic importance, is secondary to the prestige that attaches to the larger unit. This is why one often finds a wife not only urging her husband to acquire a second spouse but even aiding him by loans or gifts to make this possible.

Tensions do arise between the women who inhabit a large compound. Thirteen different ways of getting married have been recorded in this society, and in a large household those wives who are married in the same category tend to unite against all others. Competition for the regard of the husband is also a factor, when several wives try to influence the choice of an heir in favor of their own sons. Yet all the children of the compound play together, and the strength of the emotional ties between the children of the same mother more than compensates for whatever stresses may arise between brothers and sisters who share the same father but are of different mothers. Cooperation, moreover, is by no means a mere formality among the wives. Many common tasks are performed in friendly unison, and there is solidarity in the interest of women's prerogatives, or where the status of the common husband is threatened.

We may now return to the criteria to be applied in drawing judgments concerning polygamous as against monogamous families. The family structure of Dahomey is obviously a complex institution. If we but consider the possible lines of personal relations among the many individuals concerned, we see clearly how numerous are the ramifications of reciprocal right and obligation of the Dahomean family. The effectiveness of the Dahomean family is, however, patent. It has, for untold generations, performed its function of rearing the young; more than this, the very size of the group gives it economic resources and a resulting stability that might well be envied by those who live under different systems of family organization. Moral values are always difficult to establish, but at least in this society marriage is clearly distinguished from casual sex relations and from prostitution, in its supernatural sanctions and in the prestige it confers, to say nothing of the economic obligations toward spouse and prospective offspring explicitly accepted by one who enters into a marriage.

Numerous problems of adjustment do present themselves in an aggregate of this sort. It does not call for much speculation to understand the plaint of the head of one large compound when he said: "One must be something of a diplomat if one has many wives." Yet the sly digs in proverb and song, and the open quarreling, involve no greater stress than is found in any small rural community where people are also thrown closely together for long periods of time. Quarrels between co-wives are not greatly different from disputes over the back fence between neighbors. And Dahomeans who know European culture, when they argue for their system, stress the fact that it permits the individual wife to space her children in a way that is in accord with the best precepts of modern gynecology.

Thus polygamy, when looked at from the point of view of those who practice it, is seen to hold values that are not apparent from the outside. A similar case can be made for monogamy, however, when it is attacked by those who are enculturated to a different kind of family structure. And what is true of a particular phase of culture such as this, is also true of others. Evaluations are *relative* to the cultural background out of which they arise.

◆

Cultural relativism is in essence an approach to the question of the nature and role of values in culture. It represents a scientific, inductive attack on an age-old philosophical problem, using fresh, cross-cultural data, hitherto not available to scholars, gained from the study of the underlying value-systems of societies having the most diverse customs. The principle of cultural relativism, briefly stated, is as follows: *Judgments are based on experience, and experience is interpreted by each individual in terms of his own enculturation.* Those who hold for the existence of fixed values will find materials in other societies that necessitate a reinvestigation of their assumptions. Are there absolute moral standards, or are moral standards effective only as far as they agree with the orientations of a given people at a given period of their history? We even approach the problem of the ultimate nature of reality itself. Cassirer[2] holds that reality can only be experienced through the symbolism of language. Is reality, then, not defined and redefined by the ever-varied symbolisms of the innumerable languages of mankind?

Answers to questions such as these represent one of the most profound contributions of anthropology to the analysis of man's place in the world. When we reflect that such intangibles as right and wrong, normal and abnormal, beautiful and plain are absorbed as a person learns the ways of the group into which he is born, we see that we are dealing here with a process of first importance. Even the facts of the physical world are discerned through the enculturative screen, so that the perception of time, distance, weight, size, and other "realities" is mediated by the conventions of any given group.

No culture, however, is a closed system of rigid molds to which the behavior of all members of a society must conform. In stressing the psychological reality of culture, it was made plain that a culture, as such, can *do* nothing. It is but the summation of the behavior and habitual modes of thought of the persons who make up a particular society. Though by learning and habit these individuals conform to the ways of the group into which they have been born, they nonetheless vary in their reactions to the situations of living they commonly meet. They vary, too, in the degree to which they desire change, as whole cultures vary. This is but another way in which we see that culture is flexible and holds many possibilities of choice within its framework, and that to recognize the values held by a given people in no wise implies that these values are a constant factor in the lives of succeeding generations of the same group. . . .

[W]hile recognizing the role of both father and mother in procreation, many peoples have conventions of relationship that count descent on but one side of the family. In such societies, it is common for incest lines to be so arbitrarily defined that "first cousins," as we would say, on the mother's side call each other brother and sister and regard marriage with one another with horror. Yet marriage within the same degree of biological relationship on the father's side may be held not only desirable, but sometimes mandatory. This is because two persons related in this way are by definition not considered blood relatives.

The very definition of what is normal or abnormal is relative to the cultural frame of reference. As an example of this, we may take the phenomenon of possession as found among African and New World Negroes. The supreme expression of their religious experience, possession, is a psychological state wherein a displacement of personality occurs when the god "comes to the head" of the worshipper. The individual thereupon is held to be the deity himself. This phenomenon has been described in pathological terms by many students whose approach is nonanthropological, because of its surface resemblance to cases in the records of medical practitioners, psychological clinicians, psychiatrists, and others. The hysteria-like trances, where persons, their eyes tightly closed, move about excitedly and presumably without purpose or design, or roll on the ground, muttering meaningless syllables, or go into a state where their bodies achieve complete rigidity, are not difficult to equate with the neurotic and even psychotic manifestations of abnormality found in Euroamerican society.

Yet when we look beneath behavior to meaning, and place such apparently random acts in their cultural frame of reference, such conclusions become untenable. For *relative to the setting in which these possession experiences occur, they are not to be regarded as abnormal at all,* much less psychopathological. They are *culturally* patterned, and often induced by learning and discipline. The dancing or other acts of the possessed persons are so stylized that one who knows this religion can identify the god possessing a devotee by the behavior of the individual possessed. Furthermore, the possession experience does not seem to be confined to emotionally unstable persons. Those who "get the god" run the gamut of personality types found in the group. Observation of persons who frequent the cults, yet who, in the idiom of worship "have nothing in the head" and thus never experience possession, seems to show that they are far less adjusted than those who do get possessed. Finally, the nature of the possession experience in these cultures is so disciplined that it may only come to a given devotee under particular circumstances. In West Africa and Brazil the gods come only to those who have been designated in advance by the priest of their group, who lays his hands on their heads. In Haiti, for an initiate not a member of the family group giving a rite to become possessed at a ceremony is considered extremely "bad form" socially and a sign of spiritual weakness, evidence that the god is not under the control of his worshipper.

The terminology of psychopathology, employed solely for descriptive purposes, may be of some utility. But the connotation it carries of psychic instability, emotional imbalance, and departure from normality recommends the use of other words that do not invite such a distortion of cultural reality. For in these Negro societies, the meaning this experience holds for the people falls entirely in the realm of understandable, predictable, *normal* behavior. This behavior is known and recognized by all members as an experience that may come to any one of them, and is to be welcomed not only for the psychological security it affords, but also for the status, economic gain, aesthetic expression, and emotional release it vouchsafes the devotee.

⚜

The primary mechanism that directs the evaluation of culture is *ethnocentrism.* Ethnocentrism is the point of view that one's own way of life is to be preferred to all others. Flowing logically from the process of early enculturation, it characterizes the way most individuals feel about their own culture, whether or not they verbalize their feeling. Outside the stream of Euroamerican culture, particularly among nonliterate peoples, this is taken for granted and is to be viewed as a factor making for individual adjustment and social integration. For the strengthening of the ego, identification with one's own group, whose ways are implicitly accepted as best, is all-important. It is when, as in Euroamerican culture, ethnocentrism is rationalized and made the basis of programs of action detrimental to the well-being of other peoples that it gives rise to serious problems.

The ethnocentrism of nonliterate peoples is best illustrated in their myths, folk tales, proverbs, and linguistic habits. It is manifest in many tribal names whose meaning in their respective languages signifies "human beings." The inference that those to whom the name does not apply are outside this category is, however, rarely, if ever, explicitly made. When the Suriname Bush Negro, shown a flashlight, admires it and then quotes the proverb: "White man's magic isn't black man's magic," he is merely reaffirming his faith in his own culture. He is pointing out that the stranger, for all his mechanical devices, would be lost in the Guiana jungle without the aid of his Bush Negro friends.

A myth of the origin of human races, told by the Cherokee Indians of the Great Smoky Mountains, gives another instance of this kind of ethnocentrism. The Creator fashioned man by first making and firing an oven and then, from dough he had prepared, shaping three figures in human form. He placed the figures in the oven and waited for them to get done. But his impatience to see the result of this, his crowning experiment in the work of creation, was so great that he removed the first figure too soon. It was sadly underdone—pale, an unlovely color, and from it descended the white people. His second figure had fared well. The timing was accurate, the form, richly browned, that was to be the ancestor of the Indians, pleased him in every way. He so admired it, indeed, that he neglected to take out of the oven the third form, until he smelled it burning. He threw open the door, only to find this last one charred and black. It was regrettable, but there was nothing to be done; and this was the first Negro.[3]

This is the more usual form that ethnocentrism takes among many peoples —a gentle insistence on the good qualities of one's own group, without any drive to extend this attitude into the field of action. With such a point of view, the objectives, sanctioned modes of behavior, and value systems of peoples with whom one's own group comes into contact can be considered in terms of their desirability, then accepted or rejected without any reference to absolute standards. That differences in the manner of achieving commonly sought objectives may be permitted to exist without a judgment being entered on them involves a reorientation in thought for those in the Euroamerican tradition, because in this tradition, a difference in belief or behavior too often implies something is worse, or less desirable, and must be changed.

The assumption that the cultures of nonliterate peoples are of inferior quality is the end product of a long series of developments in our intellectual history. It is not often recalled that the concept of progress, that strikes so deep into our thinking, is relatively recent. It is, in fact, a unique product of our culture. It is a part of the same historic stream that developed the scientific tradition and that developed the machine, thus giving Europe and America the final word in debates about cultural superiority. "He who makes the gun-powder wields the power," runs a Dahomean proverb. There is no rebuttal to an argument, backed by cannon, advanced to a people who can defend their position with no more than spears, or bows and arrows, or at best a flint-lock gun.

With the possible exception of technological aspects of life, however, the proposition that one way of thought or action is better than another is exceedingly difficult to establish on the grounds of any universally acceptable criteria. Let us take food as an instance. Cultures are equipped differently for the production of food, so that some peoples eat more than others. However, even on the subsistence level, there is no people who do not hold certain potential foodstuffs to be unfit for human consumption. Milk, which figures importantly in our diet, is rejected as food by the peoples of southeastern Asia. Beef, a valued element of the Euroamerican cuisine, is regarded with disgust by Hindus. Nor need compulsions be this strong. The thousands of cattle that range the East African highlands are primarily wealth to be preserved, and not a source of food. Only the cow that dies is eaten—a practice that, though abhorrent to us, has apparently done no harm to those who have been following it for generations.

Totemic and religious taboos set up further restrictions on available foodstuffs, while the refusal to consume many other edible and nourishing substances is simply based on the enculturative conditioning. So strong is this conditioning that prohibited food consumed unwittingly may induce such a physiological reaction as vomiting. All young animals provide succulent meat, but the religious abhorrence of the young pig by the Mohammedan is no stronger than the secular rejection of puppy steaks or colt chops by ourselves. Ant larvae, insect grubs, locusts—all of which have caloric values and vitamin content—when roasted or otherwise cooked, or even when raw, are regarded by many peoples as delicacies. We never eat them, however, though they are equally available to us. On the other hand, some of the same peoples who feed on these with gusto regard substances that come out of tin cans as unfit for human consumption. . . .

Before we terminate our discussion of cultural relativism, it is important that we consider certain questions that are raised when the cultural-relativistic position is advanced. "It may be true," it is argued, "that human beings live in accordance with the ways they have learned. These ways may be regarded by them as best. A people may be so devoted to these ways that they are ready to fight and die for them. In terms of survival value, their effectiveness may be admitted, since the group that lives in accordance with them continues to exist. But does this mean that all systems of moral values, all concepts of right and wrong, are founded on such shifting sands that there is no need for morality, for proper behavior, for ethical codes? Does not a relativistic philosophy, indeed, imply a negation of these?"

To hold that values do not exist because they are relative to time and place is to fall prey to a fallacy that results from a failure to take into account the positive contribution of the relativistic position. For cultural relativism is a philosophy that recognizes the values set up by every society to guide its own life and that understands their worth to those who live by them, though they may differ from one's own. Instead of underscoring differences from absolute norms that, however objectively arrived at, are nonetheless the product of a given time or place, the relativistic point of view brings into relief the validity of every set of norms for the people who have them, and the values these represent.

It is essential, in considering cultural relativism, that we differentiate absolutes from universals. *Absolutes* are fixed, and, as far as convention is concerned, are not admitted to have variation, to differ from culture to culture, from epoch to epoch. *Universals,* on the other hand, are those least common denominators to be extracted from the range of variation that all phenomena of the natural or cultural world manifest. If we apply the distinction between these two concepts in drawing an answer to the points raised in our question, these criticisms are found to lose their force. To say that there is no absolute criterion of values or morals, or even, psychologically, of time or space, does not mean that such criteria, in differing *forms,* do not comprise universals in human culture. Morality is a universal, and so is enjoyment of beauty, and some standard for truth. The many forms these concepts take are but products of the particular historical experience of the societies that manifest them. In each, criteria are subject to continuous questioning, continuous change. But the basic conceptions remain, to channel thought and direct conduct, to give purpose to living.

In considering cultural relativism, also, we must recognize that it has three quite different aspects, which in most discussions of it tend to be disregarded. One of these is methodological, one philosophical, and one practical. As it has been put:

> As method, relativism encompasses the principle of our science that, in studying a culture, one seeks to attain as great a degree of objectivity as possible; that one does not judge the modes of behavior one is describing, or seek to change them. Rather, one seeks to understand the sanctions of behavior in terms of the established relationships within the culture itself, and refrains from making interpretations that arise from a preconceived frame of reference. Relativism as philosophy concerns the nature of cultural val-

ues, and, beyond this, the implications of an epistemology that derives from a recognition of the force of enculturative conditioning in shaping thought and behavior. Its practical aspects involve the application—the practice—of the philosophical principles derived from this method, to the wider, cross-cultural scene.

We may follow this reasoning somewhat further.

In these terms, the three aspects of cultural relativism can be regarded as representing a logical sequence which, in a broad sense, the historical development of the idea has also followed. That is, the methodological aspect, whereby the data from which the epistemological propositions flow are gathered, ordered and assessed, came first. For it is difficult to conceive of a systematic theory of cultural relativism—as against a generalized idea of live-and-let-live—without the pre-existence of the massive ethnographic documentation gathered by anthropologists concerning the similarities and differences between cultures the world over. Out of these data came the philosophical position, and with the philosophical position came speculation as to its implications for conduct.[4]

Cultural relativism, in all cases, must be sharply distinguished from concepts of the relativity of individual behavior, which would negate all social controls over conduct. Conformity to the code of the group is a requirement for any regularity in life. Yet to say that we have a right to expect conformity to the code of our day for ourselves does not imply that we need expect, much less impose, conformity to our code on persons who live by other codes. The very core of cultural relativism is the social discipline that comes of respect for differences—of mutual respect. Emphasis on the worth of many ways of life, not one, is an affirmation of the values in each culture. Such emphasis seeks to understand and to harmonize goals, not to judge and destroy those that do not dovetail with our own. Cultural history teaches that, important as it is to discern and study the parallelisms in human civilizations, it is no less important to discern and study the different ways man has devised to fulfill his needs.

That it has been necessary to consider questions such as have been raised reflects an enculturative experience wherein the prevalent system of morals is not only consciously inculcated, but its exclusive claim to excellence emphasized. There are not many cultures, for example, where a rigid dichotomy between good and evil, such as we have set up, is insisted upon. Rather it is recognized that good and evil are but the extremes of a continuously varied scale between these poles that produces only different degrees of greyness. We thus return to the principle enunciated earlier, that "judgments are based on experience, and experience is interpreted by each individual in terms of his enculturation." In a culture where absolute values are stressed, the relativism of a world that encompasses many ways of living will be difficult to comprehend. Rather, it will offer a field day for value judgments based on the degree to which a given body of customs resembles or differs from those of Euroamerican culture.[5]

Once comprehended, however, and employing the field methods of the scientific student of man, together with an awareness of the satisfactions the most varied bodies of custom yield, this position gives us a leverage to lift us out of the ethnocentric morass in which our thinking about ultimate values has for so long bogged down. With a means of probing deeply into all manner of differing cultural orientations, of reaching into the significance of the ways of living of different peoples, we can turn again to our own culture with fresh perspective, and an objectivity that can be achieved in no other manner.

Notes

1. Cf. M. J. Herskovits, 1938b, Vol. I, pp. 137–55, 300–51.
2. E. Cassirer, 1944, p. 25.
3. This unpublished myth was told to F. M. Olbrechts of Brussels, Belgium, in the course of field work among the Cherokee. His having made it available is gratefully acknowledged. A similar tale has been recorded from the Albany Cree, at Moose Factory, according to information received from F. Voget.
4. M. J. Herskovits, 1951, p. 24.
5. Instances of the rejection of relativism on philosophical grounds, by writers who attempt to reconcile the principle of absolute values with the diversity of known systems, are to be found in E. Vivas, 1950, pp. 27–42, and D. Bidney, 1953a, pp. 689–95, 1953b, pp. 423–9. Both of these discussions, also, afford examples of the confusion that results when a distinction is not drawn between the methodological, philosophical, and practical aspects of relativism. For a critical consideration of relativism that, by implication, recognizes these differences, see R. Redfield, 1953, pp. 144 ff.

NO

Louis P. Pojman

Ethical Relativism: Who's to Judge What's Right and Wrong?

Ethical relativism is the doctrine that the moral rightness and wrongness of actions varies from society to society and that there are no absolute universal moral standards binding on all men at all times. Accordingly, it holds that whether or not it is right for an individual to act in a certain way depends on or is relative to the society to which he belongs.

John Ladd, Ethical Relativism

In the 19th century Christian missionaries sometimes used coercion to change the customs of pagan tribal people in parts of Africa and the Pacific Islands. Appalled by the customs of public nakedness, polygamy, working on the Sabbath, and infanticide, they paternalistically went about reforming the "poor pagans." They clothed them, separated wives from their husbands in order to create monogamous households, made the Sabbath a day of rest, and ended infanticide. In the process they sometimes created malaise, causing the estranged women to despair and their children to be orphaned. The natives often did not understand the new religion, but accepted it in deference to the white man's power. The white people had guns and medicine.

Since the 19th century we've made progress in understanding cultural diversity, and now realize that the social dissonance caused by "do-gooders" was a bad thing. In the last century or so, anthropology has exposed our penchant for *ethnocentrism,* the prejudicial view that interprets all of reality through the eyes of one's own cultural beliefs and values. We have come to see enormous variety in social practices throughout the world.

For instance, Eskimos allow their elderly to die by starvation, whereas we believe that this is morally wrong. The Spartans of ancient Greece and the Dobu of New Guinea believe that stealing is morally right; but we believe it is wrong. Many cultures, past and present, have practiced or still practice infanticide. A tribe in East Africa once threw deformed infants to the hippopotamus, but our society condemns such acts. Sexual practices vary over time and clime. Some cultures permit homosexual behavior, whereas others condemn it. Some cultures, including Moslem societies, practice polygamy, while Christian cultures view it as immoral. Anthropologist Ruth Benedict describes a tribe in Melanesia that views cooperation and kindness as vices, and anthropologist Colin Turnbull has documented that the Ik in Northern Uganda have no sense of duty toward their children or parents. There are societies that make it a duty for children to kill their aging parents (sometimes by strangling).

The ancient Greek historian Herodotus (485–430 B.C.) told the story of how Darius, the king of Persia, once brought together some Callatians (Asian tribal people) and some Greeks. He asked the Callatians how they disposed of their deceased parents. They explained that they ate the bodies. The Greeks, who cremate their parents, were horrified at such barbarous behavior. No amount of money could tempt them to do such an irreverent thing. Then Darius asked the Callatians, "What should I give you to burn the bodies of your fathers at their decease?" The Callatians were utterly horrified at such barbarous behavior and begged Darius to cease from such irreverent discourse. Herodotus concluded that "Custom is the king o'er all."[1]

Today we condemn ethnocentrism as a variety of prejudice tantamount to racism and sexism. What is right in one culture may be wrong in another, what is good east of the river may be bad west of the same river, what is a virtue in one nation may be seen as a vice in another, so it behooves us not to judge others but to be tolerant of diversity.

This rejection of ethnocentrism in the West has contributed to a general shift in public opinion about morality, so that for a growing number of Westerners, consciousness-raising about the validity of other ways of life has led to a gradual erosion of belief in moral objectivism, the view that there are universal moral principles, valid for all people at all times and climes. For example, in polls taken in my ethics and introduction to philosophy classes over the past several years (in three different universities in three areas of the country) students affirmed by a 2 to 1 ratio, a version of moral relativism over moral absolutism with barely 3 percent seeing something in between these two polar opposites. Of course, I'm not suggesting that all these students have a clear understanding of what relativism entails, for many of those who say they are ethical relativists also state on the same questionnaire that "abortion, except to save the mother's life, is always wrong," that "capital punishment is always morally wrong," or that "suicide is never morally premissible." The apparent contradictions signal some confusion on the matter.

[Here] we examine the central notions of ethical relativism and look at the implications that seem to follow from it. . . .

An Analysis of Relativism

Ethical relativism holds that there are no universally valid moral principles, but rather that all moral principles are valid relative to culture or individual choice. It is to be distinguished from *moral skepticism*—the view that there are no valid moral principles at all (or at least we cannot know whether there are any)—and from all forms of *moral objectivism* or *absolutism*. John Ladd's statement . . . is a typical characterization of the theory:

> Ethical relativism is the doctrine that the moral rightness and wrongness of actions varies from society to society and that there are no absolute universal moral standards binding on all men at all times. Accordingly, it holds that whether or not it is right for an individual to act in a certain way depends on or is relative to the society to which he belongs.[2]

If we analyze this passage, we derive the following argument:

1. What is considered morally right and wrong varies from society to society, so that there are no universal moral standards held by all societies.
2. Whether or not it is right for an individual to act in a certain way depends on or is relative to the society to which he or she belongs.
3. Therefore, there are no *absolute* or objective moral standards that apply to all people everywhere and at all times.

The Diversity Thesis

The first thesis, which may be called the *diversity thesis* and identified with *cultural relativism,* is simply an anthropological thesis that acknowledges the fact that moral rules differ from society to society. As we illustrated earlier . . . , there is enormous variety in what may count as a moral principle in a given society. The human condition is malleable in the extreme, allowing any number of folkways or moral codes. As Ruth Benedict has written:

> The cultural pattern of any civilization makes use of a certain segment of the great arc of potential human purposes and motivations, just as we have seen . . . that any culture makes use of certain selected material techniques or cultural traits. The great arc along which all the possible human behaviors are distributed is far too immense and too full of contradictions for any one culture to utilize even any considerable portion of it. Selection is the first requirement.[3] . . .

The Dependency Thesis

The second thesis, the *dependency thesis,* asserts that individual acts are right and wrong depending on the nature of the society in which they occur. Morality does not exist in a vacuum; rather, what is considered morally right or wrong must be seen in a context, depending on the goals, wants, beliefs, history, and environment of the society in question. As William Graham Sumner says,

> We learn the [morals] as unconsciously as we learn to walk and hear and breathe, and [we] never know any reason why the [morals] are what they are. The justification of them is that when we wake to consciousness of life we find them facts which already hold us in the bonds of tradition, custom, and habit.[4]

Trying to see things from an independent, noncultural point of view would be like taking out our eyes in order to examine their contours and qualities. We are simply culturally determined beings.

We could, of course, distinguish both a weak and a strong thesis of dependency. The nonrelativist can accept a certain relativity in the way moral principles are *applied* in various cultures, depending on beliefs, history, and environment. For example, Orientals show respect by covering the head and uncovering the feet, whereas Occidentals do the opposite. Though both adhere to a principle of respect for deserving people, they apply the principle differently. But the ethical relativist must maintain a stronger thesis, one that insists that the very validity of the principles is a product of the culture and that different cultures will invent different valid principles. The ethical relativist maintains that even beyond the environmental factors and differences in beliefs, there are fundamental disagreements among societies.

In a sense, we all live in radically different worlds. Each person has a different set of beliefs and experiences, a particular perspective that colors all of his or her perceptions. Do the farmer, the real estate dealer, and the artist looking at the same spatiotemporal field actually see the same thing? Not likely. Their different orientations, values, and expectations govern their perceptions, so that different aspects of the field are highlighted and some features are missed. Even as our individual values arise from personal experience, so social values are grounded in the peculiar history of the community. Morality, then, is just the set of common rules, habits, and customs that have won social approval over time, so that they seem part of the nature of things, like facts. There is nothing mysterious or transcendent about these codes of behavior. They are the outcomes of our social history.

There is something conventional about *any* morality, so that every morality really depends on a level of social acceptance. Not only do various societies adhere to different moral systems, but the very same society could (and often does) change its moral views over time and place. For example, in the southern United States slavery is now viewed as immoral, whereas just over 100 years ago, it was not. We have greatly altered our views on abortion, divorce, and sexuality as well.

The conclusion—that there are no absolute or objective moral standards binding on all people—follows from the first two propositions. Cultural relativism (the diversity thesis) plus the dependency thesis yields ethical relativism in its classic form. If there are different moral principles from culture to culture and if all morality is rooted in culture, then it follows that there are no universal moral principles valid for all cultures and all people at all times.

Subjective Ethical Relativism (Subjectivism)

Some people think that even the conclusion just stated is too tame. They maintain that morality is not dependent on the society but on the individual himself or herself. As students sometimes maintain, "Morality is in the eye of the be-holder." Ernest Hemingway wrote:

So far, about morals, I know only that what is moral is what you feel good af-ter and what is immoral is what you feel bad after and judged by these moral standards, which I do not defend, the bullfight is very moral to me because I feel very fine while it is going on and have a feeling of life and death and mortality and immortality, and after it is over I feel very sad but very fine.[5]

The form of *moral subjectivism* has the sorry consequence that it makes morality a useless concept, for, on its premises, little or no interpersonal criti-cism or judgment is logically possible. Hemingway may feel good about the killing of bulls in a bullfight, whereas Albert Schweitzer or Mother Teresa would no doubt feel the opposite. No argument about the matter is possible. The only basis for judging Hemingway, or anyone else, wrong would be if he failed to live up to his own principles; however, one of Hemingway's principles could be that hypocrisy is morally permissible (he feels good about it), so that it would be im-possible for him to do wrong. For Hemingway, hypocrisy and nonhypocrisy are both morally permissible. On the basis of subjectivism it could very easily turn out that Adolf Hitler was as moral as Mahatma Gandhi, as long as each believed he was living by his chosen principles. Notions of moral good and bad, right and wrong cease to have interpersonal evaluative meaning.

In the opening days of my philosophy classes, I often find students vehe-mently defending subjective relativism. I then give the students their first test. The next class period I return all the tests, marked F even though my comments show that most of them are of a very high quality. When the students express outrage at this injustice, I answer that I have accepted subjectivism for purposes of marking the exams, in which case the principle of justice has no objective validity.

Absurd consequences follow from subjective ethical relativism. If it is cor-rect, then morality reduces to aesthetic tastes, over which there can be neither argument nor interpersonal judgment. Although many people say they hold this position, there seems to be a conflict between it and other of their moral views (e.g., that Hitler was really morally bad or that capital punishment is al-ways wrong). There seems to be a contradiction between subjectivism and the very concept of morality, which it is supposed to characterize, for morality has to do with *proper* resolution of interpersonal conflict and the amelioration of the human predicament. Whatever else it does, morality has the minimal aim of preventing a state of chaos in which life is "solitary, poor, nasty, brutish, and short." But if so, subjectivism is no help at all in doing this, for it does not rest on social *agreement* of principle (as the conventionalist maintains) or on an ob-jectively independent set of norms that bind all people for the common good.

Subjectivism treats individuals like billiard balls on a societal pool table where they meet only in radical collisions, each aimed at his or her own goal and striving to do in the others before they themselves are done in. This atom-istic view of personality is belied by the facts that we develop in families and mutually dependent communities in which we share a common language, common institutions, and similar habits, and that we often feel one another's joys and sorrows. As John Donne said, "No man is an island, entire of itself; every man is a piece of the continent."

Radical individualistic relativism seems incoherent. If so, it follows that the only plausible view of ethical relativism must be one that grounds morality in the group or culture. This form of relativism is called *conventionalism,* which we looked at earlier and to which we now return.

Conventional Ethical Relativism (Conventionalism)

Conventional ethical relativism, the view that there are no objective moral principles but rather that all valid moral principles are justified by virtue of their cultural acceptance, recognizes the social nature of morality. That is precisely its power and virtue. It does not seem subject to the same absurd consequences that plague subjectivism. Recognizing the importance of our social environment in generating customs and beliefs, many people suppose that ethical relativism is the correct ethical theory. Furthermore, they are drawn to it for its liberal philosophical stance. It seems to be an enlightened response to the sin of ethnocentricity, and it seems to entail or strongly imply an attitude of tolerance toward other cultures. As Ruth Benedict says, in recognizing ethical relativity

> we shall arrive at a more realistic social faith, accepting as grounds of hope and as new bases for tolerance the coexisting and equally valid patterns of life which mankind has created for itself from the raw materials of existence.[6]

The most famous of those holding this position is the anthropologist Melville Herskovits, who argues even more explicitly than Benedict that ethical relativism entails intercultural tolerance:

1. Morality is relative to its culture.
2. There is no independent basis for criticizing the morality of any other culture.
3. Therefore we ought to be tolerant of the moralities of other cultures.[7]

Tolerance is certainly a virtue, but is this a good argument for it? I think not. If morality is simply relative to each culture, then if the culture does not have a principle of tolerance, its members have no obligation to be tolerant. Herskovits seems to be treating the principle of tolerance as the one exception to his relativism. But from a relativistic point of view there is no more reason to be tolerant than to be intolerant, and neither stance is objectively morally better than the other.

Not only do relativists fail to offer a basis for criticizing those who are intolerant, but they cannot rationally criticize anyone who espouses what they might regard as a heinous principle. If, as seems to be the case, valid criticism supposes an objective or impartial standard, relativists cannot morally criticize anyone outside their own culture. Adolf Hitler's genocidal actions, as long as they were culturally accepted, were as morally legitimate as Mother Teresa's works of mercy. If conventional relativism is accepted, then racism, genocide of unpopular minorities, oppression of the poor, slavery, and even the advocacy of war for its own sake are as equally moral as their opposites. And if a subculture decided that starting a nuclear war was somehow morally acceptable, we could not morally criticize those people, for any actual morality, whatever its content, is as valid as every other and more valid than ideal moralities, because the latter aren't adhered to by any culture.

There are other disturbing consequences of ethical relativism. It seems to entail that reformers are always (morally) wrong, since they go against the tide of cultural standards. William Wilberforce was wrong, in the 18th century, to oppose slavery; the British were immoral in opposing suttee in India (the burning of widows on their husbands' funeral pyres, which is now illegal in India); and missionaries were immoral in opposing clitorectomies in Central Africa. The early Christians were wrong in refusing to serve in the Roman army or to bow down to Caesar, since the majority in the Roman Empire believed these acts were moral duties. In fact, Jesus himself was immoral in advocating the beatitudes and principles of the Sermon on the Mount, since it is clear that few in his time (or in ours) accepted them.

Yet we normally believe just the opposite, that the reformer is the courageous innovator who is right, who has the truth, in the face of the mindless majority. Sometimes the individual must stand alone with the truth, risking social censure and persecution. As Dr. Stockman says in Ibsen's *Enemy of the People,* after he loses the battle to declare his town's profitable polluted tourist spa unsanitary, "The most dangerous enemy of the truth and freedom among us—is the compact majority. Yes, the damned . . . majority. The majority has *might*—unfortunately—but *right* it is not. Right—are I and a few others." Yet if relativism is correct, the opposite is necessarily the case. Truth is with the crowd and error with the individual.

Similarly, conventional ethical relativism entails disturbing judgments about the law. Our normal view is that we have a prima facie duty to obey the law, because law, in general, promotes the human Good. According to most objective systems, this obligation is not absolute but rather is conditional, depending on the particular law's relation to a wider moral order. Civil disobedience is warranted in some cases in which the law seems to be in serious conflict with morality. However, if moral relativism is true, then neither law nor civil disobedience has a firm foundation. On the one hand, for society at large, civil disobedience will be morally wrong, so long as the culture agrees with the law in question. On the other hand, if you belong to the relevant subculture that doesn't recognize the particular law in question, disobedience will be morally mandated. The Ku Klux Klan, which believes that Jews, Catholics, and Blacks are evil or undeserving of high regard, are, given conventionalism, morally permitted or required to break the laws that protect these endangered groups. Why should I obey a law that my group doesn't recognize as valid?

To sum up, unless we have an independent moral basis for law, it is hard to see why we have any general duty to obey it; and unless we recognize the priority of a universal moral law, we have no firm basis to justify our acts of civil disobedience against "unjust laws." Both the validity of law and morally motivated disobedience of unjust laws are annulled in favor of a power struggle.

There is an even more basic problem with the notion that morality is dependent on cultural acceptance for its validity. The problem is that the concepts of *culture* and *society* are notoriously difficult to define, especially in a pluralistic society such as our own, in which the concepts seem rather vague. One person may belong to several societies (subcultures) with different emphases on values and arrangements of principles. A person may belong to the nation as a single society with certain values of patriotism, honor, courage, laws (including some that are controversial but have majority acceptance, such as the law on abortion). But he or she may also belong to a church that opposes some of the laws of the state. The same individual may also be an integral member of a socially mixed community in which different principles hold sway, and additionally may belong to clubs and a family that adhere to still other rules. Relativism would seem to tell us that when a person is a member of societies with conflicting moralities, that person must be judged both wrong and not wrong, whatever he or she does. For example, if Mary is a U.S. citizen and a Roman Catholic, she is wrong (qua Catholic) if she chooses to have an abortion and not wrong (qua citizen of the United States) if she acts against the teaching of the church on abortion. As a member of a racist university fraternity, the Klu Klux Klan, John has no obligation to treat his fellow African American students as equals; but as a member of the university community itself (in which the principle of equal rights is accepted), he does have that obligation; but as a member of the surrounding community (which may reject the principle of equal rights), John again has no such obligation; but then again as a member of the nation at large (which accepts the principle), he is obligated to treat his fellow citizens with respect. What is the morally right thing for John to do? The question no longer makes much sense in this moral Babel; morality has lost its action-guiding function.

Perhaps the relativist would adhere to a principle that says in such cases the individual may choose which group to belong to as primary. If Mary chooses to have an abortion, she is choosing to belong to the general society relative to that principle. And John must likewise choose among groups. The trouble with this option is that it seems to lead back to counterintuitive results. If Mafia Mike feels like killing bank president Otis Ortcutt and wants to feel good about it, he identifies with the Mafia society rather than with the general public morality. Does this justify the killing? In fact, couldn't one justify anything simply by forming a small subculture that approved of it? Charles Manson would be morally pure in killing innocents simply by virtue of forming a little coterie. How large must the group be in order to be a legitimate subculture or society? Does it need 10 or 15 people? How about just 3? Come to think about it, why can't my burglary partner and I found our own society with a morality of its own? Of course, if my partner dies, I could still claim that I was acting from an originally social set of norms. But why can't I dispense with the interpersonal agreements altogether and invent my own morality? After all, morality, on this view, is only an invention anyway. Conventionalist relativism seems to reduce to subjectivism. And subjectivism leads, as we have seen, to the demise of morality altogether. . . .

However, though we may fear the demise of morality as we have known it, this in itself may not be a good reason for rejecting relativism (that is, for judging it as false). Alas, truth may not always be edifying. But the consequences of this position are sufficiently alarming to prompt us to look carefully for some weakness in the relativist's argument. So let us examine the premises and conclusion listed earlier . . . as the three theses of relativism.

1. *The Diversity Thesis.* What is considered morally right and wrong varies from society to society, so that there are no universal moral standards held by all societies.
2. *The Dependency Thesis.* Whether or not it is right for an individual to act in a certain way depends on or is relative to the society to which he or she belongs.
3. *Ethical Relativism.* Therefore, there are no absolute or objective moral standards that apply to all people everywhere and at all times.

Does any one of these seem problematic? Let us consider the first thesis, the diversity thesis, which we have also called cultural relativism. Perhaps there is not as much diversity as anthropologists like Sumner and Benedict suppose. We can also see great similarities between the moral codes of various cultures. E. O. Wilson has identified over a score of common features,[8] and before him Clyde Kluckhohn noted some significant common ground:

> Every culture has a concept of murder, distinguishing this from execution, killing in war, and other "justifiable homicides." The notions of incest and other regulations upon sexual behavior, the prohibitions upon untruth under defined circumstances, of restitution and reciprocity, of mutual obligations between parents and children—these and many other moral concepts are altogether universal.[9]

And Colin Turnbull, whose description of the sadistic, semidisplaced Ik in Northern Uganda was seen as evidence of a people without principles of kindness and cooperation, has produced evidence that underneath the surface of this dying society is a deeper moral code, from a time when the tribe flourished, that occasionally surfaces and shows its nobler face.[10]

On the other hand, there is enormous cultural diversity, and many societies have radically different moral codes. Cultural relativism seems to be a fact; but even if it is, it does not by itself establish the truth of ethical relativism. Cultural diversity in itself is neutral relative to theories: The objectivist could concede complete cultural relativism but still defend a form of universalism, for he or she could argue that some cultures simply lack correct moral principles.

. . . [T]he first premise doesn't by itself, imply ethical relativism, and its denial doesn't disprove ethical relativism.

We turn to the crucial second thesis, the dependency thesis. . . . We distinguished between a weak and a strong thesis of dependency. The weak thesis says that the application of principles depends on the particular cultural predicament, whereas the strong thesis affirms that the principles themselves depend on that predicament. The nonrelativist can accept a certain relativity in the way moral principles are *applied* in various cultures, depending on beliefs, history, and environment. For example, a harsh environment with scarce natural resources may justify the Eskimos' brand of euthanasia to the objectivist, who in another environment would consistently reject that practice. One tribe in East Africa throws its deformed children into the river because it believes that such infants *belong* to the hippopotamus, the god of the river. We consider this a false belief, but the point is that the same principles of respect for property and for human life are operative in these contrary practices. These people differ with us only in belief, not in substantive moral principle. This is an illustration of how nonmoral beliefs (e.g., deformed children belong to the hippopotamus god), when applied to common moral principles (e.g., give to each his or her due), generate different actions in different cultures. In our own culture the difference in the nonmoral belief about the status of a fetus generates opposite moral prescriptions. So the fact that moral principles are weakly dependent doesn't show that ethical relativism is valid. In spite of this weak dependency on nonmoral factors, there could still be a set of general moral norms applicable to all cultures and even recognized in most, which are disregarded at a culture's own expense.

What the relativist needs is a strong thesis of dependency—that somehow all principles are essentially cultural inventions. But why should we choose to view morality this way? Is there anything to recommend the strong thesis over the weak thesis of dependency? The relativist may argue that in fact we lack an obvious impartial standard from which to judge. "Who's to say which culture is right and which is wrong?" But this seems to be dubious. We can reason and perform thought experiments in order to make a case for one system over another. We may not be able to *know* with certainty that our moral beliefs are closer to the truth than those of another culture or those of others within our own culture, but we may be *justified in believing* that they are. If we can be closer to the truth regarding factual or scientific matters, why can't we be closer to the truth on moral matters? Why can't a culture simply be confused or wrong about its moral perceptions? Why can't we say that a society like that of the Ik, which sees nothing wrong with enjoying watching its own children fall into fires, is less moral in that regard than the culture that cherishes children and grants them protection and equal rights? To take such a stand does not commit the fallacy of ethnocentrism, for in doing so we are seeking to derive principles through critical reason, not simply uncritical acceptance of our own mores.

Conclusion

Ethical relativism—the thesis that moral principles derive their validity from dependence on society or individual choice—seems plausible at first glance, but when scrutinized closely is seen to have some serious difficulties. Subjectivism seems to boil down to anarchistic individualism, and conventionalism fails to deal adequately with the problems of the reformer, the question of defining a culture, and the whole enterprise of moral criticism.

Notes

1. *History of Herodotus,* trans. George Rawlinson (Appleton, 1859), Bk. 3, Ch. 38.

2. John Ladd, *Ethical Relativism* (Wadsworth, 1973), p. 1.

3. Ruth Benedict, *Patterns of Culture* (New American Library, 1934), p. 257.

4. W. G. Sumner, *Folkways* (Ginn & Co., 1906), section 80, p. 76. Ruth Benedict indicates the depth of our cultural conditioning this way: "The very eyes with which we see the problem are conditioned by the long traditional habits of our own society." ["Anthropology and the Abnormal," *The Journal of General Psychology* (1934): 59–82.]

5. Ernest Hemingway, *Death in the Afternoon* (Scribners, 1932), p. 4.

6. Benedict, *Patterns of Culture,* p. 257.

7. Melville Herskovits, *Cultural Relativism* (Random House, 1972).

8. E. O. Wilson, *On Human Nature* (Bantam Books, 1979), p. 22f.

9. Clyde Kluckhohn, "Ethical Relativity: Sic et Non," *Journal of Philosophy* LII (1955).

10. Colin Turnbull, *The Mountain People* (Simon & Schuster, 1972).

POSTSCRIPT

Is Morality Relative to Culture?

Ethical relativism can be a very difficult thesis to state. It is not the same as what Pojman calls the "diversity thesis"—the thesis that what is considered right and wrong varies from society to society so that there are no universal moral standards held by all societies. The key word in the diversity thesis is *considered.* Pojman concedes that what is considered moral at one time and place is not always what is considered moral at another time and place. A nonrelativist like Pojman, however, will insist that it does not follow from the fact that people or groups disagree about what is moral (or have different opinions about what is moral) that both opinions are equally correct. Nor does it follow from that fact of disagreement that there are no universally valid moral principles. All that follows is that there is disagreement.

A relativist like Herskovits will agree that there is disagreement—at least when the parties are brought together. But since moral principles are in every case the product of a certain time and place, Herskovits considers Pojman's so-called universal moral norms pure fantasy.

One problem for the relativist who maintains that the thesis that our own perceptions, beliefs, and opinions are bound by ethnocentrism and are therefore unable to achieve any truly "objective" point of view is that the thesis of relativism seems to require just such a point of view for itself. If, on the other hand, relativistic ideas are simply those that have arisen at a certain time and place, subject to their own ethnocentrism, then we might wonder why it is that a relativist claims special status for them.

Classic social scientific views in the relativistic tradition are Ruth Benedict, *Patterns of Culture* (Pelican, 1946) and Melville J. Herskovits, *Man and His Works* (Alfred A. Knopf, 1948). The relevance of the anthropological data to philosophical issues is discussed by Kai Nielsen in "Ethical Relativism and the Facts of Cultural Relativity," *Social Research* (1966). Ethics and cultural relativity are also discussed in May Edel and Abraham Edel, eds., *Anthropology and Ethics: The Quest for Moral Understanding* (Press of Case Western Reserve University, 1968). Gilbert Harman has provided a sophisticated defense of moral relativism in his "Moral Relativism Defended," *Philosophical Review* (1975).

Further sources are David Wong, *Ethical Relativity* (University of California Press, 1984); Michael Krausz, ed., *Relativism: Interpretation and Conflict* (University of Notre Dame Press, 1989); Hugh LaFollette, "The Truth in Ethical Relativism," *Journal of Social Philosophy* (1991); and Christopher Norris, *Reclaiming Truth: A Critique of Cultural Relativism* (Duke University Press, 1996).

Recent publications include Francis J. Beckwith and Gregory Koukl, *Relativism: Feet Firmly Planted in Mid-Air* (Baker Book House, 1998); John W. Cook,

Morality and Cultural Differences (Oxford University Press, 1999); Peter Kreeft, *A Refutation of Moral Relativism: Interviews With an Absolutist* (Ignatius Press, 1999); Jane K. Cowan et al., eds., *Culture and Rights: Anthropological Perspectives* (Cambridge University Press, 2002); Neil Levy, *Moral Relativism: A Short Introduction* (Oneworld Publications, 2002); Mohammed A. Shomali, *Ethical Relativism: An Analysis of the Foundations of Morality* (Islamic College for Advanced Studies Press, 2001); and Robert Streiffer, *Moral Relativism and Reasons for Action* (Routledge, 2003).

ISSUE 2

Does Morality Need Religion?

YES: C. Stephen Layman, from *The Shape of the Good: Christian Reflections on the Foundations of Ethics* (University of Notre Dame Press, 1991)

NO: John Arthur, from "Religion, Morality, and Conscience," in John Arthur, ed., *Morality and Moral Controversies,* 4th ed. (Prentice Hall, 1996)

ISSUE SUMMARY

YES: Philosopher C. Stephen Layman argues that morality makes the most sense from a theistic perspective and that a purely secular perspective is insufficient. The secular perspective, Layman asserts, does not adequately deal with secret violations, and it does not allow for the possibility of fulfillment of people's deepest needs in an afterlife.

NO: Philosopher John Arthur counters that morality is logically independent of religion, although there are historical connections. Religion, he believes, is not necessary for moral guidance or moral answers; morality is social.

There is a widespread feeling that morality and religion are connected. One view is that religion provides a ground for morality, so without religion there is no morality. Thus, a falling away from religion implies a falling away from morality.

Such thoughts have troubled many people. The Russian novelist Dostoyevsky (1821–1881) wrote, "If there is no God, then everything is permitted." Many Americans today also believe that religious faith is important. They often maintain that even if doctrines and dogmas cannot be known for certain, religion nevertheless leads to morality and good behavior. President Dwight D. Eisenhower is reputed to have said that everyone should have a religious faith but that it did not matter what that faith was. And many daily newspapers throughout the country advise their readers to attend the church or synagogue of their choice. Apparently, the main reason why people think it is important to subscribe to a religion is that only in this way will one be able to attain morality. If there is no God, then everything is permitted and there is moral chaos. Moral chaos can be played out in societies and, on a smaller scale, within the minds of individuals. Thus, if you do not believe in God, then you will confront moral chaos; you will be liable to permit (and permit yourself to do) anything, and you will have no moral bearings at all.

Such a view seems to face several problems, however. For example, what are we to say of the morally good atheist or of the morally good but completely non-religious person? A true follower of the view that morality derives from religion might reply that we are simply begging the question if we believe that such people *could* be morally good. Such people might do things that are morally right and thus might *seem* good, the reply would go, but they would not be acting for the right reason (obedience to God). Such people would not have the same anchor or root for their seemingly moral attitudes that religious persons do.

Another problem for the view that links morality with religion comes from the following considerations: If you hold this view, what do you say of devoutly religious people who belong to religious traditions and who support moralities that are different from your own? If morality is indeed derived from religion, if different people are thus led to follow different moralities, and if the original religions are not themselves subject to judgment, then it is understandable how different people arrive at different moral views. But the views will still be different and perhaps even incompatible. If so, the statement that morality derives from religion must mean that one can derive *a* morality from *a* religion (and not that one derives morality itself from religion). The problem is that by allowing this variation among religions and moralities back into the picture, we seem to allow moral chaos back in, too.

The view that what God commands is good, what God prohibits is evil, and without divine commands and prohibitions nothing is either good or bad in itself is called the *divine command theory,* or the *divine imperative view.* This view resists the recognition of any source of good or evil that is not tied to criteria or standards of God's own creation. Such a recognition is thought to go against the idea of God's omnipotence. A moral law that applied to God but was not of God's own creation would seem to limit God in a way in which he cannot be limited. But, on the other hand, this line of thought (that no moral law outside of God's own making should apply to him) seems contrary to the orthodox Christian view that God is good. For if good means something in accordance with God's will, then when we say that God is good, we are only saying that he acts in accordance with his own will—and this just does not seem to be enough.

In the following selections, C. Stephen Layman argues that a religious perspective makes better sense of moral commitment than a secular perspective. Indeed, in his view, it is not even clear that a secular individual who followed the dictates of morality would be rational. John Arthur asserts that morality does not need a religious foundation at all and that morality is social.

C. Stephen Layman

 **YES**

Ethics and the Kingdom of God

Why build a theory of ethics on the assumption that there is a God? Why not simply endorse a view of ethics along . . . secular lines . . . ? I shall respond to these questions in [two] stages. First, I contrast the secular and religious perspectives on morality. Second, I explain why I think the moral life makes more sense from the point of view of theism [belief in God] than from that of atheism. . . .

⋅❦⋅

As I conceive it, the modern secular perspective on morality involves at least two elements. First, there is no afterlife; each individual human life ends at death. It follows that the only goods available to an individual are those he or she can obtain this side of death.[1]

Second, on the secular view, moral value is an *emergent* phenomenon. That is, moral value is "a feature of certain effects though it is not a feature of their causes" (as wetness is a feature of H_2O, but not of hydrogen or oxygen).[2] Thus, the typical contemporary secular view has it that moral value emerges only with the arrival of very complex nervous systems (viz., human brains), late in the evolutionary process. There is no Mind "behind the scenes" on the secular view, no intelligent Creator concerned with the affairs of human existence. As one advocate of the secular view puts it, "Ethics, though not consciously created [either by humans or by God], is a product of social life which has the function of promoting values common to the members of society."[3]

By way of contrast, the religious point of view (in my use of the phrase) includes a belief in God and in life after death. God is defined as an eternal being who is almighty and perfectly morally good. Thus, from the religious point of view, morality is not an emergent phenomenon, for God's goodness has always been in existence, and is not the product of nonmoral causes. Moreover, from the religious point of view, there are goods available after death. Specifically, there awaits the satisfaction of improved relations with God and with redeemed creatures.

It is important to note that, from the religious perspective, *the existence of God and life after death* are not independent hypotheses. If God exists, then at

From C. Stephen Layman, *The Shape of the Good: Christian Reflections on the Foundations of Ethics* (University of Notre Dame Press, 1991). Copyright © 1991 by University of Notre Dame Press, Notre Dame, IN 46556. Reprinted by permission.

least two lines of reasoning lend support to the idea that death is not final. While I cannot here scrutinize these lines of reasoning, I believe it will be useful to sketch them.[4] (1) It has often been noted that we humans seem unable to find complete fulfillment in the present life. Even those having abundant material possessions and living in the happiest of circumstances find themselves, upon reflection, profoundly unsatisfied. . . . [I]f this earthly life is the whole story, it appears that our deepest longings will remain unfulfilled. But if God is good, He surely will not leave our deepest longings unfulfilled provided He is able to fulfill them—at least to the extent that we are willing to accept His gracious aid. So, since our innermost yearnings are not satisfied in this life, it is likely that they will be satisfied after death.

(2) Human history has been one long story of injustice, of the oppression of the poor and weak by the rich and powerful. The lives of relatively good people are often miserable, while the wicked prosper. Now, if God exists, He is able to correct such injustices, though He does not correct all of them in the present life. But if God is also good, He will not leave such injustices forever unrectified. It thus appears that He will rectify matters at some point after death. This will involve benefits for some in the afterlife—it may involve penalties for others. (However, the . . . possibility of post-mortem punishment does not necessarily imply the possibility of hell *as standardly conceived.*)

We might sum up the main difference between the secular and religious views by saying that the only goods available from a secular perspective are *earthly* goods. Earthly goods include such things as physical health, friendship, pleasure, self-esteem, knowledge, enjoyable activities, an adequate standard of living, etc. The religious or theistic perspective recognizes these earthly goods *as good,* but it insists that there are non-earthly or *transcendent* goods. These are goods available only if God exists and there is life after death for humans. Transcendent goods include harmonious relations with God prior to death as well as the joys of the afterlife—right relations with both God and redeemed creatures.

[One secular] defense of the virtues amounts to showing that society cannot function well unless individuals have moral virtue. If we ask, "Why should we as individuals care about society?", the answer will presumably be along the following lines: "Individuals cannot flourish apart from a well-functioning society, so *morality pays for the individual."*

This defense of morality raises two questions we must now consider. First, is it misguided to defend morality by an appeal to self-interest? Many people feel that morality and self-interest are fundamentally at odds: "If you perform an act because you see that it is in your interest to do so, then you aren't doing the right thing *just because it's right.* A successful defense of morality must be a defense of duty for duty's sake. Thus, the appeal to self-interest is completely misguided." Second, *does* morality really pay for the individual? More particularly, does morality always pay in terms of earthly goods? Let us take these questions up in turn.

(1) Do we desert the moral point of view if we defend morality on the grounds that it pays? Consider an analogy with etiquette. Why should one bother with etiquette? Should one do the well-mannered thing simply for its own sake? Do we keep our elbows off the table or refrain from belching just because these things are "proper"?

To answer this question we must distinguish between the *justification of an institution* and *the justification of a particular act within that institution*. (By 'institution' I refer to any system of activities specified by rules.) This distinction can be illustrated in the case of the game (institution) of baseball. If we ask a player why he performs a particular act during a game, he will probably give an answer such as, "To put my opponent out" or "To get a home run." These answers obviously would not be relevant if the question were, "Why play baseball at all?" Relevant answers to this second question would name some advantage for the individual player, e.g., "Baseball is fun" or "It's good exercise." Thus, a justification of the institution of baseball (e.g., "It's good exercise") is quite different from a justification of a particular act within the institution (e.g., "To get a home run").

Now let's apply this distinction to our question about etiquette. If our question concerns the justification of a particular act within the institution of etiquette, then the answer may reasonably be, in effect, "This is what's proper. This is what the rules of etiquette prescribe." . . .

But plainly there are deeper questions we can ask about etiquette. Who hasn't wondered, at times, what the point of the institution of etiquette is? Why do we have these quirky rules, some of which seem to make little sense? When these more fundamental questions concerning the entire institution of etiquette are being asked, it makes no sense to urge etiquette for etiquette's sake. What is needed is a description of the human *ends* the institution fulfills— ends which play a justificatory role similar to fun or good exercise in the case of baseball. And it is not difficult to identify some of these ends. For example, the rules of etiquette seem designed, in part, to facilitate social interaction; things just go more smoothly if there are agreed upon ways of greeting, eating, conversing, etc.

If anyone asks, "Why should I as an individual bother about etiquette?", an initial reply might be: "Because if you frequently violate the rules of etiquette, people will shun you." If anyone wonders why he should care about being shunned, we will presumably reply that good social relations are essential to human flourishing, and hence that a person is jeopardizing his own best interests if he places no value at all on etiquette. Thus, in the end, a defense of the institution of etiquette seems to involve the claim that the institution of etiquette *pays* for those who participate in it; it would not be illuminating to answer the question, "Why bother about etiquette?" by saying that etiquette is to be valued for its own sake.

Now, just as we distinguish between justifying the institution of etiquette (or baseball) and justifying a particular act within the institution, so we must distinguish between justifying the institution of morality and justifying a particular act within the institution. When choosing a particular course of action we may simply want to know what's right. But a more ultimate question also cries out for an answer: "What is the point of the institution of morality, anyway? Why should one bother with it?" It is natural to respond by saying that society cannot function well without morality, and individuals cannot flourish apart from a well-functioning society. In short, defending the institution of morality involves claiming that morality pays for the individual in the long run. It seems obscurantist to preach duty for duty's sake, once the more fundamental question about the point of the institution of morality has been raised.

But if morality is defended on the grounds that it pays, doesn't this distort moral motivation? Won't it mean that we no longer do things because they are right, but rather because they are in our self-interest? No. We must bear in mind our distinction between the reasons that justify a particular act within an institution and the reasons that justify the institution itself. A baseball player performs a given act in order to get on base or put an opponent out; he does not calculate whether this particular swing of the bat (or throw of the ball) is fun or good exercise. A well-mannered person is not constantly calculating whether a given act will improve her relations with others, she simply does "the proper thing." Similarly, even if we defend morality on the grounds that it pays, it does not follow that the motive for each moral act becomes, "It will pay" for we are not constantly thinking of the philosophical issues concerning the justification of the entire system of morality; for the most part we simply do things because they are right, honest, fair, loving, etc. Nevertheless, our willingness to plunge wholeheartedly into "the moral game" is apt to be vitiated should it become clear to us that the game does not pay.

At this point it appears that the institution of morality is justified only if it pays for the individuals who participate in it. For if being moral does not pay for individuals, it is difficult to see why they should bother with it. The appeal to duty for duty's sake is irrelevant when we are asking for a justification of the institution of morality itself.

(2) But we must now ask, "Does morality in fact pay?" There are at least four reasons for supposing that morality does not pay from a *secular* perspective. (a) One problem for the secular view arises from the fact that the moral point of view involves a concern for *all* human beings—or at least for all humans affected by one's actions. Thus, within Christian theology, the parable of the good Samaritan is well known for its expansion of the category of "my neighbor." But human societies seem able to get along well without extending full moral concern to all outsiders; this is the essence of tribal morality. Thus, explorers in the 1700s found that the Sioux Indians followed a strict code in dealing with each other, but regarded themselves as free to steal horses from the Crow. Later on, American whites repeatedly broke treaties with the American Indians in a way that would not have been possible had the Indians been regarded as equals. It is no exaggeration to say that throughout much of human history tribal morality has been the morality humans lived by.

And so, while one must agree . . . that the virtues are necessary for the existence of society, it is not clear that this amounts to anything more than a defense of tribal morality. . . . From a purely secular point of view, it is unclear why the scope of moral concern must extend beyond one's society—or, more precisely, why one's concern must extend to groups of people outside of one's society *who are powerless and stand in the way of things one's society wants.* Why should the members of a modern industrial state extend full moral consideration to a tiny Amazonian tribe? . . .

(b) A second problem for secular views concerns the possibility of secret violations of moral rules. What becomes of conscientiousness when one can break the rules in secret, without anyone knowing? After all, if I can break the rules in secret, I will not cause any social disharmony. Of course, there can be no breaking of the rules in secret if there is a God of the Christian type, who knows every human thought as well as every human act. But there are cases in which it is extraordinarily unlikely that any *humans* will discover one's rule breaking. Hence, from a secular perspective, there are cases in which secret violations of morality are possible.

Consider the following case. Suppose A has borrowed some money from B, but A discovers that B has made a mistake in his records. Because of the mistake, B believes that A has already paid the money back. B even goes out of his way to thank A for prompt payment on the loan. Let us further suppose that B is quite wealthy, and hence not in need of the money. Is it in A's interest to pay the money back? Not paying the money back would be morally wrong; but would it be irrational, from a secular point of view? Not necessarily. Granted, it might be irrational in some cases, e.g., if A would have intense guilt feelings should he fail to repay the loan. But suppose A will not feel guilty because he really needs the money (and knows that B does not need it), and because he understands that secret violations belong to a special and rare category of action. Then, from a secular point of view, it is doubtful that paying the loan would be in A's interest.

The point is not that theists never cheat or lie. Unfortunately they do. The point is rather that secret violations of morality arguably pay off from a secular point of view. And so, once again, it seems that there is a "game" that pays off better (in terms of earthly goods) than the relatively idealistic morality endorsed by the great ethicists, viz., one allowing secret "violations."

(c) Even supposing that morality pays for some people, does it pay for *everyone* on the secular view? Can't there be well-functioning societies in which some of the members are "moral freeloaders"? In fact, don't all actual societies have members who maintain an appearance of decency, but are in fact highly manipulative of others? How would one show, on secular grounds, that it is in the interest of these persons to be moral? Furthermore, according to psychiatrists, some people are highly amoral, virtually without feelings of guilt or shame. Yet in numerous cases these amoral types appear to be happy. These "successful egoists" are often intelligent, charming, and able to evade legal penalties for their unconventional behavior.[5] How could one show, on secular grounds, that it is in the interests of such successful egoists to be moral? They seem to find their amoral lives amply rewarding.

(d) Another problem from the secular perspective stems from the fact that in some cases morality demands that one risk death. Since death cuts one off from all earthly goods, what sense does it make to be moral (in a given case) if the risk of death is high?

This point must be stated with care. In many cases it makes sense, from a secular point of view, to risk one's life. For example, it makes sense if the risk is small and the earthly good to be gained is great; after all, one risks one's life driving to work. Or again, risking one's life makes sense from a secular point of view if failing to do so will probably lead to profound and enduring earthly unhappiness. Thus, a woman might take an enormous risk to save her child from an attacker. She might believe that she would be "unable to live with herself" afterward if she stood by and let the attacker kill or maim her child. Similarly, a man might be willing to die for his country, because he could not bear the dishonor resulting from a failure to act courageously.

But failing to risk one's life does not always lead to profound and enduring earthly unhappiness. Many soldiers play it safe in battle when risk taking is essential for victory; they may judge that victory is not worth the personal risks. And many subjects of ruthless tyrants entirely avoid the risks involved in resistance and reform. Though it may be unpleasant for such persons to find themselves regarded as cowards, this unpleasantness does not necessarily lead to profound and enduring earthly unhappiness. It seems strained to claim that what is commonly regarded as moral courage always pays in terms of earthly goods.

At this point it appears that the institution of morality cannot be justified from a secular point of view. For, as we have seen, the institution of morality is justified only if it pays (in the long run) for the individuals who participate in it. But if by "morality" we mean the relatively idealistic code urged on us by the great moralists, it appears that the institution of morality does not pay, according to the secular point of view. This is not to say that no moral code could pay off in terms of earthly goods; a tribal morality of some sort might pay for most people, especially if it were to include conventions which skirt the problems inherent in my "secret violation" and "risk of death" cases. But such a morality would be a far cry from the morality most of us actually endorse.

Defenders of secular morality may claim that these difficulties evaporate if we look at morality from an evolutionary point of view. The survival of the species depends on the sacrifice of individuals in some cases, and the end of morality is the survival of the species. Hence, it is not surprising that being highly moral will not always pay off for individuals.

This answer is confused for two reasons. First, even if morality does have survival value for the species, we have seen that this does not by itself justify the individual's involvement in the institution of morality. In fact, it does not justify such involvement if what is best for the species is not what is best for the individual member of the species. And I have been arguing that, from a secular point of view, the interests of the species and the individual diverge.

Second, while evolution might explain why humans *feel* obligated to make sacrifices, it is wholly unable to account for genuine moral obligation. If we did not feel obligated to make sacrifices for others, it might be that the species would have died out long ago. So, moral *feelings* may have survival value. However, *feeling obligated* is not the same thing as *being obligated*. . . . Thus, to show that moral feelings have survival value is not to show that there are any actual moral obligations at all. . . . The point is, the evolutionary picture does not require the existence of real obligations; it demands only the existence of moral feelings or beliefs. Moral feelings or beliefs would motivate action even if there were in actuality no moral obligations. For example, the belief that human life is sacred may very well have survival value even if human life is not sacred. Moral obligation, as opposed to moral feeling, is thus an unnecessary postulate from the standpoint of evolution.

At this point defenders of the secular view typically make one of two moves: (i) They claim that even if morality does not pay, there remain moral truths which we must live up to; or (ii) they may claim that morality pays in subtle ways which we have so far overlooked. Let us take these claims up in turn.

(i) It may be claimed that moral obligation is just a fact of life, woven into the structure of reality. Morality may not always pay, but certain moral standards remain true, e.g., "Lying is wrong" or "Human life is sacred." These are not made true by evolution or God, but are necessary truths, independent of concrete existence, like "1 + 1 = 2" or "There are no triangular circles."

There are at least three difficulties with this suggestion. First, assuming that there are such necessary truths about morality, why should we care about them or pay them any attention? We may grant that an act is correct from the moral point of view and yet wonder whether we have good reason to participate in the institution of morality. So, even if we grant that various statements of the form "One ought to do X" are necessarily true, this does not show that the institution of morality pays off. It just says that morality is a "game" whose rules are necessary truths. . . . To defend the institution of morality simply on the grounds that certain moral statements are necessarily true is to urge duty for duty's sake. And . . . this is not an acceptable defense of the institution of morality.

Second, the idea that some moral truths are necessary comports poorly with the usual secular account. As Mavrodes points out, necessary moral truths seem to be what Plato had in mind when he spoke about the Form of the Good. And Plato's view, though not contradicted by modern science, receives no support from it either. Plato's Form of the Good is not an emergent phenomenon, but is rather woven into the very structure of reality, independently of physical processes such as evolution. So, Plato's view is incompatible with the typically modern secular view that moral value is an emergent phenomenon, coming into existence with the arrival of the human nervous system. For this reason, Plato's views have "often been taken to be congenial . . . to a religious understanding of the world."[6]

Third, it is very doubtful that there are any necessary truths of the form "One ought to do X." We have seen that the institution of morality stands unjustified if participation in it does not pay (in the long run) for individuals. And why should we suppose that there are *any* necessary moral truths if the institution of morality is unjustified? . . . [S]tatements of the form "One ought to do X" are not *necessary* truths, though they may be true *if* certain conditions are met. . . . Hence, if there are any necessary moral truths, they appear to be conditional (if-then) in form: If certain conditions exist, one ought to do X. Among the conditions, as we have seen, is the condition that doing X pays for the individual in the long run. So, it is very doubtful that there are any necessary moral truths of the form "One ought to do X."[7] The upshot is that morality is partly grounded in those features of reality which guarantee that morality pays; and the secular view lacks the metaphysical resources for making such a guarantee. . . .

(ii) But some have claimed that, if we look closely at human psychology, we can see that morality does pay *in terms of earthly goods*. For example, Plato suggested that only a highly moral person could have harmony between the various elements of his soul (such as reason and desire). Others have claimed that being highly moral is the only means to inner satisfaction. We humans are just so constituted that violations of morality never leave us with a net gain. Sure, we may gain earthly goods of one sort or another by lying, stealing, etc., but these are always outweighed by inner discord or a sense of dissatisfaction with ourselves.

There are several problems with this. First, some may doubt that moral virtue is the best route to inner peace. After all, one may experience profound inner discord when one has done what is right. It can be especially upsetting to stand up for what is right when doing so is unpopular; indeed, many people avoid "making waves" precisely because it upsets their inner peace. . . .

Second, how good is the evidence that inner peace *always* outweighs the benefits achievable through unethical action? Perhaps guilt feelings and inner discord are a reasonable price to pay for certain earthly goods. If a cowardly act enables me to stay alive, or a dishonest act makes me wealthy, I may judge that my gains are worth the accompanying guilt feelings. A quiet conscience is not everything.

Third, if inner discord or a sense of dissatisfaction stems from a feeling of having done wrong, why not reassess my standards? Therapists are familiar with the phenomenon of false guilt. For example, a married woman may feel guilty for having sex with her spouse. The cure will involve enabling the patient to view sex as a legitimate means of expressing affection. The point is that just because I feel a certain type of act is wrong, it does not follow that the only route to inner peace is to avoid the action. I also have the option of revising my standards, which may enable me to pursue self-interested goals in a less inhibited fashion. Why drag along any unnecessary moral baggage? How could it be shown, on secular grounds, that it is in my interest to maintain the more idealistic standards endorsed by the great moralists? Certainly, some people have much less idealistic standards than others, and yet seem no less happy.

By way of contrast with the secular view, it is not difficult to see how morality might pay if there is a God of the Christian type. First, God loves all humans and wants all included in his kingdom. So, a tribal morality would violate his demands, and to violate his demands is to strain one's most important personal relationship. Second, there are no secret violations of morality if God exists. Since God is omniscient, willful wrongdoing of any sort will estrange the wrongdoer from God. Third, while earthly society may be able to function pretty well even though there exists a small number of "moral freeloaders," the freeloaders themselves are certainly not attaining harmonious relations with God. Accordingly, their ultimate fulfillment is in jeopardy. Fourth, death is the end of earthly life, but it is not the end of conscious existence, according to Christianity. Therefore, death does not end one's opportunity for personal fulfillment; indeed, if God is perfectly good and omnipotent, we can only assume that the afterlife will result in the fulfillment of our deepest needs—unless we willfully reject God's efforts to supply those needs.

So, it seems to me that the moral life makes more sense from a theistic perspective than from a secular perspective. Of course, I do not claim that I have proved the existence of God, and a full discussion of this metaphysical issue would take us too far from matters at hand.[8] But if I have shown that the moral life makes more sense from a theistic perspective than from a secular one, then I have provided an important piece of evidence in favor of the rationality of belief in God. Moreover, I believe that I have turned back one objection to the Christian teleological view, namely, the allegation that theism is unnecessary metaphysical baggage.

Notes

1. It can be argued that, even from a secular perspective, some benefits and harms are available after death. For example, vindicating the reputation of a deceased person may be seen as benefiting that person. See, for example, Thomas Nagel, *Mortal Questions* (London: Cambridge University Press, 1979), pp. 1–10. But even if we grant that these are goods for the deceased, it is obvious that, from the secular point of view, such post-mortem goods cannot be consciously enjoyed by the deceased. They are not available in the sense that he will never take pleasure in them.

2. George Mavrodes, "Religion and the Queerness of Morality," in *Rationality, Religious Belief, and Moral Commitment,* ed. Robert Audi and William J. Wainwright (Ithaca, N.Y.: Cornell University Press, 1986), p. 223.

3. Peter Singer, *Practical Ethics,* (London: Cambridge University Press, 1970), p. 209.

4. For an excellent discussion of arguments for immortality, see William J. Wainwright, *Philosophy of Religion* (Belmont, Calif.: Wadsworth, 1988), pp. 99–111.

5. My source for these claims about "happy psychopaths" is Singer, *Practical Ethics,* pp. 214–216. Singer in turn is drawing from Hervey Cleckley, *The Mask of Sanity, (An Attempt to Clarify Some Issues About the So-Called Psychopathic Personality),* 5th ed. (St. Louis, Mo.: E. S. Cleckley, 1988).

6. Mavrodes, "Religion and the Queerness of Morality," p. 224. I am borrowing from Mavrodes throughout this paragraph.

7. Those acquainted with modal logic may have a question here. By a principle of modal logic, if p is a necessary truth and p necessarily implies q, then q is a necessary truth. So, if it is necessarily true that "certain conditions are met" and necessarily true that "If they are met, one ought to X," then, "One ought to do X" is a necessary truth. But I assume it is not *necessarily true* that "certain conditions are met." In my judgment it would be most implausible to suppose, e.g., that "Morality pays for humans" is a necessary truth.

8. Two fine discussions of moral arguments for theism are Robert Merrihew Adams, "Moral Arguments for Theistic Belief," in *Rationality and Religious Belief,* ed. C. F. Delaney (Notre Dame, Ind.: University of Notre Dame Press, 1979), pp. 116–140, and J. L. Mackie, *The Miracle of Theism* (Oxford: Oxford University Press, 1982), pp. 102–118.

John Arthur

Religion, Morality, and Conscience

My first and prime concern in this paper is to explore the connections, if any, between morality and religion. I will argue that in fact religion is not necessary for morality. Yet despite the lack of any logical or other necessary connection, I will claim, there remain important respects in which the two are related. In the concluding section I will discuss the notion of moral conscience, and then look briefly at the various respects in which morality is "social" and the implications of that idea for moral education. First, however, I want to say something about the subjects: just what are we referring to when we speak of morality and of religion?

Morality and Religion

A useful way to approach the first question—the nature of morality—is to ask what it would mean for a society to exist without a social moral code. How would such people think and behave? What would that society look like? First, it seems clear that such people would never feel guilt or resentment. For example, the notions that I ought to remember my parent's anniversary, that he has a moral responsibility to help care for his children after the divorce, that she has a right to equal pay for equal work, and that discrimination on the basis of race is unfair would be absent in such a society. Notions of duty, rights, and obligations would not be present, except perhaps in the legal sense; concepts of justice and fairness would also be foreign to these people. In short, people would have no tendency to evaluate or criticize the behavior of others, nor to feel remorse about their own behavior. Children would not be taught to be ashamed when they steal or hurt others, nor would they be allowed to complain when others treat them badly. (People might, however, feel regret at a decision that didn't turn out as they had hoped; but that would only be because their expectations were frustrated, not because they feel guilty.)

Such a society lacks a moral code. What, then, of religion? Is it possible that a people lacking a morality would nonetheless have religious beliefs? It seems clear that it is possible. Suppose every day these same people file into their place of worship to pay homage to God (they may believe in many gods or in one all-powerful creator of heaven and earth). Often they can be heard pray-

From John Arthur, "Religion, Morality, and Conscience," in John Arthur, ed., *Morality and Moral Controversies,* 4th ed. (Prentice Hall, 1996). Copyright © 1996 by John Arthur. Reprinted by permission of the author.

ing to God for help in dealing with their problems and thanking Him for their good fortune. Frequently they give sacrifices to God, sometimes in the form of money spent to build beautiful temples and churches, other times by performing actions they believe God would approve such as helping those in need. These practices might also be institutionalized, in the sense that certain people are assigned important leadership roles. Specific texts might also be taken as authoritative, indicating the ways God has acted in history and His role in their lives or the lives of their ancestors.

To have a moral code, then, is to tend to evaluate (perhaps without even expressing it) the behavior of others and to feel guilt at certain actions when we perform them. Religion, on the other hand, involves beliefs in supernatural power(s) that created and perhaps also control nature, the tendency to worship and pray to those supernatural forces or beings, and the presence of organizational structures and authoritative texts. The practices of morality and religion are thus importantly different. One involves our attitudes toward various forms of behavior (lying and killing, for example), typically expressed using the notions of rules, rights, and obligations. The other, religion, typically involves prayer, worship, beliefs about the supernatural, institutional forms and authoritative texts.

We come, then, to the central question: What is the connection, if any, between a society's moral code and its religious practices and beliefs? Many people have felt that morality is in some way dependent on religion or religious truths. But what sort of "dependence" might there be? In what follows I distinguish various ways in which one might claim that religion is necessary for morality, arguing against those who claim morality depends in some way on religion. I will also suggest, however, some other important ways in which the two are related, concluding with a brief discussion of conscience and moral education.

Religious Motivation and Guidance

One possible role that religion might play in morality relates to motives people have. Religion, it is often said, is necessary so that people will DO right. Typically, the argument begins with the important point that doing what is right often has costs: refusing to shoplift or cheat can mean people go without some good or fail a test; returning a billfold means they don't get the contents. Religion is therefore said to be necessary in that it provides motivation to do the right thing. God rewards those who follow His commands by providing for them a place in heaven or by insuring that they prosper and are happy on earth. He also punishes those who violate the moral law. Others emphasize less self-interested ways in which religious motives may encourage people to act rightly. Since God is the creator of the universe and has ordained that His plan should be followed, they point out, it is important to live one's life in accord with this divinely ordained plan. Only by living a moral life, it is said, can people live in harmony with the larger, divinely created order.

The first claim, then, is that religion is necessary to provide moral motivation. The problem with that argument, however, is that religious motives are far from the only ones people have. For most of us, a decision to do the right thing (if that is our decision) is made for a variety of reasons: "What if I get caught? What if somebody sees me—what will he or she think? How will I feel afterwards? Will I regret it?" Or maybe the thought of cheating just doesn't arise. We were raised to be a decent person, and that's what we are—period. Behaving fairly and treating others well is more important than whatever we might gain from stealing or cheating, let alone seriously harming another person. So it seems clear that many motives for doing the right thing have nothing whatsoever to do with religion. Most of us, in fact, do worry about getting caught, being blamed, and being looked down on by others. We also may do what is right just because it's right, or because we don't want to hurt others or embarrass family and friends. To say that we need religion to act morally is mistaken; indeed it seems to me that many of us, when it really gets down to it, don't give much of a thought to religion when making moral decisions. All those other reasons are the ones which we tend to consider, or else we just don't consider cheating and stealing at all. So far, then, there seems to be no reason to suppose that people can't be moral yet irreligious at the same time.

A second argument that is available for those who think religion is necessary to morality, however, focuses on moral guidance and knowledge rather than on people's motives. However much people may want to do the right thing, according to this view, we cannot ever know for certain what is right without the guidance of religious teaching. Human understanding is simply inadequate to this difficult and controversial task; morality involves immensely complex problems, and so we must consult religious revelation for help.

Again, however, this argument fails. First, consider how much we would need to know about religion and revelation in order for religion to provide moral guidance. Besides being sure that there is a God, we'd also have to think about which of the many religions is true. How can anybody be sure his or her religion is the right one? But even if we assume the Judeo-Christian God is the real one, we still need to find out just what it is He wants us to do, which means we must think about revelation.

Revelation comes in at least two forms, and not even all Christians agree on which is the best way to understand revelation. Some hold that revelation occurs when God tells us what he wants by providing us with His words: The Ten Commandments are an example. Many even believe, as evangelist Billy Graham once said, that the entire *Bible* was written by God using 39 secretaries. Others, however, doubt that the "word of God" refers literally to the words God has spoken, but believe instead that the *Bible* is an historical document, written by human beings, of the events or occasions in which God revealed Himself. It is an especially important document, of course, but nothing more than that. So on this second view revelation is not understood as *statements* made by God but rather as His *acts* such as leading His people from Egypt, testing Job, and sending His son as an example of the ideal life. The *Bible* is not itself revelation, it's the historical account of revelatory actions.

If we are to use revelation as a moral guide, then, we must first know what is to count as revelation—words given us by God, historical events, or both? But even supposing that we could somehow answer those questions, the problems of relying on revelation are still not over since we still must interpret that revelation. Some feel, for example, that the *Bible* justifies various forms of killing, including war and capital punishment, on the basis of such statements as "An eye for an eye." Others, emphasizing such sayings as "Judge not lest ye be judged" and "Thou shalt not kill," believe the *Bible* demands absolute pacifism. How are we to know which interpretation is correct? It is likely, of course, that the answer people give to such religious questions will be influenced in part at least by their own moral beliefs: if capital punishment is thought to be unjust, for example, then an interpreter will seek to read the *Bible* in a way that is consistent with that moral truth. That is not, however, a happy conclusion for those wishing to rest morality on revelation, for it means that their understanding of what God has revealed is itself dependent on their prior moral views. Rather than revelation serving as a guide for morality, morality is serving as a guide for how we interpret revelation.

So my general conclusion is that far from providing a short-cut to moral understanding, looking to revelation for guidance often creates more questions and problems. It seems wiser under the circumstances to address complex moral problems like abortion, capital punishment, and affirmative action directly, considering the pros and cons of each side, rather than to seek answers through the much more controversial and difficult route of revelation.

The Divine Command Theory

It may seem, however, that we have still not really gotten to the heart of the matter. Even if religion is not necessary for moral motivation or guidance, it is often claimed, religion is necessary in another more fundamental sense. According to this view, religion is necessary for morality because without God there could BE no right or wrong. God, in other words, provides the foundation or bedrock on which morality is grounded. This idea was expressed by Bishop R. C. Mortimer:

> "God made us and all the world. Because of that He has an absolute claim on our obedience. . . . From [this] it follows that a thing is not right simply because we think it is. It is right because God commands it."[1]

What Bishop Mortimer has in mind can be seen by comparing moral rules with legal ones. Legal statutes, we know, are created by legislatures; if the state assembly of New York had not passed a law limiting speed people can travel, then there would be no such legal obligation. Without the statutory enactments, such a law simply would not exist. Mortimer's view, the *divine command theory*, would mean that God has the same sort of relation to moral law as legislature has to statutes it enacts: without God's commands there would be no moral rules, just as without a legislature there would be no statutes.

Defenders of the divine command theory often add to this a further claim, that only by assuming God sits at the foundation of morality can we explain the objective difference between right and wrong. This point was forcefully argued by F. C. Copleston in a 1948 British Broadcasting Corporation radio debate with Bertrand Russell.

Copleston: . . . The validity of such an interpretation of man's conduct depends on the recognition of God's existence, obviously. . . . Let's take a look at the Commandant of the [Nazi] concentration camp at Belsen. That appears to you as undesirable and evil and to me too. To Adolf Hitler we suppose it appeared as something good and desirable. I suppose you'd have to admit that for Hitler it was good and for you it is evil.

Russell: No, I shouldn't go so far as that. I mean, I think people can make mistakes in that as they can in other things. If you have jaundice you see things yellow that are not yellow. You're making a mistake.

Copleston: Yes, one can make mistakes, but can you make a mistake if it's simply a question of reference to a feeling or emotion? Surely Hitler would be the only possible judge of what appealed to his emotions.

Russell: . . . You can say various things about that; among others, that if that sort of thing makes that sort of appeal to Hitler's emotions, then Hitler makes quite a different appeal to my emotions.

Copleston: Granted. But there's no objective criterion outside feeling then for condemning the conduct of the Commandant of Belsen, in your view. . . . The human being's idea of the content of the moral law depends certainly to a large extent on education and environment, and a man has to use his reason in assessing the validity of the actual moral ideas of his social group. But the possibility of criticizing the accepted moral code presupposes that there is an objective standard, that there is an ideal moral order, which imposes itself. . . . It implies the existence of a real foundation of God.[2]

Against those who, like Bertrand Russell, seek to ground morality in feelings and attitudes, Copleston argues that there must be a more solid foundation if we are to be able to claim truly that the Nazis were evil. God, according to Copleston, is able to provide the objective basis for the distinction, which we all know to exist, between right and wrong. Without divine commands at the root of human obligations, we would have no real reason for condemning the behavior of anybody, even Nazis. Morality, Copleston thinks, would then be nothing more than an expression of personal feeling.

To begin assessing the divine command theory, let's first consider this last point. Is it really true that only the commands of God can provide an objective basis for moral judgments? Certainly many philosophers have felt that morality rests on its own perfectly sound footing, be it reason, human nature, or natural sentiments. It seems wrong to conclude, automatically, that morality cannot rest on anything but religion. And it is also possible that morality doesn't have any foundation or basis at all, so that its claims should be ignored in favor of whatever serves our own self-interest.

In addition to these problems with Copleston's argument, the divine command theory faces other problems as well. First, we would need to say much more about the relationship between morality and divine commands. Certainly the expressions "is commanded by God" and "is morally required" do not *mean* the same thing. People and even whole societies can use moral concepts without understanding them to make any reference to God. And while it is true that God (or any other moral being for that matter) would tend to want others to do the right thing, this hardly shows that being right and being commanded by God are the same thing. Parents want their children to do the right thing, too, but that doesn't mean parents, or anybody else, can make a thing right just by commanding it!

I think that, in fact, theists should reject the divine command theory. One reason is what it implies. Suppose we were to grant (just for the sake of argument) that the divine command theory is correct, so that actions are right just because they are commanded by God. The same, of course, can be said about those deeds that we believe are wrong. If God hadn't commanded us not to do them, they would not be wrong.

But now notice this consequence of the divine command theory. Since God is all-powerful, and since right is determined solely by His commands, is it not possible that He might change the rules and make what we now think of as wrong into right? It would seem that according to the divine command theory the answer is "yes": it is theoretically possible that tomorrow God would decree that virtues such as kindness and courage have become vices while actions that show cruelty and cowardice will henceforth be the right actions. (Recall the analogy with a legislature and the power it has to change law.) So now rather than it being right for people to help each other out and prevent innocent people from suffering unnecessarily, it would be right (God having changed His mind) to create as much pain among innocent children as we possibly can! To adopt the divine command theory therefore commits its advocate to the seemingly absurd position that even the greatest atrocities might be not only acceptable but morally required if God were to command them.

Plato made a similar point in the dialogue *Euthyphro*. Socrates is asking Euthyphro what it is that makes the virtue of holiness a virtue, just as we have been asking what makes kindness and courage virtues. Euthyphro has suggested that holiness is just whatever all the gods love.

Socrates: Well, then, Euthyphro, what do we say about holiness? Is it not loved by all the gods, according to your definition?

Euthyphro: Yes.

Socrates: Because it is holy, or for some other reason?

Euthyphro: No, because it is holy.

Socrates: Then it is loved by the gods because it is holy: it is not holy because it is loved by them?

Euthyphro: It seems so.

Socrates: . . . Then holiness is not what is pleasing to the gods, and what is pleasing to the gods is not holy as you say, Euthyphro. They are different things.

Euthyphro: And why, Socrates?

Socrates: Because we are agreed that the gods love holiness because it is holy: and that it is not holy because they love it.[3]

This raises an interesting question: Why, having claimed at first that virtues are merely what is loved (or commanded) by the gods, would Euthyphro so quickly contradict this and agree that the gods love holiness *because* it's holy, rather than the reverse? One likely possibility is that Euthyphro believes that whenever the gods love something they do so with good reason, not without justification and arbitrarily. To deny this, and say that it is merely the gods' love that makes holiness a virtue, would mean that the gods have no basis for their attitudes, that they are arbitrary in what they love. Yet—and this is the crucial point—it's far from clear that a religious person would want to say that God is arbitrary in that way. If we say that it is simply God's loving something that makes it right, then what sense would it make to say God wants us to do right? All that could mean, it seems, is that God wants us to do what He wants us to do; He would have no reason for wanting it. Similarly "God is good" would mean little more than "God does what He pleases." The divine command theory therefore leads us to the results that God is morally arbitrary, and that His wishing us to do good or even God's being just mean nothing more than that God does what He does and wants whatever He wants. Religious people who reject that consequence would also, I am suggesting, have reason to reject the divine command theory itself, seeking a different understanding of morality.

This now raises another problem, however. If God approves kindness because it is a virtue and hates the Nazis because they were evil, then it seems that God discovers morality rather than inventing it. So haven't we then identified a limitation on God's power, since He now, being a good God, must love kindness and command us not to be cruel? Without the divine command theory, in other words, what is left of God's omnipotence?

But why, we may ask, is such a limitation on God unacceptable? It is not at all clear that God really can do anything at all. Can God, for example, destroy Himself? Or make a rock so heavy that He cannot lift it? Or create a universe which was never created by Him? Many have thought that God cannot do these things, but also that His inability to do them does not constitute a serious limitation on His power since these are things that cannot be done at all: to do them would violate the laws of logic. Christianity's most influential theologian, Thomas Aquinas, wrote in this regard that "whatever implies contradiction does not come within the scope of divine omnipotence, because it cannot have the aspect of possibility. Hence it is more appropriate to say that such things cannot be done than that God cannot do them."[4]

How, then, ought we to understand God's relationship to morality if we reject the divine command theory? Can religious people consistently maintain their faith in God the Creator and yet deny that what is right is right because He commands it? I think the answer to this is "yes." Making cruelty good is not like making a universe that wasn't made, of course. It's a moral limit on God rather than a logical one. But why suppose that God's limits are only logical?

One final point about this. Even if we agree that God loves justice or kindness because of their nature, not arbitrarily, there still remains a sense in which

God could change morality even having rejected the divine command theory. That's because if we assume, plausibly I think, that morality depends in part on how we reason, what we desire and need, and the circumstances in which we find ourselves, then morality will still be under God's control since God could have constructed us or our environment very differently. Suppose, for instance, that he created us so that we couldn't be hurt by others or didn't care about freedom. Or perhaps our natural environment were created differently, so that all we have to do is ask and anything we want is given to us. If God had created either nature or us that way, then it seems likely our morality might also be different in important ways from the one we now think correct. In that sense, then, morality depends on God whether or not one supports the divine command theory.

"Morality Is Social"

I have argued here that religion is not necessary in providing moral motivation or guidance, and against the divine command theory's claim that God is necessary for there to be morality at all. In this last section, I want first to look briefly at how religion and morality sometimes *do* influence each other. Then I will consider the development of moral conscience and the important ways in which morality might correctly be thought to be "social."

Nothing I have said so far means that morality and religion are independent of each other. But in what ways are they related, assuming I am correct in claiming morality does not *depend* on religion? First, of course, we should note the historical influence religions have had on the development of morality as well as on politics and law. Many of the important leaders of the abolitionist and civil rights movements were religious leaders, as are many current members of the pro-life movement. The relationship is not, however, one sided: morality has also influenced religion, as the current debate within the Catholic church over the role of women, abortion, and other social issues shows. In reality, then, it seems clear that the practices of morality and religion have historically each exerted an influence on the other.

But just as the two have shaped each other historically, so, too, do they interact at the personal level. I have already suggested how people's understanding of revelation, for instance, is often shaped by morality as they seek the best interpretations of revealed texts. Whether trying to understand a work of art, a legal statute, or a religious text, interpreters regularly seek to understand them in the best light—to make them as good as they can be, which requires that they bring moral judgment to the task of religious interpretation and understanding.

The relationship can go the other direction as well, however, as people's moral views are shaped by their religious training and beliefs. These relationships between morality and religion are often complex, hidden even from ourselves, but it does seem clear that our views on important moral issues, from sexual morality and war to welfare and capital punishment, are often influenced by our religious outlook. So not only are religious and moral practices and understandings historically linked, but for many religious people the relationship extends to the personal level—to their understanding of moral obligations as well as their sense of who they are and their vision of who they wish to be.

Morality, then, is influenced by religion (as is religion by morality), but morality's social character extends deeper even than that, I want to argue. First, of course, we possess a socially acquired language within which we think about our various choices and the alternatives we ought to follow, including whether a possible course of action is the right thing to do. Second, morality is social in that it governs relationships among people, defining our responsibilities to others and theirs to us. Morality provides the standards we rely on in gauging our interactions with family, lovers, friends, fellow citizens, and even strangers. Third, morality is social in the sense that we are, in fact, subject to criticism by others for our actions. We discuss with others what we should do, and often hear from them concerning whether our decisions were acceptable. Blame and praise are a central feature of morality.

While not disputing any of this, John Dewey has stressed another, less obvious aspect of morality's social character. Consider then the following comments regarding the origins of morality and conscience in an article he titled "Morality Is Social":

> In language and imagination we rehearse the responses of others just as we dramatically enact other consequences. We foreknow how others will act, and the foreknowledge is the beginning of judgment passed on action. We know *with* them; there is conscience. An assembly is formed within our breast which discusses and appraises proposed and performed acts. The community without becomes an forum and tribunal within, a judgment-seat of charges, assessments and exculpations. Our thoughts of our own actions are saturated with the ideas that others entertain about them. . . . Explicit recognition of this fact is a prerequisite of improvement in moral education. . . . Reflection is morally indispensable.[5]

To appreciate fully the role of society in shaping morality and influencing people's sense of responsibility, Dewey is arguing, requires appreciating the fact that to think from the moral point of view, as opposed to the selfish one, for instance, means rejecting our private, subjective perspective in favor of the view of others, envisioning how they might respond to various choices we might make. Far from being private and unrelated to others, moral conscience is in that sense "public." To consider a decision from the moral perspective, says Dewey, requires that we envision an "assembly of others" that is "formed within our breast." In that way, our moral conscience cannot be sharply distinguished from our nature as social beings since conscience invariably brings with it, or constitutes, the perspective of the other. "Is this right?" and "What would this look like were I to have to defend it to others?" are not entirely separable questions.[6]

It is important not to confuse Dewey's point here, however. He is *not* saying that what is right is finally to be determined by the reactions of actually existing other people, or even by the reaction of society as a whole. What is right or fair can never be finally decided by a vote, and might not meet the approval of any specific others. But what then might Dewey mean in speaking of such an "assembly of others" as the basis of morality? The answer is that rather than actual people or groups, the assembly Dewey envisions is hypothetical or "ideal." The "community without" is thus transformed into a "forum and tribunal within, a judgment seat of charges, assessments and exculpations." So it is through the powers of our imagination that we can meet our moral responsibilities and exercise moral judgment, using these powers to determine what morality requires by imagining the reaction of Dewey's "assembly of others."

Morality is therefore *inherently* social, in a variety of ways. It depends on socially learned language, is learned from interactions with others, and governs our interactions with others in society. But it also demands, as Dewey put it, that we know "with" others, envisioning for ourselves what their points of view would require along with our own. Conscience demands we occupy the positions of others.

Viewed in this light, God would play a role in a religious person's moral reflection and conscience since it is unlikely a religious person would wish to exclude God from the "forum and tribunal" that constitutes conscience. Rather, for the religious person conscience would almost certainly include the imagined reaction of God along with the reactions of others who might be affected by the action. Other people are also important, however, since it is often an open question just what God's reaction would be; revelation's meaning, as I have argued, is subject to interpretation. So it seems that for a religious person morality and God's will cannot be separated, though the connection between them is not the one envisioned by defenders of the divine command theory.

Which leads to my final point, about moral education. If Dewey is correct, then it seems clear there is an important sense in which morality not only can be taught but must be. Besides early moral training, moral thinking depends on our ability to imagine others' reactions and to imaginatively put ourselves into their shoes. "What would somebody (including, perhaps, God) think if this got out?" expresses more than a concern with being embarrassed or punished; it is also the voice of conscience and indeed of morality itself. But that would mean, thinking of education, that listening to others, reading about what others think and do, and reflecting within ourselves about our actions and whether we could defend them to others are part of the practice of morality itself. Morality cannot exist without the broader, social perspective introduced by others, and this social nature ties it, in that way, with education and with public discussion, both actual and imagined. "Private" moral reflection taking place independent of the social world would be no moral reflection at all; and moral education is not only possible, but essential.

Notes

1. R. C. Mortimer, *Christian Ethics* (London: Hutchinson's University Library, 1950), pp. 7–8.

2. This debate was broadcast on the "Third Program" of the British Broadcasting Corporation in 1948.

3. Plato, *Euthyphro,* tr. H. N. Fowler (Cambridge MA: Harvard University Press, 1947).

4. Thomas Aquinas, *Summa Theologica,* Part I, Q. 25, Art. 3.

5. John Dewey, "Morality Is Social" in *The Moral Writings of John Dewey,* revised edition, ed. James Gouinlock (Amherst, NY: Prometheus Books, 1994), pp. 182–4.

6. Obligations to animals raise an interesting problem for this conception of morality. Is it wrong to torture animals only because other *people* could be expected to disapprove? Or is it that the animal itself would disapprove? Or, perhaps, duties to animals rest on sympathy and compassion while human moral relations are more like Dewey describes, resting on morality's inherently social nature and on the dictates of conscience viewed as an assembly of others?

POSTSCRIPT

Does Morality Need Religion?

As Arthur notes, some of the earliest—and indeed some of the best—arguments on this issue can be found in Plato's dialogue *Euthyphro,* which was written in the fourth century B.C. His arguments were in terms of Greek religious practices and Greek gods, but we can reformulate the points and elaborate on the arguments in monotheistic terms.

One key dilemma in the original Greek version asks us to consider whether holy things (i) are holy because they please the gods or (ii) please the gods because they are holy. In monotheistic terms, the dilemma would be whether holy things (i) are holy because they please God or (ii) please God because they are holy. The question can then be broadened and the dilemma posed in terms of good things in general. We then ask whether good things are (i) good because God wills them or (ii) willed by God because they are good.

Plato believed that the gods love what is holy because it is holy (i.e., he believed the second option above), just as Christians have traditionally believed that God wills good things because they are good. Traditionally, a contrast is drawn between God, an infinite and all-good being who always wills the good, and humans, finite beings who are not all-good and do not always will the good.

We might also consider a parallel dilemma concerning truths. Are things true because God knows them, or does God know them because they are true? The traditional view is that God is all-knowing. God knows all truths because they are truths (and no truths lie outside divine knowledge), whereas people do not know all truths (and many truths lie outside human knowledge).

Nevertheless, there has also been in Christianity a tradition that the almighty power of God is not to be constrained by anything—even if we imagine that what constrains God are good things. This view holds that God creates not only good things but the very fact that a good thing (such as honesty) is good while another thing (such as false witness against your neighbor) is not. Thus, in this view, God in his power determines what is good and what is bad.

These topics are further discussed in Glenn Tinder, "Can We Be Good Without God? On the Political Meaning of Christianity," *The Atlantic Monthly* (December 1989); Richard J. Mouw, *The God Who Commands: A Study in Divine Command Ethics* (University of Notre Dame Press, 1990); E. M. Adams, *Religion and Cultural Freedom* (Temple University Press, 1993); D. Z. Phillips, ed., *Religion and Morality* (St. Martin's Press, 1996); and Paul Chamberlain, *Can We Be Good Without God? A Conversation About Truth, Morality, Culture, and a Few Other Things That Matter* (InterVarsity Press, 1996).

National Abortion and Reproductive Rights Action League

This is the home page of the National Abortion and Reproductive Rights Action League (NARAL), an organization that works to promote reproductive freedom and dignity for women and their families.

http://www.naral.org/index.html

Ultimate Pro-Life Resource List

The Ultimate Pro-Life Resource List is one of the most comprehensive listings of right-to-life resources on the Internet.

http://www.prolifeinfo.org

Literature on Reproductive Technologies

This *Ethics Updates* site contains many links to articles, interviews, associations, and other resources that are concerned with cloning.

http://ethics.acusd.edu/applied/bioethics/index.asp

PART 2

Gender, Sex, and Reproduction

*H*umans *are sexual and reproductive beings. Given this fact and the fact that humans are social beings, it is imperative to have some idea of what is socially acceptable and what is not, as well as what is expected of males and females, and what is not.*

The issues in this section do not presuppose that there is anything morally questionable about sex itself, but they do raise questions about how, in today's society, we should think about sex roles and matters of sex and reproduction.

- Does Feminism Provide a Positive Direction for Society?

- Does Pornography Violate Women's Rights?

- Is Abortion Immoral?

- Must Sex Involve Commitment?

- Should Congress Stay the Course on Education for Sexual Abstinence Until Marriage?

- Should Human Cloning Be Banned?

ISSUE 3

Does Feminism Provide a Positive Direction for Society?

YES: Ruth Sidel, from *On Her Own: Growing Up in the Shadow of the American Dream* (Viking Penguin, 1990)

NO: Elizabeth Powers, from "A Farewell to Feminism," *Commentary* (January 1997)

ISSUE SUMMARY

YES: Author and social scientist Ruth Sidel contends that although feminism has made some progress, it holds the promise of even greater progress in the future toward a more caring society.

NO: Author and educator Elizabeth Powers argues that feminism naturally leads to strong governmental enforcement of feminist demands; a devaluing of housework, childrearing, and the family; and a struggle against the biology that links women with childbirth.

Feminism seems to be a thoroughly modern view, and, for the most part, it is. In Western societies, men have dominated over women throughout history, and the situation is even more pronounced in many Eastern societies.

From the time of the ancient Greeks (when men went to the market because respectable women stayed at home) to the twentieth century (when women in America gained the right to vote in national elections in 1920), there was a nearly unbroken social tradition according to which men were regarded as superior to women in power and status. This social tradition was reflected in the intellectual tradition, so much so that the exceptions to this tradition stand out.

Two exceptional male thinkers were Plato, who held that in an ideal state the rulers would be both men and women (since there are both male and female individuals who are able to achieve wisdom and thus become good political leaders), and John Stuart Mill, who said in *The Subjection of Women* (1869), "The principle which regulates the existing social relation between the two sexes . . . is wrong in itself, and [is] now one of the chief hindrances to human improvement. . . . It ought to be replaced by a principle of perfect equality." Much more common was the view that girls should be obedient to their fathers and women should be obedient to their husbands. Sometimes there were even stronger misogynistic (antiwoman) views. What did the women of the past think about all this? For the most part, women did not have the education or social encouragement and standing to make their voices heard, so in many cases we simply do not know.

There has been a traditional sexual double standard for men and women, and the law has generally prescribed second-class citizenship for women. Nowadays we call that tradition sexist, and we tell ourselves that the situation is different. But can we rightfully say that men and women have an equitable relationship in society?

Consider, for example, the fact that most secretaries are women and most executives are men, that most doctors are men and most nurses are women, and that most kindergarten teachers are women and most university professors are men. If we are asked to picture in our minds a nurse (or a professor, or a secretary), we usually picture one of the "correct" sex. Notice that in every case it is the "male" job that has the greater social prestige and the higher pay. This raises many questions. Is it that women freely prefer to be secretaries, nurses, and kindergarten teachers, and men freely prefer to be executives, doctors, and professors? Or are there some social dynamics at work here? Do women generally seek out jobs that have lower prestige, or is lower prestige attached to the jobs because women have traditionally done them? Are people socialized differently according to their sex? Are social expectations different? Social factors aside, what differences exist between males and females anyway?

In recent history, feminists have rallied against patriarchy and male power structures. The origin of some of these power structures may have been "to keep women in their place"—their place being in the home. It is one thing to challenge this power structure by placing more women in power and prestigious positions—there are, for example, a growing number of women executives, doctors, and professors—but it is an even greater challenge to the system to aim for the destruction of the entire power structure.

In the following selections, Ruth Sidel argues that although many women choose to follow paths once closed to them, the future task of feminism is to make positive changes in the structure of society. The "more caring society" that Sidel envisions would be beneficial not just for women but for men, children, families, and society in general. Elizabeth Powers states that feminism contains within itself some very negative tendencies. She contends that if the government is to enforce feminist demands, strong governmental power is necessary. Also, if women are to pursue careers traditionally open to men, there is a danger that children and the family will suffer. Powers maintains that it is simply false to assert that women are no different from men and can simply ignore childbirth and all that it entails.

Ruth Sidel

 **YES**

Toward a More Caring Society

[T]wenty-five years after the publication of *The Feminine Mystique,* much has changed and much has remained the same. Women are attending college and graduate school in greater numbers than ever before. In the area of work, women have made great strides: the vast increase in the number of women in the labor force; the once unimaginable increase in the number of women in high-status, high-income professions; the growing acceptance, both on the part of women and on the part of many men, that women are competent, committed workers who can get the job done and achieve a considerable amount of their identity through their work roles. In keeping with their greatly increased presence in the world of work, women are often pictured by the media, by the fashion industry, even by politicians as serious, significant members of the labor force.

In recent years women have also gained greater control over their bodies. Largely because of the feminist movement, women have far greater understanding of how their bodies work, more control over their own fertility, and far greater participation in the process of childbirth. As this is being written, some of that control is under siege, particularly the right to abortion; but there have been significant strides nonetheless.

And, perhaps most important, many women recognize that they must make their own way in the world, that they must develop their own identity rather than acquire that identity through a relationship with a man. . . .

But in other areas over this quarter-century there has been very little change, and some aspects of women's lives have deteriorated dramatically. Women are still all too often depicted in advertising, in films, on television, and by the fashion industry as sex objects. Women are still encouraged to focus on their looks—their bodies, their clothes, their makeup, their image. How women are supposed to look may have changed; but the tyranny of physical attractiveness, compounded by the need to appear "fit" and youthful, is omnipresent. Even in an event such as the women's final of the 1988 U.S. Open tennis tournament, in which Steffi Graf was trying to win her fourth major tournament of the year, thereby winning the "Grand Slam"—a feat accomplished by only four other players in the history of tennis—the good looks of her opponent, Gabriela Sabatini, were mentioned numerous times by the male television announcers, who were otherwise scrupulously nonsexist. It is noteworthy that in the record-breaking four-hour-and-fifty-four-minute men's final, which pitted Mats Wilander against Ivan Lendl, there was no mention of Wilander's rugged good looks. It is not, after all, simply how well women play the game but how they look while playing that counts as well.

The area of sex is still extraordinarily problematic for young women today. Of all the mine fields women must navigate, sex is one of the most complex and treacherous. . . . [T]he pressures to have sex are enormous and the pressures not to plan for sex nearly as great. Many young women are caught in this incredible bind: some are caught by ignorance, others by the desire to be part of the group; some by fear, others by the need to be held or "loved." And many are caught by the notion that having sex is cool, sophisticated, a rite of passage somehow required in today's culture. But it is still widely seen as something you do inadvertently, almost as an afterthought, for as we have found, if a fifteen-, sixteen-, or seventeen-year-old plans for sex, goes to the local family-planning clinic for contraception, acknowledges her intention, takes responsibility for her actions, truly takes control, she is often seen by her peers, her family, even her community as deviant, as a "bad girl." To acquiesce is permissible; to choose clearly and consciously to embark on a sexual relationship is somehow reprehensible. One is reminded of many magazine advertisements that picture women being "carried away" by feeling or literally carried away by men, vignettes that are clearly metaphors for sex. Are we really saying that being carried away is appropriately feminine while being in control of one's actions is not?

But it is not only the objectification of women that remains a fact of life but the marginalization of women as well, particularly in the workplace and in positions of power. . . . [F]emale workers still occupy the lowest rungs of most occupations, including the prestigious professions they have recently entered in such large numbers. Women may have entered the labor market in record numbers in recent years, but they are still working predominantly in the lowest-paying jobs within the lowest-paying occupations.

In addition, it has become clear over the past decade that poverty dominates and determines the lives of millions of women in the United States. . . .

Within this context, within the reality of women's true economic situation, what is surprising in talking with young women from various parts of the country . . . is the narrowness of their image of success, the uniformity of their dreams. The affluent life as symbolized by the fancy car, the "house on a hill," . . . was described yearningly time and time again. . . . Success was seen, overwhelmingly, in terms of what they would be able to purchase, what kind of "life-style" they would have. The ability to consume in an upper-middle-class manner was often the ultimate goal. . . .

Given the reality of the job market for women, what will become of their dreams of affluence? Given the reality of the structure of work and the availability of child care, what will become of their image of mothering? Have these young women, in fact, been sold a false dream? Have young women become encouraged to raise their expectations, only to see those expectations unfulfilled because there has not been comparable change within society? Have the major institutions that influence public opinion—the media, advertising, the fashion industry, as well as the industries that produce consumer goods and parts of the educational establishment—fostered these rising expectations because it suits their purposes and, in some cases, their profits? Has the dream of equal opportunity for women and men, of at least partial redistribution of power both within the family and in the society at large, been coopted and commodified, turned into a sprint for consumer goods rather than a long march toward a more humane life for all of us?

Have we indeed over the last quarter-century persuaded women that they, too, are entitled to their fair share of the American Dream, in their own right, not merely as appendages to the primary players, without changing the rules of the game in ways that would permit them truly to compete and succeed? Have women, in short, been hoodwinked into believing that they can "have it all, do it all, be it all" while society itself changes minimally? And have we somehow communicated to them that they must make it on their own, recreating the myth of the rugged individualist seeking the American Dream—alone? The sheriff (or cowboy) alone but for his faithful wife (or horse); the prospector for gold, solitary and in competition with scores of others like him, obsessively searching for an often elusive fortune. . . .

Much has been written about the difficult choices women currently have: how to balance marriage and career; how to balance motherhood and career; the timing of conception; the problems of a demanding job versus the demands and joys of motherhood. But these books, articles, television programs, and occasionally films put forth a largely false message: that the majority of women in late-twentieth-century America indeed have these choices to make. The illusion is abroad in the land that a young woman can simply "choose" to postpone pregnancy and marriage, acquire the education of her choice (which should, of course, be in a field in which jobs are available and well paying), and then step into the job of her choice. At that point, if she wishes, the man of her dreams will miraculously appear (and will be single and interested in "commitment"!), and, despite years of contraception and possibly even an abortion or two, she will promptly conceive, have a healthy baby or two, and live happily ever after. But of course we know life is not like that—at least not for the vast majority of women.

Most women do not have these magnificent choices. . . .

This illusion of choice is a major impediment to the establishment of conditions that would enable women—and indeed all people—to have real choices. Young women recognize that they are likely to participate actively in both work and home, in "doing" and "caring," but they fail to recognize what they must have in order to do so: meaningful options and supports in their work lives; in childbearing, child rearing, and the structure of their families; in housing, health care, and child care; and, above all, in the values by which they live their lives. Does emphasis on fashion, consumerism, and the lives of the rich and famous create the illusion of choice while diverting attention from serious discussion of policies that would give women genuine options? . . .

For women to have real choices, we must develop a society in which women and children and indeed families of all shapes and sizes are respected and valued. Despite the mythology of American individualism, it is clear that most women cannot truly go it alone. The young women I interviewed know that they must be prepared to be part of the labor force and still be available to care for others—for children, for older family members, for friends, for lovers—but these often mutually exclusive tasks will be possible only when we develop a society that supports doing and caring. Men must take on caring functions; the society must take some of the responsibility for caring and above all must be restructured to permit, even to encourage, doing and caring. Women simply cannot do it all and cannot do it alone. . . .

[F]undamental change must be made in the workplace. Traditionally male-dominated professions cannot continue to expect their workers to function as if there were a fulltime wife and mother at home. Most male workers no longer live in that never-never land; female workers surely do not. Alternative paths to partnerships, professorships, and promotion must be developed that will neither leave women once again at the bottom of the career ladder without real power and equal rewards nor force them to choose between a demanding work life and a demanding personal life.

Nor should women have to choose a middle ground between work and mothering. . . .

We must reevaluate our system of economic rewards. Do we really want our entertainers, our stockbrokers, our corporate executives, and our divorce lawyers making millions while our nurses and day-care workers barely scrape by? Do we really want the rich to get richer while the poor get poorer and the middle class loses ground? Do we really want to tell our young women that they must play traditional male roles in order to earn a decent living and that caregiving no longer counts, is no longer worth doing? . . .

Market forces cannot be permitted to rule in all spheres of American life. If our society is to be a caring, humane place to live, to rear our children, and to grow old, we must recognize that some aspects of life—the education of our young people, health care, child care, the texture of community life, the quality of the environment—are more important than profit. We as a nation must determine our priorities and act accordingly. If teaching, the care of young children, providing nursing care, and other human services are essential to the quality of life in the United States, then we must recruit our young people into these fields and pay them what the job is really worth. Only then will we be giving them, particularly our young women, real choices. If we want nurses to care for our sick, we must indicate by decent wages and working conditions that the job is valued by society. We must give nurses and other health workers real authority, a meaningful voice in the health-care system, and then, and only then, will some of our best and brightest and most caring women and men choose to enter nursing. Whatever happened to careers in community organizing, urban planning, Legal Aid, and public-health nursing? Young women and men will be able to consider these options only if they are decently paid, have a future and some degree of security and respect.

In this fin de siècle period of U.S. history characterized (in the words of John Kenneth Galbraith) by "private affluence" and "public squalor," it may be difficult to see our way clear to putting significantly larger amounts of money into health care, community organizing, education, or even a meaningful effort to deter young people from drug abuse, but we must recognize that these issues are central to the well-being of families and thus central to the very fabric and structure of American society. . . .

[P]arents must have some time at home with their children. Why can't parents of young children work a shorter day or week and not risk losing their jobs? . . .

It must be acceptable in the United States for fathers to take leave to care for a new baby, to stay home with sick children, to leave work in time to pick up a child from day care or after-school care; for sons to attend to the needs of aging parents. It must even become acceptable for fathers to attend a school play or a Halloween party during the work day. Changing male roles may take years of resocialization and structural change within the society, but we must attempt it nonetheless. Mothers can no longer play the solitary domestic role—not while participating in the work force as well. If women are to do and to care, men must also do and care.

Perhaps a vignette from the life of one family and one work site illustrates the need to humanize the workplace. On November 21, 1985, the U.S. Senate agreed not to cast any votes between seven and nine p.m. The following letter was the reason for this unusual action:

> Dear Senator Dole:
> I am having my second-grade play tonight. Please make sure there aren't any votes between 7 and 9 so my daddy can watch me. Please come with him if you can.
> Love,
> Corinne Quayle

What is particularly remarkable about this incident is that when the final version of the Parental and Medical Leave Act was being written by the Senate Labor and Human Resources Committee, . . . J. Danforth Quayle, then a senator, vehemently opposed it and, according to one observer, "offered an amendment in committee that would assure that an employer enjoys the right to fire an employee who takes as much as one day off to be with a seriously ill child."[1] As Judy Mann, the *Washington Post* columnist who brought this incident to light, wrote: "Quayle lives by a set of special rules for the privileged and well-connected and doesn't hesitate to impose another set of rules and obligations, harsher and devoid of compassion, on those who were not to the manner born. Either he doesn't know anything about the reality of most workers' lives, or he doesn't care."[2] . . .

By demeaning the role of caregiver, society demeans all women and indeed, to one extent or another, exploits all caregivers. It also sets up the exploitation of one group of women by another. The ripples are endless: from the middle- or upper-middle-class career mother who is "stressed out" by trying to do it all to the single mother who really *is* doing it all to the day-care worker who is working in inadequate conditions earning inadequate pay to the child-care worker/domestic who is often shamefully exploited in the home, society's fundamental disregard for caregivers and for raising children diminishes us all.

Ultimately, of course, it is the children who suffer, but women at all levels suffer as well. And the poor, the nonwhite, those with least choice suffer the most.

Any society that really wants to enable women to be in control of their lives must provide a comprehensive program of sex education and contraception. . . . [M]any young women are buffeted about by conflicting attitudes toward sexuality and indeed find it exceedingly difficult to determine what they themselves think and want. By the time they figure it out, it is often too late. They are pregnant and faced with a real Hobson's choice [an apparently free choice in a situation that actually provides no alternatives]: to abort, or to have a baby at a time in their life when they are ill-prepared—economically, physically, socially, or psychologically—to care for a child. We know what it can do to both the mother and the child when the pregnancy is unplanned and the mother is unable to care for the infant properly. We must do everything possible to make every child a planned child, to make every child a wanted child.

We must learn from the experience of other industrialized countries, whose rate of unintended and teenage pregnancy is so much lower than our own. We must institute sex education in our schools at all levels. The ignorance on the part of young women is astonishing and serves no useful purpose. Moreover, in this era of AIDS and other sexually transmitted diseases, such ignorance can literally be life-threatening. We must increase the accessibility of contraceptives, whether through school-based clinics or community-based health centers. . . .

Continued access to abortion must be guaranteed. Efforts to overturn or limit women's right to abortion must be vigorously resisted. For many young women, abortion is the only barrier between them and a life of poverty and despair. Until we stop giving our young women mixed messages—that it is desirable and sometimes even de rigueur to have sex but not legitimate to protect against pregnancy—abortion remains the only resource. . . .

In addition to giving women greater choice over sex and childbearing, we must stop exploiting women as sex objects. As long as the message of jean manufacturers, cereal companies, automobile conglomerates, and perfume distributors is that women are for sale along with the product, that women are, in a very real sense, just another commodity to be bought, used, and traded in when the model wears out, both men and women will perceive women in this way. And until we enable young women to responsibly say either yes or no to sex, to understand their options and the risks involved, we are not permitting them to be in charge of their own destiny. But we cannot expect young women to take control of their own destiny unless they can see alternatives, pathways that will lead to a rewarding life.

It is ironic that young women, a group outside the cultural mainstream in at least two fundamental ways, age and gender, have internalized that most mainstream of ideologies, the American Dream. After examining the realities of women's lives today, it is clear that the American Dream, at least as conventionally conceived, cannot be the blueprint for the majority of women. . . .

We must recognize that even for most men the American Dream, with its belief in the power of the individual to shape his or her own destiny, was a myth. Men usually did not "make it" alone; they did not, as the image goes, tame the West, develop industrial America, and climb the economic ladder alone—and they certainly did not do it while being the primary caregiver for a couple of preschoolers. Most of those men who "made it" in America, whom we think of when we reaffirm our belief in the American Dream, had women beside them every step of the way—women to iron their shirts, press their pants, mend their socks, cook their meals, bring up their children, and soothe them at the end of a hard day. They did not do it alone. They *still* don't do it alone. How can women do it alone? Who is there to mend and press their clothes, cook their meals, bring up their children, and soothe them at the end of a hard day? How can women possibly make it alone when they earn 65 percent of what men earn, when housing is virtually unaffordable for millions of families, when child care is scarce and all too often second-rate or worse? And where did they get the notion that they *should* be able to make it alone? It may be progress that many young women now realize that they cannot depend on marriage and a man for their identity, their protection, their daily bread; but is it progress or is it illusion for them to believe that they can do the caring and the doing and do it all on their own in a society that has done very little to make women truly independent? . . .

We must have the courage and the wisdom as a society to recognize that we need a new vision of America for the twenty-first century, perhaps even a new American Dream. We need a vision that recognizes that we cannot survive without one another, that families must have supports in order to thrive, that women cannot make it alone any more than men ever have.

We must provide many more paths toward a gratifying, economically secure life. Traditional male occupations cannot be the only routes to the good life; traditional female work must be restructured so that it too can lead to power, prestige, and a life of plenty. And the traditional male work style must give way, for both women and men, to the recognition that work is merely one aspect of life and that private concerns, family life, leisure activities, and participation in community life help to define who we are and must be seen as important both to the individual and to the society. . . .

[W]e must develop a vision that recognizes that caring is as important as doing, that caring indeed *is* doing, and that caregivers, both paid and unpaid, are the foundation of a humane society and must be treasured and honored. We need a vision of America that recognizes that we must reorganize our social institutions—our family life, our schools, our places of work, and our communities—to enable all people to care for one another, to enable all people to work and to participate in the public life of the nation. Our courageous, insightful, persevering, and often wise young women deserve no less. Our young men deserve no less. Future generations deserve no less.

Notes

1. Judy Mann, "Some More Equal Than Others," *The Washington Post,* September 21, 1988.
2. Ibid.

NO

Elizabeth Powers

A Farewell to Feminism

She was intelligent and generous; it was a fine free nature; but what was she going to do with herself? This question was irregular, for with most women one had no occasion to ask it. . . . Isabel's originality was that she gave one an impression of having intentions of her own.

Henry James, *Portrait of a Lady*

My coming of age in the early 1970's was inextricably linked with what is variously known as feminism, the women's movement, women's liberation. It is a link by which I am much puzzled and troubled. The passing years have brought me a closer look at, so to speak, the fine print, and I shiver now when I observe the evolution that some of my closest friends from that era have undergone, spouting phrases about comparable worth and voicing the most fantastic bureaucratic visions of the future.

But in truth, if I go back to the sources—say, to a *Time* essay by Gloria Steinem in August 1970—I can see that the writing was already on the wall. Steinem, for one, had fully evolved as of that date:

> The [feminist] revolution would not take away the option of being a housewife. A woman who prefers to be her husband's housekeeper and/or hostess would receive a percentage of his pay determined by the domestic-relations courts.

Did I talk like that, advocating state control of private life, with (as Steinem went on) "free nurseries, school lunches, family cafeterias built into every housing complex"? Did I ever stand up in front of people, like the cadres of Red Guards in China, and parroting the words of Kate Millett in *Sexual Politics* (1970), demand "a permissive single standard of sexual freedom . . . uncorrupted by the crass and exploitative economic bases of traditional sexual alliances"?

As a matter of fact, I do not believe I ever said such things or even contemplated them; nor, I suspect, did most of the women who considered themselves followers of the movement. A dissertation is probably being written which will offer a demographic breakdown of leaders and followers, but my own suspicion is that the leaders were girls whose mothers had been college-educated but became full-time housewives, and so were putatively victimized by what Betty Friedan had defined as the "feminine mystique." The followers, those with backgrounds similar to mine, were not so solidly middle-class or goal-oriented, and had not yet grasped they might be leaders of anything.

We daughters of the working class or the slippery lower reaches of the middle class aspired, by and large, to a greater degree of participation in life outside the home. The shape that participation would take was uncertain. Though a number of highly motivated girls of my generation took advantage of opportunities to enter professional schools, the general affluence of the period allowed those of us who were less motivated or who came from less privileged backgrounds to engage in a lot of shopping around. In my own case, participation did not mean anything practical or even lucrative but rather "fulfillment," a realization of myself in literary and intellectual realms. It was my fortune, as Henry James wrote of Isabel Archer, to care for knowledge that was unfamiliar.

Throughout high school—I grew up in a rather cloistered environment in Kentucky—my aspirations seemed to run in thoroughly conventional directions: I wanted to be a cheerleader and prom queen and, of course, I wanted a boyfriend. But the same thing that kept me from becoming a cheerleader or prom queen also meant I was essentially dateless. I simply did not possess that combination of attributes which, for a brief time, confers unexpected grace on otherwise undeserving teenage girls. When I went to college, in 1965, still desiring to be exceptional in some way, I quickly perceived other possibilities of achievement.

This was a moment when university standards were still sacrosanct and an Ivy League institution was not the only place at which to receive a first-rate education. Though a fair number of women prominent today in public life probably graduated from women's colleges, I suspect the majority went, as I did, to schools like Indiana University (Jane Pauley, my classmate!). It was hard going for me—I was terribly uneducated when I got to college—but for the first time in my life I began to train my mind and came close to perfecting myself in something, namely, a foreign language.

Yet this youthful accomplishment, immeasurably assisted by two years of work and study in Europe, was attended by new challenges, chiefly of a social and sexual nature. Europe produced in me the same feeling that assailed Christopher Newman, the central character of Henry James's novel *The American,* in the presence of Old Master paintings: a vague self-mistrust. Possessing a fair share of Newman's innate American confidence and naturalness, but not his steady moral compass, I found myself entranced by the relaxed cultural habits that had evolved in Europe by the late 1960's. These I could not help contrasting with mid-century America's moral certitudes, centering on sex and the cold war, which now seemed to me to be a caricature of inflexibility.

Not three years before, where I came from, sex had been a matter cloaked in a great deal of mystery. I had been much fascinated by a girl I knew only by sight who became pregnant at fifteen and was married, probably shotgun-style, to her boyfriend of seventeen. Without being able to articulate it, I felt she must have been marked by her experience in a way that ordinary mortals, hewing to the straight and narrow, were not. Transgression may have resulted in shame and social denigration, but through her risk she had become an object of interest. Still, to stand outside the moral order was a fearsome prospect.

My Catholic attitudes were shot through with the fire and brimstone of other American cultural remnants—the sermons of Jonathan Edwards, Hawthorne's *The Scarlet Letter*. In an educated European of the late 1960's, such attitudes provoked only condescending smiles. Europeans, it seemed, got to have the experience minus the soul-scorching. I was ignorant in those days of the social arrangements, mainly an intensive welfare bureaucracy, that cushioned these permissive sentiments and perhaps had even helped bring them into being. Instead, in the presence of mores so different from my own, and influenced as well by superior church architecture and other evidence of cultural tradition, I came to conclude that European attitudes in the matter of sex were wiser than those of Americans. I wanted to be wise like Europeans.

⌒◉⌒

"I told you just now I'm very fond of knowledge," Isabel answered.

"Yes, of happy knowledge—of pleasant knowledge. But you haven't suffered, and you're not made to suffer. I hope you'll never see the ghost!" . . .

"I don't think that's a fault," she answered. "It's not absolutely necessary to suffer; we were not made for that."

The birth-control pill, available in Europe in the 1950's, was first approved by the FDA in 1960; the last state ban on contraception was struck down by the Supreme Court in 1965. The pill would seem to have solved the problem for which, historically, the movement for women's emancipation had struggled: freedom from constant reproduction.

Yet the pill was one of those technical achievements, like gunpowder and printing, like the desk-top computer, the effects of which flowed all over the social and political landscape. One of its effects was to alter a perilously achieved historical understanding regarding the responsibility of men to their offspring. With the pill, this responsibility was taken from them overnight. It was at this point, in 1969, returning from Europe, that I entered graduate school at the University of Texas. One of the first things I did after getting an apartment, registering for classes, and picking up my paycheck as a teaching assistant was to go to a doctor and get a prescription—even though I was still a virgin. That knowledge of which Isabel Archer spoke, which could be obtained without difficulty, had suddenly offered itself: all one had to do was take a pill 21 days in a row.

To get at some of the larger confusions engendered by this new dispensation it may be helpful to turn to a prominent book of the early women's movement, Ingrid Bengis's *Combat in the Erogenous Zone* (1972). I wonder if anyone has actually gotten to the end of this exercise in rage and self-pity; despite Bengis's avowed admiration for artists, it seems never to have occurred to *her* to shape her material or give form to her experiences. The book is instead hardly more than an accumulation of horrors, an inventory of the infallible tendency of the nicest-seeming males to take advantage of Ingrid Bengis. The gallery of villains ranges from construction workers whistling at her on the street to the boy she shared a room with who fondled her as she lay blissfully zonked out in her sleeping bag, to the Mexican restaurant owner who gave her a free meal and then demanded sex, to the truck driver who picked her up while hitchhiking and then got upset when she refused to put out.

These were experiences many of us had in the 1970's. In hindsight, the source of Bengis's rage, a rage felt by so many women of our generation, can be discerned as early as the second page of her book, where she speaks of the men (plural) she has loved. The long and the short of it is that, thanks to the pill, young American females of the 1970's were suddenly behaving with the license, but without the sensibility, of jaded aristocrats. We women instinctively knew that what we were conferring was important and had something to do with love, and, like Ingrid Bengis, we used that word when we spoke of sex. Yet the terms of the bargain between men and women had radically changed. The old bargain—sex in exchange for commitment—had issued out of conditions of what might crassly be called a balance of supply and demand. These conditions were undermined in the 1970's by the flooding of the market with casual sex.

Feminists tend to blame men for their cavalier treatment of women, but, in the realm which Goethe spoke of as *Sittlichkeit* (roughly, morals), men follow the lead of women. Young males, it turns out, will only be protective and caring of females if something is at stake. When women sleep with men they barely know, assuming on their own the responsibility for regulating reproduction, men will be equally casual. A reward not having been fought for or truly earned is not a reward for which any individual will feel more than momentary indebtedness.

No wonder the whistle of construction workers, once a sign of appreciation for rewards not yet earned, and perhaps unattainable, came to sound to us like a hiss of contempt at our availability. The resulting sense of bafflement can be gleaned from where, in her prose, Bengis stamps her foot in emphasis, and where her inimitable ellipses fall:

> *Of course* I was proud to be a woman . . . proud as well of a subtle kind of sexuality. But I was not proud of the way in which that sexuality was systematically abused in the service of something that ultimately cheapened both me and it.

By such displacements outward did rage at men become the fate of an entire generation.

⋞⊙⋟

The role of the women's movement was to turn this rage into something powerful—sisterhood. As unexpected as it may sound, the experience of becoming a feminist was, for many, akin to a sudden spiritual conversion, a radical turnaround of the kind Tolstoy described in *Confession,* in which "everything that was on the right hand of the journey is now on the left." An essay by Jane

O'Reilly, "Click! The Housewife's Moment of Truth" (from the whimsically entitled *The Girl I Left Behind,* 1980), perfectly captures the quality of transformation promised by the movement, and just as perfectly exposes its hollowness.

The essay inhabits a genre the publishing market has long catered to: morality tales in which adolescents learn the deceptiveness of appearance through painful lessons that lead them to maturity and true values. Just so, Jane O'Reilly finally grew up when she encountered women's liberation. Her book is a tale of setting aside the unimportant things, the very things she had once (in the 1950's) perceived that being a woman meant: debutante balls, identification bracelets, popularity, 75 people singing carols on Christmas Eve, drinking cocoa out of Dresden cups, real pearls. The illumination she underwent was to recognize that all these were a snare and a delusion, a cover and a preparation for deferring and submitting to men. Instead, what women needed was to become "equal members of the human society."

O'Reilly's essay contains Erma Bombeck-like hints for negotiating the transition from Cinderella-*cum*-domestic-drone to liberated human being: "(1) Decide what housework needs to be done. Then cut the list in half." In the realm of love, her language is up-to-date, *circa* 1980: "I practiced and practiced taking the sexual initiative"; "I need to get laid." But the subtext is still the same old thing: romance. It turns out Jane O'Reilly truly wanted the flowers, the passionate declarations, and all the rest. For her, too, though perhaps less grimly than for Ingrid Bengis, women's sexual liberation was a bust. The new social arrangements—here is an entry for February 29 from the *Liberated Woman's Appointment Calendar:* "Leap Year Day. Propose to the person of Your Choice"—failed.

At the end, Jane O'Reilly gives up, though she puts a brave face on it: "I now think love is somehow beside the point." Having sloughed off the demands of boyfriends, husbands, children, parents, in-laws, she is left to craft her own "lifestyle" out of the limp slogans of sisterhood:

> Nontradition has become tradition. My friends are my family, and we will provide for each other. Gathered about the [Christmas] tree will be the intact family from upstairs, the broken family from across the park, an extended family from out of town, my own reconstituted family, and the various inexplicable attachments we have all acquired along the way.

Thus, by 1980, had Kate Millett's turgid and off-putting rhetoric of revolution been refashioned into O'Reilly-style sentimentality. Moreover, this sentimentality had become a staple, peddled in magazines and books, in TV programs and movies. Seldom was it asked whether or how it could actually carry you through long-term illness, financial jeopardy, or personal crises of a truly acute nature. Instead, as many women went through affair after affair, as they failed with one Mr. Right after another, as they approached forty and saw the possibilities of a family of their own diminishing, as they found themselves living alone, scrambling for an invitation for Christmas dinner, O'Reilly's defeated alternative became more and more a necessary article of faith. . . .

The women's movement is usually seen as having grown from the movement for civil rights for blacks, and, to many people, it had to do primarily with equality of economic opportunity. From the late 1960's on, mainstream journalists dutifully trotted out the statistics concerning women's economic and professional disadvantages. Yet feminists agitating about the pay scales of lawyers or accountants were in fact after something else: a change in the very meaning of equality.

For women to be "equal," as Jane O'Reilly dimly perceived ("The point of feminism is not that the world should be the same, but that it should be different"), something more drastic than admission to medical school was required. Female biology itself would have to be interpreted as a humanly limiting condition, established not by nature but by a cabal otherwise known as the patriarchy. There was much at stake, and a 1969 article in the *Nation* spelled it out: the women's movement, intoned the writer, was dedicated "to a total restructuring of society, . . . and is not content simply to integrate women into male-defined goals and values."

This thoroughgoing radicalism, a (relatively) new aspect of the century-old movement for female emancipation, elicited criticism even on the Left. Among the opponents was the socialist and literary critic Irving Howe. In December 1970 Howe published in *Harper's* a long review-essay of Kate Millett's *Sexual Politics,* which a few months earlier had been baptized by *Time* magazine as the *Communist Manifesto* of the women's movement. Howe took the book sharply to task not only for its intellectual and literary failings but also for what he perceived as Millett's dangerous political agenda, which he considered "a parody of the Marxist vision of class struggle." In one of the nastiest literary put-downs of all time, he declared that "the emotions of women toward children don't exactly form an overwhelming preoccupation in *Sexual Politics:* there are times when one feels the book was written by a female impersonator." This was a comment, I recall, that particularly exercised me and my sisters in the movement at the time. That I had not read Millett was beside the point; it was enough that Howe attacked the woman who articulated our rage for us.

Were sexual differences amenable to the kind of social reconfiguration Millett was advocating? Howe, for one, certainly did not think so. To the contrary, he thought they should not be jettisoned on the trash heap of history in the pursuit of some bloodless ideal. In speaking of the struggles of his own parents, toiling as garment workers while raising children in wretched poverty, Howe sounded almost like a conservative. Besides suggesting that the differences between the sexes might in fact contribute to the melioration of our fallen human condition, he also defended the family as being not necessarily oppressive to women:

> That the family . . . has been coextensive with human culture itself and may
> therefore be supposed to have certain powers of endurance and to yield certain profound satisfactions to human beings other than merely satisfying
> the dominating impulses of the "master group," hardly causes Miss Millett

to skip a phrase. Nor does the thought that in at least some of its aspects the family has protected the interests of women as against those of men.

In retrospect, this may have been the moment when the Left gave way definitively to the New Left. That Howe was fighting a rear-guard action is clear from the fact that he soon withdrew from this polemical field—as did Norman Mailer, another leftist stalwart whose lone contribution to the anti-feminist canon was his 1971 *The Prisoner of Sex*. By now, moreover, both the women's movement and the New Left had begun to find a new source of legitimation in a philosophy that had sunk roots in the universities. Call it deconstruction, call it post-structuralism, its intent was to demolish the notion that there could be anything like cultural standards, or agreed-upon truths, or, it went without saying, objective sexual differences.

Today, of course, this relativism-in-the-service-of-a-new-absolutism has contaminated far more than the upper reaches of academia and the fringes of the Modern Language Association. All introductory college courses, be they in literature, sociology, anthropology, religion, etc., have become shot through with the insights of deconstruction, and an afternoon of watching Oprah is enough to demonstrate how they have filtered down into the general culture. The goal of this new orientation is, ostensibly, radical human freedom and equality, without ties to oppressive institutions of any kind, especially not to the patriarchy, that shibboleth of social reconstructionists. But what deconstruction has really done is to banish, as nothing more than a set of arbitrary conventions, the moral promptings that lead people to notice oppression in the first place, and along with them the ability to distinguish true oppression from false.

⁂

He had told her, the first evening she ever spent at Gardencourt, that if she should live to suffer enough she might some day see the ghost with which the old house was duly provided. She apparently had fulfilled the necessary condition; for the next morning, in the cold, faint dawn, she knew that a spirit was standing by her bed.

There is a cart-before-the-horse quality about feminism. An explosion of economic forces, starting after World War II, sent women into the workplace in large numbers. It was only after this process was in high gear, and when women began directly competing with men in the upper echelons, that feminism came into being. An ideology then arose to justify the unprecedented autonomy on the part of women (and perhaps to assuage some of their felt guilt over the abandonment of hearth and home) and to allocate spoils. A panoply of institutions formed in its turn, to buttress the ideology: women's-studies departments in universities, tax-exempt institutions setting themselves up as lobbyists for "women's issues," a larger and larger government bureaucracy. By now, many women have come to believe that their opportunities stem wholly from the struggles of their feminist forebears and not at all from the steady expansion of the market.

But ideology, as Karl Marx noted long ago, is replete with tensions. These tensions are in abundant evidence in an essay by Diane Johnson in a recent issue of the *New York Review of Books*. Johnson is aware of the distress signals being sent out by contemporary feminism, and she demonstrates that even a liberal like herself can recognize the ridiculousness of academic feminist highjinks:

> . . . endless testimonials, diatribes, and spurious science from people who imagine that their personal experience, the dynamics of their particular family, sexual taste, childhood trauma, and personal inclination constitute universals.

Johnson even circles back to the incommensurables of human existence, going so far as to refer to God and original sin. Since she is a novelist, such incommensurables may be on her mind.

Yet on the subject of women and women's issues, she inevitably begins from premises that are at odds with the way individuals struggle to craft their individual solutions to life's demands, a task that, ironically enough, the novel has traditionally taken it as its prerogative to illuminate. Johnson's constant use of the word "class" in connection with women alerts the reader to the non-novelistic sources of her thinking. Her enumeration of the minimal rights that feminists should urge on everyone is unalloyed bureaucratic boilerplate: personal safety, autonomy in sexual and health matters, equal pay for equal work.

Among my friends who are working women of middle age, there are very few who do not consider themselves feminists. Their attitudes, like Johnson's, are permeated by a belief in the inevitable progress of humanity—from which, they hold, women, prior to the 1960's, were excluded. They remain upbeat concerning the bureaucratic arrangements that will bring about the inevitable progress. Such has been the infiltration of feminist-think that women who 30 years ago would have recoiled from the social engineering extolled by Gloria Steinem now accept the rationale for suspending a six-year-old boy from school for sexual harassment because he has kissed a six-year-old girl.

Johnson herself adduces several sociological studies which purportedly demonstrate that all the parameters are finally lining up and settling into place. She quotes Dr. Daniel J. ("mid-life crisis") Levinson: "Humanity is now in the early phases of a transformation in the meanings of gender and the place of women and men in every society." The same doctor also holds, from the loftiest Archimedean perspective, that such gender transformation (here I am quoting Johnson) "is an irreversible historical trend which will take another century to achieve." And people think Newt Gingrich is a crackpot for spouting Alvin Toffler.

Johnson declines to question whether the "transformation in the meanings of gender" projected by Levinson is a desirable state, whether it is a state any of us would wish to morph into. An irreversible trend, after all, is an irreversible trend. But she compliments France and Scandinavia, "whose governments have committed themselves to large-scale child-care arrangements." These arrangements, like the model farms the Soviets used to allow foreign visitors to see, seem to offer evidence that rational social planning will work and that the awful dislocations and disruptions occurring all around us are only temporary and in any case justified by the march of History.

⋅⋘◉⋙⋅

But maybe Dr. Levinson is on to something. It strikes me that one of the peculiar results of the reign of feminism is that women have actually become unimportant, indeed nonessential. This has come about by feminism's making radically suspect the influence that women, *qua* women, have traditionally exercised on the souls of those with whom they come into contact. The first effective thrust was to deny that any of the endless tasks performed by women within the marriage union contributed in any way to its spiritual wholeness. Housekeeping and child-raising were transformed into a purely material operation, consisting of the kind of mindless, mechanical steps that characterize the assembly of an automobile or a computer. It is no surprise that the most ambitious women of my generation fled this scenario of drudgery, and, by extension, also avoided traditional women's occupations as they would the plague. A generation of women who would have been excellent teachers instead became attorneys, in what they were told and seemed to believe would be a net gain for humanity.

This abandonment of the female realm has also led to the production of a class that appears to be in the vanguard of the nanny state: women who "have it all," whose marriages are not so much unions as partnerships of two career paths, and whose children, once assembled and produced, are willingly turned over by them to caretakers. Most of these women have probably not dwelt on the consequences of the Faustian bargain they have struck, but their example says loudly and clearly that children are interchangeable units and that the values they learn can be equally well acquired from a Norwegian au pair and after-school public television as from parents.

Whether such women really do have it all is for them, perhaps, to say. Even so, there remains a lack of synchronicity between the highest levels of feminist achievers and ordinary women. Housework and the raising of children, denigrated by the movement and by so many elite women, is looked upon very differently by my unmarried friends, even those who call themselves feminist. They sense that the struggle to form one's life in conjunction with another—including all those horrible minutiae of daily existence that Jane O'Reilly described as the murder of a woman's soul—is a spiritual enterprise of the highest sort, involving the "discovery," as Midge Decter put it with her habitual precision in *The New Chastity* (1972), "that to be in charge of oneself also requires the courage to recognize the extent of one's frailty and dependence on others." And they sense acutely that, in declining or refusing to make those compromises of daily living-with-another, they have missed out on the greatest of human challenges and have indeed failed in point of courage. They still yearn to meet someone with whom, as the current parlance goes, they can share their life.

The tragic part is the egocentrism of their current existence, the days and years devoted to self-maintenance, with minimal effect on the lives of others. Women now get to fulfill themselves—O'Reilly's passionate wish—but they do so in the most resolute solitude. If there is any validity to what Aristotle said long ago—that one's existence has a goal toward which the soul strives—then the care of one's physical and mental self can only be a subordinate part of a larger existential plan. The women I am talking about do not have such a plan, be it marriage or children or a high-powered career. Instead of caring for the direction of their souls, they tend to their "personal space."

The greatest loss for my friends who have not married is of course the children they never had. Exhortations to self-fulfillment aside, by the time they reached forty many women of my generation were in a desperate race with their bodies. Magazines in the late 1980's began featuring articles on "Mommie Oldest," as women underwent Herculean efforts to get their aging uteruses into shape. *In vitro* fertilization, artificial insemination, hormone shots—if only they could go back and undo all those abortions!

⋅◈⋅

Here, indeed, is the great unnameable, the subject that many of us have refused to face squarely in its terrible personal dimension but that, like the purloined letter, has always been there, before our eyes. Childbirth, contraception, abortion: these dividers of women also illuminate the terrible contradictions of feminist ideology, and particularly the contention that women are no different from men.

The divide between the goals of radical, society-transforming feminism and ordinary women is inadvertently captured by Diane Johnson in her criticism of the social thinker Elizabeth Fox-Genovese, whose latest book, *Feminism Is Not the Story of My Life,* dwells precisely on this divide. Fox-Genovese, she writes, "stops just short of saying that feminists will murder infants in their cradles." Even setting partial-birth abortions aside, Johnson's refusal to see what feminism has, in fact, done in this realm is breathtaking. And because she will not acknowledge it, she must also censure Fox-Genovese for speaking of women's sexual decisions as being somehow fraught with special danger. To speak in this way, says Johnson, suggests that women are not up to "independent moral choice." But Fox-Genovese does not deny women moral choice; she merely underscores what most women have always known: that sex, for them, *is* fraught with special danger. Ingrid Bengis knew that, though it made her very angry.

I have made my way back to my starting point. Is sex merely a material manifestation, a physical fact and act, a discharge of physical tension? Does it make any difference that the man who caresses a woman's body is a man she met only a few hours before? Or is a woman's experience of sex part of a larger moral, indeed spiritual, equation? Does she require that the man with whom she shares her bed be one whose love has settled unwaveringly and discriminatingly on her? Does she expect him to take responsibility for the child she may conceive? These are the hard questions, ones that many of us have not confronted. But whenever a woman does confront them, and arrives at the latter point of view, you will probably find that she has severed her ties with feminism.

POSTSCRIPT

Does Feminism Provide a Positive Direction for Society?

Sidel argues that feminism has not been effective enough on a societal level. It has been relatively effective on an individual basis, and young women today have thoughts and hopes and dreams that women could never have entertained before the feminist movement. But Sidel states that society itself threatens to dash these hopes if it does not reform itself into what she calls a "more caring society."

Powers maintains that it is futile to pretend—as she thinks feminists do—that all the same freedoms and possibilities that have traditionally existed for men can also exist for women. She does not see the effort to grant women freedom comparable to that traditionally enjoyed by men—through the encouragement of nannies, professional child care, etc.—as a positive development. Rather, Powers asserts it threatens to alienate women from family life.

A classic work of feminism is Betty Friedan's *The Feminine Mystique,* originally published in 1963 by W. W. Norton & Company. A later edition of the work, with a new introduction, was published by Dell Publishing in 1984. A good historical overview of feminism can be found in Rosemarie Tong, *Feminist Thought: A Comprehensive Introduction* (Westview Press, 1989). Other relevant readings are Catharine MacKinnon, *Feminism Unmodified: Discourses on Life and Law* (Harvard University Press, 1987); Deborah L. Rhode, *Speaking of Sex: The Denial of Gender Inequality* (Harvard University Press, 1997); F. Carolyn Graglia, *Domestic Tranquility: A Brief Against Feminism* (Spence Publishing, 1998); Danielle Crittenden, *What Our Mothers Didn't Tell Us: Why Happiness Eludes the Modern Woman* (Simon and Schuster, 1999); Wendy Shalit, *A Return to Modesty: Discovering the Lost Virtue* (Free Press, 1999); Cathy Young, *Ceasefire! Why Women and Men Must Join Forces to Achieve True Equality* (Free Press, 1999); Rosalind Coward, *Sacred Cows* (HarperCollins, 1999); Germaine Greer, *The Whole Woman* (Alfred A. Knopf, 1999); bell hooks, *Feminism Is for Everybody: Passionate Politics* (South End Press, 2000); Carole R. McCann et al., eds., *Feminist Theory Reader: Local and Global Perspectives* (Routledge, 2002); Lynn Walter, ed., *The Greenwood Encyclopedia of Women's Issues Worldwide* (Greenwood Publishing Group, 2003); Mary Eagleton, ed., *Concise Companion to Feminist Theory* (Blackwell Publishers, 2003); and Cynthia Eller, *Am I a Woman? A Skeptic's Guide to Gender* (Beacon Press, 2003).

ISSUE 4

Does Pornography Violate Women's Rights?

YES: Rae Langton, from "Pornography, Speech Acts, and Silence," in Hugh LaFollette, ed., *Ethics in Practice: An Anthology* (Blackwell Publishers, 1997)

NO: Nadine Strossen, from *Defending Pornography: Free Speech, Sex, and the Fight for Women's Rights* (Scribner, 1995)

ISSUE SUMMARY

YES: Philosopher Rae Langton argues that an analysis of the concept of *speech acts* shows that pornography subordinates women and silences their voice. Therefore, pornography destroys political liberty and equality and should not be allowed.

NO: Nadine Strossen, president of the American Civil Liberties Union, asserts that pornography itself is a manifestation of free speech, and its presence must be accepted as part of the affirmation of the values of liberty that support all rights, including women's rights.

Many people are concerned about the prevalence of pornography in society. This is especially true today, due to the growth of the Internet, which brings words and pictures to millions of people. But, it is worthwhile to stop and ask: Why is there such a concern? Didn't the sexual revolution loosen people's ideas about sex and stretch the boundaries of what was socially acceptable? Why then should there still be any concern about pornography?

There has indeed been a social and sexual revolution. Much of the current objection is not that pornography involves "dirty pictures," but that it subordinates women. Pornography is said to be an integral part of a social system that allows for the objectification of women.

Pornography has been said by some to be a causal factor in crimes against women. This turns out to be a difficult thesis to support with scientific evidence, however, and it is very easy for someone to say, "I could watch a video of a woman being raped but I'm not going to go out and *do* it." But, consider another case. One can watch a commercial for a product and laugh at the humorous aspects of the commercial, but he or she may never buy the product simply because of a commercial. And yet the people who market a product are serious about the market research they do. They believe (and spend hundreds of thousands of dollars on the basis of their belief) that commercials are effective in getting consumers to buy their product. So maybe there are some influences on behavior that people are not even aware of.

But perhaps a more useful way of making an objection against pornography would be to state that it itself is part of the second-class status of women, that it is one of the manifestations of this status. In this view, what is objectionable about pornography is not what it causes or brings about, but what it *is*.

In the readings that follow, Rae Langton argues that pornography subordinates women and silences them by restricting their ability to speak against it. Women are thus robbed of their right of free speech. Nadine Strossen counters that pornography is itself the expression of free speech. The proper recognition of women's rights demands acceptance of pornography, not suppression.

Rae Langton

Pornography, Speech Acts, and Silence

Pornography is speech. So the courts declared in judging it protected by the First Amendment. Pornography is a kind of act. So [legal scholar] Catharine MacKinnon declared in arguing for feminist laws against it. Put these together and we have: pornography is a kind of *speech act.*

If pornography is speech, what does it say? If pornography is a kind of act, what does it do? Judge Frank Easterbrook, accepting the premises of anti-pornography legislation, gave an answer. Pornography is speech that depicts subordination. Pornography depicts women "dehumanized as sexual objects, things or commodities; enjoying pain or humiliation or rape; being tied up, cut up, mutilated, bruised, or physically hurt; in postures of sexual submission or servility or display; reduced to body parts, penetrated by objects or animals, or presented in scenarios of degradation, injury, torture; shown as filthy or inferior; bleeding, bruised or hurt in a context which makes these conditions sexual" (MacKinnon, 1987, p. 176). Pornography is a kind of act that has certain effects: depictions of subordination, said Easterbrook, "tend to perpetuate subordination. The subordinate status of women in turn leads to affront and lower pay at work, insult and injury at home, battery and rape on the streets." Easterbrook's conclusion was that pornography should be protected, since this effect "simply demonstrates the power of pornography as speech".[1] Pornography, on this view, depicts subordination, and causes it. A closer look at the feminist ordinance shows us that MacKinnon is saying something more. Before describing what pornography depicts, the ordinance begins: "We define pornography as the graphic sexually explicit subordination of women in pictures or words . . .". Besides depicting and causing subordination, pornography is, in and of itself, a form of subordination.

This aspect of the feminist legislation irritated judges and philosophers. When the drafters of the ordinance said that pornography actually *is* subordination, they were tricksters, guilty of "a certain sleight of hand", said Judge [Sarah Evans] Barker.[2] They were guilty of conceptual confusion, and their claim was "philosophically indefensible", said William Parent (1990). It is all very well to talk about what pornography depicts; and it is all very well to talk about the effects it has on the lives of women. Those ideas are not, at least, incoherent. But MacKinnon wants to say something more: she wants to attend, not simply to

From Rae Langton, "Pornography, Speech Acts, and Silence," in Hugh LaFollette, ed., *Ethics in Practice: An Anthology* (Blackwell, 1997). Revised from "Speech Acts and Unspeakable Acts," *Philosophy and Public Affairs,* vol. 22 (1993), pp. 305–330. Copyright © 1993 by Princeton University Press. Reprinted by permission of Princeton University Press.

the *content* of pornographic speech, nor simply to its *effects,* but to the *actions* constituted by it.

What she says may strike a chord of recognition amongst those who recall a philosopher who said that "to say something is to *do* something". In *How to Do Things with Words,* J. L. Austin complained of a "constant tendency in philosophy" to overlook something important: a tendency to consider the content of speech, and its effects on hearers, but to overlook the action constituted by it. Words, he said, are used to perform all kinds of actions (warning, promising, marrying . . .) which philosophers have blithely ignored.

To say something is to do quite a few different things. Here is an imaginary example (adapted from Austin, 1962, p. 101). Two men stand beside a woman. The first turns to the second, and says "Shoot her". The second man looks shocked, then raises a gun and shoots the woman. You witness the scene, and you describe it later (perhaps to the police): "The first man said to the second, 'Shoot her' meaning by 'shoot' to shoot with a gun, and referring by 'her' to the woman nearby." That report describes one aspect of what was done with those words: it captures what Austin called the *locutionary* act. To perform a locutionary act is to utter a sentence that has a particular meaning, or content. However, there is more to what you witnessed, so you describe the scene again: "By saying 'Shoot her', the first man *shocked* the second; by saying 'Shoot her', the first man *persuaded* the second to shoot the woman." That report describes what was done by saying those words, the effects of what was said: it captures what Austin called the *perlocutionary* act. But if you stop there, you will still have left something out. You will have left out what the first man did in saying what he said. In saying "Shoot her", was he making a *suggestion?* giving a word of *advice? ordering* the second man to shoot? You describe the scene yet again: "In saying 'Shoot her', the first man *ordered* the second to shoot." That report describes what Austin called the *illocutionary* act, the action performed in saying those words.

The actions listed earlier—warning, promising, marrying—are illocutionary acts. Nearly every time we say something, we do things with our words in all three ways that Austin described: we say something that has a certain content (the locution), has a certain effect (the perlocution), and is a certain act (the illocution). Austin's complaint was that the illocutionary aspect of speech is often ignored: that there is "a tendency in philosophy to elide [illocutions] in favour of the other two" (p. 103).

Now pornography is not always done with words. Yet Easterbrook's description fits the tendency of which Austin complained. Pornography depicts subordination, and causes it. That is to describe its locutionary and perlocutionary aspects. When MacKinnon says that pornography is an act of subordination, she supplies what is missing in Easterbrook's description: she describes its *illocutionary* force. Like Austin, MacKinnon wants to undermine the division between word and action. "Which is saying 'kill' to a trained guard dog, a word or an act?" she asks, in a passage that echoes Austin's example (MacKinnon, 1987, p. 156; cf. 1993, pp. 12, 21). MacKinnon has something in common with Austin, as she acknowledges (1993, p. 121), and in this [selection] I draw on Austin to illuminate and defend her feminist work.

I focus on two claims. First is the claim we just saw, that pornography *subordinates* women. Second is a claim that pornography *silences* women. This idea has an important role to play in a feminist reply to the traditional "free speech" defence of pornography. "[The] free speech of men silences the free speech of women. It is the same social goal, just other *people,*" says MacKinnon (1987, p. 156), arguing that if the law protects free speech, it should protect the speech of women. This second claim, that pornography silences women, has also been regarded as problematic: its detractors describe it as "dangerous confusion", while even sympathizers have reservations, conceding that the silence in question is "figurative", "metaphorical" (Dworkin, 1991, p. 103; Michelman, 1989, p. 294). But I want to show that the silence is literal, and that the second feminist claim is as defensible as the first.

If pornography subordinates women, it determines women's inferior civil status. Seen this way, anti-pornography legislation poses a conflict between liberty and equality: the liberty of men to produce and consume pornography, and the rights of women to equal civil status. That is how the case was seen by the courts. The claim that pornography silences women expresses a different conflict, within liberty itself. Seen this way, the ordinance poses a conflict between the liberty of men to produce and consume pornography, and the liberty of women to speak.

One liberal philosopher, Ronald Dworkin, says that only the latter feminist approach has any chance of success. Showing that pornography silences women is the only way to justify censorship, in a legal system that "assigns a preeminent place to free speech" (Dworkin, 1991, p. 108). He thinks that the feminist "silencing" argument doesn't work—it is a "confusion". I will show that it is not a confusion. Nor is the silencing argument the only possible feminist argument—there are other ways of arguing for censorship than by saying pornography silences women.

Indeed, Dworkin's own liberal theory provides a way to build a different argument for censorship, as I have shown elsewhere (Langton, 1990). We can give what Dworkin calls an argument of principle, a rights-based argument, for the conclusion that pornography ought to be prohibited. It goes something like this. A policy that permits pornography relies on the fact that many people like pornography, and would like to be able to read and watch it. (Remember that we are talking about the pornography of MacKinnon's definition, that depicts women "dehumanized as sexual objects, things, or commodities; enjoying pain or humiliation or rape", etc.) These preferences for pornography are what Dworkin would call "external" preferences, because they are preferences that depend on views about the inferior worth of other people, in particular, women. Dworkin says that when a policy relies on external preferences, the policy violates the rights of those other people. So women have rights against a policy that permits pornography. Although Dworkin himself says pornography should be permitted (1981; 1991), his own principles apparently imply that pornography should be prohibited.

My strategy in this [selection] is different, and it divides into two parts, addressing the two feminist claims about subordination and silence. What I propose, in a nutshell, is this. Once we think of pornographic images and texts as speech acts, these feminist claims are intelligible and even (on certain assumptions) plausible. Understanding how pornographic utterances are speech acts will help us understand how pornography might subordinate. Understanding how potential speech acts can be made unspeakable for women will help us understand how pornography might silence. If pornography subordinates women, it presents a conflict between liberty and equality. If pornography silences women, it presents a conflict between liberty and liberty: the free speech of men, and that of women.

I. "Pornography Subordinates"

Before seeing whether pornographic speech acts can subordinate, we need to think about speech acts, and whether they can subordinate. Our interest is in the illocutionary speech act: the action performed in saying something. A perlocutionary act (by contrast) is the action performed (not *in* but) *by* saying something: the utterance considered in terms of its effects. Austin took care to distinguish illocutions from perlocutions, and he thought that the phrases "in saying" and "by saying" were typical—though not infallible—markers of the two. Recall the earlier example. *In saying* "Shoot her", the first man *ordered* the second to shoot: that was the illocutionary act. *By saying* "Shoot her", he *shocked* the second man, and *persuaded* him to shoot: those are some of the perlocutionary acts. Another example: *In saying* "I do" I was marrying; *by saying* "I do" I greatly distressed my mother. Saying "I do" in the right context counts as, constitutes, marrying: that is the illocutionary act. It does not count as distressing my mother, even if it has that effect: that is the perlocutionary act.

Austin said that an utterance has illocutionary force of a certain kind when it satisfies certain conditions for success: he called them *felicity conditions*. Whether or not in saying "I do" the speaker is marrying depends on the felicity conditions of marriage: that the speaker intends to marry, the utterance takes place in a conventional procedure, with appropriate participants (e.g. adult heterosexual couple, unmarried, plus priest or registrar). And the hearers should *recognize* that an illocution of a certain kind is being performed; Austin called this reconition necessary for the illocution, the *uptake*. . . .

. . . Can speech be an illocutionary act that subordinates?

Yes, surely. Consider this utterance: "Blacks are not permitted to vote." Imagine that it is uttered by a legislator in Pretoria [South Africa], in the context of enacting apartheid legislation. It is a locutionary act ("Blacks" refers to blacks, etc.). It is a perlocutionary act: it will have the effect, for example, that blacks stay away from polling booths. But it is, first and foremost, an illocutionary act: it makes it the case that blacks are not permitted to vote. It subordinates blacks. So does this utterance: "Whites Only". It too is a locutionary act ("Whites" refers to whites, etc.). It has some important perlocutionary effects (keeps blacks away from white areas, etc.). But it is also an illocutionary act: it orders blacks away, welcomes whites, permits whites to act in a discriminatory way towards blacks. It is an illocutionary act that subordinates blacks. If this is right, then there is no sleight of hand, no philosophical mistake, in the idea that speech can be an illocutionary act of subordination (cf. MacKinnon, 1987, p. 202; 1993, pp. 12–14).

The speech acts of apartheid subordinate because of (at least) the following three features. They *rank* blacks as having inferior worth. They *legitimate* discriminatory behaviour on the part of whites. And they *deprive* blacks of some important powers: the power to go to certain places, the power to vote. . . . We can be glad that the example is now anachronistic.

Speech acts of this kind belong to an important subset of speech acts, *authoritative illocutions.* Some illocutions involve the authoritative delivery of a finding: for example, actions of ranking, valuing, giving a verdict. Imagine an umpire calls "Fault" at a tennis match. What does he do, in saying that word? He describes the world as he sees it. But he does more: he gives his *verdict.* Imagine a mere bystander says "Fault". He describes the world as he sees it. He says the same thing as the umpire says: they perform the same locutionary act. But the bystander's word makes no difference to the score. The umpire's does. The umpire can do more things with his words. Other authoritative illocutions confer powers and rights on people, or deprive people of powers and rights. . . . You can't order someone, or fire someone, unless you have authority. . . . The authority of the speaker gives an utterance an illocutionary force which would be otherwise absent (cf. Austin, 1962, pp. 152–6).

It is because of their authority that the speech acts of apartheid subordinate. As MacKinnon herself puts it, "*authoritatively saying* someone is inferior is largely how structures of status and differential treatment are demarcated and actualized" (MacKinnon, 1993, p. 31, emphasis added). This already tells us something about subordinating speech acts: they are speech acts whose conditions for success (felicity conditions) require that the speaker has authority. . . .

We can turn now to the main question. Pornography is said to subordinate women. It is also said to rank women as sex objects, "defined on the basis of [their] looks . . . [their] availability for sexual pleasure", and to represent degrading and abusive sexual behaviour "in such a way as to *endorse* the degradation" (MacKinnon, 1987, p. 173; Longino, 1980, p. 29). MacKinnon herself provides a range of additional illocutionary verbs:

> Pornography sexualizes rape, battery, sexual harassment . . . and child sexual abuse; it . . . *celebrates, promotes, authorizes* and *legitimates* them. (MacKinnon, 1987, p. 171, emphasis added)

These descriptions are relevant to the claim that pornography subordinates.

Recall why the speech acts of apartheid subordinate. They *rank* certain people as inferior; they *legitimate* discriminatory behaviour towards them; and they *deprive* them of some important powers and rights. The feminists just quoted say pornography has some of these features: pornography ranks women as sex objects, legitimates sexual violence. Feminists think of sexual violence not simply as harm, but as a kind of discrimination. If pornography ranks women as sex objects, and legitimates discriminatory behaviour, it is an illocutionary act of subordination. So the claim that *pornography subordinates women* makes sense: it is not confused, not "sleight of hand", not "philosophically indefensible". It makes good sense: but is it true?

There is disagreement—to put it mildly—about whether the feminist descriptions are correct. Disagreements about illocutions can be hard to resolve. Austin said that disputed speech acts need to have "a construction put upon them by judges" (p. 114), and I discuss elsewhere some different methods for resolving disagreement (Langton, 1993). However, if the argument so far is right, then we know that subordinating speech is a kind of authoritative speech. Whether you can perform authoritative speech acts depends on the authority you have. . . . So one way to help answer the question: "Does pornography subordinate?" is to ask whether it has authority. If it does, then at least one crucial felicity condition is satisfied: pornographic speech acts may then be authoritative illocutions that rank women as inferior, legitimate violence, and thus subordinate.

This question about authority may well be at the heart of the controversy about pornography. Some think pornography is the speech of a powerless minority, vulnerable to moralistic persecution. Then it seems odd to say pornographic speech is authoritative. But some think the voice of pornography is the voice of the ruling power. MacKinnon says, "the power of pornography is more like the power of the state" (1993, p. 39). Then it seems obvious that pornographic speech is authoritative—that the authors of pornographic speech are not mere bystanders to the game, but speakers whose verdict counts.

Does pornographic speech have authority? This is not really a question to be settled from the philosopher's armchair. To answer it we need to know about the role pornographers occupy as authoritative speakers about the "facts" of sex. What is important is not whether pornographic speech is generally respected, but whether it is authoritative in the domain of speech about sex. What is important is whether it is authoritative for the hearers that count: people, men, boys, who want (among other things) to discover how to act, want to know which moves in the sexual game are legitimate. What is important is whether it is authoritative for those hearers who somehow learn that violence is sexy and coercion legitimate: those who "think it is okay for a man to rape a woman if he is sexually aroused by her", who say they have raped a woman on a date, who say that they enjoy the conquest part of sex, who rank faces of women displaying pain and fear to be more sexually attractive than faces showing pleasure (Warshaw, 1988, pp. 93, 120; Wolf, 1990, pp. 162–8). In this domain, and for these hearers, perhaps pornography has the authority of a monopoly. If, as a matter of fact, pornography has authority, then the claim that pornography subordinates may be not only intelligible, but true.

II. "Pornography Silences"

If speech is action, then silence is failure to act. If pornography silences women, it prevents women from doing things with their words. Before thinking about whether pornography silences women, we need to think about how speech acts may be silenced, and whether speech acts can silence.

The ability to perform speech acts can be a measure of political power. Those who use the words "Blacks are not permitted to vote" to *prohibit* are the ones with authority. One mark of powerlessness is an inability to perform speech acts one might otherwise like to perform. We can distinguish three kinds of silence, since (following Austin) there are three kinds of act one may fail to perform.

At a first and basic level, members of a powerless group may be silent because they are intimidated. They do not protest, because they think protest is futile. They do not vote, because they fear the guns. In such cases no words are uttered at all. Speakers fail to perform even a *locutionary* act. Sometimes, however, people speak, and what they say fails to achieve the intended effects: such speakers fail to perform their intended perlocutionary act. Silencing of this second kind (perlocutionary frustration) is a common fact of life: you argue, but persuade no-one; you invite, but no-one comes to the party; you vote, hoping to oust the government, but in vain.

There is a third kind of silence: you speak, you utter words, and you fail to perform the illocutionary act that you intend. Things go wrong: your speech misfires. Silencing of this third kind I call *illocutionary disablement.*

Example (1): Warning

This example is from the philosopher Donald Davidson (1984, p. 269).

> Imagine this: the actor is acting a scene in which there is supposed to be a fire. . . . It is his role to imitate as persuasively as he can a man who is trying to warn others of a fire. "Fire!" he screams. And perhaps he adds, at the behest of the author, "I mean it! Look at the smoke!" etc. And now a real fire breaks out, and the actor tries vainly to warn the real audience. "Fire!" he screams. "I mean it! Look at the smoke!" etc.

The actor says words appropriate for warning. He gets the locutionary act exactly right. He intends to warn. But he does not warn. Something about the role he occupies prevents his utterance from counting as a warning. Something, perhaps, about the conventions of theatre constrains the speech acts he can make. The same words said with the same intentions by a member of the audience *would* count as a warning. The actor, though, has been silenced. The act of warning has been made unspeakable for him. . . .

Example (2): Voting

A white in apartheid South Africa makes marks on a piece of paper in a polling booth. A black makes marks that look the same. Their intentions are the same. But the former has done something significant. He has voted. The latter has not. Something about who he is prevents him from satisfying a crucial felicity condition. The law prevents his utterance from counting as a vote. Voting is, for him, an unspeakable act. He lacks an important political power available to other citizens. . . .

If we are interested in the silence of illocutionary disablement, we can ask about its source. When speech misfires because speakers fail to satisfy certain conditions, we can ask how those conditions came to be. MacKinnon says there can be *"words that set conditions"* (1987, p. 228), and Austin would agree. Felicity conditions can be set by other speech acts. Laws are enacted that specify the felicity conditions for . . . voting. . . . Some illocutionary acts fix the range and scope of other illocutionary acts. Some speech acts build and limit a space for other speech acts, making it possible for some people to . . . vote . . .—and impossible for other people to . . . vote. . . . Speech can thus silence by making speech acts, illocutionary acts, unspeakable.

For more informal illocutions (warning, advising, etc.) there are no enactments of legislation to "set conditions". But perhaps here too, conditions can be set by speech: by informal practices of communication that set informal rules about what counts as, for example, a warning. Here too, perhaps, there can be speech that builds and limits the space for potential speech acts, and silences those who do not satisfy the conditions.

Let us consider, now, some different examples of silence.

Example (3): Refusal

Think about the utterance "No." We know how to do things with this word. We use it, typically, to disagree, refuse, prohibit. In sexual contexts a woman sometimes uses it to refuse sex. However, in sexual contexts a woman sometimes tries to use the "No" locution to refuse sex, and it does not work. It does not work for the women who are date raped, or for the girls who are sexually forced (Wolf, 1990, pp. 166–7; Caputi, 1987, p. 119). Saying "No" sometimes doesn't work. But perhaps there are two ways in which it can fail to work. Sometimes the woman's hearer recognizes the action she performs: recognizes that she is refusing. In saying "No", she really does refuse. By saying "No", she intends to stop her hearer from continuing his advances. But the hearer goes ahead, and forces sex on her. She prohibits, but he fails to obey. She fails to achieve the (perlocutionary) goal of her refusal: her refusal is frustrated. ("Perlocutionary frustration" is too academic a label: this is simple rape.) Sometimes, perhaps, there is a different silencing. Sometimes "No", when spoken by a woman, does not *count* as the act of refusal. The hearer fails to recognize the utterance as a refusal: uptake is not secured. In saying "No" she may well intend to refuse. By saying "No" she intends to prevent sex, but she is far from doing as she intends. Since illocutionary force depends, in part, on uptake being secured, the woman fails to refuse. She is like the actor in Davidson's story, silenced as surely as the actor is silenced. He shouts "Fire!" He says the right words. He means what he says. He intends to warn. But what he says misfires. Something about him, something about the role he occupies, prevents him from warning the audience. She says "No". She says the right words. She means what she says. She intends to refuse. But what she says misfires. Something about her, something about the role she occupies, prevents her from voicing refusal. Refusal—in that context—has become unspeakable for her.

Example (4): Protest

The following appeared in a mail-order catalogue advertising "Adult Reading", flanked by such titles as "426. *Forbidden Sexual Fantasies*" and "428. *Orgy: an Erotic Experience*".

No. 427 ORDEAL: an autobiography by Linda Lovelace. With M. McGrady. The star of *Deep Throat* tells the shocking story of her enslavement in the pornographic underworld, a nightmarish ordeal of savage violence and unspeakable perversion, of thrill-seeking celebrities and sadistic criminals. For Sale to Adults Over 21 Only.

Ordeal is a book that has been cited by feminists who oppose pornography. The author, Linda Marchiano (alias Lovelace), tells the story of the making of the film *Deep Throat*. Austin remarked (p. 118) that you can perform the illocutionary act of protest a number of different ways: you can shout; you can hurl a tomato. You can also write a book in protest. *Ordeal* is an act of protest, a denunciation of the industry in which Marchiano says she was forced to perform. One can see why it is cited by anti-pornography feminists. As locutionary act *Ordeal* depicts the subordination of a woman: it depicts a woman "in scenarios of degradation, injury and torture." But it does not "endorse the degradation"; it does not "celebrate, promote, authorize and legitimate" the sexual violence. It does not appear to have pornography's illocutionary force.

Why is *Ordeal* in a mail-order catalogue, flanked by ordinary pornographic titles? Perhaps because *it is pornography after all*: here, in this context, for these intended hearers, the uptake secured is that of pornography. Marchiano says words appropriate for an act of protest. She uses the right locutions, words that graphically depict her own past subordination. She intends to protest. But her speech misfires. Something about who she is, or the role she occupies, prevents her from satisfying protest's felicity conditions, at least here. Though the threats and gags are gone, there is silence of another kind. She too is like the actor. Warning was unspeakable for him. Protest is unspeakable for her, in this context. What he tries to say comes out as "merely acted". What she tries to say comes out as pornography. Her protest has been disabled.

⟐

We can ask about the origins of the illocutionary disablement in examples (3) and (4): the disablement of the rape victim whose attempted refusal is not recognized as a refusal; the disablement of an author whose attempted protest is not recognized as protest. These misfires betray the presence of structural constraints on women's speech. The felicity conditions for refusal, for protest, are, somehow, not met. Something is robbing the speech of its intended force. Intending to refuse, intending to protest, is not enough. Pornography may be responsible for this illocutionary disablement. For if women's speech is disabled, and we ask how the disabling conditions came to be, we can reflect that felicity conditions for illocutions can be set by other speech acts. And when MacKinnon says there can be "words that set conditions", she means that *the felicity conditions for women's speech acts are set by the speech acts of pornography.*

Consider how this might apply to (3). Pornography might legitimate rape, and silence refusal, by doing something other than eroticizing refusal itself. It may simply leave no space for the refusal move in its depictions of sex. In pornography of this kind there would be all kinds of words the women depicted could use to make the consent move. "Yes" is one. "No" is just another. Here the refusal move is not eroticized: it is absent altogether. Consent is the *only* thing a woman can do with her words, in this game. Someone learning the rules from this kind of pornography might not recognize an attempted refusal. Refusal, here, would be disabled. Refusal would be made unspeakable for a woman.

How common is silencing of this kind, and the rape which accompanies it? It is hard to tell, because so few rapes are reported (and these least of all). Studies about sexual violence say that men often "refuse to take no for an answer". Perhaps they recognize the refusal, and persist in spite of it, or because of it (matching the first pattern in example (3)). Or perhaps there is something else: Naomi Wolf says (1990, 167)

> . . . boys rape and girls get raped *as a normal course of events.* The boys may even be unaware that what they are doing is wrong; violent sexual imagery may well have raised a generation of young men who can rape women without even knowing it.

If young men can rape without knowing it, then women sometimes fail to secure uptake for their attempted refusals. This is the silence of disablement. . . .

The story about *Ordeal* shows the same phenomenon. Marchiano tries to protest, but only succeeds in making more pornography. The pornographers know how to do things with her words: stories of "savage violence" and "enslavement in the pornographic underworld" are pornography to readers for whom violence has been legitimated as sex. And there is ironic truth in what the pornographers say: the violence is indeed "unspeakable" for Marchiano. If you are a woman using sexually explicit speech, describing the savage sexual violence you have suffered, and especially if you are a famous pornography star, what you say counts as pornography. Too bad if you want it to count as something else. It is an effective way to silence: not simply by depriving her speech of its intended illocutionary force, but by replacing it with a force that is its antithesis. That story is not an isolated anecdote. If MacKinnon is right, it is comparable to a similar disablement encountered by women who give testimony in court about rape and sexual harassment, and whose testimony, and descriptions of their experience, achieve the uptake appropriate to a description of "normal" sex.

If pornography sets up the rules in the language games of sex in a way that disables and silences women, then it belongs in the class of speech acts that removes powers. This, recall, was part of what it meant to be subordinating speech: so we come full circle. If pornography silences, it subordinates. And if pornography silences, it is authoritative speech. So the second feminist claim, like the first, depends on a premise about the authority of pornography—it depends on that premise for its plausibility, but not for its coherence. . . .

The claim is not metaphor; it is not confusion either. Dworkin says (1991, p. 108) it is a "confusion" to suppose that pornography silences women, because it is a confusion to "characterize certain ideas as silencing ideas". But the feminist claim is not that ideas are silencing ideas, but that acts can be silencing acts. That is no confusion. People do all kinds of thing with words: advise, warn, marry—and also silence one another. They silence by preventing other speakers from doing things with words. They can silence simply, by ordering, or threatening;

they can silence by frustrating a speaker's perlocutionary acts; they can silence by disabling a speaker's illocutionary acts, and this latter silence has been the special focus of our attention.

The claim that pornography silences is not really about ideas at all, but about people and what they do. It is common to cast ideas as the heroes of the free speech story. Free speech is a good thing, because it provides a free-market marketplace for ideas, where the best and truest ideas can win out in the end. To say that some speech silences is to describe a shopping problem: some ideas which could be on the market are not. This too is the tendency of which Austin complained: a focus on content, while ignoring the speech act performed. The claim that pornography silences women is not about ideas, but about people. Free speech is a good thing because it *enables people to act,* lets people do things with words: argue, protest, question, answer. Speech that silences is bad, not— or not just—because it restricts the ideas available on the shelves, but because it constrains people's actions. Perhaps women do have trouble developing new ideas about themselves, about sexuality, about life, when pornography has market monopoly. The market is missing out on some good ideas. But that is not the point. The point is that a woman's liberty to speak the *actions* she wants to speak has been thwarted: a woman's liberty to protest against pornography and rape, refuse sex when she wants to, argue about violence in court. The point is that while pornography sets the conditions of women's speech, women cannot do things with words, even when we think we know how. And if speech itself is more than "only words", then free speech is as well.

Notes

1. *American Booksellers, Inc.* v. *Hudnut,* 771 F2nd 329 (7th Cir. 1985).
2. *Hudnut,* 598 F. Supp. 136 (1984).

References

Austin, J. L.: *How to Do Things with Words* (London: Oxford University Press, 1962).
Bahadur, Mahomed Yusoof Khan: *Mahomedan Law,* vol. III (Calcutta: Thacker, Spink & Co., 1898).
Caputi, J.: *The Age of Sex Crime* (London: The Women's Press, 1987).
Davidson, Donald: "Communication and Convention" (1982), in *Inquiries into Truth and Interpretation* (Oxford: Oxford University Press, 1984).
Donnerstein, E., D. Linz, and S. Penrod: *The Question of Pornography: Research Findings and Policy Implications* (New York: Free Press; London: Collier Macmillan, 1987).
Dworkin, R.: "Do We Have a Right to Pornography?", *Oxford Journal of Legal Studies,* I (1981), 177–212; reprinted in *A Matter of Principle* (Cambridge, MA: Harvard University Press, 1985), pp. 335–72.
_____: "Two Concepts of Liberty", in *Isaiah Berlin: A Celebration,* ed. Edna and Avishai Margalit (London: Hogarth Press, 1991).
Habermas, J.rgen: *The Theory of Communicative Action* (Beacon Press, 1984), vol. I.
Hodkinsonü, K: *Muslim Family Law* (London: Croom Helm, 1984).
Hornsby, Jennifer: "Illocution and Its Significance", *Foundations of Speech Act Theory: Philosophical and Linguistic Perspectives,* ed. S. L. Tsohatzidis (London and New York: Routledge, 1994).

_____: "Speech Acts and Pornography", *Women's Philosophy Review,* 10 (1993), 38–45; reprinted in *The Problem of Pornography,* ed. Sue Dwyer (Belmont, CA: Wadsworth, 1995).

Jacobson, D.: "Freedom of Speech Acts? A Response to Langton", *Philosophy and Public Affairs,* 24 (1995), 64–79.

Langton, Rae: "Speech Acts and Unspeakable Acts", *Philosophy and Public Affairs,* 22 (1993), 293–330.

_____: "Whose Right? Ronald Dworkin, Women and Pornographers", *Philosophy and Public Affairs,* 19 (1990), 311–59.

Longino, H. E.: "Pornography, Oppression and Freedom: A Closer Look", in *Take Back the Night: Women on Pornography,* ed. Laura Lederer (New York: William Morrow, 1980).

Lovelace, L. with M. McGrady: *Ordeal* (Secaucus, NJ: Citadel Press, 1980).

MacKinnon, Catharine: *Feminism Unmodified* (Cambridge, MA: Harvard University Press, 1987).

_____: *Only Words* (Cambridge, MA: Harvard University Press, 1993).

Michelman, F.: "Conceptions of Democracy in American Constitutional Argument: The Case of Pornography Regulation", *Tennessee Law Review,* 56 (1989).

Parent, W. A.: "A Second Look at Pornography and the Subordination of Women", *Journal of Philosophy,* 87 (1990), 205–11.

Tribe, Laurence: *American Constitutional Law* (2nd edn) (Mineola, NY: Foundation Press, 1988), chapter 12.

Vadas, Melinda: "A First Look at the Pornography/Civil Rights Ordinance: Could Pornography be the Subordination of Women?", *Journal of Philosophy,* 84 (1987), 487–511.

Warshaw, R.: *I Never Called it Rape* (New York: Harper and Rowe, 1988).

Wolf, Naomi: *The Beauty Myth* (New York: Vintage, 1990).

 **NO**

Defending Pornography: Free Speech, Sex, and the Fight for Women's Rights

The Sex Panic and the Feminist Split

Women Having It All: Free Speech *and* Equality

> *From a feminist perspective, there is no choice between equality and freedom of expression; they are two sides of the same coin, and cannot be played off against each other any more than we can separate mind and body.*

Thelma McCormack, Director
York University Centre for Feminist Studies[1]

Since free expression about sexual issues is critically important to the women's rights cause, it is ironic that those feminists who advocate curbing such expression say they do so out of concern for women's rights. They define as pornography, and seek to suppress, sexually explicit expression that "subordinates" or "degrades" women, on the theory that this expression causes discrimination and violence against women. They argue that free speech protection for pornography is antithetical to women's rights, and therefore that we have to compromise the constitutional free speech guarantee to advance the constitutional equality guarantee. This was the major theme, for example, of Catharine MacKinnon's 1993 book *Only Words*. She declares: "The law of equality and the law of freedom of speech are on a collision course in this country."[2]

In fact, though, this line of argument is pernicious and wrongheaded. In our society, founded on the interlinked goals of liberty and equality, we all are entitled to both freedom of speech and equal opportunity under the law. Moreover, these two ideals are mutually reinforcing.

In the women's rights context, freedom of speech consistently has been the strongest weapon for countering misogynistic discrimination and violence, and censorship consistently has been a potent tool for curbing women's rights and interests. Freedom of sexually oriented expression is integrally connected with women's freedom, since women traditionally have been straitjacketed precisely in the sexual domain, notably in our ability to control our sexual and reproductive options. Accordingly, during the first wave of feminism in this century, Margaret Sanger, Mary Ware Dennett, and other pioneering birth control advocates were prosecuted (and, in some cases, convicted, fined, and imprisoned) for disseminating birth control information. Significantly, this information was held to violate *antiobscenity* statutes. Such laws were used not to promote women's equality, but rather, to erode it.

Because the American Civil Liberties Union, since its founding, has represented many women's rights activists whose free speech has been throttled—including Sanger and Dennett—its opposition to the antipornography laws endorsed by some feminists is grounded in the organization's long-standing commitment to women's rights, as well as in its consistent defense of free speech. In opposing an antipornography ordinance that Indianapolis enacted in 1984, modeled on one drafted by [Andrea] Dworkin and MacKinnon,[3] the ACLU argued that the law "unconstitutionally introduced gender-based discrimination into the First Amendment." As the ACLU's brief explained:

> The ordinance . . . presumes a natural and inevitable vulnerability of (weaker) women to the unbridled and voracious sexual appetites of (stronger) men and accordingly promises to "protect" all women. As in the past, the cost of "protection" is the perpetuation of gender-based stereotypes and the denial to women of sexually explicit material which may itself benefit women by providing information about sexuality, sexual functions, or reproduction. . . . While it is undoubtedly true that many women are victims of male violence . . . the attempt to [justify] widespread censorship on the false stereotypical assumption that all women are unable to resist male domination . . . is precisely the type of sex-based protectionism that inhibits the evolution of genuine equality between the sexes.[4]

All censorship measures throughout history have been used disproportionately to silence those who are relatively disempowered and who seek to challenge the status quo. Since women and feminists are in that category, it is predictable that any censorship scheme—even one purportedly designed to further their interests—would in fact be used to suppress expression that is especially important to their interests.

That prediction has proven accurate in our neighboring country of Canada, which in 1992 adopted the definition of pornography advocated by MacKinnon, Dworkin, and other procensorship feminists: sexually explicit expression that is "dehumanizing" or "degrading" to women.[5] The Canadian authorities have seized upon this powerful tool to suppress lesbian and gay publications and feminist works, and to harass lesbian and gay bookstores and women's bookstores. . . .

"Different Strokes for Different Folks": The Panoply of Pornographic Imagination

The fact that many women find much that excites or otherwise pleases them in commercial erotica is indicated by their large and growing share of the burgeoning market for such imagery. Women, either singly or as part of a couple, constitute more than 40 percent of the adult videotape rental audience; to put this number in perspective, it should be noted that 410 million adult videos were rented in 1991 alone, and that adult video sales and rentals have soared since then.[6] In 1987 two social scientists conducting a survey of over 26,000 female readers of *Redbook* magazine found that nearly half the respondents said they regularly watch pornographic films.[7]

Women also make up a growing portion of those who produce erotic materials. Increasing numbers of women writers, filmmakers, and magazine editors have been producing sexually explicit materials, many expressly aimed at a female audience. These include Marianna Beck, copublisher of *Libido: The Journal of Sex and Sensibility;* author Susie Bright, whose many writings include the "Cliterati" column in the *San Francisco Review of Books* and three books entitled *Herotica,* annual collections of erotic writings by and for women; filmmaker Candida Royalle, who heads Femme Productions; the Kensington Ladies Erotic Society, which has published anthologies of women's erotica; and the editors of *Bad Attitude* and *On Our Backs,* two lesbian feminist erotic magazines. In the words of Marianna Beck, who estimates that *Libido*'s readership is 40 percent female, "We're . . . depicting sex as not just something that men engage in actively while the woman somehow endures while thinking of Catherine [*sic*] MacKinnon."[8]

Pornography also has literary value. In "The Pornographic Imagination," a 1967 essay, Susan Sontag analyzes and debunks the various assumptions underlying the view that pornography can be categorically distinguished from "authentic literature":

> The ratio of authentic literature to trash in pornography may be somewhat lower than the ratio of novels of genuine literary merit to the entire volume of subliterary fiction produced for mass taste. But I doubt that it's any lower than, for instance, that of another somewhat shady subgenre with a few first-rate books to its credit, science fiction. (As literary forms, pornography and science fiction resemble each other in several interesting ways.) Anyway, the quantitative measure supplies a trivial standard. Relatively uncommon as they may be, there are writings which it seems reasonable to call pornographic—assuming that the stale label has any use at all—which, at the same time, cannot be refused accreditation as serious literature.[9]

Procensorship feminists argue that they would ban only sexual materials that are violent or subordinating. But no consensus is possible concerning which pornography can be described with such reductionist, subjective labels. By ascribing to any sexually oriented work one meaning only, and by imposing that construct on the rest of us, the feminist antipornography movement is profoundly antithetical to individualism, denying autonomy both to all the people who create expressive works and to all the people who see their works.

As writer Sallie Tisdale has stated:

> Always, the [feminist] censors are concerned with how men *act* and how women are portrayed. Women cannot make free sexual choices in that world; they are too oppressed to know that only oppression could lead them to sell sex. And I, watching, am either too oppressed to know the harm that my watching has done to my sisters . . . or else I have become the Man. And it is the Man in me who watches and is aroused. (Shame.) What a misogynistic worldview this is, this claim that women who make such choices cannot be making free choices at all. . . . Feminists against pornography have done a sad and awful thing: *They* have made women into objects.[10]

The antipornography feminists rigidly presume that all viewers, or at least all male viewers, will interpret sexual speech as conveying misogynistic messages. But many other feminists view much such speech as conveying to many viewers messages that are at worst ambiguous and at best positive. Ambiguous and positive interpretations apply to the full range of sexual speech, including violent imagery and imagery that might well be labeled "subordinating" or "degrading," such as rape scenes and scenes dramatizing the so-called rape myth—namely, that women want to be raped. . . . [W]omen have found affirmations of eroticism and empowerment in all such images, and feminist women have seen them as exploring such pro-feminist themes as liberation from conventional sexual conduct and from traditional gender roles. . . .

Degradation or Delight (or Both)

The inescapably individualized, and hence wildly divergent, interpretations that all persons bring to all sexual expression can be illustrated . . . by considering another type of such expression that, along with rape scenes, is commonly cited as a paradigmatic example of the subordinating imagery that would be banned under the antipornography feminist regime: the "come shot," in which a man ejaculates on a woman's body. In many such scenes, the woman then smears the sperm over her body and licks it. Although procensorship feminists routinely cite these as archetypal images of female degradation, this characterization is as oversimplified as every other aspect of their approach to sexual expression.

Canadian writer Wendy McElroy has suggested other interpretations of these scenes. She notes that makers of commercial erotic films often insert "come shots" simply to prove that the male *did* ejaculate, that he was "into" the sex. Likewise, the woman's response of spreading the sperm over her body or tasting it would simply demonstrate that she, too, was fully, enthusiastically involved in the sexual encounter.[11]

Many women viewers may be particularly interested in seeing come shots because men's ejaculations are usually hidden from them, occurring inside the woman's own body. As McElroy observes, to such women, the sight of male ejaculation "is as elusive as a glimpse of breast or lace panty must be to a pubescent boy. In this context, the come-shot can be interpreted in an almost romantic way: the woman wishes to share, as much as possible, in her lover's orgasm.[12] . . .

Do as They Say, Not as They Do

Procensorship feminists perforce must concede the oversimplified nature of their rhetoric denouncing the inherent dangers supposedly caused by exposure to pornography; their own experience proves that some individuals may survive exposure to pornography without any adverse impact on their attitudes and behavior toward women. Probably very few men have examined the volume of violent, misogynistic pornography with the attention that Dworkin, MacKinnon, and other procensorship advocates have lavished upon it. Katie Roiphe reports that when MacKinnon lectured at Princeton University in 1992, she "assure[d] the audience that she's seen more porn than any of us."[13] As Pete Hamill wrote:

> MacKinnon and Dworkin . . . [have] obviously pored over more pornography than the ordinary man sees in a lifetime. . . . If human beings are so weak and pornography so powerful, why aren't MacKinnon and Dworkin playing the Krafft-Ebing Music Hall with the rest of the perverts?[14]

Dworkin, MacKinnon, and their allies still maintain respect for women's equality, as they envision it, and for women's safety. Their proposed censorship regime thus is predicated on a double standard: that *they* can withstand the allegedly pernicious influence of exposure to pornography, but *others* cannot.

This double standard is typical of censorship advocates generally. . . .

Positive Aspects of Pornographic Imagery

If pornography is part of your sexuality, then you have no right to your sexuality.

Catharine MacKinnon[15]

I take this personally, the effort to repress material I enjoy—to tell me how wrong it is for me to enjoy it. Anti-pornography legislation is directed at me: as a user, as a writer. Catharine MacKinnon and Andrea Dworkin . . . are themselves prurient, scurrying after sex in every corner. They look down on me and shake a finger: Bad girl. Mustn't touch. That branch of feminism tells me my very thoughts are bad. Pornography tells me the opposite: that none of my thoughts are bad, that anything goes. . . . The message of pornography . . . is that our sexual selves are real.

Sallie Tisdale, writer[16]

Sexual Egalitarianism

Even if words and images could be interpreted literally, we would still have to reject the pornophobic feminists' simplistic stance that pornography conveys unrelentingly negative messages about women. Much commercial erotica depicts women in nonsubordinated roles, and contains images and ideas that may well be seen as positive for women and feminists.

Although Catharine MacKinnon has described pornography with characteristic oversimplification as "man's boot on woman's neck,"[17] in many films and photos, the shoe is, literally, on the other foot—rather, the woman's boot is on the man's neck, if not on an even more vulnerable section of his anatomy. The female dominatrix and male slave are familiar characters in sexually explicit materials. Taking issue with the antipornography feminists' views that women are never on top sexually, either in the real world or in erotic materials, Norman Mailer observed with his typical saltiness, "I've seen any number of pornographic films where you have girls sitting on guys' heads."[18] And feminist aficionada of erotica Sallie Tisdale emphatically corroborates this perspective: "Women in modern films are often the initiators of sex; men in such films seem perfectly content for that to be so."[19]

Many sexual materials defy traditional stereotypes of both women and pornography by depicting females as voluntarily, joyfully participating in sexual encounters with men on an equal basis. Procensorship feminists may well view a woman's apparent welcoming of sex with a man as degrading, but this is because of their negative attitudes toward women's ability to make sexual choices. Other viewers are likely to see such a scene as positive and healthy....

Men's rights activist Jack Kammer notes that "one of men's most enduring 'pornographic' fantasies is . . . about equalizing" sexual control between men and women, in a societal context in which women have often derived power from withholding sex. Accordingly, he notes:

> An archetype of male erotica is the woman who participates enthusiastically in sex, who loves male sexuality, who needs not to be cajoled, seduced or promised ulterior rewards. Erotica portraying such joyful, egalitarian sex does not demean women any more than men are denigrated by stories of women and men working cooperatively in an office where men no longer think it is their right to have women fetch them coffee. Ironically, [MacKinnon's] greatest effect may be only to enhance men's need for what she wants to suppress. The more women accept arguments about the inherent cruelty, selfishness and danger of male sexuality, the more men will need to fantasize, possibly by resorting to pornography, about women who offer egalitarian, joyful, trusting sexual companionship.[20] . . .

Unreal Rape

Just as it is vitally important to enforce criminal and societal sanctions against *real* rape—defined by University of Southern California law professor Susan Estrich, in her book of that title, as all intentional nonconsensual sex[21]—it is also vitally important *not* to enforce sanctions against *unreal* rape—words or images *describing* or *depicting* nonconsensual sex.

The distinction between the imagined and the actual, between fantasy and reality, should be crystal clear. But the feminist antipornography movement has blurred it. For example, in her 1993 book, MacKinnon writes, "In pornography, pictures and words are sex"[22] and "[s]exual words and pictures . . . have sex."[23] Indeed, the title of that book, *Only Words,* conveys MacKinnon's sarcastic dismissal of the view that pornographic words are, in fact, only words.

This confusion between expression and action is yet another common bond between feminist censors and other censors. As writer Wendy Kaminer remarked, "[I]f pornography is sex discrimination, then an editorial criticizing the President is treason."[24] (Indeed, under English common law, it was a crime to "compass"—or imagine—the death of the king;[25] the law would be moving backward toward that long discredited notion were it to adopt the feminist pro-censorship philosophy.) And Thelma McCormack retorted to the MacDworkinite charge that pornography is rape by comparing it to "the Ayatollah Khomeini saying 'The Satanic Verses' is not a work of art but an act of heresy."[26]

To MacKinnon, there are apparently no distinctions between women who are raped by actual men in real life, and female actresses in erotic productions whose rapes are simulated by male actors. Moreover, MacKinnon apparently concedes no distinction between real-life rape victims and female models who are "raped" by the cameras that simply record their nude or sexual poses. In a 1993 article in *Ms.* magazine, MacKinnon wrote, "Pornography is made from rape in film studios, on sets, in private bedrooms, in basements, in alleys, in prison cells, and in brothels."[27]

Likewise, in *Only Words,* MacKinnon asserts that women are "gang raped," "hurt and penetrated, tied and gagged, undressed and genitally spread," and even "killed . . . to make pornography," and that these violent actions are "essential . . . to make pornography."[28] It should be emphasized that, since MacKinnon defines pornography as including verbal and visual representations—for example, stories and drawings—she is claiming not only that pornography necessitates harm to actual women who serve as models or actresses for photographs or films (this claim is itself inaccurate, as discussed in the following [section]); but further, she is claiming that pornography drawn solely from the writer's or artist's imagination inevitably harms women. Again, MacKinnon conflates imagination, acting, and actuality. . . .

Many women can and do distinguish between real rape and descriptions or depictions of rape. By definition, no one wants to be raped; the very essence of this heinous crime is unwanted sex. That does not mean, though, that the unmitigatedly evil nature of real rape extends as well to unreal rape: rape fantasies, verbal descriptions of fictional rapes, paintings or sculpture depicting rape scenes, or photographs and films showing simulated rapes.

In her latest collection of women's sexual fantasies, the 1993 book *Women on Top,* Nancy Friday writes:

> The most popular guilt-avoiding device [in these fantasies] was the so-called rape fantasy—"so-called" because no rape, bodily harm, or humiliation took

place in the fantasy. It simply had to be understood that what went on was against the woman's will. Saying she was "raped" was the most expedient way of getting past the big No to sex that had been imprinted on her mind since early childhood.[29] . . .

Fantasies for Feminists and Other Freedom Fighters

[I]f social convention, backed by religion and law, confines sexuality to the heterosexual, monogamous, marital, familial, and reproductive, then the ambisexual, promiscuous, adulterous, selfish, and gratification-centered world of pornography is a charter of sexual revolution that is potentially liberating rather than confining for women.

Kathleen Sullivan
Stanford University law professor[30]

Several anthologies of feminist writings illuminate the range of messages in pornography, specifically from the viewpoints of feminists and women in general.[31] Feminist writer and literature professor Ann Snitow, who coedited one such anthology, *Powers of Desire,* has described some of porn's positive facets:

Pornography sometimes includes elements of play, as if the fear women feel toward men had evaporated and women were relaxed and willing at last. Such a fantasy—sexual revolution as *fait accompli* . . . can . . . be wishful, eager and utopian.

Porn can depict thrilling (as opposed to threatening) danger. . . . [S]ome of its manic quality . . . seems propelled by fear and joy about breaching the always uncertain boundaries of flesh and personality. . . .

Some pornography is defiant and thumbs a nose at death, at the limitations of the body and nature. . . .

Porn offers . . . a private path to arousal, an arousal that may be all too easily routed by fear or shame. . . .

[P]ornography also flouts authority, which no doubt in part explains its appeal to young boys.[32]

. . . Pornography also contains many elements that are harmonious with feminist values. As the Feminist Anti-Censorship Taskforce brief noted in the Indianapolis case, it "may convey the message that sexuality need not be tied to reproduction, men or domesticity."[33] Feminists Lisa Duggan, Nan Hunter, and Carole Vance have suggested additional profeminist aspects of pornography:

[P]ornography has served to flout conventional sexual mores, to ridicule sexual hypocrisy and to underscore the importance of sexual needs. Pornography carries many messages other than woman-hating; it advocates sexual adventure, sex outside of marriage, sex for no reason other than pleasure, casual sex, anonymous sex, group sex, voyeuristic sex, illegal sex, public sex. Some of these ideas appeal to women reading or seeing pornography, who may interpret some images as legitimating their own sense of sexual urgency or desire to be sexually aggressive. Women's experience of pornography is not as universally victimizing as the [MacKinnon-Dworkin] ordinance would have it.[34]

. . . The fact that pornography always has rebelled against conventional constraints is precisely the reason it always has provoked such anxiety among moral traditionalists and political conservatives. . . .

Just as *suppressing* sexual speech plays an essential role in *maintaining* the political, social, and economic status quo, conversely *protecting* sexual speech plays an essential role in *challenging* the status quo. . . .

Posing for Pornography: Coercion or Consent?

[M]any intelligent, self-confident women . . . have chosen to work in this lucrative industry. What sort of "feminism" is this that tells me I need "reforming" just because dancing buck naked on stage while people throw money at me is my idea of fun? By depicting sex workers as either too emotionally crippled or too stupid to escape a fate which apparently any decent woman would find unspeakably degrading, they help perpetuate the sorts of patronizing stereotypes a true women's liberation movement should strive to eradicate.

"Karen," stage name of a law student who works
as a nude dancer at New York City clubs.[35]

Antipornography feminists often seek to justify censorship by arguing that some women who pose for sexually explicit pictures or films have been forced into doing so, either through physical violence or through other types of coercion, such as fraud or duress. It is clearly illegal to coerce anyone into producing a sexual image, just as coercion is illegal in any setting. On that point, the pro-censorship and anticensorship feminists are united.

The two groups are sharply divided, though, on three related points. First, anticensorship feminists stress that the law already prohibits violence and other forms of coercion, and provides remedies when it occurs.

Second, anticensorship feminists reject the view of their procensorship counterparts that women who pose for sexual images are always and inevitably victims of coercion. Worse yet, the procensorship feminists' view that women cannot consent to pose for sexual pictures or films is antithetical to women's full and equal citizenship, relegating women to the subordinated legal status of children.

Third, anticensorship feminists stress that outlawing the production of any sexually explicit materials will decrease the protections available to women who participate in such productions. Rather than eliminating sexually explicit materials, Dworkin-MacKinnon—style laws would simply drive their production underground, where it would be impossible for models and actresses to invoke legal protections against violence and duress.

Any individuals responsible for physically assaulting women in the process of making sexually oriented materials can be criminally prosecuted as well as sued for damages. . . .

Despite the existing panoply of criminal and civil remedies for women who have been physically or psychologically abused in the production of sexual materials, procensorship feminists insist that these measures are insufficient to counter the particular type of coercion that they believe to be inevitable whenever a woman poses for such materials. Procensorship feminists conclude that—at least in the realm of sexuality and sexual expression—women can never make free, voluntary, consensual choices, and that, rather, women are *always* coerced in this context, whether they realize it or not.

But women should not be treated like children or mentally disabled persons and deprived of the right to enter into contracts for the production of sexually explicit materials. That is the end result of the MacDworkin model antipornography law, which provides that a woman's decision to pose for a sexual image should be treated as the product of coercion even under circumstances where a man's decision would be treated as voluntary and consensual. Specifically, the model law provides that proof of any of the following will *not* disprove coercion:

> that the [allegedly coerced] person actually consented to a use of the performance that is changed into pornography; or . . . that the person knew that the purpose of the acts or events in question was to make pornography; or . . . that the person showed no resistance or appeared to cooperate actively in the photographic sessions or in the sexual events that produced pornography; or . . . that the person signed a contract, or made statements affirming a willingness to cooperate in the production of pornography; or . . . that no physical force, threats, or weapons were used in the making of the pornography; or . . . that the person was paid or otherwise compensated.

This provision denies women our freedom of choice; indeed, consistent with the antisex aspect of the procensorship feminist philosophy, it presumes that women are incapable of exercising such freedom, at least as far as sex and sexual expression are concerned.

Even beyond its direct infantilization of women who voluntarily work in the sex business, this provision's "maternalistic" attitude toward women exemplifies the insultingly "matronizing" view that pervades the procensorship feminist critique of pornography. Indeed, Catharine MacKinnon and other supporters of feminist-style antipornography laws have expressly drawn analogies between women and children. MacKinnon has said: "Some of the same reasons children are granted some specific legal avenue for redress . . . also hold true for the social position of women compared to men."[36] Likewise, the proposed Minneapolis antipornography ordinance, drafted by Dworkin and MacKinnon, stated:

> Children are incapable of consenting to engage in pornographic conduct, even absent physical coercion, and therefore require special protection. By the same token, the physical and psychological well-being of women ought to be afforded comparable protection.[37]

Everyone's Looking at (Just) Linda

Some women who previously modeled or acted for pornographic publications or films have said that they were coerced to perform through physical violence. The most famous example, and one that Dworkin and MacKinnon consistently cite in an attempt to justify suppressing pornography, is Linda Marchiano, who starred in the movie *Deep Throat* under the stage name "Linda Lovelace." In her 1980 book *Ordeal,* Marchiano describes how she was raped and in other ways forced to make the film against her will.[38]

Although Linda Marchiano's *Ordeal* recounts deplorable physical and psychological abuse, which should be punished and prevented under the many existing laws that these acts clearly violated, Marchiano's ordeal provides no support for the conclusion that procensorship feminists repeatedly seek to draw from it—namely, that women who pose for pornographic materials are usually, if not inevitably, brutalized by the producers of such materials. Recently, in interviews published in *Ms.* and *The New York Times Magazine,* Dworkin and MacKinnon, respectively, cited Linda Marchiano as the sole "proof" that pornography is made by assaulting and abusing actual women.[39]

The violence and coercion that Marchiano suffered were outrageous. Yet her own account does not support the inference that producers of pornography generally inflict such violence and coercion upon the women who pose for them, for two reasons. First, in Marchiano's own case, it was not the participants in the porn industry who raped, beat, and forced her to take part in the movie, but rather, her own husband, Chuck Traynor, who had no other connection to the pornography business. Marchiano's autobiographical writings not only make clear that she experienced no abuse or force at the hands of participants in the porn industry; her writings also show that her career as a "porn star" gave her a welcome, if temporary, refuge from her husband's brutality. In *Ordeal,* Marchiano describes the sense of freedom she felt on the set of *Deep Throat,* and how she enjoyed the company of her costar, Harry Reems. She wrote, "Something was happening to me, something strange. No one was treating me like garbage. . . . We laughed a lot that first day of shooting. . . . And no one was asking me to do anything I didn't want to do."[40] Evidently threatened by Marchiano's enjoyment of her participation in *Deep Throat,* her husband brutally beat her after that first day of shooting, throwing her against the wall and kicking her for hours.

Marchiano's autobiography underscores that her subsequent contacts with the pornography industry, after she had escaped from her abusive husband, were completely voluntary. Recounting the lucrative film offers she later received to reenact the *Deep Throat* sex scenes, Marchiano wrote in her 1986 book *Out of Bondage,* "[I]f I acted in a dirty movie, I would be doing it out of need and greed. . . . I had a choice."[41] . . .

In the same vein, Leora Tanenbaum writes:

> Andrea Dworkin asks in *Ms.* magazine's recent roundtable discussion on pornography: "Why did a woman have to be brutalized to make that film [*Deep Throat*]?" The answer is: she didn't. *Ordeal* makes this clear.

In the years following the publication of *Ordeal,* though, Marchiano has been all too willing to accommodate her anti-porn sisters. When she appeared on *Geraldo* in 1988, Marchiano spoke of her experience working on *Deep Throat* in a passive voice, obfuscating the source of her coercion: "I was beaten and I was forced into it, and I had a .45 pointed at me, an M-16 semiautomatic machine gun," she told the audience. . . . Not once did she mention that the abuser was her husband.[42]

The second reason Marchiano's experience does not provide proof of abusive working conditions within the porn industry is that she speaks only for herself. Therefore, even assuming for the sake of argument—directly contrary to what she herself has written—that Marchiano had been abused by members of the pornography industry, that still would provide no basis for concluding that other sex industry workers also suffered such abuse. Nor does the fact that Marchiano's then-husband forced her to perform in *Deep Throat* support the contention that other pornography models or actresses are also performing under duress.

. . . It is as illogical to leap to the conclusion that, because of Marchiano's ordeal, all women should be "protected" against performing in pornographic films, as it would be to conclude that, because numerous Navy women were sexually abused during the 1991 Tailhook convention, all women should be "protected" against joining the Navy.

For every Linda Lovelace who was coerced to perform for a pornographic work, there is a Nina Hartley, who proclaims herself to be an exhibitionist; a Veronica Vera, who celebrates the personal growth she experienced through performing in porn films; a Candida Royalle, who proudly declares that she produces pornography "from a woman's point of view"; and countless others. Royalle, who starred in over a dozen X-rated movies before she became a director, recently commented about the antipornography feminists who want to "protect" her: "I understand their desire to help women, but they are out of touch with women in the industry."[43] Many woman who perform for pornography affirm that they do so voluntarily, and that their sister sex workers do likewise. Testifying before the Subcommittee on Juvenile Justice of the Senate Judiciary Committee, Veronica Vera, who has decades of experience with porn films as an actress and director, said that she had "never met a woman who was coerced . . . into participating" in such works.[44] The recent increase of homemade pornographic films, in which unpaid women and men voluntarily perform for others' viewing, is telling. It should not be surprising that some women willingly do for money what others willingly do even for no money.

Women who voluntarily perform for pornography resent the procensorship feminists' attempts to outlaw their chosen occupation. When the MacDworkin law was passed in Indianapolis, deeming the production of pornography a civil rights violation, one actress who appears in porn films protested, "For them to tell me I can't make films about naked men and women making love is a grotesque violation of *my* civil rights."[45] And, underscoring the debilitating impact that antipornography laws would have on *all* women, not just those who choose to work in the pornography business, Veronica Vera said,

"I don't think it would help women to beg the government to play Daddy and protect us from ourselves and then at the same time expect equality."[46]

Some sex industry workers affirm their occupational choice in explicitly feminist terms, stressing that they find it empowering as well as enjoyable. For example, Nina Hartley, who has worked in the porn business since 1983 and has hundreds of pornographic films to her credit, explains that the sex industry "provides a surprisingly flexible and supportive arena for me to grow in as a performer, both sexually and nonsexually." Proudly, she declares that "an intelligent, sexual woman could choose a job in the sex industry and not be a victim, but instead emerge even stronger and more self-confident, with a feeling, even, of self-actualization."[47]

Notes

1. Thelma McCormack, letter to the editor, *Chicago Tribune,* 28 September 1993.
2. Catharine MacKinnon, *Only Words* (Cambridge, Mass.: Harvard University Press, 1993), p. 71.
3. Indianapolis-Marion County, Indiana, General Ordinances Nos. 24 and 25 (1984), amendments to Code of Indianapolis and Marion County, Chapter 16, "Human Relations and Equal Opportunity."
4. Brief of the American Civil Liberties Union, Indiana Civil Liberties Union, and the American Civil Liberties Union of Illinois, amici curiae, *Hudnut v. American Booksellers Association* (filed in 7th Cir. 1985), p. 28.
5. *Butler v. the Queen,* 1 S. C. R. 452 (1992, Canada).
6. Heins, *Sex, Sin, and Blasphemy,* p. 35; John R. Wilke, "Porn Broker: A Publicly Held Firm Turns X-Rated Videos into a Hot Business," *Wall Street Journal,* 11 July 1994.
7. Carin Rubinstein and Carol Tavris, "Survey Results," *Redbook,* September 1987, pp. 147–49, 214–25, at p. 214.
8. Marc Speigler, "Lust Be a Lady," *New City,* 12–18 May 1994, pp. 8–9.
9. Susan Sontag, "The Pornographic Imagination," in *Styles of Radical Will* (New York: Anchor Books, 1969), p. 36.
10. Tisdale, "Talk Dirty to Me," p. 45.
11. Wendy McElroy, "Talking Sex, Not Gender," *Liberty* (in press).
12. Ibid.
13. Katie Roiphe, *The Morning After* (New York: Little, Brown, 1993), p. 151.
14. Hammill, "Women on the Verge," *Playboy,* January, 1993, p. 188.
15. Quoted in Wendy Kaminer, "Exposing the New Authoritarians," *San Francisco Examiner,* 29 November 1992.
16. Sallie Tisdale, "Talk Dirty to Me: A Woman's Taste for Pornography," *Harper's,* February 1992, pp. 37–46, at p. 45.
17. Quoted in Kathleen Sullivan, book review of *Girls Lean Back Everywhere* by Edward de Grazia, *New Republic,* 28 September 1992, pp. 35–40, at p. 39.
18. Quoted in Edward de Grazia, *Girls Lean Back Everywhere: The Law of Obscenity and the Assault on Genius* (New York: Vintage Books, 1992), p. 613.
19. Tisdale, "Talk Dirty to Me," p. 45.
20. Jack Kammer, "Men and Women: Who's Got the Power?" *The Sun* (Baltimore), 21 December 1993.
21. Susan Estrich, *Real Rape* (Boston: Harvard University Press, 1987).

22. Catharine MacKinnon, *Only Words* (Cambridge, Mass.: Harvard University Press, 1993), p. 26.

23. Ibid., p. 58.

24. Kaminer, "Exposing the New Authoritarians."

25. Statute of Treasons, 25 Edward 3 St. 5, Chap. 2 (1350), in effect until 1694.

26. Quoted in Barry Brown, "Canada's New Pornography Laws Drawing Charges of Censorship," *Buffalo News,* 10 January 1994.

27. Catharine MacKinnon, "Turning Rape into Pornography: Postmodern Genocide," *Ms.,* July/August 1993, pp. 24–30.

28. MacKinnon, *Only Words,* p. 15.

29. Nancy Friday, *Women on Top* (New York: Simon & Schuster, 1991), pp. 4–5.

30. Kathleen Sullivan, book review of *Girls Lean Back Everywhere,* p. 35.

31. Ann Snitow, Christine Stansell, and Sharon Thompson, eds., *Powers of Desire: The Politics of Sexuality* (New York: Monthly Review Press, 1983); Varda Burstyn, ed., *Women against Censorship* (Vancouver: Douglas and McIntyre, 1985); Carole S. Vance, ed., *Pleasure and Danger: Exploring Female Sexuality* (Boston: Routledge & Kegan Paul, 1984); Kate Ellis, Beth Jaker, Nan D. Hunter, Barbara O'Dair, and Abby Tallmer, eds., *Caught Looking: Feminism, Pornography, and Censorship* (East Haven, Conn.: Long River Books, 1986).

32. Ann Snitow, "Retrenchment versus Transformation: The Politics of the Anti-pornography Movement," in *Women against Censorship,* p. 107, pp. 115–16.

33. Nan D. Hunter and Sylvia Law, Brief Amici Curiae of Feminist Anti-Censorship Taskforce, *University of Michigan Journal of Law Reform* 21 (1987–88): pp. 69–136, at p. 121.

34. Lisa Duggan, Nan D. Hunter, and Carole S. Vance, "False Promises: Feminist Anti-Pornography Legislation," in *Caught Looking,* pp. 72–85, at p. 82.

35. Karen, letter to *Ms.,* May/June 1994, p. 4.

36. Quoted in Pete Hamill, "Women on the Verge of a Legal Breakdown," *Playboy,* January 1993, p. 186.

37. Wendy McElroy, "The Unholy Alliance," *Liberty,* February 1993, p. 56.

38. Leora Tanenbaum, "The Politics of Porn: Forced Arguments," *In These Times,* 7 March 1994, pp. 17–20.

39. Andrea Dworkin quoted in "Where Do We Stand on Pornography?" (Roundtable), *Ms.,* January/February 1994, pp. 32–41, 37–38; Catharine MacKinnon quoted in Fred Strebeigh, "Defining Law on the Feminist Frontier," *New York Times Magazine,* 6 October 1991.

40. Quoted in Tanenbaum, "Politics of Porn," p. 19.

41. Quoted in Dan Greenberg and Thomas H. Tobiason, "The New Legal Puritanism of Catharine MacKinnon," *Ohio State Law Journal* 54 (Fall 1993): 1375–1424, at 1402–3.

42. Tanenbaum, "Politics of Porn," p. 18.

43. Quoted ibid., p. 20.

44. Veronica Vera, testimony before the Senate Judiciary Committee, 30 October 1984.

45. Quoted in "The War against Pornography," *Newsweek,* 18 March 1985, pp. 58, 66.

46. Veronica Vera, testimony before the Senate Judiciary Committee, 30 October 1984.

47. Quoted in Tanenbaum, "Politics of Porn," p. 18.

POSTSCRIPT

Does Pornography Violate Women's Rights?

These days pornography is an issue that strongly divides feminists among themselves. (In prior times, it might have divided conservative and/or religious people from more liberal people. And even nowadays, some of the antipornography feminists form a common alliance with religious conservatives on this issue—although they disagree on almost everything else!)

The basic division is between those who see pornography as an example of the lack of social standing that women have and those who see it as just another form of free speech. The first group often argues that pornography causes violence against women, although this is not a view that Langton offers in her selection, nor does she deny the claim. Her contention is that it is not so much that pornography is a *cause* of women's mistreatment but that it is an *example* of it. As she emphasizes, it is not just the depiction of the subordination of women; rather, it is a form of subordination itself.

Defenders of pornography generally emphasize that some people (including some women) enjoy it, and that generally it is not right to limit what people enjoy, unless what they enjoy entails suffering or loss of rights for others. Pornography's defenders, like Strossen, generally emphasize the importance of the value of free speech and liberty, where consenting adults are free to act as they wish (again, so long as they do not cause harm to others).

Further literature on pornography is vast. A good place to start might be Catharine MacKinnon and Andrea Dworkin, eds., *In Harm's Way: The Pornography Civil Rights Hearings* (Harvard University Press, 1991). A variety of views can be found in Diana E. H. Russell, ed., *Making Violence Sexy: Feminist Views on Pornography* (Teachers College Press, 1993); Sallie Tisdale, *Talk Dirty to Me: An Intimate Philosophy of Sex* (Doubleday, 1994); Laura Kipnis, *Bound and Gagged: Pornography and the Politics of Fantasy in America* (Grove/Atlantic, 1996); Wendy McElroy, *XXX: A Women's Right to Pornography* (St. Martin's Press, 1997); Carol Wekesser, ed., *Pornography: Opposing Viewpoints* (Greenhaven Press, 1997); Robert M. Baird and Stuart E. Rosenbaum, eds., *Pornography: Private Right or Public Menace?* rev. ed. (Prometheus Books, 1997); Diana E. H. Russell, *Dangerous Relationships: Pornography, Misogyny and Rape* (Sage Publications, 1998); Gail Dines, Robert Jensen, and Ann Russo, *Pornography: The Production and Consumption of Inequality* (Routledge, 1998); Jane Juffer, *At Home With Pornography: Women, Sex, and Everyday Life* (New York University Press, 1998); T. Walter Herbert, *Sexual Violence and American Manhood* (Harvard University Press, 2002); and David Loftus, *Watching Sex: How Men Really Respond to Pornography* (Thunder's Mouth Press, 2003).

ISSUE 5

Is Abortion Immoral?

YES: Don Marquis, from "Why Abortion Is Immoral," *The Journal of Philosophy* (April 1989)

NO: Jane English, from "Abortion and the Concept of a Person," *Canadian Journal of Philosophy* (October 1975)

ISSUE SUMMARY

YES: Professor of philosophy Don Marquis argues that abortion is generally wrong for the same reason that killing an innocent adult human being is generally wrong: it deprives the individual of a future that he or she would otherwise have.

NO: Philosopher Jane English (1947–1978) asserts that there is no well-defined line dividing persons from nonpersons. She maintains that both the conservative and the liberal positions are too extreme and that some abortions are morally justifiable and some are not.

Abortion is a divisive topic, and discussions can easily become polarized. Here we will briefly consider some of the biological facts associated with abortion and review some relevant historical and legal matters. The selections themselves will then look at the moral issues raised by abortion.

Conception occurs when the spermatozoon of a male unites with the ovum of a female. The single cell thus formed is called a zygote. In a normal pregnancy, this zygote will multiply into several cells, travel through the fallopian tube, enter the uterus, and implant itself in the uterine wall. When implantation is complete, one to two weeks after fertilization (as the original conception is also called), we can say that the pregnancy is established and that the zygote has become an embryo. Once the placenta and umbilical cord are established, the embryo takes nourishment by means of these from the blood of the pregnant woman and quickly grows primitive limbs and organs. At eight weeks from conception, the first brain waves can be detected and the embryo is now called a fetus. So-called quickening, the first felt spontaneous movement of the fetus, occurs at around 14 or 15 weeks. The threshold of viability (the point at which the fetus can be kept alive outside the uterus) is dependent upon many factors, especially the development of the cardiopulmonary system. Depending on the level of available medical technology, viability can be reached sometime between 20 and 28 weeks. Birth generally takes place about 38 to 40 weeks after conception, although here too there is significant variation.

There are other possibilities once the spermatozoon and ovum unite. The fertilized ovum, for example, might never be implanted in the wall of the uterus and might be expelled uneventfully, and even without notice, from the body. Or the zygote might implant itself somewhere other than inside the uterus, resulting in an ectopic pregnancy. The embryo will not grow properly outside the uterus, and this kind of pregnancy can be dangerous to the mother. (In the case of an ectopic pregnancy, the Roman Catholic Church will permit an abortion to save the pregnant woman's life.) Another possibility is that the pregnancy will develop normally for a while but then end in miscarriage; this is sometimes called a spontaneous abortion.

The historic *Roe v. Wade* case, decided in 1973 by the U.S. Supreme Court in a split decision of 7−2, ruled that the nineteenth-century Texas statutes against abortion were unconstitutional. The Court divided the normal pregnancy into three trimesters and ruled as follows:

> For the stage prior to approximately the end of the first trimester, the abortion decision and its effectuation must be left to the medical judgment of the pregnant woman's attending physician. For the stage subsequent to approximately the end of the first trimester, the State, in promoting its interest in the health of the mother, may, if it chooses, regulate the abortion procedure in ways that are reasonably related to maternal health. For the stages subsequent to viability, the State, in promoting its interest in the potentiality of human life, may, if it chooses, regulate, and even proscribe, abortion except where it is necessary, in appropriate medical judgment, for the preservation of the life or health of the mother. (410 U.S. 113, 93 S. Ct. 705 [1973])

Before *Roe v. Wade*, some states permitted abortion only if a woman's life was in danger; abortion for any other reason or consideration was illegal and punishable by law. *Roe v. Wade* ruled that states do not have the right to regulate abortion procedures in any way during the first trimester of pregnancy. It is important to note that neither the Supreme Court nor the Texas statutes said anything about the relation of the woman to the fetus (or embryo) or about the reasons a woman might have for seeking an abortion.

In the following selections, Don Marquis constructs a secular argument to show that abortion is immoral. He focuses not on the present status of the fetus, but on the future status. This avoids the divisive question of whether or not the fetus is a person. Jane English counters that this question has no determinate answer. In her view, neither the standard conservative position nor the standard liberal position adequately addresses the issue of abortion.

Don Marquis  **YES**

Why Abortion Is Immoral

The view that abortion is, with rare exceptions, seriously immoral has received little support in the recent philosophical literature. No doubt most philosophers affiliated with secular institutions of higher education believe that the anti-abortion position is either a symptom of irrational religious dogma or a conclusion generated by seriously confused philosophical argument. The purpose of this essay is to undermine this general belief. This essay sets out an argument that purports to show, as well as any argument in ethics can show, that abortion is, except possibly in rare cases, seriously immoral, that it is in the same moral category as killing an innocent adult human being.

The argument is based on a major assumption. Many of the most insightful and careful writers on the ethics of abortion—such as Joel Feinberg, Michael Tooley, Mary Anne Warren, H. Tristram Engelhardt, Jr., L. W. Sumner, John T. Noonan, Jr., and Philip Devine[1]—believe that whether or not abortion is morally permissible stands or falls on whether or not a fetus is the sort of being whose life it is seriously wrong to end. The argument of this essay will assume, but not argue, that they are correct.

Also, this essay will neglect issues of great importance to a complete ethics of abortion. Some anti-abortionists will allow that certain abortions, such as abortion before implantation or abortion when the life of a woman is threatened by a pregnancy or abortion after rape, may be morally permissible. This essay will not explore the casuistry of these hard cases. The purpose of this essay is to develop a general argument for the claim that the overwhelming majority of deliberate abortions are seriously immoral.

⋅⟨⊙⟩⋅

A sketch of standard anti-abortion and pro-choice arguments exhibits how those arguments possess certain symmetries that explain why partisans of those positions are so convinced of the correctness of their own positions, why they are not successful in convincing their opponents, and why, to others, this issue seems to be unresolvable. An analysis of the nature of this standoff suggests a strategy for surmounting it.

From Don Marquis, "Why Abortion Is Immoral," *The Journal of Philosophy*, vol. 86, no. 4 (April 1989). Copyright © 1989 by The Journal of Philosophy, Inc. Reprinted by permission of the publisher and the author.

Consider the way a typical anti-abortionist argues. She will argue or assert that life is present from the moment of conception or that fetuses look like babies or that fetuses possess a characteristic such as a genetic code that is both necessary and sufficient for being human. Anti-abortionists seem to believe that (1) the truth of all of these claims is quite obvious, and (2) establishing any of these claims is sufficient to show that abortion is morally akin to murder.

A standard pro-choice strategy exhibits similarities. The pro-choicer will argue or assert that fetuses are not persons or that fetuses are not rational agents or that fetuses are not social beings. Pro-choicers seem to believe that (1) the truth of any of these claims is quite obvious, and (2) establishing any of these claims is sufficient to show that an abortion is not a wrongful killing.

In fact, both the pro-choice and the anti-abortion claims do seem to be true, although the "it looks like a baby" claim is more difficult to establish the earlier the pregnancy. We seem to have a standoff. How can it be resolved?

As everyone who has taken a bit of logic knows, if any of these arguments concerning abortion is a good argument, it requires not only some claim characterizing fetuses, but also some general moral principle that ties a characteristic of fetuses to having or not having the right to life or to some other moral characteristic that will generate the obligation or the lack of obligation not to end the life of a fetus. Accordingly, the arguments of the anti-abortionist and the pro-choicer need a bit of filling in to be regarded as adequate.

Note what each partisan will say. The anti-abortionist will claim that her position is supported by such generally accepted moral principles as "It is always prima facie seriously wrong to take a human life" or "It is always prima facie seriously wrong to end the life of a baby." Since these are generally accepted moral principles, her position is certainly not obviously wrong. The pro-choicer will claim that her position is supported by such plausible moral principles as "Being a person is what gives an individual intrinsic moral worth" or "It is only seriously prima facie wrong to take the life of a member of the human community." Since these are generally accepted moral principles, the pro-choice position is certainly not obviously wrong. Unfortunately, we have again arrived at a standoff.

Now, how might one deal with this standoff? The standard approach is to try to show how the moral principles of one's opponent lose their plausibility under analysis. It is easy to see how this is possible. On the one hand, the anti-abortionist will defend a moral principle concerning the wrongness of killing which tends to be broad in scope in order that even fetuses at an early stage of pregnancy will fall under it. The problem with broad principles is that they often embrace too much. In this particular instance, the principle "It is always prima facie wrong to take a human life" seems to entail that it is wrong to end the existence of a living human cancer-cell culture, on the grounds that the culture is both living and human. Therefore, it seems that the anti-abortionist's favored principle is too broad.

On the other hand, the pro-choicer wants to find a moral principle concerning the wrongness of killing which tends to be narrow in scope in order that fetuses will *not* fall under it. The problem with narrow principles is that they often do not embrace enough. Hence, the needed principles such as "It is prima facie seriously wrong to kill only persons" or "It is prima facie wrong to kill only rational agents" do not explain why it is wrong to kill infants or young children or the severely retarded or even perhaps the severely mentally ill. Therefore, we seem again to have a standoff. The anti-abortionist charges, not unreasonably, that pro-choice principles concerning killing are too narrow to be acceptable; the pro-choicer charges, not unreasonably, that anti-abortionist principles concerning killing are too broad to be acceptable.

Attempts by both sides to patch up the difficulties in their positions run into further difficulties. The anti-abortionist will try to remove the problem in her position by reformulating her principle concerning killing in terms of human beings. Now we end up with: "It is always prima facie seriously wrong to end the life of a human being." This principle has the advantage of avoiding the problem of the human cancer-cell culture counterexample. But this advantage is purchased at a high price. For although it is clear that a fetus is both human and alive, it is not at all clear that a fetus is a human *being*. There is at least something to be said for the view that something becomes a human being only after a process of development, and that therefore first trimester fetuses and perhaps all fetuses are not yet human beings. Hence, the anti-abortionist, by this move, has merely exchanged one problem for another.[2]

The pro-choicer fares no better. She may attempt to find reasons why killing infants, young children, and the severely retarded is wrong which are independent of her major principle that is supposed to explain the wrongness of taking human life, but which will not also make abortion immoral. This is no easy task. Appeals to social utility will seem satisfactory only to those who resolve not to think of the enormous difficulties with a utilitarian account of the wrongness of killing and the significant social costs of preserving the lives of the unproductive.[3] A pro-choice strategy that extends the definition of 'person' to infants or even to young children seems just as arbitrary as an anti-abortion strategy that extends the definition of 'human being' to fetuses. Again, we find symmetries in the two positions and we arrive at a standoff.

There are even further problems that reflect symmetries in the two positions. In addition to counterexample problems, or the arbitrary application problems that can be exchanged for them, the standard anti-abortionist principle "It is prima facie seriously wrong to kill a human being," or one of its variants, can be objected to on the grounds of ambiguity. If 'human being' is taken to be a *biological* category, then the anti-abortionist is left with the problem of explaining why a merely biological category should make a moral difference. Why, it is asked, is it any more reasonable to base a moral conclusion on the number of chromosomes in one's cells than on the color of one's skin?[4] If 'human being', on the other hand, is taken to be a *moral* category, then the claim that a fetus is a human being cannot be taken to be a premise in the anti-abortion argument, for it is precisely what needs to be established. Hence, either the anti-abortionist's main category is a morally irrelevant, merely biological category, or it is of no use to the anti-abortionist in establishing (non-circularly, of course) that abortion is wrong.

Although this problem with the anti-abortionist position is often noticed, it is less often noticed that the pro-choice position suffers from an analogous problem. The principle "Only persons have the right to life" also suffers from an ambiguity. The term 'person' is typically defined in terms of psychological characteristics, although there will certainly be disagreement concerning which characteristics are most important. Supposing that this matter can be settled, the pro-choicer is left with the problem of explaining why *psychological* characteristics should make a *moral* difference. If the pro-choicer should attempt to deal with this problem by claiming that an explanation is not necessary, that in fact we do treat such a cluster of psychological properties as having moral significance, the sharp-witted anti-abortionist should have a ready response. We do treat being both living and human as having moral significance. If it is legitimate for the pro-choicer to demand that the anti-abortionist provide an explanation of the connection between the biological character of being a human being and the wrongness of being killed (even though people accept this connection), then it is legitimate for the anti-abortionist to demand that the pro-choicer provide an explanation of the connection between psychological criteria for being a person and the wrongness of being killed (even though that connection is accepted).[5] . . .

[T]he pro-choicer cannot any more escape her problem by making person a purely moral category than the anti-abortionist could escape by the analogous move. For if person is a moral category, then the pro-choicer is left without the resources for establishing (noncircularly, of course) the claim that a fetus is not a person, which is an essential premise in her argument. Again, we have both a symmetry and a standoff between pro-choice and anti-abortion views.

Passions in the abortion debate run high. There are both plausibilities and difficulties with the standard positions. Accordingly, it is hardly surprising that partisans of either side embrace with fervor the moral generalizations that support the conclusions they preanalytically favor, and reject with disdain the moral generalizations of their opponents as being subject to inescapable difficulties. It is easy to believe that the counterexamples to one's own moral principles are merely temporary difficulties that will dissolve in the wake of further philosophical research, and that the counterexamples to the principles of one's opponents are . . . straightforward. . . . This might suggest to an impartial observer (if there are any) that the abortion issue is unresolvable.

There is a way out of this apparent dialectical quandary. The moral generalizations of both sides are not quite correct. The generalizations hold for the most part, for the usual cases. This suggests that they are all *accidental* generalizations, that the moral claims made by those on both sides of the dispute do not touch on the *essence* of the matter.

This use of the distinction between essence and accident is not meant to invoke obscure metaphysical categories. Rather, it is intended to reflect the rather atheoretical nature of the abortion discussion. If the generalization a partisan in the abortion dispute adopts were derived from the reason why ending the life of a human being is wrong, then there could not be exceptions to that generalization unless some special case obtains in which there are even more powerful countervailing reasons. Such generalizations would not be merely accidental generalizations; they would point to, or be based upon, the essence of the wrongness of killing, what it is that makes killing wrong. All this suggests that a necessary condition of resolving the abortion controversy is a more theoretical account of the wrongness of killing. After all, if we merely believe, but do not understand, why killing adult human beings such as ourselves is wrong, how could we conceivably show that abortion is either immoral or permissible?

⋅⃝⋅

In order to develop such an account, we can start from the following unproblematic assumption concerning our own case: it is wrong to kill *us*. Why is it wrong? . . .

What primarily makes killing wrong is neither its effect on the murderer nor its effect on the victim's friends and relatives, but its effect on the victim. The loss of one's life is one of the greatest losses one can suffer. The loss of one's life deprives one of all the experiences, activities, projects, and enjoyments that would otherwise have constituted one's future. Therefore, killing someone is wrong, primarily because the killing inflicts (one of) the greatest possible losses on the victim. To describe this as the loss of life can be misleading, however. The change in my biological state does not by itself make killing me wrong. The effect of the loss of my biological life is the loss to me of all those activities, projects, experiences, and enjoyments which would otherwise have constituted my future personal life. These activities, projects, experiences, and enjoyments are either valuable for their own sakes or are means to something else that is valuable for its own sake. Some parts of my future are not valued by me now, but will come to be valued by me as I grow older and as my values and capacities change. When I am killed, I am deprived both of what I now value which would have been part of my future personal life, but also what I would come to value. Therefore, when I die, I am deprived of all of the value of my future. Inflicting this loss on me is ultimately what makes killing me wrong. This being the case, it would seem that what makes killing *any* adult human being prima facie seriously wrong is the loss of his or her future.[6] . . .

The claim that what makes killing wrong is the loss of the victim's future is directly supported by two considerations. In the first place, this theory explains why we regard killing as one of the worst of crimes. Killing is especially wrong, because it deprives the victim of more than perhaps any other crime. In the second place, people with AIDS or cancer who know they are dying believe, of course, that dying is a very bad thing for them. They believe that the loss of a future to them that they would otherwise have experienced is what makes their premature death a very bad thing for them. A better theory of the wrongness of killing would require a different natural property associated with killing which better fits with the attitudes of the dying. What could it be?

The view that what makes killing wrong is the loss to the victim of the value of the victim's future gains additional support when some of its implications are examined. In the first place, it is incompatible with the view that it is wrong to kill only beings who are biologically human. It is possible that there exists a different species from another planet whose members have a future like ours. Since having a future like that is what makes killing someone wrong, this theory entails that it would be wrong to kill members of such a species. Hence, this theory is opposed to the claim that only life that is biologically human has great moral worth, a claim which many anti-abortionists have seemed to adopt. This opposition, which this theory has in common with personhood theories, seems to be a merit of the theory.

In the second place, the claim that the loss of one's future is the wrong-making feature of one's being killed entails the possibility that the futures of some actual nonhuman mammals on our own planet are sufficiently like ours that it is seriously wrong to kill them also. Whether some animals do have the same right to life as human beings depends on adding to the account of the wrongness of killing some additional account of just what it is about my future or the futures of other adult human beings which makes it wrong to kill us. No such additional account will be offered in this essay. Undoubtedly, the provision of such an account would be a very difficult matter. Undoubtedly, any such account would be quite controversial. Hence, it surely should not reflect badly on this sketch of an elementary theory of the wrongness of killing that it is indeterminate with respect to some very difficult issues regarding animal rights.

In the third place, the claim that the loss of one's future is the wrong-making feature of one's being killed does not entail, as sanctity of human life theories do, that active euthanasia is wrong. Persons who are severely and incurably ill, who face a future of pain and despair, and who wish to die will not have suffered a loss if they are killed. It is, strictly speaking, the value of a human's future which makes killing wrong in this theory. This being so, killing does not necessarily wrong some persons who are sick and dying. Of course, there may be other reasons for a prohibition of active euthanasia, but that is another matter. Sanctity-of-human-life theories seem to hold that active euthanasia is seriously wrong even in an individual case where there seems to be good reason for it independently of public policy considerations. This consequence is most implausible, and it is a plus for the claim that the loss of a future of value is what makes killing wrong that it does not share this consequence.

In the fourth place, the account of the wrongness of killing defended in this essay does straightforwardly entail that it is prima facie seriously wrong to kill children and infants, for we do presume that they have futures of value. Since we do believe that it is wrong to kill defenseless little babies, it is important that a theory of the wrongness of killing easily account for this. Personhood theories of the wrongness of killing, on the other hand, cannot straightforwardly account for the wrongness of killing infants and young children.[7] Hence, such theories must add special ad hoc accounts of the wrongness of killing the young. The plausibility of such ad hoc theories seems to be a function of how desperately one wants such theories to work. The claim that the primary wrong-making feature of a killing is the loss to the victim of the value of its future accounts for the wrongness of killing young children and infants directly; it makes the wrongness of such acts as obvious as we actually think it is. This is a further merit of this theory. Accordingly, it seems that this value of a future-like-ours theory of the wrongness of killing shares strengths of both sanctity-of-life and personhood accounts while avoiding weaknesses of both. In addition, it meshes with a central intuition concerning what makes killing wrong.

The claim that the primary wrong-making feature of a killing is the loss to the victim of the value of its future has obvious consequences for the ethics of abortion. The future of a standard fetus includes a set of experiences, projects, activities, and such which are identical with the futures of adult human beings and are identical with the futures of young children. Since the reason that is sufficient to explain why it is wrong to kill human beings after the time of birth is a reason that also applies to fetuses, it follows that abortion is prima facie seriously morally wrong. . . .

✦❦✦

How complete an account of the wrongness of killing does the value of a future-like-ours account have to be in order that the wrongness of abortion is a consequence? This account does not have to be an account of the necessary conditions for the wrongness of killing. Some persons in nursing homes may lack valuable human futures, yet it may be wrong to kill them for other reasons. Furthermore, this account does not obviously have to be the sole reason killing is wrong where the victim did have a valuable future. This analysis claims only that, for any killing where the victim did have a valuable future like ours, having that future by itself is sufficient to create the strong presumption that the killing is seriously wrong. . . .

✦❦✦

In this essay, it has been argued that the correct ethic of the wrongness of killing can be extended to fetal life and used to show that there is a strong presumption that any abortion is morally impermissible. If the ethic of killing adopted here entails, however, that contraception is also seriously immoral, then there would appear to be a difficulty with the analysis of this essay.

But this analysis does not entail that contraception is wrong. Of course, contraception prevents the actualization of a possible future of value. Hence, it follows from the claim that futures of value should be maximized that contraception is prima facie immoral. This obligation to maximize does not exist, however; furthermore, nothing in the ethics of killing in this paper entails that it does. The ethics of killing in this essay would entail that contraception is wrong only if something were denied a human future of value by contraception. Nothing at all is denied such a future by contraception, however. . . .

At the time of contraception, there are hundreds of millions of sperm, one (released) ovum and millions of possible combinations of all of these. There is no actual combination at all. Is the subject of the loss to be a merely possible combination? Which one? This alternative does not yield an actual subject of harm either. Accordingly, the immorality of contraception is not entailed by the loss of a future-like-ours argument simply because there is no nonarbitrarily identifiable subject of the loss in the case of contraception.

ᐁᐤᐣ

The purpose of this essay has been to set out an argument for the serious presumptive wrongness of abortion subject to the assumption that the moral permissibility of abortion stands or falls on the moral status of the fetus. Since a fetus possesses a property, the possession of which in adult human beings is sufficient to make killing an adult human being wrong, abortion is wrong. This way of dealing with the problem of abortion seems superior to other approaches to the ethics of abortion, because it rests on an ethics of killing which is close to self-evident, because the crucial morally relevant property clearly applies to fetuses, and because the argument avoids the usual equivocations on 'human life', 'human being', or 'person'. The argument rests neither on religious claims nor on Papal dogma. It is not subject to the objection of "speciesism." Its soundness is compatible with the moral permissibility of euthanasia and contraception. It deals with our intuitions concerning young children.

Finally, this analysis can be viewed as resolving a standard problem—indeed, *the* standard problem—concerning the ethics of abortion. Clearly, it is wrong to kill adult human beings. Clearly, it is not wrong to end the life of some arbitrarily chosen single human cell. Fetuses seem to be like arbitrarily chosen human cells in some respects and like adult humans in other respects. The problem of the ethics of abortion is the problem of determining the fetal property that settles this moral controversy. The thesis of this essay is that the problem of the ethics of abortion, so understood, is solvable.

Notes

1. Feinberg, "Abortion," in *Matters of Life and Death: New Introductory Essays in Moral Philosophy,* Tom Regan, ed. (New York: Random House, 1986), pp. 256–293; Tooley, "Abortion and Infanticide," *Philosophy and Public Affairs,* II, 1 (1972): 37–65; Tooley, *Abortion and Infanticide* (New York: Oxford, 1984); Warren, "On the Moral and Legal Status of Abortion," *The Monist,* I.VII, 1 (1973): 43–61; Engelhardt, "The Ontology of Abortion," *Ethics,* I, XXXIV, 3 (1974):217–234; Sumner, *Abortion and Moral Theory* (Princeton: University Press, 1981); Noonan, "An Almost Absolute Value in History," in *The Morality of Abortion: Legal and Historical Perspectives,* Noonan, ed. (Cambridge: Harvard, 1970); and Devine, *The Ethics of Homicide* (Ithaca: Cornell, 1978).

2. For interesting discussions of this issue, see Warren Quinn, "Abortion: Identity and Loss," *Philosophy and Public Affairs,* XIII, 1 (1984):24–54; and Lawrence C. Becker, "Human Being: The Boundaries of the Concept," *Philosophy and Public Affairs,* IV, 4 (1975):334–359.

3. For example, see my "Ethics and the Elderly: Some Problems," in Stuart Spicker, Kathleen Woodward, and David Van Tassel, eds., *Aging and the Elderly: Humanistic Perspectives in Gerontology* (Atlantic Highlands, NJ: Humanities, 1978), pp. 341–355.

4. See Warren, *op. cit.,* and Tooley, "Abortion and Infanticide."

5. This seems to be the fatal flaw in Warren's treatment of this issue.

6. I have been most influenced on this matter by Jonathan Glover, *Causing Death and Saving Lives* (New York: Penguin, 1977), ch. 3; and Robert Young, "What Is So Wrong with Killing People?" *Philosophy,* LIV, 210 (1979):515–528.

7. Feinberg, Tooley, Warren, and Engelhardt have all dealt with this problem.

Abortion and the Concept of a Person

The abortion debate rages on. Yet the two most popular positions seem to be clearly mistaken. Conservatives maintain that a human life begins at conception and that therefore abortion must be wrong because it is murder. But not all killings of humans are murders. Most notably, self-defense may justify even the killing of an innocent person.

Liberals, on the other hand, are just as mistaken in their argument that since a fetus does not become a person until birth, a woman may do whatever she pleases in and to her own body. First, you cannot do to as you please with your own body if it affects other people adversely.[1] Second, if a fetus is not a person, that does not imply that you can do to it anything you wish. Animals, for example, are not persons, yet to kill or torture them for no reason at all is wrong.

At the center of the storm has been the issue of just when it is between ovulation and adulthood that a person appears on the scene. Conservatives draw the line at conception, liberals at birth. In this paper I first examine our concept of a person and conclude that no single criterion can capture the concept of a person and no sharp line can be drawn. Next I argue that if a fetus is a person, abortion is still justifiable in many cases; and if a fetus is not a person, killing it is still wrong in many cases. To a large extent, these two solutions are in agreement. I conclude that our concept of a person cannot and need not bear the weight that the abortion controversy has thrust upon it.

The several factions in the abortion argument have drawn battle lines around various proposed criteria for determining what is and what is not a person. For example, Mary Anne Warren[2] lists five features (capacities for reasoning, self-awareness, complex communication, etc.) as her criteria for personhood and argues for the permissibility of abortion because a fetus falls outside this concept. Baruch Brody[3] uses brain waves. Michael Tooley[4] picks having-a-concept-of-self as his criterion and concludes that infanticide and abortion are justifiable, while the killing of adult animals is not. On the other side, Paul Ramsey[5] claims a certain gene structure is the defining characteristic. John Noonan[6] prefers conceived-of-humans and presents counterexamples to various other candidate criteria. For instance, he argues against viability as the criterion because the newborn and infirm would then be nonpersons, since they cannot live without the aid of others. He rejects any criterion that calls

From Jane English, "Abortion and the Concept of a Person," *Canadian Journal of Philosophy,* vol. 5, no. 2 (October 1975), pp. 233–243. Copyright © 1975 by *Canadian Journal of Philosophy.* Reprinted by permission.

upon the sorts of sentiments a being can evoke in adults on the grounds that this would allow us to exclude other races as nonpersons if we could just view them sufficiently unsentimentally.

These approaches are typical: foes of abortion propose sufficient conditions for personhood which fetuses satisfy, while friends of abortion counter with necessary conditions for personhood which fetuses lack. But these both presuppose that the concept of a person can be captured in a strait jacket of necessary and/or sufficient conditions.[7] Rather, "person" is a cluster of features, of which rationality, having a self concept and being conceived of humans are only part.

What is typical of persons? Within our concept of a person we include, first, certain biological factors: descended from humans, having a certain genetic makeup, having a head, hands, arms, eyes, capable of locomotion, breathing, eating, sleeping. There are psychological factors: sentience, perception, having a concept of self and of one's own interests and desires, the ability to use tools, the ability to use language or symbol systems, the ability to joke, to be angry, to doubt. There are rationality factors: the ability to reason and draw conclusions, the ability to generalize and to learn from past experience, the ability to sacrifice present interests for greater gains in the future. There are social factors: the ability to work in groups and respond to peer pressure, the ability to recognize and consider as valuable the interests of others, seeing oneself as one among "other minds," the ability to sympathize, encourage, love, the ability to evoke from others the responses of sympathy, encouragement, love, the ability to work with others for mutual advantage. Then there are legal factors: being subject to the law and protected by it, having the ability to sue and enter contracts, being counted in the census, having a name and citizenship, the ability to own property, inherit, and so forth.

Now the point is not that this list is incomplete, or that you can find counterinstances to each of its points. People typically exhibit rationality, for instance, but someone who was irrational would not thereby fail to qualify as a person. On the other hand, something could exhibit the majority of these features and still fail to be a person, as an advanced robot might. There is no single core of necessary and sufficient features which we can draw upon with the assurance that they constitute what really makes a person; there are only features that are more or less typical.

This is not to say that no necessary or sufficient conditions can be given. Being alive is a necessary condition for being a person, and being a U.S. Senator is sufficient. But rather than falling inside a sufficient condition or outside a necessary one, a fetus lies in the penumbra region where our concept of a person is not so simple. For this reason I think a conclusive answer to the question whether a fetus is a person is unattainable.

Here we might note a family of simple fallacies that proceed by stating a necessary condition for personhood and showing that a fetus has that characteristic. This is a form of the fallacy of affirming the consequent. For example, some have mistakenly reasoned from the premise that a fetus is human (after all, it is a human fetus rather than, say, a canine fetus), to the conclusion that it is a human. Adding an equivocation on "being," we get the fallacious argument that since a fetus is something both living and human, it is a human being.

Nonetheless, it does seem clear that a fetus has very few of the above family of characteristics, whereas a newborn baby exhibits a much larger proportion of them—and a two-year-old has even more. Note that one traditional antiabortion argument has centered on pointing out the many ways in which a fetus resembles a baby. They emphasize its development ("It already has ten fingers . . .") without mentioning its dissimilarities to adults (it still has gills and a tail). They also try to evoke the sort of sympathy on our part that we only feel toward other persons ("Never to laugh . . . or feel the sunshine?"). This all seems to be a relevant way to argue, since its purpose is to persuade us that a fetus satisfies so many of the important features on the list that it ought to be treated as a person. Also note that a fetus near the time of birth satisfies many more of these factors than a fetus in the early months of development. This could provide reason for making distinctions among the different stages of pregnancy, as the U.S. Supreme Court has done.[8]

Historically, the time at which a person has been said to come into existence has varied widely. Muslims date personhood from fourteen days after conception. Some medievals followed Aristotle in placing ensoulment at forty days after conception for a male fetus and eighty days for a female fetus.[9] In European common law since the seventeenth century, abortion was considered the killing of a person only after quickening, the time when a pregnant woman first feels the fetus move on its own. Nor is this variety of opinions surprising. Biologically, a human being develops gradually. We shouldn't expect there to be any specific time or sharp dividing point when a person appears on the scene.

For these reasons I believe our concept of a person is not sharp or decisive enough to bear the weight of a solution to the abortion controversy. To use it to solve that problem is to clarify *obscurum per obscurius* [to clarify what is obscure by what is more obscure].

Next let us consider what follows if a fetus is a person after all. Judith Jarvis Thomson's landmark article, "A Defense of Abortion,"[10] correctly points out that some additional argumentation is needed at this point in the conservative argument to bridge the gap between the premise that a fetus is an innocent person and the conclusion that killing it is always wrong. To arrive at this conclusion, we would need the additional premise that killing an innocent person is always wrong. But killing an innocent person is sometimes permissible, most notably in self-defense. Some examples may help draw out our intuitions or ordinary judgments about self-defense.

Suppose a mad scientist, for instance, hypnotized innocent people to jump out of the bushes and attack innocent passers-by with knives. If you are so attacked, we agree you have a right to kill the attacker in self-defense, if killing him is the only way to protect your life or to save yourself from serious injury. It does not seem to matter here that the attacker is not malicious but himself an innocent pawn, for your killing of him is not done in a spirit of retribution but only in self-defense.

How severe an injury may you inflict in self-defense? In part this depends upon the severity of the injury to be avoided: you may not shoot someone merely to avoid having your clothes torn. This might lead one to the mistaken conclusion that the defense may only equal the threatened injury in severity; that to avoid death you may kill, but to avoid a black eye you may only inflict a black eye or the equivalent. Rather, our laws and customs seem to say that you may create an injury somewhat, but not enormously, greater than the injury to be avoided. To fend off an attack whose outcome would be as serious as rape, a severe beating or the loss of a finger, you may shoot; to avoid having your clothes torn, you may blacken an eye. . . .

Some cases of pregnancy present a parallel situation. Though the fetus is itself innocent, it may pose a threat to the pregnant woman's well-being, life prospects or health, mental or physical. If the pregnancy presents a slight threat to her interests, it seems self-defense cannot justify abortion. But if the threat is on a par with a serious beating or the loss of a finger, she may kill the fetus that poses such a threat, even if it is an innocent person. If a lesser harm to the fetus could have the same defensive effect, killing it would not be justified. It is unfortunate that the only way to free the woman from the pregnancy entails the death of the fetus (except in very late stages of pregnancy). Thus a self-defense model supports Thomson's point that the woman has a right only to be freed from the fetus, not a right to demand its death.[11] . . .

Thanks to modern technology, the cases are rare in which pregnancy poses as clear a threat to a woman's bodily health as an attacker brandishing a switchblade. How does self-defense fare when more subtle, complex and long-range harms are involved?

To consider a somewhat fanciful example, suppose you are a highly trained surgeon when you are kidnapped by the hypnotic attacker. He says he does not intend to harm you but to take you back to the mad scientist who, it turns out, plans to hypnotize you to have a permanent mental block against all your knowledge of medicine. This would automatically destroy your career which would in turn have a serious adverse impact on your family, your personal relationships and your happiness. It seems to me that if the only way you can avoid this outcome is to shoot the innocent attacker, you are justified in so doing. You are defending yourself from a drastic injury to your life prospects. I think it is no exaggeration to claim that unwanted pregnancies (most obviously among teenagers) often have such adverse life-long consequences as the surgeon's loss of livelihood.

Several parallels arise between various views on abortion and the self-defense model. Let's suppose further that these hypnotized attackers only operate at night, so that it is well known that they can be avoided completely by the considerable inconvenience of never leaving your house after dark. One view is that since you could stay home at night, therefore if you go out and are selected by one of these hypnotized people, you have no right to defend yourself. This parallels the view that abstinence is the only acceptable way to avoid pregnancy. Others might hold that you ought to take along some defense such as Mace which will deter the hypnotized person without killing him, but that if this defense fails, you are obliged to submit to the resulting injury, no matter how severe it is. This parallels the view that contraception is all right but abortion is always wrong, even in cases of contraceptive failure.

A third view is that you may kill the hypnotized person only if he will actually kill you, but not if he will only injure you. This is like the position that abortion is permissible only if it is required to save a woman's life. Finally we have the view that it is all right to kill the attacker, even if only to avoid a very slight inconvenience to yourself and even if you knowingly walked down the very street where all these incidents have been taking place without taking along any Mace or protective escort. If we assume that a fetus is a person, this is the analogue of the view that abortion is always justifiable, "on demand."

The self-defense model allows us to see an important difference that exists between abortion and infanticide, even if a fetus is a person from conception. Many have argued that the only way to justify abortion without justifying infanticide would be to find some characteristic of personhood that is acquired at birth. Michael Tooley, for one, claims infanticide is justifiable because the really significant characteristics of person[hood] are acquired some time after birth. But all such approaches look to characteristics of the developing human and ignore the relation between the fetus and the woman. What if, after birth, the presence of an infant or the need to support it posed a grave threat to the woman's sanity or life prospects? She could escape this threat by the simple expedient of running away. So a solution that does not entail the death of the infant is available. Before birth, such solutions are not available because of the biological dependence of the fetus on the woman. Birth is the crucial point not because of any characteristics the fetus gains, but because after birth the woman can defend herself by a means less drastic than killing the infant. Hence self-defense can only be used to justify abortion without necessarily thereby justifying infanticide.

On the other hand, supposing a fetus is not after all a person, would abortion always be morally permissible? Some opponents of abortion seem worried that if a fetus is not a full-fledged person, then we are justified in treating it in any way at all. However, this does not follow. Nonpersons do get some consideration in our moral code, though of course they do not have the same rights as persons have (and in general they do not have moral responsibilities), and though their interests may be overridden by the interests of persons. Still, we cannot just treat them in any way at all.

Treatment of animals is a case in point. It is wrong to torture dogs for fun or to kill wild birds for no reason at all. It is wrong Period, even though dogs and birds do not have the same rights persons do. However, few people think it is wrong to use dogs as experimental animals, causing them considerable suffering in some cases, provided that the resulting research will probably bring discoveries of great benefit to people. And most of us think it all right to kill birds for food or to protect our crops. People's rights are different from the consideration we give to animals, then, for it is wrong to experiment on people, even if others might later benefit a great deal as a result of their suffering. You might volunteer to be a subject, but this would be supererogatory; you certainly have a right to refuse to be a medical guinea pig.

But how do we decide what you may or may not do to nonpersons? This is a difficult problem, one for which I believe no adequate account exists. You do not want to say, for instance, that torturing dogs is all right whenever the sum of its effects on people is good—when it doesn't warp the sensibilities of the torturer so much that he mistreats people. If that were the case, it would be all right to torture dogs if you did it in private, or if the torturer lived on a desert island or died soon afterward, so that his actions had no effect on people. This is an inadequate account, because whatever moral consideration animals get, it has to be indefeasible, too. It will have to be a general proscription of certain actions, not merely a weighing of the impact on people on a case-by-case basis. . . .

An ethical theory must operate by generating a set of sympathies and attitudes toward others which reinforces the functioning of . . . moral principles. Our prohibition against killing people operates by means of certain moral sentiments including sympathy, compassion and guilt. But if these attitudes are to form a coherent set, they carry us further; we tend to perform supererogatory actions, and we tend to feel similar compassion toward person-like nonpersons.

It is crucial that psychological facts play a role here. Our psychological constitution makes it the case that for our ethical theory to work, it must prohibit certain treatment of nonpersons which are significantly person-like. If our moral rules allowed people to treat some person-like nonpersons in ways we do not want people to be treated, this would undermine the system of sympathies and attitudes that makes the ethical system work. . . . Thus it makes sense that it is those animals whose appearance and behavior are most like those people that get the most consideration in our moral scheme.

It is because of "coherence of attitudes," I think, that the similarity of a fetus to a baby is very significant. A fetus one week before birth is so much like a newborn baby in our psychological space that we cannot allow any cavalier treatment of the former while expecting full sympathy and nurturative support for the latter. Thus, I think that antiabortion forces are indeed giving their strongest arguments when they point to the similarities between a fetus and a baby, and when they try to evoke our emotional attachment to and sympathy for the fetus. An early horror story from New York about nurses who were expected to alternate between caring for six-week premature infants and disposing of viable 24-week aborted fetuses is just that—a horror story. These beings are so much alike that no one can be asked to draw a distinction and treat them so very differently.

Remember, however, that in the early weeks after conception, a fetus is very much unlike a person. It is hard to develop these feelings for a set of genes which doesn't yet have a head, hands, beating heart, response to touch or the ability to move by itself. Thus it seems to me that the alleged "slippery slope" between conception and birth is not so very slippery. In the early stages of pregnancy, abortion can hardly be compared to murder for psychological reasons, but in the latest stages it is psychologically akin to murder.

Another source of similarity is the bodily continuity between fetus and adult. Bodies play a surprisingly central role in our attitudes toward persons. One has only to think of the philosophical literature on how far physical identity suffices for personal identity or Wittgenstein's remark that the best picture of the human soul is the human body. Even after death, when all agree the body is no longer a person, we will observe elaborate customs of respect for the human body; like people who torture dogs, necrophiliacs are not to be trusted with people.[12] So it is appropriate that we show respect to a fetus as the body continuous with the body of the person. This is a degree of resemblance to persons that animals cannot rival. . . .

Even if a fetus is not a person, abortion is not always permissible, because of the resemblance of a fetus to a person. I agree with Thomson that it would be wrong for a woman who is seven months pregnant to have an abortion just to avoid having to postpone a trip to Europe. In the early months of pregnancy when the fetus hardly resembles a baby at all, then, abortion is permissible whenever it is in the interests of the pregnant woman or her family. The reasons would only need to outweigh the pain and inconvenience of the abortion itself. In the middle months, when the fetus comes to resemble a person, abortion would be justifiable only when the continuation of the pregnancy or the birth of the child would cause harms—physical, psychological, economic or social—to the woman. In the late months of pregnancy, even on our current assumption that a fetus is not a person, abortion seems to be wrong except to save a woman from significant injury or death.

The Supreme Court has recognized similar gradations in the alleged slippery slope stretching between conception and birth. To this point, the present paper has been a discussion of the moral status of abortion only, not its legal status. In view of the great physical, financial and sometimes psychological costs of abortion, perhaps the legal arrangement most compatible with the proposed moral solution would be the absence of restrictions, that is, so-called abortion "on demand."

So I conclude, first, that application of our concept of a person will not suffice to settle the abortion issue. After all, the biological development of a human being is gradual. Second, whether a fetus is a person or not, abortion is justifiable early in pregnancy to avoid modest harms and seldom justifiable late in pregnancy except to avoid significant injury or death.[13]

Notes

1. We also have paternalistic laws which keep us from harming our own bodies even when no one else is affected. Ironically, antiabortion laws were originally designed to protect pregnant women from a dangerous but tempting procedure.

2. Mary Anne Warren, "On the Moral and Legal Status of Abortion," *Monist* 57 (1973), p. 55.

3. Baruch Brody, "Fetal Humanity and the Theory of Essentialism," in Robert Baker and Frederick Elliston, eds., *Philosophy and Sex* (Buffalo, N.Y., 1975).

4. Michael Tolley, "Abortion and Infanticide," *Philosophy and Public Affairs* 2 (1982).

5. Paul Ramsey, "The Morality of Abortion," in James Rachels, ed., *Moral Problems* (New York, 1971).

6. John Noonan, "Abortion and the Catholic Church: A Summary History," *Natural Law Forum* 12 (1967), pp. 125–131.

7. Wittgenstein has argued against the possibility of so capturing the concept of a game, *Philosophical Investigations* (New York, 1958), § 66.

8. Not because the fetus is partly a person and so has some of the rights of persons, but rather because of the rights of person-like nonpersons. This I discuss . . . below.

9. Aristotle himself was concerned, however, with the different question of when the soul takes form. For historical data, see Jimmye Kimmey, "How the Abortion Laws Happened," Ms. 1 (April 1973), pp. 48ff, and John Noonan, *loc. cit.*

10. J. J. Thomson, "A Defense of Abortion," *Philosophy and Public Affairs* 1 (1971).

11. *Ibid.,* p. 62.

12. On the other hand, if they can be trusted with people, then our moral customs are mistaken. It all depends on the facts of psychology.

13. I am deeply indebted to Larry Crocker and Arthur Kuflik for their constructive comments.

POSTSCRIPT

Is Abortion Immoral?

Whether or not a fetus can be considered a person is often at the center of the abortion issue. Marquis, however, does not find that a direct approach to this question breaks the deadlock that is characteristic of many discussions of the morality of abortion. Instead he argues that the effect of aborting a fetus, which is the loss of that fetus's future experiences, is the reason why abortion is immoral. Marquis considers this loss of future experiences to be the reason why killing adult human beings is wrong, and he carries the logic over to fetuses.

English also does not consider the question, Is a fetus a person? to be a key one, because, first, even if the fetus is *not* a person, this does not imply that we may do anything to it that we like. Second, even if it *is* a person, this does not mean that abortion may always be ruled out. Not only is the question not decisive, English asserts, but it has no *right* answer. She does not mean that there really is a right answer but we do not know it; she means instead that our concepts (including the concept of a person) do not have clear boundaries. Likewise, we might ask, when does a baby become a child? Again, there is no right answer. The problem is not that babies turn into children without our being able to catch them in the act. There is no right answer because the concepts in our language (such as *baby* and *child*) do not have sharply defined boundaries. Thus, when we ask whether or not a fetus is a person, instead of finding out that it is or is not, we find out that it has some of the features of a person but that it lacks other features.

Judith Jarvis Thomson, in her ground-breaking article "In Defense of Abortion," *Philosophy and Public Affairs* (Fall 1971), argues that, from the premise that the fetus is a person with a right to life, it does not follow that a woman cannot disconnect herself from it and terminate an unwanted pregnancy. Suppose, she says, that you wake up one day to find yourself medically attached to a famous violinist who would die if you detached yourself. A violinist is a person and has a right to life. Does it then follow, asks Thomson, that you may not detach yourself from this unwanted arrangement?

Further readings on this issue are Joel Feinberg, *The Problem of Abortion,* 2d ed. (Wadsworth, 1984); Laurence Tribe, *Abortion: The Clash of Absolutes* (W. W. Norton, 1990); Bonnie Steinbock, *Life Before Birth: The Moral and Legal Status of Embryos and Fetuses* (Oxford University Press, 1992); Frances Myrna Kamm, *Creation and Abortion: An Essay in Moral and Legal Philosophy* (Oxford University Press, 1992); Robert M. Baird and Stuart E. Rosenbaum, eds., *The Ethics of Abortion: Pro-Life vs. Pro-Choice,* 2d ed. (Prometheus Books, 1993); Eva R. Rubin, ed., *The Abortion Controversy: A Documentary History* (Greenwood Press, 1994); Bhavani Sitaraman, *The Middleground: The American Public and the Abortion Debate* (Garland, 1994); Laurie Shrage, *Moral Dilemmas of Feminism: Prostitution, Adul-*

tery, and Abortion (Routledge, 1994); Ian Shapiro, ed., *Abortion: The Supreme Court Decisions* (Hackett, 1995); Peter Korn, *Lovejoy: A Year in the Life of an Abortion Clinic* (Atlantic Monthly Press, 1996); Patrick Lee, *Abortion and Unborn Human Life* (Catholic University of America Press, 1996); Janet Hadley, *Abortion: Between Freedom and Necessity* (Temple University Press, 1996); Eileen McDonagh, *Breaking the Abortion Deadlock: From Choice to Consent* (Oxford University Press, 1996); Kathy Rudy, *Beyond Pro-Life and Pro-Choice: Moral Diversity in the Abortion Debate* (Beacon Press, 1997); Donald T. Chitchlow, ed., *The Politics of Abortion in Historical Perspective* (Pennsylvania State Press, 1996); Katha Pollitt, "Abortion in American History," *The Atlantic Monthly* (May 1997); and Louis Pojman and Francis Beckwith, eds., *The Abortion Controversy: 25 Years After Roe v. Wade: A Reader,* 2d ed. (Wadsworth Publishing Company, 1998).

On RU-486 (sometimes called the "abortion pill"), see Janice G. Raymond, Renate Klein, and Lynette J. Dumble, *RU 486: Myths, Misconceptions, and Morals* (Institute on Women and Technology, 1991), and Lawrence Ladder, *A Private Matter: RU-486 and the Abortion Crisis* (Prometheus Books, 1995).

A CD-ROM on abortion is J. Douglas Butler, ed., *Abortion and Reproductive Rights* (J. Douglas Butler, Inc., 1997).

Recent publications include Lawrence Becker et al., eds., *Encyclopedia of Ethics,* 2d ed. (Routledge, 2002); Edwin C. Hui, *At the Beginning of Life: Dilemmas in Theological Bioethics* (InterVarsity Press, 2002); David Boonin, *A Defense of Abortion* (Cambridge University Press, 2002); and Laurie J. Shrage, *Abortion and Social Responsibility: Depolarizing the Debate* (Oxford University Press, 2003).

ISSUE 6

Must Sex Involve Commitment?

YES: Vincent C. Punzo, from *Reflective Naturalism* (Macmillan, 1969)

NO: Alan H. Goldman, from "Plain Sex," *Philosophy and Public Affairs* (Princeton University Press, 1977)

ISSUE SUMMARY

YES: Philosopher Vincent C. Punzo maintains that the special intimacy of sex requires a serious commitment that is for the most part not required in other human activities.

NO: Philosopher Alan H. Goldman argues for a view of sex that is completely separate from any cultural or moral ideology that might be attached to it.

For many people, sex and morality are interconnected. Some complain that talk about sex, such as in sex education classes, is worse than worthless—it is downright corrupt—if it is divorced from talk about morality. Yet, with the exception of specialized concepts such as sexual harassment, most contemporary moral philosophers have very little to say about sex. In part, this may be due to the modern idea that many traditional beliefs about sex are steeped in superstitious, prejudiced, or misguided views that are in need of scientific correction.

In the traditional thought of ancient and medieval times, the stage of the world contains a large backdrop that is intended to make sense of the place of humans in the world. Ancient Greek philosophers created metaphysical theories and medieval theologians created religious theories to explain the role and purpose of humankind. According to both ancient and medieval views, humans are different from animals and thought to possess traits beyond the physical, which ground this difference. However, the modern and scientific view is that humans have no special metaphysical or supernatural standing above animals. Humans are simply a part of nature. This is not an attempt to provide another backdrop, but instead an attempt to eliminate all backdrops, so that people can be viewed in a more realistic manner. This view supports the idea that sexual urges are simply a part of our nature.

Consider a different example. Eating habits are also considered to be a part of our nature, but traditionalists would remind us that we have to eat the correct foods from a nutritional standpoint. We have to direct our eating habits with reason—we cannot simply eat whatever we feel like whenever we want to. Traditionalists view eating as something beyond the process of digestion. Sexual intercourse has its own physical processes, and, like eating, also involves more than just the physical. Sex involves the use of self-control and reason.

Modernists may argue that in many ways the analogy with eating fails. In the past, eating habits were only minimally affected by superstitious or false ideas, whereas sexual practices were greatly affected.

What we are left with today are elements of ancient, medieval, and modern thought. When it comes to sex, it is clear that modern scientific views have a contribution to make; but it is not clear whether we can simply do away with all previous ideas about sex.

In the following selections, Vincent C. Punzo argues for the view that sex, since it involves the highest level of human intimacy, must involve commitment. Alan H. Goldman counters that a concept of "plain sex" helps us to understand sex for what it is—something that does not need moral ideas attached to it.

Morality and Human Sexuality

If one sees man's moral task as being simply that of not harming anyone, that is if one sees this task in purely negative terms, he will certainly not accept the argument to be presented in the following section. However, if one accepts the notion of the morality of aspiration, if one accepts the view that man's moral task involves the positive attempt to live up to what is best in man, to give reality to what he sees to be the perfection of himself as a human subject, the argument may be acceptable.

Sexuality and the Human Subject

[Previous discussion] has left us with the question as to whether sexual intercourse is a type of activity that is similar to choosing a dinner from a menu. The question is of utmost significance in that one's view of the morality of premarital intercourse seems to depend on the significance that one gives to the sexual encounter in human life. Those such as [John] Wilson and [Eustace] Chesser who see nothing immoral about the premarital character of sexual intercourse seem to see sexual intercourse as being no different from myriad of other purely aesthetic matters. This point is seen in Chesser's questioning of the reason for demanding permanence in the relationship of sexual partners when we do not see such permanence as being important to other human relationships.[1] It is also seen in his asking why we raise a moral issue about premarital coition when two people may engage in it, with the resulting social and psychological consequences being no different than if they had gone to movie.[2]

Wilson most explicitly makes a case for the view that sexual intercourse does not differ significantly from other human activities. He holds that people think that there is a logical difference between the question "Will you engage in sexual intercourse with me?" and the question, "Will you play tennis with me?" only because they are influenced by the acquisitive character of contemporary society.[3] Granted that the two questions may be identical from the purely formal perspective of logic, the ethician must move beyond this perspective to a consideration of their content. Men and women find themselves involved in many different relationships: for example, as buyer-seller, employer-employee, teacher-student, lawyer-client, and partners or competitors in certain games

From Vincent C. Punzo, *Reflective Naturalism* (Macmillan, 1969). Copyright © 1969 by Vincent C. Punzo. Reprinted by permission of Prentice Hall, Inc., Upper Saddle River, NJ.

such as tennis or bridge. Is there any morally significant difference between these relationships and sexual intercourse? We cannot examine all the possible relationships into which a man and woman can enter, but we will consider the employer-employee relationship in order to get some perspective on the distinctive character of the sexual relationship.

A man pays a woman to act as his secretary. What rights does he have over her in such a situation? The woman agrees to work a certain number of hours during the day taking dictation, typing letters, filing reports, arranging appointments and flight schedules, and greeting clients and competitors. In short, we can say that the man has rights to certain of the woman's services or skills. The use of the word "services" may lead some to conclude that this relationship is not significantly different from the relationship between a prostitute and her client in that the prostitute also offers her "services."

It is true that we sometimes speak euphemistically of a prostitute offering her services to a man for a sum of money, but if we are serious about our quest for the difference between the sexual encounter and other types of human relationships, it is necessary to drop euphemisms and face the issue directly. The man and woman who engage in sexual intercourse are giving their bodies, the most intimate physical expression of themselves, over to the other. Unlike the man who plays tennis with a woman, the man who has sexual relations with her has literally entered her. A man and woman engaging in sexual intercourse have united themselves as intimately and as totally as is physically possible for two human beings. Their union is not simply a union of organs, but is as intimate and as total a physical union of two selves as is possible of achievement. Granted the character of this union, it seems strange to imply that there is no need for a man and woman to give any more thought to the question of whether they should engage in sexual intercourse than to the question of whether they should play tennis.

In opposition to Wilson, I think that it is the acquisitive character of our society that has blinded us to the distinction between the two activities. Wilson's and Chesser's positions seem to imply that exactly the same moral considerations ought to apply to a situation in which a housewife is bartering with a butcher for a few pounds of pork chops and the situation in which two human beings are deciding whether sexual intercourse ought to be an ingredient of their relationship. So long as the butcher does not put his thumb on the scale in the weighing process, so long as he is truthful in stating that the meat is actually pork, so long as the woman pays the proper amount with the proper currency, the trade is perfectly moral. Reflecting on sexual intercourse from the same sort of economic perspective, one can say that so long as the sexual partners are truthful in reporting their freedom from contagious venereal diseases and so long as they are truthful in reporting that they are interested in the activity for the mere pleasure of it or to try out their sexual techniques, there is nothing immoral about such activity. That in the one case pork chops are being exchanged for money whereas in the other the decision concerns the most complete and intimate merging of one's self with another makes no difference to the moral evaluation of the respective cases.

It is not surprising that such a reductionistic outlook should pervade our thinking on sexual matters, since in our society sexuality is used to sell everything from shave cream to underarm deodorants, to soap, to mouthwash, to cigarettes, and to automobiles. Sexuality has come to play so large a role in our commercial lives that it is not surprising that our sexuality should itself come to be treated as a commodity governed by the same moral rules that govern any other economic transaction.

Once sexuality is taken out of this commercial framework, once the character of the sexual encounter is faced directly and squarely, we will come to see that Doctor Mary Calderone has brought out the type of questions that ought to be asked by those contemplating the introduction of sexual intercourse into their relationships: "How many times, and how casually, are you willing to invest a portion of your total self, and to be the custodian of a like investment from the other person, without the sureness of knowing that these investments are being made for keeps?"[4] These questions come out of the recognition that the sexual encounter is a definitive experience, one in which the physical intimacy and merging involves also a merging of the nonphysical dimensions of the partners. With these questions, man moves beyond the negative concern with avoiding his or another's physical and psychological harm to the question of what he is making of himself and what he is contributing to the existential formation of his partner as a human subject.

If we are to make a start toward responding to Calderone's questions we must cease talking about human selfhood in abstraction. The human self is an historical as well as a physical being. He is a being who is capable of making at least a portion of his past an object of his consciousness and thus is able to make this past play a conscious role in his present and in his looking toward the future. He is also a being who looks to the future, who faces tomorrow with plans, ideals, hopes, and fears. The very being of a human self involves his past and his movement toward the future. Moreover, the human self is not completely shut off in his own past and future. Men and women are capable of consciously and purposively uniting themselves in a common career and venture. They can commit themselves to sharing the future with another, sharing it in all its aspects—in its fortunes and misfortunes, in its times of happiness and times of tragedy. Within the lives of those who have so committed themselves to each other, sexual intercourse is a way of asserting and confirming the fullness and totality of their mutual commitment.

Unlike those who have made such a commitment and who come together in the sexual act in the fullness of their selfhood, those who engage in premarital sexual unions and who have made no such commitment act as though they can amputate their bodily existence and the most intimate physical expression of their selfhood from their existence as historical beings. Granting that there may be honesty on the verbal level in that two people engaging in premarital intercourse openly state that they are interested only in the pleasure of the activity, the fact remains that such unions are morally deficient because they lack existential integrity in that there is a total merging and union on a physical level, on the one hand, and a conscious decision not to unite any other dimension of themselves, on the other hand. Their sexual union thus involves a "depersonalization" of their bodily existence, an attempt to cut off the most intimate physical expression of their respective selves from their very selfhood. The mutual agreement of premarital sex partners is an agreement to merge with the other not as a self, but as a body which one takes unto oneself, which one possesses in a most intimate and total fashion for one's own pleasure or designs, allowing the other to treat oneself in the same way. It may be true that no physical or psychological harm may result from such unions, but such partners have failed to existentially incorporate human sexuality, which is at the very least the most intimate physical expression of the human self, into the character of this selfhood.

In so far as premarital sexual unions separate the intimate and total physical union that is sexual intercourse from any commitment to the self in his historicity, human sexuality, and consequently the human body, have been fashioned into external things or objects to be handed over totally to someone else, whenever one feels that he can get possession of another's body, which he can use for his own purposes.[5] The human body has thus been treated no differently from the pork chops spoken of previously or from any other object or commodity, which human beings exchange and haggle over in their day-to-day transactions. One hesitates to use the word that might be used to capture the moral value that has been sacrificed in premarital unions because in our day the word has taken on a completely negative meaning at best, and, at worst, it has become a word used by "sophisticates" to mock or deride certain attitudes toward human sexuality. However, because the word "chastity" has been thus abused is no reason to leave it in the hands of those who have misrepresented the human value to which it gives expression.

The chaste person has often been described as one intent on denying his sexuality. The value of chastity as conceived in this section is in direct opposition to this description. It is the unchaste person who is separating himself from his sexuality, who is willing to exchange human bodies as one would exchange money for tickets to a baseball game—honestly and with no commitment of self to self. Against this alienation of one's sexuality from one's self, an alienation that makes one's sexuality an object, which is to be given to another in exchange for his objectified sexuality, chastity affirms the integrity of the self in his bodily and historical existence. The sexuality of man is seen as an integral part of his subjectivity. Hence, the chaste man rejects depersonalized sexual relations as a reduction of man in his most intimate physical being to the status of an object or pure instrument for another. He asserts that man is a subject and end in himself, not in some trans-temporal, nonphysical world, but in the historical-physical world in which he carries on his moral task and where he finds his fellow man. He will not freely make of himself in his bodily existence a thing to be handed over to another's possession, nor will he ask that another treat his own body in this way. The total physical intimacy of sexual intercourse will be an expression of total union with the other self on all levels of their beings. Seen from this perspective, chastity is one aspect of man's attempt to attain existential integrity, to accept his body as a dimension of his total personality.

In concluding this section, it should be noted that I have tried to make a case against the morality of premarital sexual intercourse even in those cases in which the partners are completely honest with each other. There is reason to question whether the complete honesty, to which those who see nothing immoral in such unions refer, is as a matter of fact actually found very often among premarital sex partners. We may well have been dealing with textbook cases which present these unions in their best light. One may be pardoned for wondering whether sexual intercourse often occurs under the following conditions: "Hello, my name is Josiah. I am interested in having a sexual experience with you. I can assure you that I am good at it and that I have no communicable disease. If it sounds good to you and if you have taken the proper contraceptive precautions, we might have a go at it. Of course, I want to make it clear to you that I am interested only in the sexual experience and that I have no intention of making any long-range commitment to you." If those, who defend the morality of premarital sexual unions so long as they are honestly entered into, think that I have misrepresented what they mean by honesty, then they must specify what they mean by an honest premarital union. . . .

Marriage as a Total Human Commitment

The preceding argument against the morality of premarital sexual unions was not based on the view that the moral character of marriage rests on a legal certificate or on a legal or religious ceremony. The argument was not directed against "preceremonial" intercourse, but against premarital intercourse. Morally speaking, a man and woman are married when they make the mutual and total commitment to share the problems and prospects of their historical existence in the world. Although marriages are not to be identified with ceremonies, the words used in marriage ceremonies have captured the character of marriage in the promise which the partners make to each other to join their lives "for better, for worse, for richer, for poorer, in sickness and in health, till death do us part."

. . . The commitment that constitutes marriage is a total commitment of one person to another person of the opposite sex. To understand the character of such commitment, it is necessary to know something about the being of those involved in the commitment; for if it is to be truly total, the commitment must be as rich as the being of those who have made it. It is at this point that the historical character of the human self's existence becomes important. A total commitment to another means a commitment to him in his historical existence. Such a commitment is not simply a matter of words or of feelings, however strong. It involves a full existential sharing on the part of two beings of the burdens, opportunities, and challenges of their historical existence.

Granted the importance that the character of their commitment to each other plays in determining the moral quality of a couple's sexual encounter, it is clear that there may be nothing immoral in the behavior of couples who engage in sexual intercourse before participating in the marriage ceremony. For example, it is foolish to say that two people who are totally committed to each other and who have made all the arrangements to live this commitment are immoral if they engage in sexual intercourse the night before the marriage ceremony. Admittedly this position can be abused by those who have made a purely verbal commitment, a commitment which will be carried out in some vague and ill-defined future. At some time or other, they will unite their two lives totally by setting up house together and by actually undertaking the task of meeting the economic, social, legal, medical responsibilities that are involved in living this commitment. Apart from the reference to a vague and amorphous future time when they will share the full responsibility for each other, their commitment presently realizes itself in going to dances, sharing a box of popcorn at Saturday night movies, and sharing their bodies whenever they can do so without taking too great a risk of having the girl become pregnant.

Having acknowledged that the position advanced in this section can be abused by those who would use the word "commitment" to rationalize what is an interest only in the body of the other person, it must be pointed out that neither the ethician nor any other human being can tell two people whether they actually have made the commitment that is marriage or are mistaking a "warm glow" for such a commitment. There comes a time when this issue falls out of the area of moral philosophy and into the area of practical wisdom. . . .

The characterization of marriage as a total commitment between two human beings may lead some to conclude that the marriage ceremony is a wholly superfluous affair. It must be admitted that people may be morally married without having engaged in a marriage ceremony. However, to conclude from this point that the ceremony is totally meaningless is to lose sight of the social character of human beings. The couple contemplating marriage do not exist in a vacuum, although there may be times when they think they do. Their existences reach out beyond their union to include other human beings. By making their commitment a matter of public record, by solemnly expressing it before the law and in the presence of their respective families and friends and, if they are religious people, in the presence of God and one of his ministers, they sink the roots of their commitment more deeply and extensively in the world in which they live, thus taking steps to provide for the future growth of their commitment to each other. The public expression of this commitment makes it more fully and more explicitly a part of a couple's lives and of the world in which they live.

Notes

1. Eustace Chesser, *Unmarried Love* (New York: Pocket Books, 1965), p. 29.
2. *Op. cit.,* pp. 35–36; see also p. 66.
3. John Wilson, *Logic and Sexual Morality* (Baltimore, Md.: Penguin Books, 1965), p. 67, note 1.
4. Mary Steichen Calderone, "The Case for Chastity," *Sex in America,* ed. by Henry Anatole Grunwald (New York: Bantam Books, 1964), p. 147.
5. The psychoanalyst Rollo May makes an excellent point in calling attention to the tendency in contemporary society to exploit the human body as if it were only a machine. Rollo May, "The New Puritanism," *Sex in America,* pp. 161–164.

Alan H. Goldman

 **NO**

Plain Sex

Several recent articles on sex herald its acceptance as a legitimate topic for analytic philosophers (although it has been a topic in philosophy since Plato). One might have thought conceptual analysis unnecessary in this area; despite the notorious struggles of judges and legislators to define pornography suitably, we all might be expected to know what sex is and to be able to identify at least paradigm sexual desires and activities without much difficulty. Philosophy is nevertheless of relevance here if for no other reason than that the concept of sex remains at the center of moral and social consciousness in our, and perhaps any, society. Before we can get a sensible view of the relation of sex to morality, . . . social regulation, and marriage, we require a sensible analysis of the concept itself; one which neither understates its animal pleasure nor overstates its importance within a theory or system of value. I say "before," but the order is not quite so clear, for questions in this area, as elsewhere in moral philosophy, are both conceptual and normative at the same time. Our concept of sex will partially determine our moral view of it, but as philosophers we should formulate a concept that will accord with its proper moral status. What we require here, as elsewhere, is "reflective equilibrium," a goal not achieved by traditional and recent analyses together with their moral implications. Because sexual activity, like other natural functions such as eating or exercising, has become imbedded in layers of cultural, moral, and superstitious superstructure, it is hard to conceive it in its simplest terms. But partially for this reason, it is only by thinking about plain sex that we can begin to achieve this conceptual equilibrium.

I shall suggest here that sex continues to be misrepresented in recent writings, at least in philosophical writings, and I shall criticize the predominant form of analysis which I term "means-end analysis." Such conceptions attribute a necessary external goal or purpose to sexual activity, whether it be reproduction, the expression of love, simple communication, or interpersonal awareness. They analyze sexual activity as a means to one of these ends, implying that sexual desire is a desire to reproduce, to love or be loved, or to communicate with others. All definitions of this type suggest false views of the relation of sex to . . . morality by implying that sex which does not fit one of these models or fulfill one of these functions is in some way deviant or incomplete.

From Alan H. Goldman, "Plain Sex," *Philosophy and Public Affairs*, vol. 6, no. 3 (Spring 1977). Copyright © 1977 by Princeton University Press. Reprinted by permission of Princeton University Press.

The alternative, simpler analysis with which I will begin is that sexual desire is desire for contact with another person's body and for the pleasure which such contact produces; sexual activity is activity which tends to fulfill such desire of the agent. Whereas Aristotle and [others] were correct in holding that pleasure is normally a byproduct rather than a goal of purposeful action, in the case of sex this is not so clear. The desire for another's body is, principally among other things, the desire for the pleasure that physical contact brings. On the other hand, it is not a desire for a particular sensation detachable from its causal context, a sensation which can be derived in other ways. This definition in terms of the general goal of sexual desire appears preferable to an attempt to more explicitly list or define specific sexual activities, for many activities such as kissing, embracing, massaging, or holding hands may or may not be sexual, depending upon the context and more specifically upon the purposes, needs, or desires into which such activities fit. The generality of the definition also represents a refusal (common in recent psychological texts) to overemphasize orgasm as the goal of sexual desire or genital sex as the only norm of sexual activity. . . .

Central to the definition is the fact that the goal of sexual desire and activity is the physical contact itself, rather than something else which this contact might express. By contrast, what I term "means-end analyses" posit ends which I take to be extraneous to plain sex, and they view sex as a means to these ends. Their fault lies not in defining sex in terms of its general goal, but in seeing plain sex as merely a means to other separable ends. I term these "means-end analyses" for convenience, although "means-separable-end analyses," while too cumbersome, might be more fully explanatory. The desire for physical contact with another person is a minimal criterion for (normal) sexual desire, but is both necessary and sufficient to qualify normal desire as sexual. Of course, we may want to express other feelings through sexual acts in various contexts; but without the desire for the physical contact in and for itself, or when it is sought for other reasons, activities in which contact is involved are not predominantly sexual. Furthermore, the desire for physical contact in itself, without the wish to express affection or other feelings through it, is sufficient to render sexual the activity of the agent which fulfills it. Various activities with this goal alone, such as kissing and caressing in certain contexts, qualify as sexual even without the presence of genital symptoms of sexual excitement. The latter are not therefore necessary criteria for sexual activity. . . .

Our definition of sex in terms of the desire for physical contact may appear too narrow in that a person's personality, not merely her or his body, may be sexually attractive to another, and in that looking or conversing in a certain way can be sexual in a given context without bodily contact. Nevertheless, it is not the contents of one's thoughts per se that are sexually appealing, but one's personality as embodied in certain manners of behavior. Furthermore, if a person is sexually attracted by another's personality, he or she will desire not just further conversation, but actual sexual contact. While looking at or conversing with someone can be interpreted as sexual in given contexts it is so when intended as preliminary to, and hence parasitic upon, elemental sexual interest. Voyeurism or viewing a pornographic movie qualifies as a sexual activity, but only as an imaginative substitute for the real thing (otherwise a deviation from the norm as expressed in our definition). The same is true of masturbation as a sexual activity without a partner.

That the initial definition indicates at least an ingredient of sexual desire and activity is too obvious to argue. We all know what sex is, at least in obvious cases, and do not need philosophers to tell us. My preliminary analysis is meant to serve as a contrast to what sex is not, at least, not necessarily. I concentrate upon the physically manifested desire for another's body, and I take as central the immersion in the physical aspect of one's own existence and attention to the physical embodiment of the other. One may derive pleasure in a sex act from expressing certain feelings to one's partner or from awareness of the attitude of one's partner, but sexual desire is essentially desire for physical contact itself: it is a bodily desire for the body of another that dominates our mental life for more or less brief periods. Traditional writings were correct to emphasize the purely physical or animal aspect of sex; they were wrong only in condemning it. This characterization of sex as an intensely pleasurable physical activity and acute physical desire may seem to some to capture only its barest level. But it is worth distinguishing and focusing upon this least common denominator in order to avoid the false views of sexual morality . . . which emerge from thinking that sex is essentially something else.

One common position views sex as essentially an expression of love or affection between the partners. It is generally recognized that there are other types of love besides sexual, but sex itself is taken as an expression of one type, sometimes termed "romantic" love.[1] Various factors again ought to weaken this identification. First, there are other types of love besides that which it is appropriate to express sexually, and "romantic" love itself can be expressed in many other ways. I am not denying that sex can take on heightened value and meaning when it becomes a vehicle for the expression of feelings of love or tenderness, but so can many other usually mundane activities such as getting up early to make breakfast on Sunday, cleaning the house, and so on. Second, sex itself can be used to communicate many other emotions besides love, and, as I will argue below, can communicate nothing in particular and still be good sex.

On a deeper level, an internal tension is bound to result from an identification of sex, which I have described as a physical-psychological desire, with love as a long-term, deep emotional relationship between two individuals. As this type of relationship, love is permanent, at least in intent, and more or less exclusive. A normal person cannot deeply love more than a few individuals even in a lifetime. We may be suspicious that those who attempt or claim to love many love them weakly if at all. Yet, fleeting sexual desire can arise in relation to a variety of other individuals one finds sexually attractive. It may even be, as some have claimed, that sexual desire in humans naturally seeks variety, while this is obviously false of love. For this reason, monogamous sex, even if justified, almost always represents a sacrifice or the exercise of self-control on the part of the spouses, while monogamous love generally does not. There is no such thing as casual love in the sense in which I intend the term "love." It may occasionally happen that a spouse falls deeply in love with someone else (especially when sex is conceived in terms of love), but this is relatively rare in comparison to passing sexual desires for others; and while the former often indicates a weakness or fault in the marriage relation, the latter does not.

If love is indeed more exclusive in its objects than is sexual desire, this explains why those who view sex as essentially an expression of love would again tend to hold a repressive or restrictive sexual ethic. . . . [T]here may be good reasons for reserving the total commitment of deep love to the context of marriage and family—the normal personality may not withstand additional divisions of ultimate commitment and allegiance. There is no question that marriage itself is best sustained by a deep relation of love and affection; and even if love is not naturally monogamous, the benefits of family units to children provide additional reason to avoid serious commitments elsewhere which weaken family ties. It can be argued similarly that monogamous sex strengthens families by restricting and at the same time guaranteeing an outlet for sexual desire in marriage. But there is more force to the argument that recognition of a clear distinction between sex and love in society would help avoid disastrous marriages which result from adolescent confusion of the two when sexual desire is mistaken for permanent love, and would weaken damaging jealousies which arise in marriages in relation to passing sexual desires. The love and affection of a sound marriage certainly differs from the adolescent romantic variety, which is often a mere substitute for sex in the context of a repressive sexual ethic.

In fact, the restrictive sexual ethic tied to the means-end analysis in terms of love . . . has failed to be consistent. At least, it has not been applied consistently, but forms part of the double standard which has curtailed the freedom of women. The inconsistency in the sexual ethic typically attached to the sex-love analysis, according to which it has generally been taken with a grain of salt when applied to men, is simply another example of the impossibility of tailoring a plausible moral theory in this area to a conception of sex which builds in conceptually extraneous factors.

I am not suggesting here that sex ought never to be connected with love or that it is not a more significant and valuable activity when it is. Nor am I denying that individuals need love as much as sex and perhaps emotionally need at least one complete relationship which encompasses both. Just as sex can express love and take on heightened significance when it does, so love is often naturally accompanied by an intermittent desire for sex. But again love is accompanied appropriately by desires for other shared activities as well. What makes the desire for sex seem more intimately connected with love is the intimacy which is seen to be a natural feature of mutual sex acts. Like love, sex is held to lay one bare psychologically as well as physically. Sex is unquestionably intimate, but beyond that the psychological toll often attached may be a function of the restrictive sexual ethic itself, rather than a legitimate apology for it. The intimacy involved in love is psychologically consuming in a generally healthy way, while the psychological tolls of sexual relations, often including embarrassment as a correlate of intimacy, are too often the result of artificial sexual ethics and taboos. The intimacy involved in both love and sex is insufficient in any case in light of previous points to render a means-end analysis in these terms appropriate.

. . . To the question of what morality might be implied by my analysis, the answer is that there are no moral implications whatever. Any analysis of sex which imputes a moral character to sex acts in themselves is wrong for that reason. There is no morality intrinsic to sex, although general moral rules apply to the treatment of others in sex acts as they apply to all human relations. We can speak of a sexual ethic as we can speak of a business ethic, without implying that business in itself is either moral or immoral or that special rules are required to judge business practices which are not derived from rules that apply elsewhere as well. Sex is not in itself a moral category, although like business it invariably places us into relations with others in which moral rules apply. It gives us opportunity to do what is otherwise recognized as wrong, to harm others, deceive them or manipulate them against their wills. Just as the fact that an act is sexual in itself never renders it wrong or adds to its wrongness if it is wrong on other grounds (sexual acts towards minors are wrong on other grounds, as will be argued below), so no wrong act is to be excused because done from a sexual motive. If a "crime of passion" is to be excused, it would have to be on grounds of temporary insanity rather than sexual context (whether insanity does constitute a legitimate excuse for certain actions is too big a topic to argue here). Sexual motives are among others which may become deranged, and the fact that they are sexual has no bearing in itself on the moral character, whether negative or exculpatory, of the actions deriving from them. Whatever might be true of war, it is certainly not the case that all's fair in love or sex.

Our first conclusion regarding morality and sex is therefore that no conduct otherwise immoral should be excused because it is sexual conduct, and nothing in sex is immoral unless condemned by rules which apply elsewhere as well. The last clause requires further clarification. Sexual conduct can be governed by particular rules relating only to sex itself. But these precepts must be implied by general moral rules when these are applied to specific sexual relations or types of conduct. The same is true of rules of fair business, ethical medicine, or courtesy in driving a car. In the latter case, particular acts on the road may be reprehensible, such as tailgating or passing on the right, which seem to bear no resemblance as actions to any outside the context of highway safety. Nevertheless their immorality derives from the fact that they place others in danger, a circumstance which, when avoidable, is to be condemned in any context. This structure of general and specifically applicable rules describes a reasonable sexual ethic as well. To take an extreme case, rape is always a sexual act and it is always immoral. A rule against rape can therefore be considered an obvious part of sexual morality which has no bearing on nonsexual conduct. But the immorality of rape derives from its being an extreme violation of a person's body, of the right not to be humiliated, and of the general moral prohibition against using other persons against their wills, not from the fact that it is a sexual act.

The application elsewhere of general moral rules to sexual conduct is further complicated by the fact that it will be relative to the particular desires and preferences of one's partner (these may be influenced by and hence in some sense include misguided beliefs about sexual morality itself). This means that there will be fewer specific rules in the area of sexual ethics than in other areas of conduct, such as driving cars, where the relativity of preference is irrelevant to the prohibition of objectively dangerous conduct. More reliance will have to be placed upon the general moral rule, which in this area holds simply that the preferences, desires, and interests of one's partner or potential partner ought to be taken into account. This rule is certainly not specifically formulated to govern sexual relations; it is a form of the central principle of morality itself. But when applied to sex, it prohibits certain actions, such as molestation of children, which cannot be categorized as violations of the rule without at the same time being classified as sexual. I believe this last case is the closest we can come to an action which is wrong *because* it is sexual, but even here its wrongness is better characterized as deriving from the detrimental effects such behavior can have on the future emotional and sexual life of the naive victims, and from the fact that such behavior therefore involves manipulation of innocent persons without regard for their interests. Hence, this case also involves violation of a general moral rule which applies elsewhere as well. . . .

I suggested earlier that in addition to generating confusion regarding the rightness or wrongness of sex acts, false conceptual analyses of the means-end form cause confusion about the value of sex to the individual. My account recognizes the satisfaction of desire and the pleasure this brings as the central psychological function of the sex act for the individual. Sex affords us a paradigm of pleasure, but not a cornerstone of value. For most of us it is not only a needed outlet for desire but also the most enjoyable form of recreation we know. Its value is nevertheless easily mistaken by being confused with that of love, when it is taken as essentially an expression of that emotion. Although intense, the pleasures of sex are brief and repetitive rather than cumulative. They give value to the specific acts which generate them, but not the lasting kind of value which enhances one's whole life. The briefness of these pleasures contributes to their intensity (or perhaps their intensity makes them necessarily brief), but it also relegates them to the periphery of most rational plans for the good life.

By contrast, love typically develops over a long term relation; while its pleasures may be less intense and physical, they are of more cumulative value. The importance of love to the individual may well be central in a rational system of value. And it has perhaps an even deeper moral significance relating to the identification with the interests of another person, which broadens one's possible relationships with others as well. Marriage is again important in preserving this relation between adults and children, which seems as important to the adults as it is to the children in broadening concerns which have a tendency to become selfish. Sexual desire, by contrast, is desire for another which is nevertheless essentially self-regarding. Sexual pleasure is certainly a good for the individual, and for many it may be necessary in order for them to function in a reasonably cheerful way. But it bears little relation to those other values just discussed, to which some analyses falsely suggest a conceptual connection. . . .

The position I have taken in this paper against those concepts is not totally new. Something similar to it is found in Freud's view of sex, which of course was genuinely revolutionary, and in the body of writings deriving from Freud to the present time. But in his revolt against romanticized and repressive conceptions, Freud went too far—from a refusal to view sex as merely a means to a view of it as the end of all human behavior, although sometimes an elaborately disguised end. This pansexualism led to the thesis (among others) that repression was indeed an inevitable and necessary part of social regulation of any form, a strange consequence of a position that began by opposing the repressive aspects of the means-end view. Perhaps the time finally has arrived when we can achieve a reasonable middle ground in this area, at least in philosophy if not in society.

Note

1. Even Bertrand Russell, whose writing in this area was a model of rationality, at least for its period, tends to make this identification and to condemn plain sex in the absence of love: "sex intercourse apart from love has little value, and is to be regarded primarily as experimentation with a view to love." *Marriage and Morals* (New York: Bantam, 1959), p. 87.

POSTSCRIPT

Must Sex Involve Commitment?

It is clear that Punzo and Goldman differ fundamentally in their approach to sex and commitment. Goldman maintains that a concept of "plain sex" can be used to view sex without cultural and moral ideology. Punzo's approach counters the idea that an important human concept like sex can be separated from ideology.

A further question is whether men and women regard this issue in different ways. Traditionally, there has been a cultural demand that commitment is required before engaging in sex. However, a "double standard" exists that lets men practice sex in the absence of commitment without cultural disapproval. On the other hand, women are more likely to be viewed as "immoral" if they engage in sex without commitment. If the double standard is to be replaced by a unified standard, should this be one that includes commitment?

Sources relevant to this topic include Russell Vannoy, *Sex Without Love: A Philosophical Exploration* (Prometheus Books, 1981); G. Sidney Buchanan, *Morality, Sex and the Constitution: A Christian Perspective on the Power of Government to Regulate Private Sexual Conduct Between Consenting Adults* (University Press of America, 1985); G. Frankson, *Sex and Morality* (Todd & Honeywell, 1987); Joseph Monti, *Arguing About Sex: The Rhetoric of Christian Sexual Morality* (State University of New York Press, 1995); John Marshall Townsend, *What Women Want—What Men Want: Why the Sexes Still See Love and Commitment So Differently* (Oxford University Press, 1998); and J. Gordon Muir, *Sex, Politics, and the End of Morality* (Pentland Press, 1998).

ISSUE 7

Should Congress Stay the Course on Education for Sexual Abstinence Until Marriage?

YES: Joe S. McIlhaney, from "Should Congress Stay the Course on Education for Sexual Abstinence Until Marriage? Yes," *Insight on the News* (May 20, 2002)

NO: James Wagoner, from "Should Congress Stay the Course on Education for Sexual Abstinence Until Marriage? No," *Insight on the News* (May 20, 2002)

ISSUE SUMMARY

YES: Joe S. McIlhaney, president of the Medical Institute for Sexual Health, argues that the idea of "safe sex" is a dangerous myth that has led to an epidemic of sexually transmitted diseases (STDs) among young people. He states that condoms are not effective on certain common but incurable STDs.

NO: James Wagoner, president of Advocates for Youth, maintains that abstinence-only sex education programs are unrealistic and ineffective. Young people, he asserts, must also know about contraception in order to help prevent unwanted pregnancies, STDs, and HIV/AIDS.

Young people are of course concerned about the problems that are connected with sexual activity—e.g., unwanted pregnancies and STDs (some of which are curable and some of which are not). At the same time, they are subject to strong biological urges as well as to peer pressure to "be cool." This is a dangerous combination.

Meanwhile, in addition to the details or particulars of an individual's situation, there are social problems to consider. We worry about the rate of teenage pregnancy, about the spread of HIV/AIDS, and about political questions having to do with the separation of church and state, the proper role of public education, and so on. This occurs against a fairly Puritanistic background but at a time when out-of-wedlock births in the United States are at an all-time high (and rising), at a time when unprotected sex can be fatal, and at a time when even nonfatal sexually transmitted diseases are widespread.

Traditionally, education about these matters was supposed to be the province of the home (and perhaps the church or synagogue). But the social and political questions have driven what were once private concerns into the public arena. If education is supposed to prepare young people for life, and life presents sexual dangers that are great—both for the individual and for the community, then, many argue, education should face these dangers and supply young people with the knowledge necessary to come to grips with them. Many can agree with this in the abstract, but once we start to talk about sex education that involves an abstinence-only approach, or instruction in the proper use of condoms, or discussion of the spread of AIDS, people start to disagree. Sometimes the disagreement can be about matters of fact. One could question, for example, just how effective condoms really are in controlling the spread of STDs. One could ask for facts about the spread of HIV/AIDS or about the effectiveness of abstinence-only programs. And some of these disagreements can be settled by data and science. But sooner or later we run into disagreements of value, where there are questions of good or bad, right or wrong—questions that seem to go beyond the scope of science and its (presumably) value-free data. Suppose that the use of condoms could be shown to be 100 percent effective in preventing unwanted pregnancies and 100 percent effective in preventing the spread of STDs, the AIDS virus, etc. That still would not directly refute a person who nevertheless holds that it is sinful or wrong to use condoms. Moreover, we can identify a third kind of disagreement in which the first two are intermingled: here we have *ideological* disagreement.

The authors of the following selections present their cases as grounded in matters of fact, not ideology. Joe S. McIlhaney and James Wagoner both believe that if one pays attention to the facts, then one will be better able to determine the better policy. McIlhaney stresses the dangers inherent in a reliance on condoms. In his view, teaching and promoting sexual abstinence until marriage is the most responsible course of action. Wagoner argues that young people who are going to have sex need to know the facts about contraception and the use of condoms in order to prevent the spread of STDs and the AIDS virus.

Joe S. McIlhaney  **YES**

The Myth of 'Safe Sex' Has Led to an Epidemic of STDs Among Young People

The term "abstinence-only education" is a straw man built by apologists for what may be the greatest public-health failure in our country's history: the so-called "safe-sex" approach to sexually transmitted diseases (STDs). "Abstinence-only" suggests that abstinence-education programs speak only about abstinence and never mention the words "contraception" or "condoms." This is not true. What these programs do is tell young people the full truth, which includes the facts about sexual activity and contraception.

Indeed, it's not an exaggeration to say that abstinence education arms young people with the information they need to make the healthiest decision about their own sexual well-being. On the other side is comprehensive sexuality education, which tells kids that if they are just sure to use a condom, everything will be fine. As we will see, that is far from the truth.

In 1996, I testified before the House Ways and Means subcommittee on Human Resources on the proposed Welfare Reform Act. My message then was that STDs and nonmarital pregnancies were hurting far more people in society than most members of Congress and other Americans realized. To its credit, in an effort constructively and meaningfully to deal with these pregnancy and disease problems, Congress funded abstinence education with $50 million per year for five years through the Title V provision of the Welfare Reform Act. This funding has helped more than 700 abstinence-education programs nationwide devote serious and much-needed attention to these problems.

Today, as Congress works to reauthorize welfare reform, we find ourselves with both good news and bad news. The good news is that there is credible evidence showing that abstinence education is having an impact. More young people are living abstinent lifestyles and fewer teens are getting pregnant. Today, more than half of all high-school students are virgins. Beginning in 1990, the number of teens becoming pregnant began declining. Today the United States has its lowest teen birthrate since the 1950s, and teen-pregnancy rates are lower than they have been at any time since 1976.

Trend data showing declining sexual activity among adolescents and declining teen-pregnancy rates reveal a societal shift in a positive direction. It is reasonable to conclude that one contributing factor is the concomitant increase in abstinence-education programs, though how large of a contributing factor is unknown. Some specific programs, such as the one in Monroe County, N.Y., and the Best Friends program in inner-city Washington, show a very marked decline in pregnancy rates.

But the bad news is that we still have an enormous problem. Sexually transmitted infections are highly prevalent among adolescents. Three million to 4 million STDs are contracted yearly by 15- to 19-year-olds, and another 5 million to 6 million STDs are contracted annually by 20- to 24-year-olds. Approximately 6 percent of adolescent females tested at family planning clinics and 9 percent of female U.S. Army recruits (12.2 percent of 17-year-olds) are infected with chlamydia trachomatis; 5.6 percent of 12- to 19-year-olds and 17 percent of 20- to 29-year-olds are infected with herpes simplex virus type 2 (which causes genital herpes).

And whereas in the 1960s only two STDs were of real concern, we now are aware of more than 25. It is clear that, if and when young people begin sexual activity prior to marriage, they are at very high risk of acquiring an STD.

One's age at the onset of sexual activity is a very strong predictor of the lifetime number of sexual partners. And an individual's risk of contracting an STD is linked strongly to his or her lifetime number of sexual partners. One reason STDs have become so prevalent among young people is that, in spite of the recent trend toward later sexual initiation, we previously had experienced a trend toward earlier sexual initiation.

In addition, a major shift has occurred during the last three decades. The diseases primarily infecting young people no longer are syphilis and gonorrhea, which frequently are symptomatic and treatable with penicillin. Today's young people are infected mainly with viral diseases such as human papillomavirus (HPV), herpes and the unusual bacterium, chlamydia. Viral diseases cannot be cured—only managed.

The STD that has become the most common is HPV. The most recent major study shows that 50 percent of sexually active women between the ages of 18 and 22 are infected with HPV. The National Institutes of Health Workshop on the Scientific Evidence on Condom Effectiveness for STD Prevention reported that there is no evidence that condoms reduce the sexual transmission of HPV. In addition, researchers at Johns Hopkins University in Baltimore, upon completing a study of STD prevalence at an adolescent clinic, found reinfection rates of chlamydia in adolescent girls to be so high that they recommended testing every sexually active adolescent girl in the United States every six months for chlamydia infection (regardless of reported condom use).

Many have suggested that so-called "abstinence plus"—dual-message programs discussing abstinence while also teaching about contraception—is the appropriate answer to the twin epidemics of STDs and out-of-wedlock pregnancies. Yet for many years just such programs have been the predominant approach to sexuality education. And what did we see during these years? A genuine epidemic of STDs is devastating our young people.

There have been many studies of dual-message educational programs. Only a handful of these studies have found any significant impact on any behavioral or health outcome. And most of these have made only "statistically significant" impacts (not practically significant impacts) on behavioral outcomes that may or may not result in reducing STDs or unwanted pregnancies.

Only two of the Centers for Disease Control and Prevention's (CDC's) "Programs That Work" have reported statistically significant delays in the initiation of sexual activity, and only one has reported a truly substantial impact on this outcome. Recently, and to the acclaim of the media, a study reported a reduction in pregnancy rates among participants in a teen-pregnancy-prevention program. The intervention made no impact on rates of sexual activity and did not even measure STD rates. And the impact on teen pregnancy was almost entirely attributable to injectable contraceptive use, which provides no risk reduction for HIV or any other STD. Additionally, this intervention was so expensive per student that it cannot be considered a reasonable option in most settings. Finally, not a single one of the CDC's so-called Programs That Work even has investigated its impact on STD or pregnancy rates!

Additionally, "safer-sex" programs do not even address the problem of out-of-wedlock pregnancy, which is a significant risk factor for poverty, welfare dependence and other social problems. At best, these programs may encourage young people to wait before having sex; there rarely, if ever, is any mention of the importance of actually being abstinent until marriage.

In spite of the recent decline in teen-pregnancy rates, there has been a steady increase in the proportion of births occurring to unmarried teens. Similarly, the proportion of all births occurring out of wedlock has risen dramatically in the last few decades. In 1999, 33 percent of all births in the United States occurred to unmarried women, compared with just 18 percent in 1980. Could this increase be related to the lack of an emphasis on marriage in our classrooms during that period?

Much has been made of the fact that many parents and sexuality-education teachers believe it is necessary to teach kids very directly how to use condoms and contraceptives. Clearly, parents care about their adolescent children and desperately want to protect them from harm.

Unfortunately, far too many parents are inadequately informed about the problems of contraceptive and condom use. How many parents know, for example, that condoms do not appear to reduce the risk of infection with HPV, which is the cause of almost all cervical cancer and most abnormal Pap smears? Do most parents understand that even with 100 percent consistent condom use, their sexually active adolescents are at risk of contracting one of the other prevalent STDs? Do parents understand that for many STDs, if condoms are not used 100 percent of the time it is little or no better than not using a condom at all, ever?

If America's parents knew the facts—and these are scientifically supported facts, not conjecture nor ideology—we are sure they would agree with us: Their children need to hear that the only reliable way to protect themselves from an STD that can have lifelong, physically and emotionally painful ramifications, is to abstain from sexual activity.

With STD prevalence among young people continuing at high levels, condoms clearly are not eliminating the risk of any STD or a continued increase in the proportion of births occurring to unwed mothers. This is abundant evidence that the "safer-sex" paradigm, despite more than 20 years and a variety of education programs designed to promote condom use, has not solved the problem.

Since new research is beginning to suggest that abstinence education can address these problems effectively, it is important that we continue the effort begun in 1996 and allow these programs sufficient time to keep proving their effectiveness. Doing so will ensure that research and evaluation can continue so that we can learn how this option is best delivered, and how abstinence education can best protect young people.

We recognize that we do not yet have sufficient data positively to determine the degree of effectiveness of abstinence education. But results are promising. The national evaluation of abstinence programs by Mathematica will be completed in 2005. If we do not continue with the current level of funding, or if we change the focus of the programs funded under the Welfare Reform Act, we will lose an invaluable opportunity to learn how we effectively can help young people avoid sexual activity—a risk behavior at least as detrimental to their health as the use of alcohol, drugs and tobacco.

This is not about politics or ideology. This is about medicine, science and data. All of which tell us the old approaches aren't working, not when millions of adolescents are contracting STDs. We owe it to our young people fully to explore and evaluate the abstinence-education approach, and that means continuing the effort first funded by Congress in 1996.

James Wagoner

NO

Young People Also Must Know About Contraception to Help Prevent Pregnancies, STDs, and HIV

Each and every day in the United States some 10,000 teens contract a sexually transmitted disease (STD), 2,400 get pregnant and, tragically, 55 contract HIV. The issues surrounding these problems are complex and defy simplistic solutions.

Fortunately, there is a wealth of public-health research on the issue of sex education, and it overwhelmingly points in one direction: Young people need strong messages and information about both abstinence and contraception to safeguard their health and save their lives.

Yet, for the last six years Congress has put ideology before science and politics before public health. In 1996, in a little-noticed provision of the Welfare Reform Act, Congress appropriated $250 million over five years for abstinence-only-until-marriage programs—programs that censor information about contraception and prohibit educators from honestly answering students' questions about contraception and condoms for the prevention of pregnancy, STDs and HIV.

Every year since 2000, Congress has increased funding for these unproven and ineffective programs. In the course of the next few months, Congress will consider reauthorization of the Welfare Reform Act and, with it, Title V, Section 510, which appropriates funds for these misguided abstinence-only programs.

Congress' overly simplistic "just-say-no" approach to teens and sex is unrealistic and dangerous. The facts: The average age of puberty in this country is 12. The average age of marriage is 26. Almost 70 percent of teens have had sex by the time they reach age 18 and 90 percent of Americans report they were not virgins on their wedding night.

Censoring vital information that young people need to protect their health endangers their lives. People younger than age 25 currently account for 50 percent of all new cases of HIV in the United States. Yet, one-third of the secondary schools in the United States limit the sex education available to students to information only about abstinence.

Complicating the issue further is "data" bandied about by organizations that have sprung up around the sex-education debate. Sadly, some of these organizations misrepresent their mission, fabricate data and distort the science to confuse the public. Congress must begin to rely on nationally respected research and science-based organizations that have dedicated themselves for decades to the health and well-being of young people to guide the direction of public-health policy.

The American Medical Association, the American Nurses Association, the American Academy of Pediatrics, the Society for Adolescent Medicine and more than 100 other leading public-health and medical institutions support comprehensive sex education—education that includes information about both abstinence and contraception.

In fact, in September 2000 the Institute of Medicine (IOM), created by Congress to advise the nation on scientific issues, released a report calling on that very body "to eliminate requirements that public funds be used for abstinence-only education." The IOM further recommended "age-appropriate comprehensive sex education and condom-availability programs in schools" to help young people reduce their risk of contracting HIV. Later that same month, the Office of National AIDS Policy released a report concurring. It stated, "it is a matter of grave concern that there is such a large incentive to adopt unproven abstinence-only approaches. Effective programs identified to date provide information about safer sex, condoms and contraception, in addition to encouraging abstinence."

For those concerned that teaching young people about contraception will make them have sex, research again is clear. Numerous studies, including those by the National Campaign to Prevent Teen Pregnancy, the World Health Organization and the IOM, have found that programs that teach about both abstinence *and* contraception do not encourage sexual activity.

Further, the IOM report, *No Time to Lose,* concluded that programs that teach young people about abstinence and contraception demonstrate more success than do abstinence-only programs in delaying sexual activity among youth who have not had sex, and at improving contraceptive use among teens when they do become sexually active.

Those on the other side of this debate—the Heritage Foundation, Focus on the Family and the Medical Institute for Sexual Health, among others—would have us believe otherwise. Yet, no study ever has been published in a peer-reviewed journal demonstrating the effectiveness of the abstinence-only approach.

Instead, the far right touts the "success" of these programs in papers they write and disseminate themselves. For example, in a recent paper targeted at Capitol Hill by the Heritage Foundation, Robert Rector lists "effective" abstinence-only programs. The first among them is a brief description of "virginity pledges"—a program in which young people sign a card pledging to remain "chaste" until marriage. Scientific evaluations of this program do show that the pledge can delay sexual initiation for some young people.

What Rector fails to include in his paper, however, is that the pledge does not work for most young people. In response to the Heritage Foundation's report, Peter Bearman, the researcher who evaluated these pledges, wrote to Rector, "I note that your review of my paper extracts one of the core findings from my research, but not the others." He adds, "The pledge does not work in all contexts. In fact, where more than 30 percent of adolescents in a community have pledged there is no pledge effect." He goes on to say, "those who pledge and break their promise are less likely to contracept at first intercourse. There is no long-term benefit to pledging in terms of pregnancy reduction, unless pledgers use contraception at first intercourse. Therefore it seems obvious to me that all adolescents should learn how to protect themselves. This is a finding you did not report."

While some in Congress seem uncertain about the difference between educating young people about the importance of abstinence and limiting education to abstinence-only, parents are clear. A poll by the National Campaign to Prevent Teen Pregnancy shows that a majority of adults and teens support both greater emphasis on encouraging teens not to have sex and greater emphasis on contraception.

A national poll by the Kaiser Family Foundation further revealed that 85 percent of parents want schools to teach information about condoms, and 90 percent want schools to teach about other forms of birth control. An Advocates for Youth/SEICUS poll conducted by Hickman/Brown Associates further indicates that 70 percent of adults oppose federal funding for abstinence-only education.

The United States continues to have the highest teen-age pregnancy, birth and abortion rates, and one of the highest rates of STDs, in the industrialized world. The United States has nearly 11 times the teen birthrate of the Netherlands, more than 74 times the teen gonorrhea rate of France and nearly eight times the abortion rate of Germany. Why are public-health outcomes for teens so much better in these countries than in America? The answer is that these European countries have pragmatic, research-based policies and an open, honest approach to sex education in the home and at school.

Does all this openness lead to promiscuity? To the contrary, European teens in these countries begin having sex at about the same time or later than American teens. They also have fewer sexual partners and use contraception more consistently than their American peers.

So what exactly should Congress do? Clearly it is time for a change! The American public wants a more comprehensive and realistic approach to adolescent sexual health. Teens say that they need more information about both abstinence and contraception. Research shows that comprehensive sex education—education that includes information about both abstinence and contraception—is the most effective for young people.

Congress must act as the research and the public directs and not stay the course on abstinence-only education. At the very least, Congress should mandate that all sex education be medically accurate.

Congress should amend Title V, Section 510 of the Welfare Reform Act and rescind all federal funds allocated to abstinence-only programs. Finally,

Congress should pass the Family Life Education Act (HR 3469) and appropriate funds for scientifically proved comprehensive sex education.

American teens deserve medically accurate, realistic and honest information about sex. Anything less in the era of HIV/AIDS not only is naïve and misguided, but irresponsible and dangerous.

POSTSCRIPT

Should Congress Stay the Course on Education for Sexual Abstinence Until Marriage?

The issues here are very complex. One has to think about what teenagers themselves want and need, what parents desire for their children, what responsibilities the government has with respect to public education, what are the scientific facts of the situation, and a host of other variables (including what kind of message we are sending). Moreover, part of the "given" in the situation demands that we are cognizant of what people *believe* is true—the truth is irrelevant; what matters is that it drives the peer pressure on teens and other unmarried people. Any policy that public schools adopt must take place in the social world in which myths and peer pressure do have an influence. Saying that the schools must take cognizance of this fact does not mean that they should perpetrate the myths; on the contrary, the schools might have to fight the myths. Likewise for peer pressure: If schools send one message, but peer pressure is running in the opposite direction, the original message may not get through at all.

One ironic aspect of this issue is that parents are supposed to be the source for much important information and value orientations that are transmitted to their children, and yet this whole area, although extremely important, is one that parents and children are often the least comfortable talking about. Young people often get their information—and encouragement to act in potentially life-changing ways—from their friends, the media, etc. If schools are going to take sex education seriously, then it seems that more than scientific knowledge will be needed. There must be awareness not only of the scientific facts but also of the social world in which people live and interact.

The following readings are selected with an eye toward that wide expanse of knowledge and concern. See Kristine M. Napier, *The Power of Abstinence* (Avon Books, 1996); Richard A. Panzer, *Condom Nation: Blind Faith, Bad Science* (Center for Educational Media, 1997); Lisa Marr, *Sexually Transmitted Diseases: A Physician Tells You What You Need to Know* (Johns Hopkins University Press, 1999); Paul Joannides, *The Guide to Getting It On! (The Universe's Coolest and Most Informative Book About Sex)*, 3rd ed. (Goofy Foot Press, 2000); Alexander McKay, *Sexual Ideology and Schooling: Towards Democratic Sexuality Education* (State University of New York Press, 2000); Kristen Anderson, *The Truth About Sex by High School Senior Girls* (Kristen Anderson, 2001); Jesus Cruz et al., *A Hard*

Choice: Sexual Abstinence in an Out-of-Control World (Hensley Publishing, 2002); Meg Meeker, *Epidemic: How Teen Sex Is Killing Our Kids* (Lifeline Press, 2002); David Campos, *Sex, Youth and Sex Education: A Reference Handbook* (ABC-CLIO, 2002); and James W. Button and Barbara Ann Rienzo, *The Politics of Youth, Sex, and Health Care in American Schools* (Haworth Hospitality Press, 2003).

ISSUE 8

Should Human Cloning Be Banned?

YES: George J. Annas, from "Why We Should Ban Human Cloning," *The New England Journal of Medicine* (July 9, 1998)

NO: John A. Robertson, from "Human Cloning and the Challenge of Regulation," *The New England Journal of Medicine* (July 9, 1998)

ISSUE SUMMARY

YES: Law professor George J. Annas argues that human cloning devalues people by depriving them of their uniqueness and that it would radically alter the idea of what it is to be human.

NO: Law professor John A. Robertson maintains that there should not be a complete ban on human cloning but that regulatory policy should be focused on ensuring that it is performed in a responsible manner.

T he issue of human cloning requires careful consideration. Each person is believed to be uniquely valuable. Also, many prefer to differentiate humans from animals. If it is proven that the same technology that allows for the cloning of sheep can also be applied to the cloning of humans, both of these ideas are brought into question. In light of animal cloning, the existence of humans seems to be based on the very same biological processes that exist in sheep and other animals. And if there can be such a thing as human cloning, what happens to the idea that we are all unique? What happens to the idea that we all have our individual lives to lead, and that each person is responsible for his or her own choices?

Moreover, cloning can change ideas about reproduction. In cloning, no male is required. Consider the case of Dolly, the sheep cloned from the cell of an adult ewe. An egg cell, taken from a female sheep, had its nucleus removed; this was replaced with the nucleus of a cell taken from another female sheep. Then the result was implanted and grew in the uterus of a third female sheep, who eventually gave birth to Dolly. Normally, a newborn has genetic input from both the father's side and the mother's side. The original egg cell that was used in Dolly's case contributed almost nothing in this regard. The nucleus from the cell of the second sheep contained virtually all of the genetic input for Dolly.

Identical twins are familiar cases of human beings who, like clones, share a common genetic input. When environmental factors connected with identical twins are closely the same, and when they have similar clothes, haircut, etc., they can be difficult to tell apart. But when the environmental factors that impinge on their lives are quite different—as in the case of twins separated at birth—the twins can be quite different in obvious physical ways.

Physical aspects such as height have both genetic and environmental inputs; two people with the same genes can easily have different heights if environmental conditions (e.g., their diets) are different.

In some ways, clones are like identical twins, but in many cases there would be far less resemblance between clones than between identical twins, since they would be subject to very different environmental factors. Being conceived and born at different times—perhaps years or even decades apart from each other—they may have radically different environmental input.

Human cloning can be seen as beneficial. Cloning may provide another way for people to utilize technological assistance in reproduction. For example, a couple who could not have children naturally might consider a range of options, including cloning. Some maintain that is a relatively innocent use of human cloning, and can benefit those who are infertile.

Some object to cloning by citing other possible scenarios. Suppose a person wanted numerous clones of himself or herself. Suppose a sports star desires a clone who would then be expected to achieve greatness in sports. Suppose parents want a replacement for a child that they had lost, or want a child who could serve as a bone marrow or organ donor. These cases give some pause, since the motivation for cloning appears to be questionable.

To counter this argument, it is stated that proper regulation would prevent these types of scenarios from occurring. Instead, cloning would be performed only under the correct circumstances, and would promote scientific progress.

In the following selections, George J. Annas argues that human cloning radically undermines our beliefs in human uniqueness and self-identity. John A. Robertson counters that human cloning, if properly regulated, should be allowed to occur.

George J. Annas

Why We Should Ban Human Cloning

In February [1998] the U.S. Senate voted 54 to 42 against bringing an anticloning bill directly to the floor for a vote.[1] During the debate, more than 16 scientific and medical organizations, including the American Society of Reproductive Medicine and the Federation of American Societies for Experimental Biology, and 27 Nobel prize–winning scientists, agreed that there should be a moratorium on the creation of a human being by somatic nuclear transplants. What the groups objected to was legislation that went beyond this prohibition to include cloning human cells, genes, and tissues. An alternative proposal was introduced by Senator Edward M. Kennedy (D-Mass.) and Senator Dianne Feinstein (D-Calif.) and modeled on a 1997 proposal by President Bill Clinton and his National Bioethics Advisory Commission. It would, in line with the views of all of these scientific groups, outlaw attempts to produce a child but permit all other forms of cloning research.[2,3] Because the issue is intimately involved with research with embryos and abortion politics, in many ways the congressional debates over human cloning are a replay of past debates on fetal-tissue transplants[4] and research using human embryos.[5] Nonetheless, the virtually unanimous scientific consensus on the advisability of a legislative ban or voluntary moratorium on the attempt to create a human child by cloning justifies deeper discussion of the issue than it has received so far.

It has been more than a year since embryologist Ian Wilmut and his colleagues announced to the world that they had cloned a sheep.[6] No one has yet duplicated their work, raising serious questions about whether Dolly the sheep was cloned from a stem cell or a fetal cell, rather than a fully differentiated cell.[7] For my purpose, the success or failure of Wilmut's experiment is not the issue. Public attention to somatic-cell nuclear cloning presents an opportunity to consider the broader issues of public regulation of human research and the meaning of human reproduction.

Cloning and Imagination

In the 1970s, human cloning was a centerpiece issue in bioethical debates in the United States.[8,9] In 1978, a House committee held a hearing on human cloning in response to the publication of David Rorvik's *In His Image: The Cloning of a*

Man.[10] All the scientists who testified assured the committee that the supposed account of the cloning of a human being was fictional and that the techniques described in the book could not work. The chief point the scientists wanted to make, however, was that they did not want any laws enacted that might affect their research. In the words of one, "there is no need for any form of regulation, and it could only in the long run have a harmful effect."[11] The book was an elaborate fable, but it presented a valuable opportunity to discuss the ethical implications of cloning. The failure to see it as a fable was a failure of imagination. We normally do not look to novels for scientific knowledge, but they provide more: insights into life itself.[12]

This failure of imagination has been witnessed repeatedly, most recently in 1997, when President Clinton asked the National Bioethics Advisory Commission to make recommendations about human cloning. Although acknowledging in their report that human cloning has always seemed the stuff of science fiction rather than science, the group did not commission any background papers on how fiction informs the debate. Even a cursory reading of books like Aldous Huxley's *Brave New World,* Ira Levin's *The Boys from Brazil,* and Fay Weldon's *The Cloning of Joanna May,* for example, would have saved much time and needless debate. Literary treatments of cloning inform us that cloning is an evolutionary dead end that can only replicate what already exists but cannot improve it; that exact replication of a human is not possible; that cloning is not inherently about infertile couples or twins, but about a technique that can produce an indefinite number of genetic duplicates; that clones must be accorded the same human rights as persons that we grant any other human; and that personal identity, human dignity, and parental responsibility are at the core of the debate about human cloning.

We might also have gained a better appreciation of our responsibilities to our children had we examined fiction more closely. The reporter who described Wilmut as "Dolly's laboratory father,"[13] for example, probably could not have done a better job of conjuring up images of Mary Shelley's *Frankenstein* if he had tried. Frankenstein was also his creature's father and god; the creature told him, "I ought to be thy Adam." As in the case of Dolly, the "spark of life" was infused into the creature by an electric current. Shelley's great novel explores virtually all the noncommercial elements of today's debate.

The naming of the world's first cloned mammal also has great significance. The sole survivor of 277 cloned embryos (or "fused couplets"), the clone could have been named after its sequence in this group (for example, C-137), but this would only have emphasized its character as a laboratory product. In stark contrast, the name Dolly (provided for the public and not used in the scientific report in *Nature,* in which she is identified as 6LL3) suggests a unique individual. Victor Frankenstein, of course, never named his creature, thereby repudiating any parental responsibility. The creature himself evolved into a monster when he was rejected not only by Frankenstein, but by society as well. Naming the world's first mammal clone Dolly was meant to distance her from the Frankenstein myth both by making her something she is not (a doll) and by accepting "parental" responsibility for her.

Unlike Shelley's world, the future envisioned in Huxley's *Brave New World,* in which all humans are created by cloning through embryo splitting and conditioned to join a specified worker group, was always unlikely. There are much more efficient ways of creating killers or terrorists (or even soldiers and workers) than through cloning. Physical and psychological conditioning can turn teenagers into terrorists in a matter of months, so there is no need to wait 18 to 20 years for the clones to grow up and be trained themselves. Cloning has no real military or paramilitary uses. Even clones of Adolf Hitler would have been very different people because they would have grown up in a radically altered world environment.

Cloning and Reproduction

Even though virtually all scientists oppose it, a minority of free-marketers and bioethicists have suggested that there might nonetheless be some good reasons to clone a human. But virtually all these suggestions themselves expose the central problem of cloning: the devaluing of persons by depriving them of their uniqueness. One common example suggested is cloning a dying or recently deceased child if this is what the grieving parents want. A fictional cover story in the March 1998 issue of *Wired,* for example, tells the story of the world's first clone.[14] She is cloned from the DNA of a dead two-week-old infant, who died from a mitochondrial defect that is later "cured" by cloning with an enucleated donor egg. The closer one gets to the embryo stage, the more cloning a child looks like the much less problematic method of cloning by "twinning" or embryo splitting. And proponents of cloning tend to want to "naturalize" and "normalize" asexual replication by arguing that it is just like having "natural" twins.

Embryo splitting might be justified if only a few embryos could be produced by an infertile couple and all were implanted at the same time (since this does not involve replicating an existing and known genome). But scenarios of cloning by nuclear transfer have involved older children, and the only reason to clone an existing human is to create a genetic replica. Using the bodies of children to replicate them encourages all of us to devalue children and treat them as interchangeable commodities. For example, thanks to cloning, the death of a child need no longer be a singular human tragedy but, rather, can be an opportunity to try to replicate the no longer priceless (or irreplaceable) dead child. No one should have such dominion over a child (even a dead or dying child) as to use his or her genes to create the child's child.

Cloning would also radically alter what it means to be human by replicating a living or dead human being asexually to produce a person with a single genetic parent. The danger is that through human cloning we will lose something vital to our humanity, the uniqueness (and therefore the value and dignity) of every human. Cloning represents the height of genetic reductionism and genetic determinism.

Population geneticist R.C. Lewontin has challenged my position that the first human clone would also be the first human with a single genetic parent by arguing that, instead, "a child by cloning has a full set of chromosomes like anyone else, half of which were derived from a mother and half from a father. It happens that these chromosomes were passed through another individual, the cloning donor, on the way to the child. That donor is certainly not the child's 'parent' in any biological sense, but simply an earlier offspring of the original parents."[15] Lewontin takes genetic reductionism to perhaps its logical extreme. People become no more than containers of their parents' genes, and their parents have the right to treat them not as individual human beings, but rather as human embryos—entities that can be split and replicated at their whim without any consideration of the child's choice or welfare. Children (even adult children), according to Lewontin's view, have no say in whether they are replicated or not, because it is their parents, not they, who are reproducing. This radical redefinition of reproduction and parenthood, and the denial of the choice to procreate or not, turns out to be an even stronger argument against cloning children than its biologic novelty. Of course, we could require the consent of adults to be cloned—but why should we, if they are not becoming parents?

Related human rights and human dignity would also prohibit using cloned children as organ sources for their father or mother original. Nor is there any constitutional right to be cloned in the United States that is triggered by marriage to someone with whom an adult cannot reproduce sexually, because there is no tradition of asexual replication and because permitting asexual replication is not necessary to safeguard any existing concept of ordered liberty (rights fundamental to ordered liberty are the rights the Supreme Court sees as essential to individual liberty in our society).

Although it is possible to imagine some scenarios in which cloning could be used for the treatment of infertility, the use of cloning simply provides parents another choice for choice's sake, not out of necessity. Moreover, in a fundamental sense, cloning cannot be a treatment for infertility. This replication technique changes the very concept of infertility itself, since all humans have somatic cells that could be used for asexual replication and therefore no one would be unable to replicate himself or herself asexually. In vitro fertilization, on the other hand, simply provides a technological way for otherwise infertile humans to reproduce sexually.

John Robertson argues that adults have a right to procreate in any way they can, and that the interests of the children cannot be taken into account because the resulting children cannot be harmed (since without cloning the children would not exist at all).[16] But this argument amounts to a tautology. It applies equally to everyone alive; none of us would exist had it not been for the precise and unpredictable time when the father's sperm and the mother's egg met. This biologic fact, however, does not justify a conclusion that our parents had no obligations to us as their future children. If it did, it would be equally acceptable, from the child's perspective, to be gestated in a great ape, or even a cow, or to be composed of a mixture of ape genes and human genes.

The primary reason for banning the cloning of living or dead humans was articulated by the philosopher Hans Jonas in the early 1970s. He correctly noted that it does not matter that creating an exact duplicate of an existing person is impossible. What matters is that the person is chosen to be cloned because of some characteristic or characteristics he or she possesses (which, it is hoped, would also be possessed by the genetic copy or clone). Jonas argued that cloning is always a crime against the clone, the crime of depriving the clone of his or her "existential right to certain subjective terms of being"—particularly, the "right to ignorance" of facts about his or her origin that are likely to be "paralyzing for the spontaneity of becoming himself" or herself.[17] This advance knowledge of what another has or has not accomplished with the clone's genome destroys the clone's "condition for authentic growth" in seeking to answer the fundamental question of all beings, "Who am I?" Jonas continues: "The ethical command here entering the enlarged stage of our powers is: never to violate the right to that ignorance which is a condition of authentic action; or: to respect the right of each human life to find its own way and be a surprise to itself."[17]

Jonas is correct. His rationale, of course, applies only to a "delayed genetic twin" or "serial twin" created from an existing human, not to genetically identical twins born at the same time, including those created by cloning with use of embryo splitting. Even if one does not agree with him, however, it is hypocritical to argue that a cloning technique that limits the liberty and choices of the resulting child or children can be justified on the grounds that cloning expands the liberty and choices of would-be cloners.[18]

Moratoriums and Bans on Human Cloning

Members of the National Bioethics Advisory Commission could not agree on much, but they did conclude that any current attempt to clone a human being should be prohibited by basic ethical principles that ban putting human subjects at substantial risk without their informed consent. But danger itself will not prevent scientists and physicians from performing first-of-their-kind experiments— from implanting a baboon's heart in a human baby to using a permanent artificial heart in an adult—and cloning techniques may be both safer and more efficient in the future. We must identify a mechanism that can both prevent premature experimentation and permit reasonable experimentation when the facts change.

The mechanism I favor is a broad-based regulatory agency to oversee human experimentation in the areas of genetic engineering, research with human embryos, xenografts, artificial organs, and other potentially dangerous boundary-crossing experiments.[19] Any such national regulatory agency must be composed almost exclusively of nonresearchers and nonphysicians so it can reflect public values, not parochial concerns. Currently, the operative American ethic seems to be that if any possible case can be imagined in which a new technology might be useful, it should not be prohibited, no matter what harm might result. One of the most important procedural steps Congress should take in setting up a federal agency to regulate human experimentation would be to put the burden of proof on those who propose to undertake novel experiments (including cloning) that risk harm and call deeply held social values into question.

This shift in the burden of proof is critical if society is to have an influence over science.[20] Without it, social control is not possible. This model applies the precautionary principle of international environmental law to cloning and other potentially harmful biomedical experiments involving humans. The principle requires governments to protect the public health and the environment from realistic threats of irreversible harm or catastrophic consequences even in the absence of clear evidence of harm.[21] Under this principle, proponents of human cloning would have the burden of proving that there was some compelling contravailing need to benefit either current or future generations before such an experiment was permitted (for example, if the entire species were to become sterile). Thus, regulators would not have the burden of proving that there was some compelling reason not to approve it. This regulatory scheme would depend on at least a de facto, if not a de jure, ban or moratorium on such experiments and a mechanism such as my proposed regulatory agency that could lift the ban. The suggestion that the Food and Drug Administration (FDA) can substitute for such an agency is fanciful. The FDA has no jurisdiction over either the practice of medicine or human replication and is far too narrowly constituted to represent the public in this area. Some see human cloning as inevitable and uncontrollable.[22,23] Control will be difficult, and it will ultimately require close international cooperation. But this is no reason not to try—any more than a recognition that controlling terrorism or biologic weapons is difficult and uncertain justifies making no attempt at control.

On the recommendation of the National Bioethics Advisory Commission, the White House sent proposed anti-cloning legislation to Congress in June 1997. The Clinton proposal receded into obscurity until early 1998, when a Chicago physicist, Richard Seed, made national news by announcing that he intended to raise funds to clone a human. Because Seed acted like a prototypical "mad scientist," his proposal was greeted with almost universal condemnation.[24] Like the 1978 Rorvik hoax, however, it provided another opportunity for public discussion of cloning and prompted a more refined version of the Clinton proposal: the Feinstein–Kennedy bill. We can (and should) take advantage of this opportunity to distinguish the cloning of cells and tissues from the cloning of human beings by somatic nuclear transplantation[25] and to permit the former while prohibiting the latter. We should also take the opportunity to fill in the regulatory lacuna that permits any individual scientist to act first and consider the human consequences later, and we should use the controversy over cloning as an opportunity to begin an international dialogue on human experimentation.

References

1. U.S. Senate. 144 Cong. Rec. S561–S580, S607–S608 (1998).
2. S. 1611 (Feinstein–Kennedy Prohibition on Cloning of Human Beings Act of 1998).
3. Cloning human beings: report and recommendations of the National Bioethics Advisory Commission. Rockville, Md.: National Bioethics Advisory Commission, June 1997.
4. Annas GJ, Elias S. The politics of transplantation of human fetal tissue. N Engl J Med 1989;320:1079–82.
5. Annas GJ, Caplan A, Elias S. The politics of human embryo research—avoiding ethical gridlock. N Engl J Med 1996;334:1329–32.

6. Wilmut I, Schnieke AE, McWhir J, Kind AJ, Campbell KH. Viable offspring derived from fetal and adult mammalian cells. Nature 1997;385:810–3.
7. Butler D. Dolly researcher plans further experiments after challenges. Nature 1998;391:825–6.
8. Lederberg J. Experimental genetics and human evolution. Am Naturalist 1966;100:519–31.
9. Watson JD. Moving toward the clonal man. Atlantic Monthly. May 1971:50–3.
10. Rorvik DM. In his image: the cloning of a man. Philadelphia: J.B. Lippincott, 1978.
11. Development in cell biology and genetics, cloning. Hearings before the Subcommittee on Health and the Environment of the Committee on Interstate and Foreign Commerce of the U.S. House of Representatives, 95th Congress, 2d Session, May 31, 1978.
12. Chomsky N. Language and problems of knowledge: the Managua lectures. Cambridge, Mass.: MIT Press, 1988.
13. Montalbano W. Cloned sheep is star, but not sole project, at institute. Los Angeles Times. February 25, 1997:A7.
14. Kadrey R. Carbon copy: meet the first human clone. Wired. March 1998:146–50.
15. Lewontin RC. Confusion over cloning. New York Review of Books. October 23, 1997:20–3.
16. Robertson JA. Children of choice: freedom and the new reproductive technologies. Princeton, N.J.: Princeton University Press, 1994:169.
17. Jonas H. Philosophical essays: From ancient creed to technological man. Englewood Cliffs, N.J.: Prentice-Hall, 1974:162–3.
18. Annas GJ. Some choice: law, medicine and the market. New York: Oxford University Press, 1998:14–5.
19. Annas GJ. Regulatory models for human embryo cloning: the free market, professional guidelines, and government restrictions. Kennedy Inst Ethics J 1994;4:235–49.
20. Hearings before the U.S. Senate Subcommittee on Public Health and Safety, 105th Congress, 1st Session, March 12, 1997. (Or see: http://www.busph.bu.edu/depts/lw/clonetest.htm.)
21. Cross FB. Paradoxical perils of the precautionary principle. Washington Lee Law Rev 1996;53:851–925.
22. Kolata GB. Clone: the road to Dolly, and the path ahead. New York: W. Morrow, 1998.
23. Silver LM. Remaking Eden: cloning and beyond in a brave new world. New York: Avon Books, 1997.
24. Knox RA. A Chicagoan plans to offer cloning of humans. Boston Globe. January 7, 1998:A3.
25. Kassirer JP, Rosenthal NA. Should human cloning research be off limits? N Engl J Med 1998;338:905–6.

NO

John A. Robertson

Human Cloning and the
Challenge of Regulation

The birth of Dolly, the sheep cloned from a mammary cell of an adult ewe, has initiated a public debate about human cloning. Although cloning of humans may never be clinically feasible, discussion of the ethical, legal, and social issues raised is important. Cloning is just one of several techniques potentially available to select, control, or alter the genome of offspring.[1-3] The development of such technology poses an important social challenge: how to ensure that the technology is used to enhance, rather than limit, individual freedom and welfare.

A key ethical question is whether a responsible couple, interested in rearing healthy offspring biologically related to them, might ethically choose to use cloning (or other genetic-selection techniques) for that purpose. The answer should take into account the benefits sought through the use of the techniques and any potential harm to offspring or to other interests.

The most likely uses of cloning would be far removed from the bizarre or horrific scenarios that initially dominated media coverage.[4] Theoretically, cloning would enable rich or powerful persons to clone themselves several times over, and commercial entrepreneurs might hire women to bear clones of sports or entertainment celebrities to be sold to others to rear. But current reproductive techniques can also be abused, and existing laws against selling children would apply to those created by cloning.

There is no reason to think that the ability to clone humans will cause many people to turn to cloning when other methods of reproduction would enable them to have healthy children. Cloning a human being by somatic-cell nuclear transfer, for example, would require a consenting person as a source of DNA, eggs to be enucleated and then fused with the DNA, a woman who would carry and deliver the child, and a person or couple to raise the child. Given this reality, cloning is most likely to be sought by couples who, because of infertility, a high risk of severe genetic disease, or other factors, cannot or do not wish to conceive a child.

Several plausible scenarios can be imagined. Rather than use sperm, egg, or embryo from anonymous donors, couples who are infertile as a result of

From John A. Robertson, "Human Cloning and the Challenge of Regulation," *The New England Journal of Medicine,* vol. 339, no. 2 (July 9, 1998), pp. 119–122. Copyright © 1998 by The Massachusetts Medical Society. Reprinted by permission.

gametic insufficiency might choose to clone one of the partners. If the husband were the source of the DNA and the wife provided the egg that received the nuclear transfer and then gestated the fetus, they would have a child biologically related to each of them and would not need to rely on anonymous gamete or embryo donation. Of course, many infertile couples might still prefer gamete or embryo donation or adoption. But there is nothing inherently wrong in wishing to be biologically related to one's children, even when this goal cannot be achieved through sexual reproduction.

A second plausible application would be for a couple at high risk of having offspring with a genetic disease.[5] Couples in this situation must now choose whether to risk the birth of an affected child, to undergo prenatal or preimplantation diagnosis and abortion or the discarding of embryos, to accept gamete donation, to seek adoption, or to remain childless. If cloning were available, however, some couples, in line with prevailing concepts of kinship, family, and parenting, might strongly prefer to clone one of themselves or another family member. Alternatively, if they already had a healthy child, they might choose to use cloning to create a later-born twin of that child. In the more distant future, it is even possible that the child whose DNA was replicated would not have been born healthy but would have been made healthy by gene therapy after birth.

A third application relates to obtaining tissue or organs for transplantation. A child who needed an organ or tissue transplant might lack a medically suitable donor. Couples in this situation have sometimes conceived a child coitally in the hope that he or she would have the correct tissue type to serve, for example, as a bone marrow donor for an older sibling.[6,7] If the child's disease was not genetic, a couple might prefer to clone the affected child to be sure that the tissue would match.

It might eventually be possible to procure suitable tissue or organs by cloning the source DNA only to the point at which stem cells or other material might be obtained for transplantation, thus avoiding the need to bring a child into the world for the sake of obtaining tissue.[8] Cloning a person's cells up to the embryo stage might provide a source of stem cells or tissue for the person cloned. Cloning might also be used to enable a couple to clone a dead or dying child so as to have that child live on in some closely related form, to obtain sufficient numbers of embryos for transfer and pregnancy, or to eliminate mitochondrial disease.[5]

Most, if not all, of the potential uses of cloning are controversial, usually because of the explicit copying of the genome. As the National Bioethics Advisory Commission noted, in addition to concern about physical safety and eugenics, somatic-cell cloning raises issues of the individuality, autonomy, objectification, and kinship of the resulting children.[5] In other instances, such as the production of embryos to serve as tissue banks, the ethical issue is the sacrifice of embryos created solely for that purpose.

Given the wide leeway now granted couples to use assisted reproduction and prenatal genetic selection in forming families, cloning should not be rejected in all circumstances as unethical or illegitimate. The manipulation of embryos and the use of gamete donors and surrogates are increasingly common. Most fetuses conceived in the United States and Western Europe are now screened for genetic or chromosomal anomalies. Before conception, screening to identify carriers of genetic diseases is widespread.[9] Such practices also deviate from conventional notions of reproduction, kinship, and medical treatment of infertility, yet they are widely accepted.

Despite the similarity of cloning to current practices, however, the dissimilarities should not be overlooked. The aim of most other forms of assisted reproduction is the birth of a child who is a descendant of at least one member of the couple, not an identical twin. Most genetic selection acts negatively to identify and screen out unwanted traits such as genetic disease, not positively to choose or replicate the genome as in somatic-cell cloning.[3] It is not clear, however, why a child's relation to his or her rearing parents must always be that of sexually reproduced descendant when such a relationship is not possible because of infertility or other factors. Indeed, in gamete donation and adoption, although sexual reproduction is involved, a full descendant relation between the child and both rearing parents is lacking. Nor should the difference between negative and positive means of selecting children determine the ethical or social acceptability of cloning or other techniques. In both situations, a deliberate choice is made so that a child is born with one genome rather than another or is not born at all.

Is cloning sufficiently similar to current assisted-reproduction and genetic-selection practices to be treated similarly as a presumptively protected exercise of family or reproductive liberty?[10] Couples who request cloning in the situations I have described are seeking to rear healthy children with whom they will have a genetic or biologic tie, just as couples who conceive their children sexually do. Whether described as "replication" or as "reproduction," the resort to cloning is similar enough in purpose and effects to other reproduction and genetic-selection practices that it should be treated similarly. Therefore, a couple should be free to choose cloning unless there are compelling reasons for thinking that this would create harm that the other procedures would not cause.[10]

The concern of the National Bioethics Advisory Commission about the welfare of the clone reflects two types of fear. The first is that a child with the same nuclear DNA as another person, who is thus that person's later-born identical twin, will be so severely harmed by the identity of nuclear DNA between them that it is morally preferable, if not obligatory, that the child not be born at all.[5] In this case the fear is that the later-born twin will lack individuality or the freedom to create his or her own identity because of confusion or expectations caused by having the same DNA as another person.[5,11]

This claim does not withstand the close scrutiny that should precede interference with a couple's freedom to bear and rear biologically related children.[10] Having the same genome as another person is not in itself harmful, as widespread experience with monozygotic twins shows. Being a twin does not deny either twin his or her individuality or freedom, and twins often have a special intimacy or closeness that few non-twin siblings can experience.[12] There is no reason to think that being a later-born identical twin resulting from cloning would change the overall assessment of being a twin.

Differences in mitochondria and the uterine and childhood environment will undercut problems of similarity and minimize the risk of overidentification with the first twin. A clone of Smith may look like Smith, but he or she will not be Smith and will lack many of Smith's phenotypic characteristics. The effects of having similar DNA will also depend on the length of time before the second twin is born, on whether the twins are raised together, on whether they are informed that they are genetic twins, on whether other people are so informed, on the beliefs that the rearing parents have about genetic influence on behavior, and on other factors. Having a previously born twin might in some circumstances also prove to be a source of support or intimacy for the later-born child.

The risk that parents or the child will overly identify the child with the DNA source also seems surmountable. Would the child invariably be expected to match the phenotypic characteristics of the DNA source, thus denying the second twin an "open future" and the freedom to develop his or her own identity?[5,11,13] In response to this question, one must ask whether couples who choose to clone offspring are more likely to want a child who is a mere replica of the DNA source or a child who is unique and valued for more than his or her genes. Couples may use cloning in order to ensure that the biologic child they rear is healthy, to maintain a family connection in the face of gametic infertility, or to obtain matched tissue for transplantation and yet still be responsibly committed to the welfare of their child, including his or her separate identity and interests and right to develop as he or she chooses.

The second type of fear is that parents who choose their child's genome through somatic-cell cloning will view the child as a commodity or an object to serve their own ends.[5] We do not view children born through coital or assisted reproduction as "mere means" just because people reproduce in order to have company in old age, to fulfill what they see as God's will, to prove their virility, to have heirs, to save a relationship, or to serve other selfish purposes.[14] What counts is how a child is treated after birth. Self-interested motives for having children do not prevent parents from loving children for themselves once they are born.

The use of cloning to form families in the situations I have described, though closely related to current assisted-reproduction and genetic-selection practices, does offer unique variations. The novelty of the relation—cloning in lieu of sperm donation, for example, produces a later-born identical twin raised by the older twin and his spouse—will create special psychological and social challenges. Can these challenges be successfully met, so that cloning produces net good for families and society? Given the largely positive experience with assisted-reproduction techniques that initially appeared frightening, cautious optimism is justified. We should be able to develop procedures and guidelines for cloning that will allow us to obtain its benefits while minimizing its problems and dangers.

In the light of these considerations, I would argue that a ban on privately funded cloning research is unjustified and likely to hamper important types of research.[8] A permanent ban on the cloning of human beings, as advocated by the Council of Europe and proposed in Congress, is also unjustified.[15,16] A more limited ban—whether for 5 years, as proposed by the National Bioethics Advisory Commission and enacted in California, or for 10 years, as in the bill of Senator Dianne Feinstein (D-Calif.) and Senator Edward M. Kennedy (D-Mass.) that is now before Congress—is also open to question.[5,17,18] Given the early state of cloning science and the widely shared view that the transfer of cloned embryos to the uterus before the safety and efficacy of the procedure has been established is unethical, few responsible physicians are likely to offer human cloning in the near future.[5] Nor are profit-motivated entrepreneurs, such as Richard Seed, likely to have many customers for their cloning services until the safety of the procedure is demonstrated.[19] A ban on human cloning for a limited period would thus serve largely symbolic purposes. Symbolic legislation, however, often has substantial costs.[20,21] A government-imposed prohibition on privately funded cloning, even for a limited period, should not be enacted unless there is a compelling need. Such a need has not been demonstrated.

Rather than seek to prohibit all uses of human cloning, we should focus our attention on ensuring that cloning is done well. No physician or couple should embark on cloning without careful thought about the novel relational issues and child-rearing responsibilities that will ensue. We need regulations or guidelines to ensure safety and efficacy, fully informed consent and counseling for the couple, the consent of any person who may provide DNA, guarantees of parental rights and duties, and a limit on the number of clones from any single source.[10] It may also be important to restrict cloning to situations where there is a strong likelihood that the couple or individual initiating the procedure will also rear the resulting child. This principle will encourage a stable parenting situation and minimize the chance that cloning entrepreneurs will create clones to be sold to others.[22] As our experience grows, some restrictions on who may serve as a source of DNA for cloning (for example, a ban on cloning one's parents) may also be defensible.[10]

Cloning is important because it is the first of several positive means of genetic selection that may be sought by families seeking to have and rear healthy, biologically related offspring. In the future, mitochondrial transplantation, germ-line gene therapy, genetic enhancement, and other forms of prenatal genetic alteration may be possible.[3,23,24] With each new technique, as with cloning, the key question will be whether it serves important health, reproductive, or family needs and whether its benefits outweigh any likely harm. Cloning illustrates the principle that when legitimate uses of a technique are likely, regulatory policy should avoid prohibition and focus on ensuring that the technique is used responsibly for the good of those directly involved. As genetic knowledge continues to grow, the challenge of regulation will occupy us for some time to come.

References

1. Silver LM. Remaking Eden: cloning and beyond in a brave new world. New York: Avon Books, 1997.
2. Walters L, Palmer JG. The ethics of human gene therapy. New York: Oxford University Press, 1997.
3. Robertson JA. Genetic selection of offspring characteristics. Boston Univ Law Rev 1996;76:421–82.
4. Begley S. Can we clone humans? Newsweek. March 10, 1997:53–60.

5. Cloning human beings: report and recommendations of the National Bioethics Advisory Commission. Rockville, Md.: National Bioethics Advisory Commission, June 1997.

6. Robertson JA. Children of choice: freedom and the new reproductive technologies. Princeton, N.J.: Princeton University Press, 1994.

7. Kearney W, Caplan AL. Parity for the donation of bone marrow: ethical and policy considerations. In: Blank RH, Bonnicksen AL, eds. Emerging issues in biomedical policy: an annual review. Vol. 1. New York: Columbia University Press, 1992:262–85.

8. Kassirer JP, Rosenthal NA. Should human cloning research be off limits? N Engl J Med 1998;338:905–6.

9. Holtzman NA. Proceed with caution: predicting genetic risks in the recombinant DNA era. Baltimore: Johns Hopkins University Press, 1989.

10. Robertson JA. Liberty, identity, and human cloning. Texas Law Rev 1998;77:1371–456.

11. Davis DS. What's wrong with cloning? Jurimetrics 1997;38:83–9.

12. Segal NL. Behavioral aspects of intergenerational human cloning: what twins tell us. Jurimetrics 1997;38:57–68.

13. Jonas H. Philosophical essays: from ancient creed to technological man. Englewood Cliffs, N.J.: Prentice-Hall, 1974:161.

14. Heyd D. Genethics: moral issues in the creation of people. Berkeley: University of California Press, 1992.

15. Council of Europe. Draft additional protocol to the Convention on Human Rights and Biomedicine on the prohibition of cloning human beings with explanatory report and Parliamentary Assembly opinion (adopted September 22, 1997). XXXVI International Legal Materials 1415 (1997).

16. Human Cloning Prohibition Act, H.R. 923, S.1601 (March 5, 1997).

17. Act of Oct. 4, 1997, ch. 688, 1997 Cal. Legis. Serv. 3790 (West, WESTLAW through 1997 Sess.).

18. Prohibition on Cloning of Human Beings Act, S. 1602, 105th Cong. (1998).

19. Stolberg SG. A small spark ignites debate on laws on cloning humans. New York Times. January 19, 1998:A1.

20. Gusfield J. Symbolic crusade: status politics and the American temperance movement. Urbana: University of Illinois Press, 1963.

21. Wolf SM. Ban cloning? Why NBAC is wrong. Hastings Cent Rep 1997;27(5):12.

22. Wilson JQ. The paradox of cloning. The Weekly Standard. May 26, 1997:23–7.

23. Zhang J, Grifo J, Blaszczyk A, et al. In vitro maturation of human preovulatory oocytes reconstructed by germinal vesicle transfer. Fertil Steril 1997;68: Suppl:S1. abstract.

24. Bonnicksen AL. Transplanting nuclei between human eggs: implications for germ-line genetics. Politics and the Life Sciences. March 1998:3–10.

POSTSCRIPT

Should Human Cloning Be Banned?

The social and legal debates about cloning are appropriate because the technology is so fundamentally groundbreaking. Note that, as much as Annas and Robertson disagree in the preceding readings, neither would think it advisable for human cloning to proceed in a totally unregulated way.

One problem that might seem small at first but is quite serious is that we do not have a good way of assimilating the new ideas of cloning into our vocabulary and thought. For example, we think of a baby as having both a father and a mother. But a clone would be made from a single person. The clone and the single original person would both have the same set of genes. This set of genes comes from the parents of the original person, who are also the parents, as viewed from a biological standpoint, of the clone. So, this creates a situation in which people can have children when they are very old or even after death. Moreover, if the original person and the clone share genes, then they seem like identical twins. But they could be of vastly different ages; in fact, one of the "twins" could be an adoptive parent of the other.

Some say that the fact that cloning doesn't fit into our normal system for making sense of family relationships is due to the fact that cloning upsets the system in a fundamental way. This view holds that human cloning causes people to be viewed as objects instead of being viewed as unique individuals. But others will say that the fact that our traditional vocabulary is inadequate to the situation only shows that we are unprepared for this new situation, not that human cloning should be totally banned.

For the original bioethics report discussed by both Annas and Robertson, see *Cloning Human Beings: Report and Recommendations of the National Bioethics Advisory Commission* (Gem Publications, 1998). A variety of views about cloning can be found in Gregory E. Pence, *Who's Afraid of Human Cloning?* (Rowman & Littlefield, 1998); Glenn McGee, ed., *The Human Cloning Debate* (Berkeley Hills Books, 1998); James C. Hefley and Lane P. Lester, *Human Cloning: Playing God or Scientific Progress?* (Fleming H. Revell, 1998); Gregory E. Pence, ed., *Flesh of My Flesh: The Ethics of Cloning Humans: A Reader* (Rowman & Littlefield, 1998); Martha Nussbaum and Cass R. Sunstein eds., *Clones and Clones: Facts and Fantasies About Human Cloning* (W. W. Norton, 1998); M. L. Rantala and Arthur J. Milgram, eds., *Cloning: For and Against* (Open Court, 1999); Lori B. Andrews, *The Clone Age: Adventures in the New World of Reproductive Technology* (Henry Holt, 1999); Michael C. Brannigan, ed., *Ethical Issues in Human Cloning: Cross-Disciplinary Perspectives* (Seven Bridges Press, 2000); and Leon R. Kass, *Human Cloning and Human Dignity: The Report of the President's Council on Bioethics* (Public Affairs, 2002).

On the Internet . . .

DRCNet Online Library of Drug Policy

The Drug Reform Coordination Network (DRCN) sponsors this site of links to drug policy organizations and studies.

http://druglibrary.org

Punishment and the Death Penalty

This *Ethics Updates* site contains discussion forums, court decisions, statistical resources, and Internet resources on capital punishment.

http://ethics.acusd.edu/Applied/deathpenalty/

Euthanasia and End-of-Life Decisions

This *Ethics Updates* site contains discussion questions, court decisions, statistical resources, and Internet resources on euthanasia.

http://ethics.acusd.edu/Applied/Euthanasia/

PART 3

Law and Society

*I*t is part of the social nature of human beings that we live in groups. And this requires that we have laws or rules that govern our behavior and interpersonal interactions. Morality and shared values can be positive tools for social living. One presupposition in a democratic society is that social differences must be settled by open discussion, argument, and persuasion—not by force. The issues in this section include some of those that have strongly divided our own society and some that challenge existing social institutions and practices.

- Should the Government Support Faith-Based Charities?

- Should There Be Payment for Body Parts?

- Should Drugs Be Legalized?

- Is It Morally Permissible to Eat Meat?

- Is Affirmative Action Fair?

- Should the Supreme Court Prohibit Racial Preferences in College Admissions?

- Are African Americans Owed Reparations for Slavery?

- Should Hate-Crime Laws Explicitly Protect Sexual Orientation?

- Should Handguns Be Banned?

- Should the Death Penalty Be Retained?

- Should Physician-Assisted Suicide Be Legalized by the States?

ISSUE 9

Should the Government Support Faith-Based Charities?

YES: Ronald J. Sider and Heidi Rolland Unruh, from "'No Aid to Religion?' Charitable Choice and the First Amendment," in E. J. Dionne, Jr., and John J. DiIulio, Jr., eds., *What's God Got to Do With the American Experiment?* (Brookings Institution Press, 2000)

NO: Melissa Rogers, from "The Wrong Way to Do Right: A Challenge to Charitable Choice," in E. J. Dionne, Jr., and John J. DiIulio, Jr., eds., *What's God Got to Do With the American Experiment?* (Brookings Institution Press, 2000)

ISSUE SUMMARY

YES: Ronald J. Sider, president of Evangelicals for Social Action, and Heidi Rolland Unruh, project analyst for Evangelicals for Social Action, argue that the First Amendment, which prohibits the establishment of religion, should not stand in the way of the equal treatment of all religious sects. In particular, religious charities that refrain from proselytizing should be included among those charities that receive government assistance.

NO: Melissa Rogers, general counsel at the Baptist Joint Committee on Public Affairs, contends that entanglements between government and religious entities are dangerous and should not be encouraged. Government support of faith-based charities, in her opinion, will bring government oversight and regulation to the religious entity and will open the door to numerous abuses.

All sides can agree that there are social ills that need to be addressed, e.g., problems of homelessness, poverty, drug dependence, etc. Faith-based organizations stand ready to address these matters. So, the question naturally arises as to why they should or should not address them.

One immediate concern is the First Amendment—the first part of the Bill of Rights, which reads:

Congress shall make no law respecting an establishment of religion, or prohibiting the free exercise thereof; or abridging the freedom of speech, or of the press; or the right of the people peaceably to assemble, and to petition the government for a redress of grievances.

The first part—about the establishment of religion—has always been rather strongly construed as the government should not sponsor or provide money for religious activities. America's founding fathers were well aware of the religious strife, and even religious warfare, that had plagued Europe in the time before the Constitution of the United States was drawn up. And they were clearly focused on setting up a new nation that would avoid many of the problems—religious intolerance among them—that had caused social divisiveness and trouble. The second part of the First Amendment says that Congress shall not prohibit the free exercise of religion. So the idea was not to jettison religion completely—on the grounds that it led to intolerance and war—but to jettison the intolerance, so that there could be freedom of religion. In order to guarantee this freedom, Thomas Jefferson said that there should be a "wall of separation" between church and state.

The formation of the United States and the drawing up of the Constitution were great opportunities to put some of the troublesome aspects of European history behind and start over with a clean slate. Whereas European countries had had state religions and numerous traditions (for example, hereditary privileges) that had developed over time, the United States specifically ruled out the idea of a state religion (and hereditary privileges).

Today, many Americans fall into the Bible-believing category—but others are Buddhists, Moslems, atheists, Hindus, etc. Many Americans are inspired by their religious faith to practice charity. Most would agree that the charitable programs of faith-based organizations are major forces of social good in the United States.

But what about the idea of the government funding faith-based organizations? On the one hand, faith-based charities are doing good, addressing problems (such as homelessness, poverty, and drug dependence), problems with which the government is concerned. So it seems natural to many that the government should fund these organizations. But, on the other hand, it can be argued that because they are *faith*-based, the wall of separation between church and state is violated. It is not clear that the *material* aspects of what faith-based organizations are doing can be definitively separated from the *spiritual* aspects.

In the following selections, Ronald J. Sider and Heidi Rolland Unruh argue in support of government funding of faith-based charities. It is important that the state should not favor one religion over another nor hand people over to faith-based charities that will then proceed to recruit the individuals. Melissa Rogers argues against government involvement with faith-based organizations and warns of the dangers that such involvement could foster.

Ronald J. Sider and
Heidi Rolland Unruh

 **YES**

"No Aid to Religion?"
Charitable Choice and
the First Amendment

As government struggles to solve a confounding array of poverty-related social problems—deficient education, un- and underemployment, substance
abuse, broken families, substandard housing, violent crime, inadequate health
care, crumbling urban infrastructures—it has turned increasingly to the private
sector, including a wide range of faith-based agencies. As described in Stephen
Monsma's *When Sacred and Secular Mix,* public funding for nonprofit organizations with a religious affiliation is surprisingly high. Of the faith-based child
service agencies Monsma surveyed, 63 percent reported that more than 20 percent of their budget came from public funds.

Government's unusual openness to cooperation with the private religious
sector arises in part from public disenchantment with its programs but also
from an increasingly widespread view that the nation's acute social problems
have moral and spiritual roots. Acknowledging that social problems arise both
from unjust socioeconomic structures and from misguided personal choices,
scholars, journalists, politicians, and community activists are calling attention
to the vital and unique role that religious institutions play in social restoration.

Though analysis of the outcomes of faith-based social services is at yet
incomplete, the available evidence suggests that some of those services may
be more effective and cost-efficient than similar secular and government
programs. One oft-cited example is Teen Challenge, the world's largest residen-
tial drug rehabilitation program, with a documented rehabilitation rate of
86 percent—a vastly higher success rate than most other programs, at a substantially lower cost. Multiple studies identify religion as a key variable in reducing
health risk factors, keeping marriages together, and escaping the downward
spiral of gangs, drugs, and prison that overwhelms many young, urban African-
American males.

"'No Aid to Religion?' Charitable Choice and the First Amendment," in E. J. Dionne, Jr., and John J.
DiIulio, Jr., eds., *What's God Got to Do With the American Experiment?* (Brookings Institution Press,
2000). Copyright © 2000 by The Brookings Institution. Reprinted by permission. Notes omitted.

The New Cooperation and the Courts

The potential of public-private cooperative efforts involving religious agencies has been constrained by traditional First Amendment interpretation. The ruling interpretive principle on public funding of religious nonprofits—following the metaphor of the wall of separation between church and state, as set forth in *Everson v. Board of Education* (1947)—has been "no aid to religion." While most court cases have involved funding for religious elementary and secondary schools, clear implications have been drawn for other types of "pervasively sectarian" organizations. A religiously affiliated institution may receive public funds—but only if it is not too religious.

Application of the no-aid policy by the courts, however, has been confusing. The Supreme Court has provided no single, decisive definition of "pervasively sectarian" to determine which institutions qualify for public funding, and judicial tests have been applied inconsistently. Rulings attempting to separate the sacred and secular aspects of religiously based programs often appear arbitrary from a faith perspective and at worst border on impermissible entanglement. As a result of this legal confusion, some agencies receiving public funds pray openly with their clients, while other agencies have been banned even from displaying religious symbols. Faith-based child welfare agencies have greater freedom in incorporating religious components than religious schools working with the same population. Only a few publicly funded religious agencies have been challenged in the courts, but such leniency may not continue. The lack of legal recourse leaves agencies vulnerable to pressures from public officials and community leaders to secularize their programs.

The Supreme Court's restrictive rulings on aid to religious agencies stand in tension with the government's movement toward greater reliance on private sector social initiatives. If the no-aid principle were applied consistently against all religious agencies now receiving public funding—such as churches with government-funded food programs or day care agencies—government provision of social services would face significant setbacks. This ambiguous state of affairs for public-private cooperation has created a climate of mistrust and misunderstanding, in which faith-based agencies are reluctant to expose themselves to risk of lawsuits, civic authorities are confused about what is permissible, and multiple pressures push religious organizations into hiding or compromising their identity, while at the same time many public officials and legislators are willing to look the other way when effective faith-based social service programs include religious content.

Fortunately, an alternative principle of First Amendment interpretation, which Monsma identifies as the "equal treatment" strain, has been emerging in the Supreme Court. This line of reasoning—as in *Widmar v. Vincent* (1981) and *Rosenberg v. Rector* (1995)—holds that public access to facilities or benefits cannot exclude religious groups. Although the principle has not yet been applied to funding for social service agencies, it could be a precedent for defending cooperation between government and faith-based agencies where the offer of funding is available to any qualifying agency.

The section of the 1996 welfare reform law known as Charitable Choice paves the way for this cooperation by prohibiting government from discriminating against nonprofit applicants for certain types of social service funding (whether by grant, contract, or voucher) on the basis of their religious nature. Charitable Choice also shields faith-based agencies receiving federal funding from governmental pressures to alter their religious character—among other things, ensuring their freedom to display religious symbols and to hire staff who share their religious perspective. Charitable Choice prohibits religious nonprofits from using government funds for "inherently religious" activities defined as "sectarian worship, instruction, or proselytization"—but allows them to raise money from nongovernment sources to cover the costs of any such activities they choose to integrate into their program. Clearly, Charitable Choice departs from the dominant "pervasively sectarian" standard for determining eligibility for government funding, which has restricted the funding of thoroughly religious organizations. It makes religiosity irrelevant to the selection of agencies for public-private cooperative ventures and emphasizes instead the public goods to be achieved by cooperation. At the same time, Charitable Choice protects clients' First Amendment rights by ensuring that services are not conditional on religious preference, that client participation in religious activities is voluntary, and that an alternative nonreligious service provider is available.

The First Amendment and the Case for Charitable Choice

Does Charitable Choice violate the First Amendment's nonestablishment and free exercise clauses? We think not. As long as participants in faith-based programs freely choose those programs over a "secular" provider and may opt out of particular religious activities within the program, no one is coerced to participate in religious activity, and freedom of religion is preserved. As long as government is equally open to funding programs rooted in any religious perspective—whether Islam, Christianity, philosophic naturalism, or no explicit faith perspective—government is not establishing or providing preferential benefits to any specific religion or to religion in general. As long as religious institutions maintain autonomy over such crucial areas as program content and staffing, the integrity of their identity and mission is maintained. As long as agencies are required to account for grant and contract funds in accordance with the ban on expenditures for inherently religious activities, no taxpayer need fear that taxes are paying for religion. While Charitable Choice may increase interactions between government and religious institutions, these interactions do not in themselves violate the First Amendment. Charitable Choice is designed precisely to discourage such interactions from leading to impermissible entanglement or establishment of religion.

Not only does Charitable Choice not violate proper church-state relations, it strengthens First Amendment protections. In the current context of extensive government funding for a wide array of social services, limiting government funds to allegedly "secular" programs actually offers preferential treatment to one specific religious worldview.

In setting forth this argument, we distinguish four types of social service providers. First are secular providers who make no explicit reference to God or any ultimate values. People of faith may work in such an agency—say, a job training program that teaches job skills and work habits—but staff use only current techniques from the social and medical sciences without reference to religious faith. Expressing explicit faith commitments of any sort is considered inappropriate.

Second are religiously affiliated providers (of any religion) who incorporate little inherently religious programming and rely primarily on the same medical and social science methods as a secular agency. Such a program may be historically rooted in a faith community; a staff with strong theological reasons for their involvement; religious symbols may be present. A religiously affiliated job training program might be housed in a church, and clients might be informed about the church's religious programs and about the availability of a chaplain's services. But the content of the training curriculum would be very similar to that of a secular program.

Third are exclusively faith-based providers whose programs rely on inherently religious activities, making little or no use of techniques from the medical and social sciences. An example would be a prayer support group and seminar on biblical principles of work for job seekers.

Fourth are holistic faith-based providers who combine techniques from the medical and social sciences with inherently religious components such as prayer, worship, and the study of sacred texts. A holistic job training program might incorporate explicitly biblical principles into a curriculum that teaches job skills and work habits and invite clients to pray with program staff.

Everyone agrees that public funding of only the last two types of providers would constitute government establishment of religion. But if government (because of the "no aid to religion" principle) funds only secular programs, is this a properly neutral policy?

Not really, for two reasons. First, given the widespread public funding for private social services, if government funds only secular programs, it puts all faith-based programs at a disadvantage. Government would tax everyone—both religious and secular—and then fund only allegedly secular programs. Government-run or government-funded programs would be competing in the same fields with faith-based programs lacking access to such support.

Second, secular programs are not religiously neutral. Implicitly, purely "secular" programs convey the message that nonreligious technical knowledge and skills are sufficient to address social problems such as low job skills and single parenthood. Implicitly, they teach the irrelevance of a spiritual dimension to human life. Although secular programs may not explicitly uphold the tenets of philosophical naturalism and the belief that nothing exists except the natural order, implicitly they support such a worldview. Rather than being religiously neutral, "secular" programs implicitly convey a set of naturalistic beliefs about the nature of persons and ultimate reality that serve the same function as religion. Vast public funding of only secular programs means government bias in favor of one particular quasi-religious perspective, namely, philosophical naturalism.

The fact that religiously affiliated agencies (type two) have received large amounts of funding in spite of the "no aid to religion" principle poses another problem. These agencies often claim a clear religious identity—in the agency's history or name, in the religious identity and motivations of sponsors and some staff, in the provision of a chaplain, or in visible religious symbols. By choice or in response to external pressures, however, little in their program content and methods distinguishes many of these agencies from their fully secular counterparts. Prayer, spiritual counseling, Bible studies, and invitations to join a faith community are not featured; in fact, most such agencies would consider inherently religious activities inappropriate to social service programs.

Millions of public dollars have gone to support the social service programs of religiously affiliated agencies. There are three possible ways to understand this apparent potential conflict with the "no aid to religion" principle. Perhaps these agencies are finally only nominally religious, and in fact are essentially secular institutions, in which case their religious sponsors should be raising questions. Or perhaps they are more pervasively religious than they have appeared to government funders, in which case the government should have withheld funding.

The third explanation may be that these agencies are operating with a specific, widely accepted worldview that holds that people may need God for their spiritual well-being, but that their social problems can be addressed exclusively through medical and social science methods. Spiritual nurture, in this worldview, is important in its place but has no direct bearing on achieving public goods like drug rehabilitation or overcoming welfare dependency. Such a worldview acknowledges the spiritual dimension of persons and the existence of a transcendent realm outside of nature. But it also teaches (whether explicitly or implicitly) a particular understanding of God and persons, by addressing people's social needs independently of their spiritual nature. By allowing aid to flow only to the religiously affiliated agencies holding this understanding, government in effect has given preferential treatment to a particular religious worldview.

Holistic faith-based agencies (type four), however, operate on the belief that no area of a person's life, whether psychological, physical, social, or economic, can be adequately addressed in isolation from the spiritual. Agencies operating out of this worldview consider the explicitly spiritual components of their programs—used in conjunction with conventional, secular social service methods—as fundamental to their ability to achieve the secular social goals desired by government. Government has in the past considered such agencies ineligible for public funding, though they may provide the same services as their religiously affiliated counterparts.

Some claim that channeling public funds through a holistic religious program threatens the First Amendment, while funding religiously affiliated agencies does not. To the contrary, the pervasively sectarian standard has also constituted a genuine, though more subtle, establishment of religion, because it supports one type of religious worldview while penalizing holistic beliefs. It should not be the place of government to judge between religious worldviews, but this is what the no-aid principle has required the courts to do. Selective religious perspectives on the administration of social services are deemed permissible for government to aid. Those who believe that explicitly religious content does not play a central role in addressing social problems are free to act on this belief with government support; those who believe that spiritual nurture is an integral aspect of social transformation are not.

The alternative is to pursue a policy that discriminates neither against nor in favor of any religious perspective. Charitable Choice enables the government to offer equal access to benefits to any faith-based nonprofit, as long as the money is not used for inherently religious activities and the agency provides the social benefits desired by government. Charitable Choice does not ask governmental bodies to decide which agencies are too religious. It clearly indicates the types of "inherently religious" activities that are off limits for government funding. The government must continue to make choices about which faith-based agencies will receive funds, but eligibility for funding is to be based on an agency's ability to provide specific public goods, rather than on its religious character. Charitable Choice moves the focus of church-state interactions away from the religious beliefs and practices of social service agencies and onto the common goals of helping the poor and strengthening the fabric of public life.

A Model for Change

Our treasured heritage of religious freedom demands caution as we contemplate new forms of church-state cooperation, but caution does not preclude change if the benefits promise to outweigh the dangers. Indeed, change is required if the pervasively sectarian standard is actually biased in favor of some religious perspectives and against others.

For church and state to cooperate successfully, both must remain true to their roles and mission. Religious organizations must refrain from accepting public funds if that means compromising their beliefs and undermining their effectiveness and integrity. Fortunately, Charitable Choice allows faith-based agencies to maintain their religious identity while expanding the possibilities for constructive cooperation between church and state in addressing the nation's most serious social problems.

NO

The Wrong Way to Do Right: A Challenge to Charitable Choice

The 2000 presidential election has reinvigorated a very old debate—what is required of a nation for religious freedom to prosper? Presidential candidates Governor George W. Bush and Vice President Al Gore are encouraging new partnerships between faith-based organizations and the government to solve pressing social problems. Without question, their goals are laudable—religion should play a greater role in improving the lives of the less fortunate. But their proposals would needlessly sacrifice a measure of religious freedom.

Both candidates' proposals arise from the "charitable choice" provision first made law as part of the massive overhaul of the welfare system in 1996. That provision popularized the term "faith-based organization" and proposed a dramatic revision of the law of church and state.

Before 1996, instead of being known as faith-based organizations, religious organizations generally were known by one of two labels drawn from court decisions. A religiously affiliated entity is a group that has ties to religion but is set up to perform secular social services. These groups, such as Catholic Charities and Lutheran Services in America, have long received public funding. A "pervasively sectarian" organization, on the other hand, is a term the Supreme Court has used to refer to "an institution in which religion is so pervasive that a substantial portion of its functions are subsumed in a religious mission." Pervasively religious groups would include, for example, houses of worship or a drug rehabilitation ministry that relies on acceptance of the gospel in its treatment program. While the Supreme Court has ruled that religiously affiliated entities may receive tax funds, the Court generally has barred the flow of tax funds to pervasively religious organizations.

Why has the Supreme Court traditionally refused to permit tax funds to flow to pervasively religious organizations like churches? Because religion pervades these entities, public funding for any part of them becomes unconstitutionally advancing religion itself. In a 1988 case the Court specifically warned against allowing tax funds to flow to pervasively religious social service organizations. Justice Rehnquist, writing for the Court, observed, "There is a risk that direct government funding, even if it is designated for specific secular purposes, may nonetheless advance the pervasively sectarian institution's 'religions mission.'" The Court also has noted that, to the extent the government attempts to separate sacred from secular in an entity like a church, it risks becoming excessively entangled with religion, which also violates the Constitution.

Charitable choice, however, attempts to obliterate any legal distinction between religiously affiliated and pervasively religious organizations, allowing both to receive tax funds. As governor, George W. Bush signed an executive order urging state agencies to use the charitable choice provision of the welfare reform law. Bush commented that "for too long government has excluded churches and synagogues from the delivery of welfare." In his presidential campaign, Bush has called for "making 'charitable choice' explicitly applicable to all federal laws that authorize the government to use non-governmental entities to provide services to beneficiaries with federal dollars," and has pledged to remove all barriers to the use of federal funds by faith-based groups. Vice President Gore has also explicitly embraced the charitable choice concept and called for its extension.

The presidential candidates' endorsements of these schemes, however, don't make them constitutional or advisable. By allowing tax funds to flow to churches and other pervasively religious entities, charitable choice allows the state to advance religion and risks excessive church-state entanglement. And, contrary to the claims of charitable choice proponents, recent Supreme Court rulings allowing some discrete, government-provided educational aids for students at public, private, and parochial schools don't come close to constitutionalizing these schemes. Further, charitable choice creates other clear risks for religion and religious liberty.

Two things are often lacking in the debate on this issue. One is an examination of the dangers these new partnerships create for churches and other pervasively religious groups. The other is consideration of some alternatives for boosting religion's role in the delivery of social services. Charitable choice is neither the best nor the only way for religious organizations to serve the less fortunate.

One immutable consequence of receiving tax funds is that regulation goes along with it. The government will regulate tax-subsidized social service providers, even if they are houses of worship. Some regulation is specified in the charitable choice provision itself. For example, the charitable choice provision requires providers (including churches and other religious missions) to submit to an audit. Charitable choice providers also must refrain from using contract money for "sectarian worship, instruction or proselytization." Vice President Gore has articulated what appears to be a similar "safeguard," insisting that the government "must continue to prohibit direct proselytizing as part of any publicly funded efforts."

Proponents of these schemes have not begun to explain how such safeguards would be implemented. How will the government define "direct proselytizing," much less ensure that a church isn't using public money to do it? Adequate enforcement of this safeguard in a church or like institution will put it on a collision course with the constitutional prohibition against excessive church-state entanglements. On the other side of the coin, how will the government fund programs that are successful precisely because of their religious content without resulting in unconstitutional state support for religion itself?

The regulation specified in charitable choice, however, is clearly the floor rather than the ceiling of relevant regulation for tax-funded religious ministries. Other regulation generally follows tax money. Even though religious ministries will likely agree with the goals of these laws, proving compliance with it by filing annual compliance reports, waiving rights of confidentiality, and submitting to governmental investigations may take a large toll on religious autonomy. And one news report of fraud by some rogue group, claiming to be a church, will lead to tighter restrictions.

Proponents of tax-subsidized church ministries correctly point out that they have taken steps to try to preserve religious organizations' independence. Vice President Gore insists that faith-based organizations can perform their social service "*with* public funds—and without having to alter the religious character that is so often the key to their effectiveness." The charitable choice provision states that the religious organizations that receive tax funds will nevertheless retain "control over the definition, development, practice and expression of its religious beliefs." Governor Bush promises that he will go even farther to try to free tax-subsidized, faith-based organizations from regulation.

Religious ministries, however, have reason to be wary. It is far from clear that the protections for religious social service providers that are part of charitable choice will withstand judicial scrutiny or be interpreted in ways that won't diminish religious autonomy. Indeed, a charitable choice proponent, Representative Nancy Johnson (R-Conn.), recently admitted: "Yes, there will be red tape. Churches who choose to receive Federal money will be regulated. If they do not like it, I cannot help it. If there are Federal dollars, you are accountable."

And, of course, litigation often follows regulation. There are likely to be multiple legal challenges based on the applicable regulation as well as the constitutionality of various aspects of the law. In 1989, for example, one court refused to allow the Salvation Army to fire an employee who was a Wiccan because the employee's salary was paid substantially with tax money. And a lawsuit has recently been filed against a tax-subsidized Baptist children's home because it fired an employee when it learned she was a lesbian. How will these cases square with the charitable choice provision that attempts to allow tax-subsidized religious providers to discriminate on the basis of religion in hiring? Time-consuming litigation will tell.

Another danger of tax-funded religious ministries is the prospect that churches and other religious ministries could come to be viewed as administrative centers of government benefits and services. This could require houses of worship to terminate certain benefits, report on individuals, and otherwise police the system. Nothing could be farther from the church's historic identity as sanctuary. Moreover, other core elements of government programs may directly conflict with religious doctrine. The new welfare law's heavy emphasis on personal responsibility rather than communal sharing of burdens is contrary to some biblical precepts. And some religious persons may be torn between their own religious-based conviction that mothers of young children should stay at home and the welfare law's insistence that welfare mothers enter the job force.

Participation in these new partnerships also will diminish religion's prophetic witness, which sometimes includes the obligation to criticize those in power. It should come as no surprise when recipients of government subsidies are hesitant to criticize those who are paying the bills.

These new partnerships further threaten to drag religion into the political process of governmental appropriations. If lawmaking is like sausage-making, then the appropriations process is akin to the production of the cheapest, most questionable sausage in town. Religion enters this political fray at its peril. There is simply not enough tax money to fund every religious group in this country. Thus, the government will have to pick and choose when it awards grants and contracts. Elected officials will find it almost impossible to resist playing politics with religion. Houses of worship may compete against one another for government contracts, and, all too often, only majority faiths will prevail. While the government cannot heal all of the religious divisions in our country, it should not be in the business of driving us farther apart. As our founders recognized, passing out government tax money to churches will do just that.

Other serious implementation problems remain. How do we ensure, for example, that welfare beneficiaries will truly have the ability to reject religious options, especially when the charitable choice provision of the welfare reform law does not even require that beneficiaries be given notice that they have the right to a secular alternative? Churches should be concerned not only about their own autonomy but also about religious freedom and justice for all.

Can religious organizations simply refuse government funding if it begins to harm their ministries? Theoretically, yes. But once the new building is constructed and the program is expanded, it will be difficult to wean oneself from tax funding. Moreover, the risk of tax-subsidized church ministries isn't limited to the individual recipient of the funds. Allowing tax funds to flow to houses of worship creates a dangerous, far-reaching precedent. It flies in the face of our nation's historic recognition that religion is different and must be treated differently in many circumstances. Religion is subject to special limitations at times (for example, pervasively religious institutions like churches may not receive tax funding), and at times religion enjoys special accommodations from the government (for example, religious organizations may discriminate on the basis of religion in hiring). These principles are the yin and yang of religious freedom, ensuring a healthy separation of the institutions of church and state, which affords each maximum freedom to pursue its distinct agenda.

Upsetting this balance will have serious consequences. Asking the government to treat churches the same as everything else in the area of tax-funded social services (to fund houses of worship like everything else) will come back to haunt us in other areas. Ultimately, it will undercut a wide range of protections for religion from government.

For all these reasons, we should be extremely careful about financial partnerships between the government and religious organizations. Instead of racing to tack charitable choice to every stream of federal and state social service funding, legislators should study how charitable choice is being implemented already. Instead of assuming that religion and religious liberty will be strengthened by providing tax subsidies to houses of worship and other pervasively religious groups, legislators ought to call hearings to explore the profound constitutional dangers and policy concerns raised by charitable choice. And, instead of allowing charitable choice to monopolize the discussion regarding church-state cooperation in the provision of social services, legislators and policy makers ought to explore the many other ways in which religious institutions and government may cooperate. While charitable choice is the wrong way to do right, there are many right ways for church and state to do right together.

Of course, the government should maintain a strong safety net for those in need—in today's society, religious and other private organizations cannot be expected to shoulder this burden alone. But church and state may work cooperatively in several ways.

First, legislatures should pass bills that provide enhanced tax incentives for charitable giving. This money could then be directed by individual taxpayers to the charities (including houses of worship) of their choice with no regulatory strings attached. Congress is currently considering the Charitable Giving Tax Relief Act (H.R. 1310), which would increase charitable giving by approximately $3 billion a year by allowing nonitemizers to deduct 50 percent of their charitable contributions over $500 annually. The Clinton administration and Governor Bush have endorsed this concept. Additional private funding for the programs of houses of worship may come from denominational appeals, charitable foundation grants, or even corporate sponsorships. Vice President Gore's idea of encouraging corporate matching funds for employees' gifts to religious organizations also is a laudable one.

Second, houses of worship and governmental officials should share information about needs and programs. Many houses of worship are uniquely situated to understand the community around them and to serve as incubators and motivators for an array of helpful social service projects. We can and should capitalize on these strengths without setting up new pipelines between federal and state treasuries and church coffers. The government may publicize the good work that private religious and other social service groups are doing and make referrals to these groups when appropriate.

Third, churches may choose to play a cooperative role with the state in certain volunteer programs. Along with other community groups, for example, religious institutions may participate in government-organized, volunteer mentoring projects as long as the government does not promote religion.

Fourth, houses of worship and other pervasively religious entities that haven't already done so should consider spinning off separate affiliates that are not thoroughly religious. Tax funding for these religiously affiliated entities is uncontroversial from a constitutional standpoint. Organizations that enter into these arrangements should realize that they will have to play by the rules that apply to other tax-funded social service providers. They should use tax money for secular services, not for religious activities. Catholic Charities and Lutheran Services in America have been doing this work for years.

These are just a few of the ways in which church and state may cooperate without creating funding ties that bind.

In his speech on the role of faith-based organizations, Vice President Gore caricatured the tensions underlying this issue. He said that "national leaders have been trapped in a dead-end debate" between "false choices: hollow secularism or right-wing religion."

This rhetoric buys into an old saw that is widespread, convenient, and dead wrong. "Hollow secularists" aren't the only ones concerned about scrupulously maintaining the boundaries between the institutions of church and state. Many people of faith urge enforcement of these boundaries precisely because they value religion and religious freedom so much.

Respecting these boundaries does not mean that religion and politics don't mix. It does not mean church and state can't cooperate. It does not require reflexive resistance to new ideas on the church-state landscape. But respecting church-state boundaries does require resisting proposals that seriously and unnecessarily threaten the foundations of religious liberty in this country.

Our country is the most religiously vibrant in the world. This is no accident. Unlike so many other nations, religion in America relies on voluntary gifts, rather than compulsory tax funds. Unlike religion abroad, religion in this country is largely free from government direction and regulation. Charitable choice would undercut these foundations, causing religious freedom to suffer.

We must fight hopelessness and poverty. We can and should do so without sacrificing religious liberty.

POSTSCRIPT

Should the Government Support Faith-Based Charities?

The authors of the selections on faith-based charities do not take issue with the idea that faith-based charities have done a lot of good. That much is admitted by both sides. The focus of the contention is on whether the government should fund the groups. Two lines of criticism of this idea have been raised, one primarily secular, and one primarily religious. Both lines of criticism tend to be wary of the use of government funds by religious groups, but the secular line is concerned about what this means for government and the religious line is concerned about what this means for religion.

Many consider that even if it is admitted that the groups are doing a lot of good, they are also spreading their faith and preaching their word since that is part of what faith-based groups do. In fact, in some particular cases it seems very difficult or impossible to separate out the purely secular from the purely religious aspects of the work of faith-based charities. (For example, suppose a church group helps poor people get employment so that they can take care of themselves and get their lives back on track. Does "taking care of themselves" involve taking care of both material and spiritual matters? Does part of "getting back on track" involve increased religious faith?) Secular critics are worried that the government will end up supporting particular religious ideas, which, if the "wall of separation" is to be maintained, it should not do.

Even if the purely secular aspects can be separated out from the religious aspects, there remains the other line of criticism from the religious point of view. This line of criticism is concerned about what the impact might be for religious groups if the government puts more money into faith-based charities. The good that the faith-based groups have done has been work that the groups have done on their own. But to get the government involved necessarily entails complications. There will be some amount of government control, for example. And if funding for the work of the groups comes from taxes, the funds will be required of all of us, since we must all pay taxes. But, in the absence of government support, the funds are voluntarily given and individuals will be free to give money or not. Also, the groups can proceed to use the money as they see fit. Part of the original value of what the groups do, some assert, is that they operate on a voluntary basis. But if tax money is involved, the voluntary aspect is lost.

What is more important, that the work of faith-based charities is funded or how this work is funded? Do the benefits achieved from faith-based charities outweigh the risks associated with government funding? Some argue that it is the end result that matters most.

ISSUE 10

Should There Be Payment for Body Parts?

YES: Michael B. Gill and Robert M. Sade, from "Paying for Kidneys: The Case Against Prohibition," *Kennedy Institute of Ethics Journal* (March 2002)

NO: David J. Rothman, from "The International Organ Traffic," *The New York Review of Books* (March 26, 1998)

ISSUE SUMMARY

YES: Assistant professor Michael B. Gill and professor of surgery Robert M. Sade maintain that healthy people should be allowed to sell one of their kidneys while they are still alive. They contend that it is not intrinsically wrong for a healthy person to sell a kidney, nor does selling body parts have the potential to exploit the poor.

NO: Professor of history David J. Rothman counters that payment for organs exploits the poor and benefits the wealthy. He asserts that it is doubtful that the sellers of the organs give their informed consent. Therefore, argues Rothman, body parts are turned into mere commodities, and this is degrading to people.

To properly understand this issue, there are some important facts to consider. First, the supply of organs—particularly kidneys, on which Michael B. Gill and Robert M. Sade focus in their selection—is vastly lower than the demand. This is so not only in the United States but on a worldwide basis. In America, people who need and want a new kidney have to be put on a waiting list. In the meantime, they may be able to use a dialysis machine. This is a noncurative procedure, which must be performed on a regular basis—sometimes three times a week for several hours. Unless people who need new kidneys receive them, the dialysis machine must become a regular part of their lives—forever. Secondly, when an organ such as a kidney is transplanted into someone selected for transplantation, numerous parties receive compensation for the services they render. Thousands of dollars are paid to physicians and hospitals and the nonprofit organizations that procure the organs, for example. But many argue that donors must be *donors*: they must *give* the organ and must not receive compensation of any kind (except perhaps a small amount for their time or for their own expenses). Finally, Gill and Sade concentrate their discussion on receiving payment for *kidneys* only. They argue that human beings normally have two kidneys but can easily live with one, as long as it is a functioning kidney.

Many think that there is something wrong, perhaps something distasteful, with buying or selling an organ. By contrast, *donating* an organ is often regarded as an extremely worthy—even heroic—act. Moreover, since 1984 and the passage of the National Organ Transplantation Act, it has been a federal offense to buy or sell organs. Moreover, to *receive* an organ through transplantation is thought to be extremely beneficial, not distasteful or shameful at all. So there is a bit of irony in this situation. A donor can give a kidney to a recipient, and both of them will be thought well of, but we tend to look askance at a situation in which money changes hands.

And yet, from one point of view it seems only fair for the person who gives up a kidney to be compensated for doing so. Everyone else involved in the transplant situation seems to have benefited or has been compensated. Apparently, the donor is supposed to be motivated by pure altruism and not at all by money. This works well when the donor and the recipient are close relations. It is not infrequent for transplantations to occur between family members. (What parent would not give a kidney to a son or daughter who desperately needed one?) But there remains the problem of the general societal lack of organs for transplantation.

In the following selections, Gill and Sade argue that payment should be made for kidneys. They do not mean that people could bypass the waiting list and simply buy a kidney if they needed one or that wealthy buyers could rise to the top of the list by outbidding poorer buyers. Gill and Sade limit their argument to the view that payment should be made to the person whose kidney is used. On the other side, David J. Rothman argues against all forms of buying and selling organs or even using "free" ones from executed prisoners. He raises the question of whether or not poor people or condemned prisoners can really grant free consent, a condition that most would agree should be required for organ donation.

Michael B. Gill and Robert M. Sade

Paying for Kidneys:
The Case Against Prohibition

Our society places a high priority on value pluralism and individual autonomy. With few constraints, people make personal decisions regarding what they wish to buy and sell based on their own values. There are laws prohibiting certain kinds of trade; these laws are generally aimed at preventing commercial interactions that are associated with serious harms. Payment to living organ donors has been perceived to be just such a harmful transaction.

The Uniform Anatomical Gift Act (UAGA), originally approved by the National Conference of Commissioners on Uniform State Laws in 1968, was intended to permit individuals to specify their desire to donate organs at the time of their deaths (Uniform Anatomical Gift Act, *Uniform Laws Annotated* 8, 1972). Although the framers of the proposed act considered the possibility that a market for organs could develop, they did not conclude that buying and selling organs was intrinsically wrong. The UAGA was, in fact, silent on the question of payment for organs. Yet, today, every major organization that has an official position on the matter maintains that payment for organs is unequivocally unethical and must be legally prohibited. Why did this shift occur?

In the early 1980s, transplantation was expanding rapidly due to the introduction of improved immunosuppressive drugs. The need for a national system of organ procurement and allocation was identified and codified in the National Organ Transplantation Act (NOTA) of 1984 (Public Law No. 98–507, amended by Public Law No. 100–607 and Public Law No. 101–616). At the same time, organ brokerage began to develop (U.S. Congress 1984, pp. 238–56). A strongly adverse public reaction to this development led to the inclusion in NOTA of a prohibition against the provision of any "valuable consideration" in exchange for a transplantable organ. Thus, all forms of payment for organs were made illegal, based on the ethical judgment that the harms of allowing payment substantially outweighed the benefits (Childress 1996).

We believe that possible harms arising from allowing payment for organs have been overstated, and that healthy people should be allowed to sell one of their kidneys while they are alive—that kidney sales by living people ought to be legal. In what follows, we will present the case for the legalization of live kidney

From Michael B. Gill and Robert M. Sade, "Paying for Kidneys: The Case Against Prohibition," *Kennedy Institute of Ethics Journal*, vol. 12, no. 1 (March 2002), pp. 17–34, 39. Copyright © 2002 by The Johns Hopkins University Press. Reprinted by permission. Notes and references omitted.

sales and answer objections to it. We confine our discussion to kidneys because the kidney is a paired organ that can be removed safely with little impact on the health of the donor. Kidney transplantation, moreover, is by far the most common of all transplants, and the discrepancy between kidney supply and need is the greatest. (Our argument does, however, bear on the sale of parts of other, nonpaired, organs, as we discuss in the section entitled "The *Prima Facie* Case for Kidney Sales.")

In presenting our case, we start by making several important preliminary points. We then present an initial argument for allowing healthy people to sell one of their kidneys. This initial argument is not conclusive in itself, but we think that it constitutes a powerful *prima facie* or presumptive case for not prohibiting kidney sales. Next we address the view that kidney sales are intrinsically wrong. Finally, we address the objection that kidney sales are wrong because paying for organs is exploitative. We hope to show that there are very good reasons for overturning the prohibition on payment for kidneys, and that neither the "intrinsically wrong" objections nor the worries about exploitation withstand careful scrutiny.

Preliminary Points

First, we are arguing for the claim that it ought to be legal for a person to *be paid* for one of his or her kidneys. We are not arguing that it ought to be legal for a potential recipient to *buy* a kidney in an open market. We propose that the buyers of kidneys be the agencies in charge of kidney procurement or transplantation; that is, we propose that such agencies should be allowed to use financial incentives to acquire kidneys. We assume that allocation of kidneys will be based on medical criteria, as in the existing allocation system for cadaveric organs. Kidneys will not be traded in an unregulated market. A similar system is currently in place for blood products: a person can receive money for providing blood products, but one's chances of receiving blood are distinct from one's financial status. We further note that transplant recipients or their agents—e.g., insurance companies, Medicaid—pay for organs now, compensating the organ procurement organization that organizes the organ retrieval, the surgeon who removes the organ, the hospital where the organ is procured, and so forth. The only component of the organ procurement process not currently paid is the most critical component, the possessor of the kidney, who is *sine qua non* for organ availability.

Second, we believe the legalization of kidney sales will increase the number of kidneys that are transplanted each year and thus save the lives of people who would otherwise die. We base this belief on two views that seem to us very plausible: first, that financial incentives will induce some people to give up a kidney for transplantation who would otherwise not have done so; and second, that the existence of financial incentives will not decrease significantly the current level of live kidney donations. The first view seems to us to follow from the basic idea that people are more likely to do something if they are going to get paid for it. The second view seems to us to follow from the fact that a very large majority of live kidney donations occur between family members and the idea that the motivation of a sister who donates a kidney to a brother, or a parent who donates a kidney to a child, will not be altered by the existence of financial incentives. Although we think these views are plausible, we acknowledge that there is no clear evidence that they are true. If subsequent research were to establish that the legalization of kidney sales would lead to a decrease in the number of kidneys that are transplanted each year, some of the arguments we make would be substantially weakened.

Third, we are arguing for allowing payment to living kidney donors, but many of the kidneys available for transplantation come from cadavers. We believe that payment for cadaveric organs also ought to be legalized, but we will not discuss that issue here. If we successfully make the case for allowing payment to living donors, the case for payment for cadaveric kidneys should follow easily.

The *Prima Facie* Case for Kidney Sales

With these preliminary points in mind, we will proceed to the initial argument for permitting payment for kidneys. This argument is based on two claims: the "good donor claim" and the "sale of tissue claim."

The good donor claim contends that it is and ought to be legal for a living person to donate one of his or her kidneys to someone else who needs a kidney in order to survive. These donations typically consist of someone giving a kidney to a sibling, spouse, or child, but there are also cases of individuals donating to strangers. Such donations account for about half of all kidney transplants. Our society, moreover, does not simply *allow* such live kidney donations. Rather, it actively praise and encourage them. We typically take them to be morally unproblematic cases of saving a human life.

The sale of tissue claim contends that it is and ought to be legal for living persons to sell parts of their bodies. We can sell such tissues as hair, sperm, and eggs, but the body parts we focus on here are blood products. A kidney is more like blood products than other tissues because both are physical necessities: people need them in order to survive. Our proposed kidney sales are more like the sale of blood products in that both involve the market only in acquisition and not in allocation: the current system pays people for plasma while continuing to distribute blood products without regard to patients' economic status, just as we propose for kidneys. We do not typically praise people who sell their plasma as we do people who donate a kidney to save the life of a sibling. At the same time, most people do not brand commercial blood banks as moral abominations. We generally take them to be an acceptable means of acquiring a resource that is needed to save lives. It is doubtful, for instance, that there would be widespread support for the abolition of payment for plasma if the result were a reduction in supply so severe that thousands of people died every year for lack of blood products.

If both the good donor claim and the sale of tissue claim are true, we have at least an initial argument, or *prima facie* grounds, for holding that payment for kidneys ought to be legal. The good donor claim implies that it ought to be legal for a living person to decide to transfer one of his or her kidneys to someone else, while the sale of tissue claim implies that it ought to be legal for a living person to decide to transfer part of his or her body to someone else for money. It thus seems initially plausible to hold that the two claims together imply that it ought to be legal for a living person to decide to transfer one of his or her kidneys to someone else for money.

Of course, there seems to be an obvious difference between donating a kidney and selling one: motive. Those who donate typically are motivated by benevolence or altruism, while those who sell typically are motivated by monetary self-interest. The sale of tissue claim suggests, however, that this difference on its own is irrelevant to the question of whether kidney sales ought to be legal, because the sale of tissue claim establishes that it ought to be legal to transfer a body part in order to make money. If donating a kidney ought to be legal (the good donor claim), and if the only difference between donating a kidney and selling one is the motive of monetary self-interest, and if the motive of monetary self-interest does not on its own warrant legal prohibition (the sale of tissue claim), then the morally relevant part of the analogy between donating and selling should still obtain and we still have grounds for holding that selling kidneys ought to be legal.

There is also an obvious difference between selling a kidney and selling plasma: the invasiveness of the procedure. Phlebotomy for sale of plasma is simple and quick, with no lasting side effects, while parting with a kidney involves major surgery and living with only one kidney thereafter. It is very unlikely, however, that there will be any long-term ill effects from the surgery itself or from life with a single kidney. Indeed, the laws allowing live kidney donations presuppose that the risk to donors is very small and thus morally acceptable. The good donor claim implies, then, that the invasiveness of the procedure of transferring a kidney is not in and of itself a sufficient reason to legally prohibit live kidney transfer. If the only difference between selling plasma and selling a kidney is the risk of the procedure, and if that risk does not constitute grounds for prohibiting live kidney transfers, then the morally relevant part of the analogy between selling plasma and selling a kidney still should obtain and we still have grounds for holding that kidney sales ought to be legal.

The point of the preceding two paragraphs is this: if we oppose the sale of kidneys because we think it is too dangerous, then we also should oppose live kidney donations. But we do not oppose live kidney donations because we realize that the risks are acceptably low and worth taking in order to save lives. So, it is inconsistent to oppose selling kidneys because of the possible dangers while at the same time endorsing the good donor claim. Similarly, if we oppose kidney sales because we think people should not sell body parts, then we should also oppose commercial blood banks. But most people do not oppose blood banks because they realize that the banks play an important role in saving lives. So, it is inconsistent to oppose selling kidneys because it involves payment while at the same time endorsing the sale of tissue claim.

The considerable emotional resistance to permitting kidney sales may be based on a combination of distaste for payment and worry about risk. But if neither of these concerns on its own constitutes defensible grounds for opposing payment, then it seems unlikely that the two of them together will do so.

This initial argument does not imply that we should legalize the sale of hearts and livers. The initial argument holds only that, if it is medically safe for living people to donate an organ, then people should also be allowed to sell that organ. But it is not medically safe for a living person to donate his or her heart or liver. Our reliance on the good donor claim does, however, commit us to the idea that if it is morally correct to allow someone to donate an organ or part of an organ, then it is morally correct to allow someone to sell that organ or organ part. If, therefore, it is morally correct to allow people to donate liver lobes and parts of lungs, then, according to our initial argument, it ought to be legal for a person to sell a liver lobe or part of a lung as well.

Our proposal does not address the purchase of kidneys, which is a separate question. Many of the arguments against legalizing the purchase of kidneys do not apply to the sale of kidneys. For example, one argument against permitting the buying of kidneys is that it will lead to fewer kidneys for transplantation overall. Another argument is that while allowing individuals to purchase kidneys might not reduce the overall number of kidneys available for transplantation, it will reduce the number of *donated* kidneys and harm the poor who will not be able to afford to buy a kidney. Both arguments rest on empirical claims that are often stated as fact, yet have no supporting evidence. Even if the empirical claims were accurate, moreover, their moral importance could be disputed. Perhaps there are powerful moral reasons to legalize the buying of organs even if doing so leads to fewer organs overall or reduces the chances of a poor person's receiving a kidney transplant. Then again, perhaps a negative effect on the overall supply of kidneys or on the transplantation prospects for the poor will turn out to be a conclusive reason not to legalize the buying of kidneys. The important point is that our proposal will not be affected either way. As already noted in our preliminary points, our proposal can be reasonably expected both to increase the overall number of kidneys for transplantation and to increase the chances that a poor person who needs a kidney will receive one. Therefore, in arguing for the legalization of kidney sales, we put aside the separate question of whether buying kidneys ought to be legal as well.

Many people continue to oppose kidney sales, however, and some do so directly in the face of the good donor claim and the sale of tissue claim. For them, there are two possible methods of attack. First, they can argue that there is a morally relevant intrinsic difference between kidney sales and both kidney donations and plasma sales, the considerations offered above notwithstanding. Second, they can argue that while there might be nothing intrinsically wrong with selling kidneys considered in isolation, the real world circumstances under which these sales would take place would inevitably lead to exploitation. In the next section, we will examine the view that selling kidneys is intrinsically wrong, and, in the subsequent section, the view that kidney sales lead to exploitation.

The Intrinsic Immorality of Selling Organs

The Kantian View

The most common reason offered for the intrinsic wrongness of paying people for kidneys is that doing so violates the dignity of human beings or is incompatible with proper respect for persons. This opposition to kidney sales is usually grounded in the second formulation of Kant's categorical imperative, which tells us that we should never treat humanity, whether in ourselves or in others, merely as a means (Kant 1983, p. 36). But by selling a kidney, according to this Kantian reasoning, we are treating humanity in ourselves merely as a means. Mario Morelli (1999, p. 320) summarizes the position in this way:

> The question that needs to be addressed is why, on a Kantian view, selling a body part is not respecting one's humanity, whereas donating a kidney may not be objectionable, at least sometimes. The short answer is, I think, that selling oneself or part of oneself is always treating oneself as a mere means. It is treating oneself as an object with a market price, and thus a commodity. The transaction, the selling, is done for the receipt of the money to be obtained. One's humanity, one's body, is being treated only as a means and not as an end in itself. It is not simply the giving up of a body part that is objectionable: it is giving it up for the reason of monetary gain. However, there are forms of alienation of the body, such as donation of a kidney to save another's life, that would not violate the principle. . . . One is not using oneself as a mere means if one donates a kidney for such beneficent purposes.

In the Kantian view, then, to sell one's kidney is to violate a duty to oneself; it is to violate the duty not to treat the humanity in oneself merely as a means (see Chadwick 1989, pp. 131–34; Kass 1992, p. 73).

Unfortunately, this Kantian view seems to condemn not only kidney sales but also the sale of plasma. Cynthia Cohen has attempted to solve this problem by drawing a distinction between essential parts of the body and nonessential parts. She writes, "[A]ny part that is necessary for the functioning of the whole person, Kant asserts, is endowed with the dignity of that person. Kidneys and testicles are such essential body parts; hair [and presumably a pint of plasma] is not" (Cohen 1999, p. 292). Cohen (p. 294) continues,

> To sell human beings and those bits and pieces integral to them as embodied selves is to violate that which is essential to them. . . . [A]s it violates human dignity to sell whole persons, so, too, it violates that dignity to sell body parts integral to whole persons. Thus, it is ethically acceptable to sell human hair, for this accoutrement is not integral to the functioning of the whole person, but it is not ethically acceptable to sell vital organs. . . .

We have a duty to treat humanity in ourselves as an end, according to this Kantian view. And while selling nonessential body parts does not violate that duty, selling essential body parts does.

The Flaws in the Kantian View

There are two problems with this approach. First, even if selling a kidney does violate a Kantian duty to oneself, this still would not justify a legal prohibition on kidney sales; second, it is doubtful that selling a kidney does violate a Kantian duty to oneself.

Even if selling a kidney does violate a Kantian duty to oneself, it is still far from clear that we are justified in having laws and public policies against payment for kidneys. We generally do not use the law to enforce duties to oneself, and the Kantian opponents of kidney sales have not explained why we should use the law to enforce a duty to oneself in this particular case (see Dworkin 1994, pp. 155–61; Radcliffe-Richards 1996, pp. 384–87).

We can put the dubiousness of basing opposition to payment for kidneys on Kantian duties to oneself in terms of two different senses of autonomy. The first sense of autonomy is a thin sense—autonomy as noninterference. According to this sense, people are acting autonomously when they make their own self-regarding decisions free from interference by others. This sense of autonomy is neutral on the nature of the decisions that people make and on the decision-making processes that they go through: if people are not harming someone else, on the thin, noninterference conception of autonomy, then they should be left alone to do whatever they want, regardless of what it is or why they choose to do it. The second sense of autonomy is the robust Kantian notion of autonomy as self-legislation. According to this view, people respect their own autonomy only when they are motivated by rational moral law. This sense of autonomy is definitely *not* neutral on the nature of a person's decision or decision-making process. Even if an action is entirely self-regarding, it can still violate Kantian autonomy if it fails to live up to certain very high standards of self-respect or if it is grounded in the wrong kind of motive.

The thin sense of autonomy implies that we should legalize kidney sales, for the decision to sell a kidney is self-regarding, so the noninterference model tells us that each person should be allowed to make his or her own decision. According to Morelli (1999, p. 320) and Cohen (1999, p. 294), the robust Kantian sense of autonomy implies that it is wrong to sell a kidney because doing so involves the wrong kind of motive and thus violates the rational moral law. But even if Morelli and Cohen are right and selling a kidney does violate Kant's categorical imperative, this will not prove that kidney sales ought to be illegal. For the robust Kantian sense of autonomy is not the proper guide for governmental legislation. We do not make laws to enforce the Kantian duty to respect humanity in oneself. Governmental law making is, rather, primarily geared toward the promotion of autonomy in the thin, noninterference sense.

The concept of informed consent is instructive here. Over the course of the last 50 years or so, we have developed laws on informed consent to ensure that individual patients have the liberty to make their own decisions about what will happen to their bodies. The value underlying these laws is the noninterference sense of autonomy (see President's Commission 1982, p. 6). Do our informed consent laws have as their goal the promotion of robust Kantian duties to oneself? No, they do not. In fact, the goal of informed consent laws is to *prevent* the imposition of robust moral views on the individual. Were we to try to use the law to enforce Kantian duties to self, we would have to discard a great deal of informed consent legislation, for informed consent legislation is intended to allow people to make decisions on the basis of their own views of personal morality, regardless of whether their views accord with Kantianism. Because views of Kantian duties to self should have no role in legislative decisions about informed consent in general, they should not have any role in legislative decisions about kidney sales in particular.

But that is not the worst of it for the Kantian opposition to selling kidneys. The worst of it is that there is no good reason to think that selling a kidney violates even the robust Kantian sense of autonomy.

Kant says that we ought not to treat humanity in ourselves merely as a means. But my kidney is not my humanity. Humanity—what gives us dignity and intrinsic value—is our ability to make rational decisions (see Hill 1992, pp. 38–41), and a person can continue to make rational decisions with only one kidney. Thus, Cohen's distinction between essential and nonessential parts does not help her case, for a person can function perfectly well with a single kidney and so a second kidney cannot be essential to personhood. Selling a kidney does not destroy or even seriously compromise what Kant says is intrinsically valuable and dignified (see Nelson 1991, p. 69).

The problem with the Kantian opposition shows up clearly when we consider the claim by Morelli (1999, pp. 318–24) and Cohen (1999, pp. 292–95) that kidney sales are immoral because they violate "bodily integrity." If we take "bodily integrity" in its most literal sense, then selling a kidney clearly violates it. But such literal violations occur whenever a person sells or donates plasma or gives a kidney to a relative, so opponents must not be claiming that it is wrong to engage in any activity that breaks the surface of the flesh and extracts a part of the body. What, then, is the sense in which selling a kidney violates "bodily integrity" but selling other body parts does not? As Morelli (1999, p. 321) tries to explain it,

> . . . a reasonably strong case can be made for the value of bodily integrity in terms of the Kantian principle of respect for the persons, insofar as human persons are embodied. After all, it is undeniable that our existence as rational and autonomous beings and the exercise of our powers of rationality and autonomy are dependent to a considerable extent on our physical well-being. . . . [But] what we do to or with our bodies can . . . constitute or contribute to the impairment of our capacities for rationality and autonomy.

The underlying moral idea is that it violates one's humanity to engage in activities that "impair" one's "rationality and autonomy." That is why suicide and excessive drug use are wrong. There is, however, no reason to believe that selling a kidney impairs one's rationality and autonomy in any significant respect. The medical data provide no evidence that individuals who have given away a kidney suffer any grave limitations or restrictions on their future decision making.

The reason that even a Kantian should accept kidney sales stands out sharply when we contrast that activity with suicide and selling oneself into slavery. Suicide and selling oneself into slavery clearly violate the Kantian duty to oneself. They violate this duty by destroying one's humanity through annihilation of the ability to make rational decisions. But while death and slavery are incompatible with rational decision making, selling a kidney is not. A kidney seller may be incapacitated while recovering from surgery, but many acceptable activities (such as contracted labor and military service) involve giving up decision making in the short term for long-term benefit. Nor are the kidney seller's future options significantly limited: there are few, if any, intellectual side effects or physical sequelae. And the fact that two athletes (Sean Elliot and Pete Chilcutt) have played in the National Basketball Association with only one kidney makes it difficult to argue that having one kidney compromises the normal range of physical activity.

There is, moreover, an additional problem facing those who would try to find Kantian grounds for opposing kidney sales while allowing kidney donations. Kant argued that the moral status of an action was based entirely on the motive behind it. A person who sells a kidney, however, may have motives that do much better on the Kantian scale than those of a person who donates a kidney. A living donor, for instance, could be motivated entirely by illogical guilt and an irrationally low estimation of self-worth, or by an emotional need for grateful adoration, or by a desire to indebt and manipulate someone else. A kidney seller, by contrast, may be motivated by the idea that he ought to save someone else's life if it is in his power and that he ought to earn the money necessary to pay for his child's education. Needless to say, we do not mean to cast aspersions on the motives of those who donate their kidneys, nor to suggest that all those who sell their kidneys will have morally admirable motives. We mean merely to highlight another way in which Kantian moral theory fails to justify both the practice of kidney donation and the prohibition on kidney sales. Kant's moral theory, concerned as it is with motive, has its place in the first-person deliberations of moral agents; it is ill-equipped to draw the third-person legal distinctions that the opponents of kidney sales want to maintain.

So far, the discussion of Kant has focused on duties to self. One might wonder, however, whether the doctor who performs the operation to remove a kidney from a healthy person violates a Kantian duty to others, by treating the person who is selling the kidney as a mere means. But if persons do not violate their own humanity when they decide to have a kidney removed, it is hard to see how a doctor can be violating a person's humanity by assisting in its removal. It seems that the doctor's actions have an end in which the other person can "share," and if another person can "share in the end of the very same action," then the person performing the action is not, according to Kant, violating the humanity of the other (Kant 1964, p. 97). Recall, moreover, that those opposed to organ sales must give reasons against organ sales that do not also lead to the condemnation of live organ donations. It is, once again, difficult to see how someone can argue—without begging the question of whether kidney sales are intrinsically wrong—that a doctor who performs the operation to remove the kidney from a live donor is treating that person as an end while a doctor who performs the same operation to remove the kidney from a seller is treating that person merely as a means. (Some people might believe that legalizing kidney sales will violate humanity by leading to exploitation or coercion, a matter that can be addressed adequately only by attending to large-scale real-world societal conditions, not by looking at isolated hypothetical cases. We examine this type of argument in the subsequent section on exploitation.)

The "Kidneys Are Not Property" Claim

The problems with the Kantian opposition also plague the related objection that kidneys cannot legitimately be sold because they are not *property*—that is, not possessions that are ours to sell. Selling a kidney, according to this objection, is morally equivalent to selling a person. And just as the latter violates fundamental moral restrictions on property and ownership, so too does the former. Charles Fried (1978, p. 142) has this idea in mind when he says that "when a man sells his body he does not sell what is his, he sells himself," as does Cohen (1999, p. 294) when she writes:

> [H]uman beings and their integral parts are not the sorts of objects that can become the property of others, even if their market equivalent is given in exchange. . . . To sell human beings and those bits and pieces integral to them as embodied selves is to violate that which is essential to them.

In a certain sense, selling one's body may be equivalent to selling oneself, for one may not be able to exist without one's body. It may even make sense to say that one is one's body. If I sell my body to someone else, then that person will have total control over my body, and a person who has total control over my body has something very close to total control over me. When I cede total control of my body to someone else, in other words, I have, in effect, enslaved myself, which is clearly a Kantian violation.

But although Cohen and Fried are right to say that the sale of one's body is morally equivalent to self-enslavement, it is a mistake to go on to claim that kidney sales are wrong in the same way (Cohen 1999, p. 295). The error is to equate selling one's kidney with selling one's *entire* body. A person who sells a kidney still has the rest of his or her body left. The seller can continue to control his or her own destiny. Indeed, the money from the sale of a kidney may enhance the range of choices for the seller by increasing rather than decreasing the capacity to control the future. That one's *entire* body is not the sort of thing that should ever become property does not imply that a *part* of one's body can never become property (see Andrews 1986, p. 37; Campbell 1992, p. 36).

None of what we have said so far is meant to establish that selling a kidney must accord with a universal view of duties to oneself. Undoubtedly, many people believe that selling a kidney would be the wrong thing for them to do. Other people no doubt believe that selling a kidney is right for them. We have seen no justification—Kantian or otherwise—for using the law to impose the view of the first group upon the second.

Exploitation

Much of the opposition to payment for kidneys is based not simply on Kantian duties to self but on the real-world circumstances in which such a practice would occur. A market in kidneys, it is said, will inevitably be exploitative, and for this reason it should be prohibited. Some of the worries about exploitation are fueled by stories in the popular press of the international black market in kidneys. Such stories typically involve desperately poor people from underdeveloped countries selling their kidneys to wealthy individuals from developed countries. The wealthy individuals pay very large sums for an uncertain product; the poor people receive their payment and are hastily returned to their desperate lives with poor medical follow-up and without one of their kidneys (see Finkel 2001, pp. 28–31).

The international black market in kidneys is worthy of moral condemnation, and the popular press has been right to expose it. But the horrible stories do not constitute justification for a blanket rejection of payment for kidneys in this country because there are two crucial differences between the international black market and the legal domestic program we propose.

First, in our proposal the medical setting in which legal kidney transfer would take place is that of contemporary transplantation, safe and medically sophisticated. Screening would select only potential kidney sellers whose kidneys are suitable for transfer and whose medical condition predicts minimal risk. Follow-up care would be scrupulous. Sellers would receive exactly the same medical attention and treatment that living kidney donors now receive in this country. The people to whom the kidneys are transferred will also receive the same medical attention and treatment that kidney recipients currently receive.

Second, the domestic program we propose involves money only in the acquisition of kidneys, unlike the international black market. Allocation of kidneys would be based on medical criteria, as it is today. No private individual would be able to buy a kidney outside the system. Poor individuals will have just as much chance of receiving one of the kidneys.

Disproportionate Burden

These two differences between an international black market and a legal domestic program will not, however, alter everyone's belief that payment for kidneys is exploitative. The problem, as some will continue to believe, is that even if the *benefits* are spread evenly across the economic spectrum, the *burdens* will still fall disproportionately on the poor. For it is the poor who will sell, not the rich, and there has to be something deeply morally wrong with a proposal that results in the neediest parting with a kidney while the fortunate do not.

Though this objection seems solid, the reasoning behind it is vague. When the ideas underlying the objection are clarified, it turns out to be much less substantive than it initially appears.

There are two ways of understanding the objection. First, one can hold that kidney sales are morally unacceptable no matter who does the selling and that the proposal to legalize such sales is especially pernicious because the poor will be disproportionately affected. Second, one can hold that kidney sales *per se* are morally unobjectionable, but that we know in the real world the sellers will be disproportionately poor, and this economic disproportionality makes the proposal morally unacceptable. We will examine these two versions of the objection in order.

If payment for kidneys were morally unacceptable no matter who did the selling, then it would be especially offensive that the sellers are disproportionately poor; an activity that victimizes everyone it touches is made worse when those affected are especially vulnerable. The problem with this objection, however, is that it assumes without argument that such payments are morally unacceptable and thus ought to be illegal, when the moral and legal status of kidney sales is just what is under dispute. The objection thus begs the question. Of course, many people believe there are independent reasons for thinking that paying for kidneys is immoral and ought to be illegal, regardless of who receives the payment. But they have to articulate and defend those reasons before they can legitimately claim that economic factors will make matters worse. Pointing out that most kidney sellers will be poor will not on its own strengthen a weak argument for the intrinsic wrongness of allowing kidney sales.

The second way of understanding the objection contends that paying for kidneys might not be intrinsically wrong, but such sales ought not be allowed because the resulting situation in which the poor sell and the rich do not would be morally unacceptable. Some people might be drawn to this objection by a concern for equality, believing that it is morally unacceptable to implement any policy that widens the gap between rich and poor. An egalitarian principle of this sort requires argument, but even if we grant for the moment the essential importance of equality, it still does not speak against paying for kidneys. If paying for kidneys is legalized, the ratio of poor people with only one kidney to rich people with only one kidney probably will increase. The kind of equality that matters to egalitarians, however, concerns not the presence of one kidney versus two but economic and political power. There is no reason to think that allowing payment for kidneys will worsen the economic or political status of kidney sellers in particular or of poor people in general. To equate the selling of a kidney with being worse off is to beg the question once again.

It might seem more promising to cast this objection in terms of consent and coercion. No one should give up a kidney without freely consenting to do so. According to this objection, however, the people who sell their kidneys will be so desperate that their decision to sell will be neither reasonable nor rational and therefore should not be counted as instances of free consent. Poverty will, in effect, coerce people into selling their kidneys, and it is clearly immoral to take advantage of others' poverty in this way. The fact that we can find people desperate enough for money to do something they would not otherwise do is no justification for allowing them to do it (Abouna et al. 1990, p. 166).

In this view, the amount of money involved is what vitiates true consent to sell a kidney. This concern about money could come in two guises. One could claim that paying for kidneys will be coercively exploitative because the sellers will be paid too little money, or one could claim that paying for kidneys will be coercively exploitative because the sellers will be paid too much.

Those who hold that the payment will be too low point to the international black market, where payment for a kidney is often five thousand dollars or less (see Finkel 2001, pp. 28–31). Considering the surgery the sellers must undergo, this is taken to be a relative pittance, and certainly not enough to alter in any serious and long-lasting way the dire circumstances that force people to sell their kidneys in the first place. In this view, selling a kidney for five thousand dollars is so manifestly unreasonable that anyone who agrees to do it must be too desperate to give truly informed consent.

One way of responding to this concern is to mandate that kidney sellers receive a much higher sum. Some may object, however, that if the sum is too high, it will unfairly manipulate people into making irrational decisions. Large sums of money can tempt people to do what is wrong to do (Sells 1991, p. 20).

Clearly, though, the concern that people will be paid too little or too much for a kidney is not fatal to the case for payment. There are two ways to view this element of the exploitation issue. First, there is a certain amount of money that is universally too much to pay for a kidney, and a certain amount that is too little. Second, there is no objective way to decide universally the question of the monetary value of a kidney. In the first case, a universally nonexploitative payment can be established by setting the fee so that sellers are reasonably compensated without being unduly tempted to abandon their principles. We are not arguing that kidney sales be left entirely up to an unregulated market, so we do not rule out the idea that the price could be adjusted to ensure fairness and consent. The second case holds that personal values and circumstances make it impossible to set a single dollar amount for a kidney that would be reasonable and nonexploitative for all potential sellers of kidneys. Personal needs and values, regional economy, and numerous other factors will create wide variations in the payment level at which a person will choose to part with a kidney. The best one can do, such a position suggests, is to set the price of a kidney at a level that would persuade a sufficient number of sellers to relieve the kidney shortage (Barnett, Blair, and Kaserman 1992, pp. 373–74).

These solutions, however, will leave unsatisfied some of those who believe selling kidneys to be coercively exploitative. The decision to sell a kidney, these people will argue, is always unreasonable or irrational, no matter what the price, and so no one can ever truly and freely consent to do it. There is something crucially wrong with the decision to sell a kidney, regardless of whether one is paid one thousand dollars or one million. But to hold that it is irrational or unreasonable to sell a kidney no matter what the price is to revert once again to the view that selling a kidney is intrinsically wrong. It is asserting that kidney sales would be wrong even if practiced by people across the economic spectrum and abandoning the idea that what would make kidney sales wrong is that only poor people will sell. Now many people do believe that it would be wrong to allow kidney sales no matter who engages in them. As we have argued above, however, that belief requires justification, and until that justification is provided, the fact that poor people would be more likely than rich people to sell their kidneys does not on its own constitute a moral objection to the legalization of kidney sales.

Moreover, the good donor claim makes it very difficult to show that it will always be irrational or unreasonable to sell a kidney, no matter who does the selling. If it can be rational and reasonable for a person to decide to donate a kidney to a relative or to a stranger, it is difficult to imagine why it must always be irrational and unreasonable to sell a kidney. It seems plausible that a live seller can gain from the sale something intangible that is equal in value to what a live donor gains. Indeed, it is quite plausible that a living seller can gain exactly what a living donor gains—the satisfaction of saving a life, or of significantly improving the life prospects of another—*plus* a financial reward. If it is rational or reasonable for a living person to donate a kidney, then it seems that it would also be rational or reasonable for a living person to sell a kidney when the seller receives from the transaction the same benefit as the donor plus more.

Perhaps some opponents will continue to maintain that the mere fact that only the poor will sell is clear evidence of the coercively exploitative nature of paying for kidneys, the considerations above notwithstanding. Such opponents might base their argument on the idea that an act that no wealthy person would ever agree to must have some essentially rebarbative quality that always makes it wrong to inflict on the poor. The opposition might, in other words, hold this principle: if the only people who will agree to X are poor, then X must be an activity to which no one can truly and freely consent.

The problem with this principle is that it is inconsistent with many of the jobs that employ a large percentage of our population. A wealthy person rarely will choose to clean toilets for a living, or to pick strawberries. But this does not prove that it is immoral to allow people to do these jobs. Of course we should be concerned about the wages and conditions of custodians and field hands. But the solution is to take measures to ensure fair wages and tolerable conditions, not to ban public toilets and commercially grown strawberries. Similarly, if we are concerned about the price and safety of kidney sales and removal, then the answer is not to ban them but to make them as fair and safe as possible.

Can the surgical procedure associated with kidney sales ever truly be safe? We think it can be. There are risks, to be sure, but they can be minimized so that the procedure will pose less of a threat to the seller than do many jobs and activities that our society currently allows. Live kidney donation is now not merely allowed but actively encouraged precisely because these risks can be minimized. In our proposal, potential sellers will be screened and monitored just as carefully as potential donors are, so that the risks to the former should be no greater than the risks to the latter. . . .

Conclusion

Undoubtedly, many people will continue to oppose kidney sales, regardless of the arguments we have offered. Many people will continue to find the sale of a kidney repugnant, a feeling that rational argumentation alone may be incapable of dislodging (Kass 1992, pp. 84–85). But we should not let this feeling of repugnance hold hostage our moral thinking. For a great many things we now hold in the highest esteem—including organ transplantation itself—occasioned strong repugnance in times past.

Still, it is there in our psyche and hard to shake—the sense that there is something unsavory, something sharply distasteful, about paying perfectly healthy individuals to submit to a major operation and to live thereafter without one of their internal organs. The mind flinches at the thought of what such individuals will endure for money. This reaction, however, may be the result of restricted vision, for there is another part of the story, another image that we must attend to before we can honestly say that we are responding to the matter in its entirety. The other part of the story is the people waiting for kidneys—the people who will live if they receive a kidney or die, or at least suffer needlessly, if they do not. A complete emotional response requires that we frame in our mind an image of these sick people, as well as of their families and friends, that is just as vivid as our image of the healthy kidney sellers.

When we complete the picture, we may find that our feelings of repugnance begin to soften, and perhaps to dissipate. Such imaginative exercises should not substitute for rational moral arguments, but they may help pave the way for a fair consideration of those arguments.

NO

David J. Rothman

The International Organ Traffic

Over the past fifteen years, transplanting human organs has become a standard and remarkably successful medical procedure, giving new life to thousands of people with failing hearts, kidneys, livers, and lungs. But very few countries have sufficient organs to meet patients' needs. . . .

This lack of available organs arouses desperation and rewards greed. . . . The international commerce in organs is unregulated, indeed anarchic. We know a good deal about trafficking in women and children for sex. We are just beginning to learn about the trafficking in organs for transplantation.

1.

The routes that would-be organ recipients follow are well known to both doctors and patients. Italians (who have the lowest rate of organ donation in Europe) travel to Belgium to obtain their transplants; so do Israelis, who lately have also been going to rural Turkey and bringing their surgeon along with them. Residents of the Gulf States, Egyptians, Malaysians, and Bangladeshis mainly go to India for organs. In the Pacific, Koreans, Japanese, and Taiwanese, along with the residents of Hong Kong and Singapore, fly to China. Less frequently, South Americans go to Cuba and citizens of the former Soviet Union go to Russia. Americans for the most part stay home, but well-to-do foreigners come to the United States for transplants, and some centers allot up to 10 percent of their organs to them.

All of these people are responding to the shortages of organs that followed on the discovery of cyclosporine in the early 1980s. Until then, transplantation had been a risky and experimental procedure, typically a last-ditch effort to stave off death; the problem was not the complexity of the surgery but the body's immune system, which attacked and rejected the new organ as though it were a foreign object. Cyclosporine moderated the response while not suppressing the immune system's reactions to truly infectious agents. As a result, in countries with sophisticated medical programs, kidney and heart transplantation became widely used and highly successful procedures. . . .

Transplantation spread quickly from developed to less developed countries. By 1990, kidneys were being transplanted in nine Middle Eastern, six

From David J. Rothman, "The International Organ Traffic," *The New York Review of Books* (March 26, 1998), pp. 14–17. Copyright © 1998 by NYREV, Inc. Reprinted by permission of *The New York Review of Books*.

201

South American, two North African, and two sub-Saharan African countries. Kidney transplants are by far the most common, since kidney donors can live normal lives with one kidney, while kidneys are subject to disease from a variety of causes, including persistent high blood pressure, adult diabetes, nephritis (inflammation of vessels that filter blood), and infections, which are more usually found in poor countries. (It is true that the donor runs the risk that his remaining kidney will become diseased, but in developed countries, at least, this risk is small.) The transplant techniques, moreover, are relatively simple. Replacing one heart with another, for example, is made easier by the fact that the blood-carrying vessels that must be detached from the one organ and reattached to the other are large and relatively easy to handle. (A transplant surgeon told me that if you can tie your shoes, you can transplant a heart.)

Fellowships in American surgical programs have enabled surgeons from throughout the world to master the techniques and bring them home. Countries such as India and Brazil built transplant centers when they might have been better advised to invest their medical resources in public health and primary care. For them the centers are a means for enhancing national prestige, for persuading their surgeons not to leave the country, and for meeting the needs of their own middle-class citizens.

In China, more than fifty medical centers report they perform kidney transplants, and in India hundreds of clinics are doing so. Reliable information on the success of these operations is hard to obtain, and there are reports that hepatitis and even AIDS have followed transplant operations. But according to physicians I have talked to whose patients have traveled to India or China for a transplant, and from published reports within these countries, some 70 to 75 percent of the transplants seem to have been successful.[1]

With patient demand for transplantation so strong and the medical capacity to satisfy it so widespread, shortages of organs were bound to occur. Most of the doctors and others involved in early transplants expected that organs would be readily donated as a gift of life from the dead, an exchange that cost the donor nothing and brought the recipient obvious benefits. However, it turns out that powerful cultural and religious taboos discourage donation, not only in countries with strong religious establishments but in more secular ones as well. The issue has recently attracted the attention of anthropologists, theologians, and literary scholars, and some of their findings are brought together in the fascinating collection of essays, *Organ Transplantation: Meanings and Realities.*[2]

In the Middle East, it is rare to obtain organs from cadavers. Islamic teachings emphasize the need to maintain the integrity of the body after death, and although some prominent religious leaders make an exception for transplants, others refuse. An intense debate occurred . . . in Egypt when the government-appointed leader of the most important Sunni Muslim theological faculty endorsed transplantation as an act of altruism, saying that permitting it was to accept a small harm in order to avoid a greater harm—the same rationale that allows a Muslim to eat pork if he risks starvation. But other clerics immediately objected, and there is no agreement in favor of donation.

In Israel, Orthodox Jewish precepts define death exclusively as the failure of the heart to function, not the cessation of brain activity, a standard that makes it almost impossible to retrieve organs. The primary purpose of statutes defining death as the absence of brain activity is to ensure that organs to be transplanted are continuously supplied with oxygen and nutrients; in effect, the patient is declared dead, and a respirator keeps the heart pumping and the circulatory system working until the organs have been removed, whereupon the respirator is disconnected. Some rabbis give precedence to saving a life and would therefore accept the standard of brain death for transplantation. But overall rates of donation in Israel are very low. The major exceptions are kibbutz members, who tend to be community-minded, as well as other secular Jews.

In much of Asia, cultural antipathy to the idea of brain death and, even more important, conceptions of the respect due elders, have practically eliminated organ transplantation. For all its interest in new technology and its traditions of gift-giving, Japan has only a minuscule program, devoted almost exclusively to transplanting kidneys from living related donors. As the anthropologist Margaret Lock writes: "The idea of having a deceased relative whose body is not complete prior to burial or cremation is associated with misfortune, because in this situation suffering in the other world never terminates."[3] For tradition-minded Japanese, moreover, death does not take place at a specific moment. The process of dying involves not only the heart and brain but the soul, and it is not complete until services have been held on the seventh and forty-ninth days after bodily death. It takes even longer to convert a deceased relative into an ancestor, all of which makes violating the integrity of the body for the sake of transplantation unacceptable.

Americans say they favor transplantation but turn out to be very reluctant to donate organs. Despite countless public education campaigns, organ donation checkoffs on drivers' licenses, and laws requiring health professionals to ask families to donate the organs of a deceased relative, the rates of donation have not risen during the past five years and are wholly inadequate to the need. . . . One recent study found that when families were asked by hospitals for permission to take an organ from a deceased relative, 53 percent flatly refused. . . .

2.

If organs are in such short supply, how do some countries manage to fill the needs of foreigners? The answers vary. Belgium has a surplus of organs because it relies upon a "presumed consent" statute that probably would be rejected in every American state. Under its provisions, you must formally register your unwillingness to serve as a donor; otherwise, upon your death, physicians are free to transplant your organs. To object you must go to the town hall, make your preference known, and have your name registered on a national computer roster; when a death occurs, the hospital checks the computer base, and unless your name appears on it, surgeons may use your organs, notwithstanding your family's objections. I was told by health professionals in Belgium that many citizens privately fear that if they should ever need an organ, and another patient simultaneously needs one as well, the surgeons will check the computer and give the organ to the one who did not refuse to be a donor. There is no evidence that surgeons actually do this; still many people feel it is better to be safe than sorry, and so they do not register any objections.

One group of Belgian citizens, Antwerp's Orthodox Jews, have nonetheless announced they will not serve as donors, only as recipients, since they reject the concept of brain death. An intense, unresolved rabbinic debate has been taking place over the ethics of accepting but not giving organs. Should the Jewish community forswear accepting organs? Should Jews ask to be placed at the bottom of the waiting list? Or should the Jewish community change its position so as to reduce the prospect of fierce hostility or even persecution?

Because its system of presumed consent has worked so well, Belgium has a surplus of organs and will provide them to foreigners. However, it will not export them, say, to Milan or Tel Aviv, which would be entirely feasible. Instead, it requires that patients in need of a transplant come to Belgium, which then benefits from the surgical fees paid to doctors and hospitals.

Not surprisingly, money counts even more in India, which has an abundant supply of kidneys because physicians and brokers bring together the desperately poor with the desperately ill. The sellers include impoverished villagers, slum dwellers, power-loom operators, manual laborers, and daughters-in-law with small dowries. The buyers come from Egypt, Kuwait, Oman, and other Gulf States, and from India's enormous middle class (which numbers at least 200 million). They readily pay between $2,500 and $4,000 for a kidney (of which the donor, if he is not cheated, will receive between $1,000 and $1,500) and perhaps two times that for the surgery. From the perspective of patients with end-stage renal disease, there is no other choice. For largely cultural reasons, hardly any organs are available from cadavers; dialysis centers are scarce and often a source of infection, and only a few people are able to administer dialysis to themselves at home (as is also the case in the US). Thus it is not surprising that a flourishing transplant business has emerged in such cities as Bangalore, Bombay, and Madras.

The market in organs has its defenders. To refuse the sellers a chance to make the money they need, it is said, would be an unjustifiable form of paternalism. Moreover, the sellers may not be at greater risk living with one kidney, at least according to US research. A University of Minnesota transplant team compared seventy-eight kidney donors with their siblings twenty years or more after the surgery took place, and found no significant differences between them in health; indeed, risk-conscious insurance companies do not raise their rates for kidney donors.[4] And why ban the sale of kidneys when the sale of other body parts, including semen, female eggs, hair, and blood, is allowed in many countries? The argument that these are renewable body parts is not persuasive if life without a kidney does not compromise health. Finally, transplant surgeons, nurses, and social workers, as well as transplant retrieval teams and the hospitals, are all paid for their work. Why should only the donor and the donor's family go without compensation?

But because some body parts have already been turned into commodities does not mean that an increasing trade in kidneys and other organs is desirable. To poor Indians, as Margaret Radin, professor of law at Stanford, observes, "Commodification worries may seem like a luxury. Yet, taking a slightly longer view, commodification threatens the personhood of everyone, not just those who can now afford to concern themselves about it." Many of the poor Indians who sell their organs clearly feel they have had to submit to a degrading practice in order to get badly needed sums of money. They would rather not have parts of their body cut out, an unpleasant experience at best, and one that is probably more risky in Bombay than in Minnesota. Radin concludes: "Desperation is the social problem that we should be looking at, rather than the market ban. . . . We must rethink the larger social context in which this dilemma is embedded."[5]

In 1994, perhaps for reasons of principle or because of public embarrassment—every world medical organization opposes the sale of organs—a number of Indian states, including the regions of Bombay, Madras, and Bangalore, outlawed the practice, which until then had been entirely legal. But the laws have an egregious loophole so that sales continue almost uninterrupted. A detailed and persuasive report in the December 26, 1997, issue of *Frontline,* one of India's leading news magazines, explains how the new system works.[6] The legislation permits donations from persons unrelated to the recipient if the donations are for reasons of "affection or attachment," and if they are approved by "authorization committees." These conditions are easily met. Brokers and buyers coach the "donors" on what to say to the committee—that he is, for example, a cousin and that he has a (staged) photograph of a family gathering to prove it, or that he is a close friend and bears great affection for the potential recipient. Exposing these fictions would be simple enough, but many committees immediately approve them, unwilling to block transactions that bring large sums to hospitals, surgeons, and brokers.

Accurate statistics on kidney transplantation in India are not available, but *Frontline* estimates that about one third of transplants come from living, unrelated donors; four years after the new law went into effect, the rate of transplantation has returned to its earlier levels. It is true that not every hospital participates in the charade, that the market in kidneys is less visible than it was, and it may well be that fewer foreigners are coming to India for a transplant. But the lower classes and castes in India, already vulnerable to so many other abuses, continue to sell their organs. As *Frontline* reports, many donors who sell their organs do so because they are badly in debt; and before long they are again in debt.

3.

China is at the center of the Pacific routes to organ transplantation because it has adopted the tactic of harvesting the organs of executed prisoners. In 1984, immediately after cyclosporine became available, the government issued a document entitled "Rules Concerning the Utilization of Corpses or Organs from the Corpses of Executed Prisoners." Kept confidential, the new law provided that organs from executed prisoners could be used for transplants if the prisoner agreed, if the family agreed, or if no one came to claim the body. (Robin Munro of Human Rights Watch/Asia brought the law to light.) That the law lacks an ethical basis according to China's own values is apparent from its stipulations. "The use of corpses or organs of executed prisoners must be kept strictly secret," it stated, "and attention must be paid to avoiding negative repercussions." The cars used to retrieve organs from the execution grounds cannot bear health department insignia; the people involved in obtaining organs are not permitted to wear white uniforms. In my own interviews with Chinese transplant surgeons, none would admit to the practice; when I showed them copies of the law, they shrugged and said it was news to them.

But not to other Asian doctors. Physicians in Japan, Hong Kong, Singapore, and Taiwan, among other countries, serve as travel agents, directing their patients to hospitals in Wuhan, Beijing, and Shanghai. The system is relatively efficient. Foreigners do not have to wait days or weeks for an organ to be made available; executions can be timed to meet market needs and the supply is more than adequate. China keeps the exact number of executions secret but Amnesty International calculates on the basis of executions reported in newspapers that there are at least 4,500 a year, and perhaps three to four times as many. Several years ago a heart transplant surgeon told me that he had just been invited to China to perform a transplant; accustomed to long waiting periods in America, he asked how he could be certain that a heart would be available when he arrived. His would-be hosts told him they would schedule an execution to fit with his travel schedule. He turned down the invitation. In February [1998] the FBI arrested two Chinese nationals living in New York for allegedly soliciting payment for organs from executed prisoners to be transplanted in China.

China's system also has its defenders. Why waste the organs? Why deprive prisoners of the opportunity to do a final act of goodness? But once again, the objections should be obvious. The idea that prisoners on death row—which in China is a miserable hovel in a local jail—can give informed consent to their donations is absurd. Moreover, there is no way of ensuring that the need for organs might not influence courtroom verdicts. A defendant's guilt may be unclear, but if he has a long criminal record, why not condemn him so that a worthy citizen might live?

To have physicians retrieve human organs at an execution, moreover, subverts the ethical integrity of the medical profession. There are almost no reliable eyewitness accounts of Chinese practices, but until 1994, Taiwan also authorized transplants of organs from executed prisoners, and its procedures are probably duplicated in China. Immediately before the execution, the physician sedates the prisoner and then inserts both a breathing tube in his lungs and a catheter in one of his veins. The prisoner is then executed with a bullet to his head; the physician immediately moves to stem the blood flow, attach a respirator to the breathing tube, and inject drugs into the catheter so as to increase blood pressure and cardiac output. With the organs thus maintained, the body is transported to a hospital where the donor is waiting and the surgery is performed. The physicians have become intimate participants in the executions; instead of protecting life, they are manipulating the consequences of death.

The motive for all such practices is money. The Europeans, Middle Easterners, and Asians who travel to China, India, Belgium, and other countries pay handsomely for their new organs and in hard currencies. Depending on the organization of the particular health care system and the level of corruption, their fees will enrich surgeons or medical centers, or both. Many of the surgeons I interviewed were quite frank about how important the income from transplants was to their hospitals, but they were far more reluctant to say how much of it they kept for themselves. Still, a leading transplant surgeon in Russia is well known for his vast estate and passion for horses. His peers in India and China may be less ostentatious but not necessarily less rich. They will all claim to be doing good, rescuing patients from near death.

4.

The international trade in organs has convinced many of the poor, particularly in South America, that they or their children are at risk of being mutilated and murdered. Stories are often told of foreigners who arrive in a village, survey the scene, kidnap and murder several children, remove their organs for sale abroad, and leave the dissected corpses exposed in the graveyard. In Guatemala in 1993 precisely such fears were responsible for one innocent American woman tourist being jailed for a month, and another being beaten to death.

Villagers' anxieties are shared by a number of outside observers who believe that people are being murdered for their organs. The author of the report of a transplant committee of the European Parliament unequivocally asserted that

> Organized trafficking in organs exists in the same way as trafficking in drugs. It involved killing people to remove organs which can be sold at a profit. To deny the existence of such trafficking is comparable to denying the existence of ovens and gas chambers during the last war.[7]

So, too, the rapporteur of a UN committee on child welfare circulated a questionnaire asserting that "the sale of children is mainly carried out for the purpose of organ transplantation." It then asked: "To what extent and in what ways and forms do these violations of children's rights exist in your country? Please describe."[8]

The stories of organ snatching have an American version. I have heard it from my students, read about it on e-mail, been told about it with great conviction by a Moscow surgeon, and been asked about it by more than a dozen journalists. According to the standard account, a young man meets an attractive woman in a neighborhood bar; they have a few drinks, go back to her place, whereupon he passes out and then wakes up the next morning to find a sewn-up wound on his side. When he seeks medical attention, he learns that he is missing a kidney.

Although there have been sporadically reported stories of robberies of kidneys from people in India, I have not found a single documented case of abduction, mutilation, or murder for organs, whether in North or South America. I was in Guatemala in 1993 when the atrocities are alleged to have occurred, and heard seemingly reliable people say there was convincing evidence for them. I stayed long enough to see every claim against the two American women tourists proven false. Nevertheless, as the anthropologist Nancy Scheper-Hughes argues, the villagers' fears and accusations are understandable in the light of their everyday experience. The bodies of the poor are ordinarily treated so contemptuously that organ snatching does not seem out of character. In Guatemala, babies are regularly kidnapped for sale abroad in the adoption market. Local doctors and health workers admitted to me that "fattening houses" have been set up so that kidnapped babies would be more attractive for adoption.

But it is extremely dangerous to investigate the adoption racket, since highly placed officials in the government and military take a cut of the large sums of money involved. Moreover, Scheper-Hughes continues, if street children in Brazil can be brazenly murdered without recrimination, it is not far-fetched for slum dwellers to believe that the organs of the poor are being removed for sale abroad. And since girls and boys can be kidnapped with impunity to satisfy an international market in sex, why not believe they are also kidnapped to satisfy an international market for organs?[9]

In truth, medical realities make such kidnappings and murder highly unlikely. The rural villages and the urban apartments in which transplants are alleged to secretly take place do not have the sterile environment necessary to remove or implant an organ. Organs from children are too small to be used in adults. And however rapacious health care workers may seem, highly trained and medically sophisticated teams of surgeons, operating room nurses, anesthesiologists, technicians, and blood transfusers are not likely to conspire to murder for organs or accept them off the street. Had they done so, at least one incident would have come to light during the past fifteen years.

5.

The well-documented abuses are bad enough. Is there some way of diminishing them? The Bellagio Task Force, an international group including transplant surgeons, human rights activists, and social scientists, has made several proposals that might be effective if they could be carried out.[10]

Almost all major national and international medical bodies have opposed the sale of organs and the transplantation of organs from executed prisoners; but none of the medical organizations has been willing to take action to enforce their views. The World Medical Association in 1984, 1987, and 1994 condemned "the purchase and sale of human organs for transplantation." But it asks "governments of all countries to take effective steps," and has adopted no measures of its own. It has also criticized the practice of using organs from executed prisoners without their consent; but it fails to ask whether consent on death row can be meaningful. The association leaves it to national medical societies to "severely discipline the physicians involved." Neither it nor any other medical organization has imposed sanctions on violators.

The Bellagio Task Force has posed several challenges to the international medical societies. What would happen if they took their proclaimed principles seriously, established a permanent monitoring body, and kept close surveillance on organ donation practices? What if they threatened to withhold training fellowships from countries which tolerated exploitative practices? What if they refused to hold international meetings in those countries, and, as was the case with South Africa under apartheid, did not allow physicians from those countries to attend their meetings? Why, moreover, couldn't the Novartis company, the manufacturer of cyclosporine, insist that it would sell its product only to doctors and hospitals that meet strict standards in obtaining organs? Such measures would be likely to have a serious effect, certainly in India, probably even in China. But as with the organs themselves, the willingness of doctors to use the moral authority of medicine as a force for change has, so far, been in short supply.

Notes

1. Xia Sui-sheng, "Organ Transplantation in China: Retrospect and Prospect," *Chinese Medical Journal,* 105 (1992), pp. 430–432.

2. Edited by Stuart J. Youngner, Renée C. Fox, and Laurence J. O'Connell (University of Wisconsin Press, 1996).

3. "Deadly Disputes: Ideologies and Brain Death in Japan," in Youngner et al., *Organ Transplantation,* pp. 142–167.

4. John S. Najarian, Blanche M. Chavers, Lois E. McHugh, and Arthur J. Matas, "20 Years or More of Follow-Up of Living Kidney Donors," *Lancet,* 340 (October 3, 1992), pp. 807–809.

5. Margaret Jane Radin, *Contested Commodities* (Harvard University Press, 1996), p. 125.

6. "Kidneys Still for Sale," *Frontline,* 14 (December 13–26, 1997), pp. 64–79.

7. This and other examples of lending credence to the rumors may be found in the United States Information Agency Report of December 1994, "The Child Organ Trafficking Rumor," written by Todd Leventhal.

8. Vitit Muntarbhorn, "Sale of Children," Report of the Special Rapporteur to the United Nations Commission on Human Rights, January 12, 1993.

9. Nancy Scheper-Hughes, "Theft of Life: The Globalization of Organ Stealing Rumours," *Anthropology Today,* 12 (June 1996), pp. 3–11.

10. D.J. Rothman, E. Rose, et al., "The Bellagio Task Force Report on Transplantation, Bodily Integrity, and the International Traffic in Organs," *Transplantation Proceedings,* 29 (1997), pp. 2739–2745. I am currently serving as chair of the Bellagio group.

POSTSCRIPT

Should There Be Payment for Body Parts?

This is a complicated issue. Gill and Sade attempt to narrow the focus of the question of payment for body parts to its most acceptable formulation, so that it only addresses kidney donation. The authors appeal to our sense of fairness in including the kidney seller among those who receive compensation for the kidney. Gill and Sade also speak to our strong sense that sellers are *autonomous* and therefore in a position to make up their own minds and decide what they want to do.

Rothman discusses some of the real-world phenomena that lie behind Gill and Sade's assumptions. For example, he describes some of the religious and cultural beliefs that prevent the use of organs from the deceased. If such beliefs close off the possibility of using the organs of the dead for transplantation, how can we expect these beliefs to allow *living* people to give up their organs? In addition, Rothman raises questions about the presumed autonomy of the sellers. In desperation, poor people might *say* that they freely consent to the sale of their organs. But desperately poor people might do many things—for example, they might do something that their religion forbids, making them less autonomous than one might think.

For further sources, see Leon R. Kass, "Organs for Sale? Propriety, Property, and the Price of Progress," *The Public Interest* (Spring 1992); Richard A. Epstein, "Organ Transplants: Is Relying on Altruism Costing Lives?" *The American Enterprise* (November–December 1993); Stephen J. Spurr, "The Proposed Market for Human Organs," *Journal of Health Politics, Policy, and Law* (Spring 1993); Roger W. Evans, "Organ Procurement: Expenditures and the Role of Financial Incentives," *Journal of the American Medical Association* (June 23, 1993); and Frank A. Sloan, "Organ Procurement: Expenditures and the Role of Financial Incentives—Commentary," *Journal of the American Medical Association* (June 23, 1993).

More recent publications include Arthur L. Caplan and Daniel H. Coelho, eds., *The Ethics of Organ Transplants: The Current Debate* (Prometheus Books, 1999); Robert M. Veatch, *Transplantation Ethics* (Georgetown University Press, 2001); Norman Levinsky, ed., *Ethics and the Kidney* (Oxford University Press, 2001); Tom Koch, *Scarce Goods: Justice, Fairness, and Organ Transplantation* (Praeger Publishers, 2001); Ronald Munson, *Raising the Dead: Organ Transplants, Ethics, and Society* (Oxford University Press, 2002); and Stuart J. Youngner, ed., *Transplanting Human Tissue: Ethics, Policy, and Practice* (Oxford University Press, 2003).

ISSUE 11

Should Drugs Be Legalized?

YES: David Boaz, from "A Drug-Free America—or a Free America?" *U.C. Davis Law Review* (Spring 1991)

NO: David T. Courtwright, from "Should We Legalize Drugs? No," *American Heritage* (February/March 1993)

ISSUE SUMMARY

YES: Political analyst David Boaz argues that in a free country, people have the right to ingest whatever substances they choose without governmental interference. Moreover, as our national experience with Prohibition shows, attempts at restricting substances create more problems than they solve.

NO: Professor of history David T. Courtwright maintains that the complete legalization of drugs is morally irresponsible. Moreover, controlled legalization will not work. Easy access to drugs through complete legalization will lead to more drug abuse and more drug addiction, and legally controlled access will result in a new black market.

No one can deny that the use of psychoactive substances has a great impact on society today—from the health effects of cigarettes to the criminal activity of street-corner crack dealers. In many ways, the greatest impact is from the smuggling, trafficking, and consumption of illegal drugs. These practices entail or lead to bribery, inner-city crime, babies born addicted to drugs such as crack, and a host of other social ills.

America has been waging a "war on drugs" that is supposed to address (if not solve) these problems. But the problems still exist, and the war on drugs has been going on for some time now. Critics wonder how effective the war is. Severe critics would say that the so-called war on drugs is not working at all and that it is time to try another approach.

Some have called for the legalization of drugs. If drugs were legal, advocates say, their sale and use could be regulated and controlled. The government would be able to raise revenue through taxation (instead of having huge drug profits go to organized crime), the quality and quantity of the drugs could be officially monitored, and much inner-city street crime could be eliminated. On the other hand, even after legalization, there would still be many drug addicts (perhaps even more of them), "crack babies," and other victims of drug use.

Proponents of drug legalization must offer a realistic plan for the legal market they propose. At least two elements should be addressed. First, what exactly is meant by *legalization*? Substances that are legal are not necessarily available at all times to everyone. Alcohol, for example, is a legal substance, but when and where and to whom it may be sold are all regulated by federal and local authorities. And some currently legal drugs are available only by prescription. Secondly, some further clarification is needed about what is meant by *drugs*. Much talk about drugs is very vague. Caffeine and nicotine are common drugs, but since they are already legal, we might say that we are considering here only illegal drugs. But why are some drugs legal and some illegal?

Prohibition (when the status of alcohol was changed from legal to illegal) is one of the useful test cases that people on both sides of this issue can appeal to. It is useful because although we cannot experiment with changing the legal status of some drugs for a limited time to see what would happen, Prohibition is a historical reality. Prohibition became effective on January 16, 1920, and was repealed December 5, 1933. During this time, the Constitution was amended to outlaw "the manufacture, sale, or transportation of intoxicating liquors within . . . the United States." Also outlawed was all import and export of these items. During Prohibition, many of the problems that we now associate with the modern drug world existed: smuggling, official corruption, murder, large amounts of money being made by violent criminals, and organized criminal networks. The general public could, with a little effort—and in some cases with very little effort—buy and consume the very products that were against the law. And what was bought on the black market had no guarantees with respect to health or safety.

In the following selections, David Boaz and David T. Courtwright use the historical experience with alcohol and other drugs as a source of lessons for today's drug problem, but they draw very different conclusions. Boaz argues that the government does not have the right to prohibit people from using substances that they wish to use. Governmental programs that are meant to control the use of certain substances are misguided. These efforts are responsible for the creation of black markets and an increase in drug-related crime. Moreover, they do not succeed in keeping the substances out of the hands of people who want them. Courtwright, on the other hand, argues that drug legalization would be far more problematic than its proponents realize and would lead to an increase in drug abuse and drug addiction.

David Boaz

 **YES**

A Drug-Free America—or a Free America?

Introduction: The Drug Problem

Human beings have used mind-altering substances throughout recorded history. Why? . . . Perhaps because we fail to love one another as we should. Perhaps because of the social pressure for success. Perhaps because—and this is what really irks the prohibitionists—we enjoy drugs' mind-altering effects.

Though the reasons for drug use are numerous, the governmental response has been singular: almost as long as humans have used drugs, governments have tried to stop them. In the sixteenth century the Egyptian government banned coffee. In the seventeenth century the Czar of Russia and the Sultan of the Ottoman Empire executed tobacco smokers. In the eighteenth century England tried to halt gin consumption and China penalized opium sellers with strangulation.

The drug prohibition experiment most familiar to Americans is the prohibition of alcohol in the 1920s. The period has become notorious for the widespread illegal consumption of alcohol and the resultant crime. Movies such as *Some Like It Hot* typify the popular legend of the era. The failure of Prohibition, however, is not just legendary. Consumption of alcohol probably fell slightly at the beginning of Prohibition but then rose steadily throughout the period. Alcohol became more potent, and there were reportedly more illegal speakeasies than there had been legal saloons. More serious for nondrinkers, the per capita murder rate and the assault-by-firearm rate both rose throughout Prohibition.

Most of the same phenomena are occurring with today's prohibition of marijuana, cocaine, and heroin. Use of these drugs has risen and fallen during the seventy-seven years since Congress passed the Harrison Narcotics Act [designed to curb opium trafficking], with little relationship to the level of enforcement. In the past decade, the decade of the "War on Drugs," use of these drugs seems to have declined, but no faster than the decline in the use of the legal drugs alcohol and tobacco. In the 1980s Americans became more health- and fitness-conscious, and use of all drugs seems to have correspondingly decreased. Drug prohibition, however, has not stopped thirty million people from trying cocaine and sixty million people from trying marijuana. Prohibition also has not stopped the number of heroin users from increasing by one hundred fifty percent and the

From David Boaz, "A Drug-Free America—or a Free America?" *U.C. Davis Law Review,* vol. 24 (1991). Copyright © 1991 by The Regents of the University of California. Reprinted by permission. Some notes omitted.

number of cocaine users from increasing by ten thousand percent. Moreover, prohibition has not kept drugs out of the hands of children: in 1988 fifty-four percent of high school seniors admitted to having tried illicit drugs; eighty-eight percent said it was fairly easy or very easy to obtain marijuana; and fifty-four percent said the same about cocaine.

Although drug prohibition has not curtailed drug use, it has severely limited some fundamental American liberties. Programs such as "Zero Tolerance," which advocates seizing a car or boat on the mere allegation of a law enforcement official that the vehicle contains drugs, ignore the constitutional principle that a person is innocent until proven guilty.

In attempting to fashion a solution to "the drug problem," one first needs to define the problem society is trying to solve. If the problem is the age-old human instinct to use mind-altering substances, then the solution might be God, or evolution, or stronger families, or Alcoholics Anonymous. History suggests, however, that the solution is unlikely to be found in the halls of Congress. If, on the other hand, the problem is the soaring murder rate, the destruction of inner-city communities, the creation of a criminal subculture, and the fear millions of Americans experience on their own streets, then a solution may well be found in Congress—not in the creation of laws but in their repeal.

This Article proposes that the repeal of certain laws will force individuals to take responsibility for their actions; the repeal of other laws will provide individuals the right to make important decisions in their lives free from outside interference. Together these changes will create the society in which drugs can, and must, be legalized. Legalization of drugs, in turn, will end the need for the government to make the intrusions into our fundamental rights as it does so often in its War on Drugs.

The Futility of Prohibition

A. The War on Drugs

Prohibition of drugs is not the solution to the drug problem. [Since 1981] the United States has waged a "War on Drugs." The goals of this War were simple: prohibit the cultivation or manufacture of drugs, prohibit the import of drugs, and prohibit the use of drugs. As the aforementioned statistics demonstrate, the War has not achieved its goals.

Prohibitionists, however, sometimes claim that the United States has not yet "really fought a drug war." The prohibitionists argue that a "true drug war" would sharply lower drug use. They feel that the government has not fully committed itself to winning this battle. One need only look at the War on Drug's record, however, to see the commitment.

- Congress passed stricter anti-drug laws in 1984, 1986, and 1988. Congress and state legislators steadily increased penalties for drug law violations, mandating jail time even for first offenders, imposing large civil fines, seizing property, denying federal benefits to drug law violators, and evicting tenants from public housing.

- Federal drug war outlays tripled between 1980 and 1988, and the federal government spent more than $20 billion on anti-drug activities during the decade. Adjusted for inflation, the federal government spends ten times as much on drug-law enforcement every year as it spent on Prohibition enforcement throughout the Roaring Twenties.
- Police officers made more than one million drug law arrests in 1989, more than two-thirds of them for drug possession.
- The number of drug busts tripled during the 1980s, and the number of convictions doubled.
- America's prison population more than doubled between 1981 and 1990, from 344,283 to 755,425. Prisons in thirty-five states and the District of Columbia are under court orders because of overcrowding or poor conditions. An increasing percentage of these prisoners are in jail for nonviolent drug law violations.
- The armed services, Coast Guard, and Civil Air Patrol became more active in the drug fight, providing search and pursuit planes, helicopters, ocean interdiction, and radar. Defense Department spending on the War on Drugs rose from $200 million in 1988 to $800 million in 1990.
- The Central Intelligence Agency (CIA) and National Security Agency began using spy satellites and communications listening technology as part of the drug war. The CIA also designed a special Counter Narcotics Center.
- The federal government forced drug testing upon public employees and required contractors to establish "drug-free" workplaces. Drug testing has also expanded among private companies.
- Seizures of cocaine rose from 2,000 kilograms in 1981 to 57,000 kilograms in 1988.

Despite this enormous effort, drugs are more readily available than ever before. The War on Drugs has failed to achieve its primary goal of diminishing the availability and use of drugs.

B. Prohibition Creates Financial Incentives

One reason for the failure of the War on Drugs is that it ignores the fact that prohibition sets up tremendous financial incentives for drug dealers to supply the demand. Prohibition, at least initially, reduces the supply of the prohibited substance and thus raises the price. In addition, a large risk premium is added onto the price. One has to pay a painter more to paint the Golden Gate Bridge than to paint a house because of the added danger. Similarly, drug dealers demand more money to sell cocaine than to sell alcohol. Those who are willing to accept the risk of arrest or murder will be handsomely—sometimes unbelievably—rewarded.

Drug dealers, therefore, whatever one may think of them morally, are actually profit-seeking entrepreneurs. Drug researcher James Ostrowski points out that "[t]he public has the false impression that drug enforcers are highly innovative, continually devising new schemes to catch drug dealers. Actually, the reverse is true. The dealers, like successful businessmen, are usually one step ahead of the 'competition.' "[1]

New examples of the drug dealers' entrepreneurial skills appear every day. For example, partly because the Supreme Court upheld surveillance flights over private property to look for marijuana fields, marijuana growers have been moving indoors and underground. The Drug Enforcement Administration seized about 130 indoor marijuana gardens in California in 1989; by November the figure for 1990 was 259.

Overseas exporters have also been showing off their entrepreneurial skills. Some have been sending drugs into the United States in the luggage of children traveling alone, on the assumption that authorities will not suspect children and will go easy on them if they are caught. Others have concealed drugs in anchovy cans, bean-sprout washing machines, fuel tanks, and T-shirts. At least one man surgically implanted a pound of cocaine in his thighs. Some smugglers swallow drugs before getting on international flights. Professor Ethan Nadelmann has explained the spread of overseas exporters as the "push-down/pop-up factor": push down drug production in one country, and it will pop up in another.[2] For example, Nadelmann notes that "Colombian marijuana growers rapidly expanded production following successful eradication efforts in Mexico during the mid-1970s. Today, Mexican growers are rapidly taking advantage of recent Colombian government successes in eradicating marijuana."

Prohibition of drugs creates tremendous profit incentives. In turn, the profit incentives induce drug manufacturers and dealers to creatively stay one step ahead of the drug enforcement officials. The profit incentives show the futility of eradication, interdiction, and enforcement and make one question whether prohibition will ever be successful. . . .

Individual Rights

Many of the drug enforcement ideas the prohibitionists suggest trample upon numerous constitutional and natural rights. In any discussion of government policies, it is necessary to examine the effect on natural rights for one simple reason: Individuals have rights that governments may not violate. In the Declaration of Independence, Thomas Jefferson defined these rights as life, liberty, and the pursuit of happiness. I argue that these inviolable rights can actually be classified as one fundamental right: Individuals have the right to live their lives in any way they choose so long as they do not violate the equal rights of others. To put this idea in the drug context, what right could be more basic, more inherent in human nature, than the right to choose what substances to put in one's own body? Whether it is alcohol, tobacco, laetrile, AZT, saturated fat, or cocaine, this is a decision that the individual should make, not the government. This point seems so obvious to me that it is, to borrow Jefferson's words, self-evident.

The prohibitionists, however, fail to recognize this fundamental freedom. They advance several arguments in an effort to rebut the presumption in favor of liberty. First, they argue, drug users are responsible for the violence of the drug trade and the resulting damage to innocent people. The erstwhile Drug

Czar, William Bennett, when asked how his nicotine addiction differed from a drug addiction, responded, "I didn't do any drive-by shootings."[3] Similarly former First Lady Nancy Reagan said, "The casual user may think when he takes a line of cocaine or smokes a joint in the privacy of his nice condo, listening to his expensive stereo, that he's somehow not bothering anyone. But there is a trail of death and destruction that leads directly to his door. I'm saying that if you're a casual drug user, you are an accomplice to murder."[4]

The comments of both Mr. Bennett and Mrs. Reagan, however, display a remarkable ignorance about the illegal-drug business. Drug use does not cause violence. Alcohol did not cause the violence of the 1920s, Prohibition did. Similarly drugs do not cause today's soaring murder rates, drug prohibition does. The chain of events is obvious: drug laws reduce the supply and raise the price of drugs. The high price causes addicts to commit crimes to pay for a habit that would be easily affordable if obtaining drugs was legal. The illegality of the business means that business disputes—between customers and suppliers or between rival suppliers—can be settled only through violence, not through the courts. The violence of the business then draws in those who have a propensity—or what economists call a comparative advantage—for violence. When Congress repealed Prohibition, the violence went out of the liquor business. Similarly, when Congress repeals drug prohibition, the heroin and cocaine trade will cease to be violent. As columnist Stephen Chapman put it, "the real accomplices to murder" are those responsible for the laws that make the drug business violent.[5]

Another prohibitionist argument against the right to take drugs is that drug use affects others, such as automobile accident victims and crack babies. With regard to the former, certainly good reasons exist to strictly penalize driving (as well as flying or operating machinery) while under the influence of drugs. It hardly seems appropriate, however, to penalize those who use drugs safely in an attempt to stop the unsafe usage. As for harm to babies, this is a heart-rending problem (though perhaps not as large a problem as is sometimes believed). Again, however, it seems unnecessary and unfair to ban a recreational drug just because it should not be used during pregnancy. Moreover, drug-affected babies have one point in common with driving under the influence: misuse of legal drugs (alcohol, tobacco, codeine, caffeine) as well as illegal drugs, contribute to both problems. Thus, if society wants to ban cocaine and marijuana because of these drugs' potential for misuse, society should logically also ban alcohol, tobacco, and similar legal drugs.

The question of an individual right to use drugs comes down to this: If the government can tell us what we can put into our own bodies, what can it not tell us? What limits on government action are there? We would do well to remember Jefferson's advice: "Was the government to prescribe to us our medicine and diet, our bodies would be in such keeping as our souls are now."[6]

The Solution: Re-establish Individual Responsibility

For the past several decades a flight from individual responsibility has taken place in the United States. Intellectuals, often government funded, have concocted a whole array of explanations as to why nothing that happens to us is our own fault. These intellectuals tell us that the poor are not responsible for their poverty, the fat are not responsible for their overeating, the alcoholic are not responsible for their drinking. Any attempt to suggest that people are sometimes responsible for their own failures is denounced as "blaming the victim."

These nonresponsibility attitudes are particularly common in discussions of alcohol, tobacco, and other drugs. Development of these attitudes probably began in the 1930s with the formulation of the classic disease theory of alcoholism. The disease theory holds that alcoholism is a disease that the alcoholic cannot control. People have found it easy to apply the theory of addiction to tobacco, cocaine, heroin, even marijuana. In each case, according to the theory, people get "hooked" and simply cannot control their use. Author Herbert Fingarette, however, stated that "*no* leading research authorities accept the classic disease concept [for alcoholism]."[7] Many scientists, though, believe it is appropriate to mislead the public about the nature of alcoholism in order to induce what they see as the right behavior with regard to alcohol.

In the popular press the addiction theory has spread rapidly. Popular magazines declare everything from sex to shopping to video games an addiction that the addicted person has no power to control. As William Wilbanks said, the phrase "I can't help myself" has become the all-purpose excuse of our time.[8]

The addiction theory has also gained prominence in discussions of illegal drugs. Both prohibitionists and legalizers tend to be enamored of the classic notion of addiction. Prohibitionists say that because people cannot help themselves with respect to addictive drugs, society must threaten them with criminal sanctions to protect them from their own failings. Legalizers offer instead a "medical model": treat drug use as a disease, not a crime. The legalizers urge that the billions of dollars currently spent on drug enforcement be transferred to treatment programs so that government can supply "treatment on demand" for drug addicts.

Despite the popular affection for the addiction theory, numerous commentators denounce the theory. For example, addiction researcher Stanton Peele deplores the effects of telling people that addictive behavior is uncontrollable:

> [O]ne of the best antidotes to addiction is to teach children responsibility and respect for others and to insist on ethical standards for everyone—children, adults, addicts. Crosscultural data indicate, for instance, that when an experience is defined as uncontrollable, many people experience such loss of control and use it to justify their transgressions against society. For example, studies find that the "uncontrollable" consequences of alcohol consumption vary from one society to another, depending upon cultural expectations.[9]

. . . The United States requires . . . more reforms—in addition to drug legalization—to create the kind of society in which people accept responsibility for their actions. . . .

Americans might take . . . steps to restore traditional notions of individual responsibility. Laws regarding drugs should only punish persons who violate the rights of others; private actions should go unpunished. Thus, laws should strictly punish those who drive while under the influence of alcohol or other drugs. Intoxication, moreover, should not be a legal defense against charges of theft, violence, or other rights violations, nor should a claim of "shopping addiction" excuse people from having to pay their debts. Physicians, intellectuals, and religious leaders should recognize that the denial of responsibility has gone too far, and they should begin to stress the moral value of individual responsibility, the self-respect such responsibility brings, and the utilitarian benefits of living in a society in which all persons are held responsible for the consequences of their actions.

Conclusion

Society cannot really make war on drugs, which are just chemical substances. Society can only wage wars against people, in this case people who use and sell drugs. Before America continues a war that has cost many billions of dollars and many thousands of lives—more than eight thousand lives per year even before the skyrocketing murder rates of the past few years—Americans should be sure that the benefits exceed the costs. Remarkably, all of the high-ranking officers in the Reagan administration's drug war reported in 1988 that they knew of no studies showing that the benefits of prohibition exceeded the costs.

There is a good reason for the lack of such a study. Prohibition is futile. We cannot win the War on Drugs. We cannot even keep drugs out of our prisons. Thus, we could turn the United States into a police state, and we still would not win the War on Drugs. The costs of prohibition, however, are very real: tens of billions of dollars a year, corruption of law enforcement officials, civil liberties abuses, the destruction of inner-city communities, black-market murders, murders incident to street crime by addicts seeking to pay for their habit, and the growing sense that our major cities are places of uncontrollable violence.

Hundreds, perhaps thousands, of years of history teach us that we will never make our society drug-free. In the futile attempt to do so, however, we may well make our society unfree.

Notes

1. Ostrowski, *Thinking About Drug Legalization,* 121 Pol'y Analysis, May 25, 1989, at 34. . . .

2. Nadelmann, *The Case for Legalization,* 92 Pub. Interest 3, 9 (1988). . . .

3. Isikoff, *Bennett Rebuts Drug Legalization Ideas,* Washington Post, Dec. 12, 1989, at A10, col. 1.

4. Chapman, *Nancy Reagan and the Real Villains in the Drug War,* Chicago Tribune, Mar. 6, 1988, § 4, at 3, col. 1. . . .

5. Chapman, *supra* note 4.

6. T. Jefferson, *Notes on Virginia,* in The Life and Selected Writings of Thomas Jefferson 187, 275 (1944).

7. H. Fingarette, Heavy Drinking at 3 (1988) (emphasis in original). . . .

8. Wilbanks, *The New Obscenity,* 54 Vital Speeches of the Day 658, 658–59 (1988).

9. *See generally* S. Peele, *Control Yourself,* Reason, Feb. 1990, at 25.

 **NO**

Should We Legalize Drugs? No

One thing that all parties in the American drug-policy debate agree on is that they want to eliminate the traffic in illicit drugs and the criminal syndicates that control it. There are two divergent strategies for achieving this end: the drug war and drug legalization, or, more precisely, controlled legalization, since few people want the government to simply abandon drug control and proclaim laissez faire.

The drug war was launched during the Reagan administration. It is actually the fourth such campaign, there having been sustained legislative and governmental efforts against drug abuse between 1909 and 1923, 1951 and 1956, and 1971 and 1973. What distinguishes the current war is that it is more concerned with stimulants like cocaine than with opiates, it is larger, and—no surprise in our age of many zeros—it is much more expensive.

The war against drugs has included the treatment of addicts and educational programs designed to discourage new users, but the emphasis has been on law enforcement, with interdiction, prosecution, imprisonment, and the seizure of assets at the heart of the campaign. The news from the front has been mixed. Price and purity levels, treatment and emergency-room admissions, urinalyses, and most other indices of drug availability showed a worsening of the problem during the 1980s, with some improvement in 1989 and 1990. The number of casual cocaine users has recently declined, but cocaine addiction remains widespread, affecting anywhere from about 650,000 to 2.4 million compulsive users, depending on whose definitions and estimates one chooses to accept. There has been some success in stopping marijuana imports—shipments of the drug are relatively bulky and thus easier to detect—but this has been offset by the increased domestic cultivation of high-quality marijuana, which has more than doubled since 1985. Heroin likewise has become both more available and more potent than it was in the late 1970s.

But cocaine has been the drug of greatest concern. Just how severe the crisis has become may be gauged by federal cocaine seizures. Fifty years ago the annual haul for the entire nation was 1 or 2 pounds, an amount that could easily be contained in the glove compartment of a car. As late as 1970 the total was under 500 pounds, which would fit in the car's trunk. In fiscal year 1990 it was

235,000 pounds—about the weight of 60 mid-size cars. And this represented a fraction, no more than 10 percent, of what went into the nostrils and lungs and veins of the approximately seven million Americans who used cocaine during 1990. Worse may be in store. Worldwide production of coca surged during 1989 to a level of 225,000 metric tons, despite U.S. efforts to eradicate cultivation. Global production of opium, marijuana, and hashish has likewise increased since President Reagan formally declared war on drugs in 1986.

◦◦◦◦

The greatest obstacle to the supply-reduction strategy is the enormous amount of money generated by the illicit traffic. Drug profits have been used to buy off foreign and domestic officials and to secure protection for the most vulnerable stages of the drug-cultivation, -manufacturing, and -distribution process. These profits also hire various specialists, from assassins to money launderers to lawyers, needed to cope with interlopers; they pay for technological devices ranging from cellular phones to jet planes; and they ensure that should a trafficker die or land in jail, there will be no shortage of replacements.

It is hardly surprising that these stubborn economic realities, together with the drug war's uneven and often disappointing results, have led several commentators to question the wisdom of what they call the prohibition policy. What is unprecedented is that these disenchanted critics include mayors, prominent lawyers, federal judges, nationally syndicated columnists, a congressman, a Princeton professor, and a Nobel laureate in economics. They espouse variations of a position that is often called controlled legalization, meaning that the sale of narcotics should be permitted under conditions that restrict and limit consumption, such as no sales to minors, no advertising, and substantial taxation. They cite the numerous advantages of this approach: several billion dollars per year would be realized from tax revenues and savings on law enforcement; crime would diminish because addicts would not have to hustle to keep themselves supplied with drugs; the murders associated with big-city drug trafficking would abate as lower-cost, legal drugs drive the traffickers out of business. Because these drugs would be of known quality and potency, and because they would not have to be injected with shared needles, the risk of overdose and infection would drop. The issue of foreign complicity in the drug traffic, which has complicated American diplomatic relations with many countries, would disappear. Under a policy of controlled legalization, it would be no more criminal or controversial to import coca from Colombia than to import coffee.

The more candid of the legalization proponents concede that these advantages would be purchased at the cost of increased drug abuse. Widespread availability, lower prices, and the elimination of the criminal sanction would result in more users, some of whom would inevitably become addicts. But how many more? Herbert Kleber, a treatment specialist and former deputy director of the Office of National Drug Control Policy, has argued that there would be between twelve and fifty-five million addicted users if cocaine and heroin were legally available. While it is impossible to anticipate the exact magnitude of the increase, history does support Kleber's argument. In countries like Iran or Thailand, where narcotics have long been cheap, potent, and readily available, the prevalence of addiction has been and continues to be quite high. Large quantities of opium sold by British and American merchants created a social disaster in nineteenth-century China; that Chinese sailors and immigrants subsequently introduced opium smoking to Britain and America is a kind of ironic justice. Doctors, who constantly work with and around narcotics, have historically had a very serious addiction problem: estimates of the extent of morphine addiction among American physicians at the turn of the century ran from 6 percent to an astonishing 23 percent. In a word, exposure matters.

Kleber has also attacked the crime-reduction rationale by pointing out that addicts will generally use much more of an illicit substance if the cost is low. They would spend most of their time using drugs and little of it working, thus continuing to resort to crime to acquire money. If the total number of addicts rose sharply as availability increased, total crime would also increase. There would be less crime committed by any single addict but more crime in the aggregate.

The debate over decriminalization is, in essence, an argument about a high-stakes gamble, and so far the opponents represent the majority view. At the close of the 1980s, four out of every five Americans were against the legalization of marijuana, let alone cocaine. But if the drug war produces another decade of indifferent results, growing disillusionment could conceivably prompt experiments in controlled legalization.

⁂

The controlled-legalization argument rests on the assumption that legal sales would largely eliminate the illicit traffic and its attendant evils. The history of drug use, regulation, and taxation in the United States suggests otherwise. The very phrase *controlled legalization* implies denying certain groups access to drugs. Minors are the most obvious example. No one advocates supplying narcotics to children, so presumably selling drugs to anyone under twenty-one would remain a criminal offense, since that is the cutoff point for sales of beverage alcohol. Unfortunately, illicit drug abuse in this century has become concentrated among the young—that is, among the very ones most likely to be made exceptions to the rule of legal sales.

Until about 1900 the most common pattern of drug dependence in the United States was opium or morphine addiction, brought about by the treatment of chronic diseases and painful symptoms. Addicts were mainly female, middle-class, and middle-aged or older; Eugene O'Neill's mother, fictionalized as Mary Tyrone in *Long Day's Journey into Night,* was one. Habitual users of morphine, laudanum, and other medicinal opiates in their adolescence were extremely rare, even in big cities like Chicago.

Another pattern of drug use was nonmedical and had its roots in marginal, deviant, and criminal subcultures. The "pleasure users," as they were sometimes called, smoked opium, sniffed cocaine, injected morphine and cocaine in combination, or, after 1910, sniffed or injected heroin. Nonmedical addicts began much younger than their medical counterparts. The average age of addiction (not first use, which would have been lower still) for urban heroin addicts studied in the 1910s was only nineteen or twenty years. They were also more likely to be male than those whose addiction was of medical origin, and more likely to have been involved in crime.

Initially the pleasure users were the smaller group, but during the first two decades of [the twentieth] century—the same period when the police approach to national drug control was formulated—the number of older, docile medical addicts steadily diminished. There were several reasons: doctors became better educated and more conservative in their use of narcotics; the population grew healthier; patent-medicine manufacturers were forced to reveal the contents of their products; and the numerous morphine addicts who had been created in the nineteenth century began to age and die off. Drug use and addiction became increasingly concentrated among young men in their teens and twenties, a pattern that continues to this day.

In 1980, 44 percent of drug arrests nationwide were of persons under the age of twenty-one. There were more arrests among teen-agers than among the entire population over the age of twenty-five; eighteen-year-olds had the highest arrest rate of any age group. By 1987 the proportion of those arrested under twenty-one had declined to 25 percent. This was partly due to the aging of the population and to the effects of drug education on students. . . .

So, depending on timing and demographic circumstances, at least a quarter and perhaps more than a third of all drug buyers would be underage, and there would be a great deal of money to be made by selling to them. The primary source of supply would likely be diversion—adults legally purchasing drugs and selling them to customers below the legal age. The sellers (or middlemen who collected and then resold the legal purchases) would make a profit through marking up or adulterating the drugs, and there might well be turf disputes and hence violence. Some of the dealers and their underage purchasers would be caught, prosecuted, and jailed, and the criminal-justice system would still be burdened with drug arrests. The black market would be altered and diminished, but it would scarcely disappear.

Potential for illegal sales and use extends far beyond minors. Pilots, police officers, fire fighters, drivers of buses, trains, taxis, and ambulances, surgeons, active-duty military personnel, and others whose drug use would jeopardize public safety would be denied access to at least some drugs, and those of them who did take narcotics would be liable to criminal prosecution, as would their suppliers. Pregnant women would also pose a problem. Drugs transmitted to fetuses can cause irreversible and enormously costly harm. Federal and local governments may soon be spending billions of dollars a year just to prepare the impaired children of addicts for kindergarten. Society has the right and the obligation to stop this neurological carnage, both because it cruelly handicaps innocents and because it harms everyone else through higher taxes and health-insurance premiums. Paradoxically, the arguments for controlled legalization might lead to denying alcohol and tobacco to pregnant women along with narcotics. Alcohol and tobacco can also harm fetal development, and several legalization proponents have observed that it is both inconsistent and unwise to treat them as if they were not dangerous because they are legal. If cocaine is denied to pregnant women, why not alcohol too? The point here is simply that every time one makes an exception for good and compelling reasons—every time one accents the "controlled" as opposed to the "legalization"—one creates the likelihood of continued illicit sales and use.

The supposition that this illegal market would be fueled by diversion is well founded historically. There has always been an undercurrent of diversion, especially in the late 1910s and 1920s, when black-market operators like Legs Diamond got their supplies not so much by smuggling as by purchases from legitimate drug companies. One possible solution is to require of all legal purchasers that which is required of newly enrolled methadone patients: consumption of the drug on the premises. Unfortunately, unlike methadone, heroin and cocaine are short-acting, and compulsive users must administer them every few hours or less. . . . Confining the use of heroin or cocaine or other street drugs to clinics would be a logistical nightmare. But the alternative, take-home supplies, invites illegal sales to excluded groups.

Another historical pattern of black-market activity has been the smuggling of drugs to prisoners. Contraband was one of the reasons the government built specialized narcotic hospitals in Lexington, Kentucky, and Fort Worth, Texas, in the 1930s. Federal wardens wanted to get addicts out of their prisons because they were constantly conniving to obtain smuggled drugs. But when drug-related arrests multiplied after 1965 and the Lexington and Fort Worth facilities were closed, the prisons again filled with inmates eager to obtain drugs. Birch Bayh, chairing a Senate investigation of the matter in 1975, observed that in some institutions young offenders had a more plentiful supply of drugs than they did on the outside.

Since then more jails have been crammed with more prisoners, and these prisoners are more likely than ever to have had a history of drug use. In 1989, 60 to 80 percent of male arrestees in twelve large American cities tested positive for drugs. It is hard to imagine a controlled-legalization system that would permit sales to prisoners. Alcohol, although a legal drug, is not sold licitly in prisons, and for good reason, as more than 40 percent of prisoners were under its influence when they committed their crimes. If drugs are similarly denied to inmates, then the contraband problem will persist. If, moreover, we insist that our nearly three million parolees and probationers remain clean on the theory that drug use aggravates recidivism, the market for illegal sales would be so much the larger.

By now the problem should be clear. If drugs are legalized, but not for those under twenty-one, or for public-safety officers, or transport workers, or military personnel, or pregnant women, or prisoners, or probationers, or parolees, or psychotics, or any of several other special groups one could plausibly name, then just exactly who is going to buy them? Noncriminal adults, whose drug use is comparatively low to begin with? Controlled legalization entails a dilemma. To the extent that its controls are enforced, some form of black-market activity will persist. If, on the other hand, its controls are not enforced and drugs are easily diverted to those who are underage or otherwise ineligible, then it is a disguised form of wholesale legalization and as such morally, politically, and economically unacceptable.

One of the selling points of controlled legalization was also one of the decisive arguments for the repeal of Prohibition: taxation. Instead of spending billions to suppress the illicit traffic, the government would reap billions by imposing duties on legitimate imports and taxes on domestically manufactured drugs. Not only could these revenues be earmarked for drug treatment and education programs, but they would also increase the prices paid by the consumer, thus discouraging consumption, especially among adolescents.

The United States government has had extensive historical experience with the taxation of legal narcotics. In the nineteenth and early twentieth centuries, opium was imported and subject to customs duties. The imports were assigned to one of three categories. The first was crude opium, used mainly for medicinal purposes and for the domestic manufacture of morphine. Foreign-manufactured morphine, codeine, and heroin made up the second class of imports, while the third was smoking opium, most of it prepared in Hong Kong and shipped to San Francisco.

﹒◈﹒

The imposts [taxes] on these imported drugs fluctuated over the years, but they were generally quite stiff. From 1866 to 1914 the average ad valorem duty [calculated according to value] on crude opium was 33 percent; for morphine or its salts, 48 percent. From 1866 to 1908 the average duty on smoking opium was an extraordinarily high 97 percent. This last was in the nature of a sin tax; congressmen identified opium smoking with Chinese coolies, gamblers, pimps, and prostitutes and wished to discourage its importation and use.

These customs duties produced revenue; they also produced widespread smuggling, much of it organized by violent criminal societies like the Chinese tongs. The smugglers were as ingenious as their latter-day Mafia counterparts. They hid their shipments in everything from hollowed-out lumber to snake cages. Avoiding the customs collectors, they saved as much as three dollars a pound on crude opium, three dollars an ounce on morphine, and twelve dollars a pound on smoking opium. Twelve dollars seems a trifling sum by modern standards, hardly worth the risk of arrest, but in the nineteenth century it was more than most workers earned in a week. Someone who smuggled in fifty pounds of smoking opium in 1895 had gained the equivalent of a year's wages. One knowledgeable authority estimated that when the duty on smoking opium was near its peak, the amount smuggled into the United States was nearly twice that legally imported and taxed. Something similar happened with eighteenth-century tobacco imports to the British Isles. More than a third of the tobacco consumed in England and Scotland circa 1750 had been clandestinely imported in order to avoid a duty of more than five pence per pound. The principle is the same for domestically produced drugs: if taxes are sufficiently onerous, an illegal supply system will spring up. Moonshining existed before and after, as well as during, Prohibition.

The obvious solution is to set taxes at a sufficiently low level to discourage smuggling and illegal manufacturing. But again there is a dilemma. The most important illicit drugs are processed agricultural products that can be grown in several parts of the world by peasant labor. They are not, in other words, intrinsically expensive. Unless they are heavily taxed, legal consumers will be able to acquire them at little cost, less than ten dollars for a gram of cocaine. If drugs are that cheap, to say nothing of being 100 percent pure, the likelihood of a postlegalization epidemic of addiction will be substantially increased. But if taxes are given a stiff boost to enhance revenues and limit consumption, black marketeers will reenter the picture in numbers proportionate to the severity of the tax.

Tax revenues, like drugs themselves, can be addictive. In the twelve years after the repeal of Prohibition, federal liquor tax revenues ballooned from 259 million to 2.3 billion dollars. The government's dependence on this money was one important reason anti-liquor forces made so little progress in their attempts to restrict alcohol consumption during World War II. Controlled drug legalization would also bring about a windfall in tax dollars, which in an era of chronic deficits would surely be welcomed and quickly spent. Should addiction rates become too high, a conflict between public health and revenue concerns would inevitably ensue.

When both proponents and opponents of controlled legalization talk about drug taxes, they generally assume a single level of taxation. The assumption is wrong. The nature of the federal system permits state and local governments to levy their own taxes on drugs in addition to the uniform federal customs and excise taxes. This means that total drug taxes, and hence the prices paid by consumers, will vary from place to place. Variation invites interstate smuggling, and if the variation is large enough, the smuggling can be extensive and involve organized crime.

The history of cigarette taxation serves to illustrate this principle. In 1960 state taxes on cigarettes were low, between zero and eight cents per pack, but after 1965 a growing number of states sharply increased cigarette taxes in response to health concerns and as a politically painless way of increasing revenue. Some states, mainly in the Northeast, were considerably more aggressive than others in raising taxes. By 1975 North Carolina purchasers were paying thirty-six cents per pack while New Yorkers paid fifty-four cents. The price was higher still in New York City because of a local levy that reached eight cents per pack (as much as the entire federal tax) at the beginning of 1976.

Thus was born an opportunity to buy cheap and sell dear. Those who bought in volume at North Carolina prices and sold at New York (or Connecticut, or Massachusetts) prices realized a substantial profit, and by the mid-1970s net revenue losses stood at well over three hundred million dollars a year. Much of this went to organized crime, which at one point was bootlegging 25 percent of the cigarettes sold in New York State and *half* of those sold in New York City. The pioneer of the illegal traffic, Anthony Granata, established a trucking company with thirty employees operating vehicles on a six-days-a-week basis. Granata's methods—concealed cargoes, dummy corporations, forged documents, fortresslike warehouses, bribery, hijacking, assault, and homicide—were strikingly similar to those used by illicit drug traffickers and Prohibition bootleggers.

⋯

Although high-tax states like Florida or Illinois still lose millions annually to cigarette bootleggers, the 1978 federal Contraband Cigarette Act and stricter law enforcement and accounting procedures have had some success in reducing over-the-road smuggling. But it is relatively easy to detect illegal shipments of cigarettes, which must be smuggled by the truckload to make a substantial amount of money. Cocaine and heroin are more compact, more profitable, and very easy to conceal. Smuggling these drugs to take advantage of state tax differentials would consequently be much more difficult to detect and deter. If, for example, taxed cocaine retailed in Vermont for ten dollars a gram and in New York for twelve dollars a gram, anyone who bought just five kilograms at Vermont prices, transported them, and sold them at New York prices would realize a profit of ten thousand dollars. Five kilograms of cocaine can be concealed in an attaché case.

⋯

Of course, if all states legalized drugs and taxed them at the same rate, this sort of illegal activity would not exist, but it is constitutionally and politically unfeasible to ensure uniform rates of state taxation. And federalism poses other challenges. Laws against drug use and trafficking have been enacted at the local, state, and federal levels. It is probable that if Congress repeals or modifies the national drug laws, some states will go along with controlled legalization while others will not. Nevada, long in the legalizing habit, might jettison its drug laws, but conservative Mormon-populated Utah might not. Alternately, governments could experiment with varying degrees of legalization. Congress might decide that anything was better than the current mayhem in the capital and legislate a broad legalization program for the District of Columbia. At the same time, Virginia and Maryland might experiment with the decriminalization of marijuana, the least risky legalization option, but retain prohibition of the non-medical use of other drugs. The result would again be smuggling, whether from Nevada to Utah or, save for marijuana, from the District of Columbia to the surrounding states. It is hard to see how any state that chose to retain laws against drugs could possibly stanch the influx of prohibited drugs from adjacent states that did not. New York City's futile attempts to enforce its strict gun-control laws show how difficult it is to restrict locally that which is elsewhere freely available.

I referred earlier to the legalization debate as an argument about a colossal gamble, whether society should risk an unknown increase in drug abuse and addiction to eliminate the harms of drug prohibition, most of which stem from illicit trafficking. "Take the crime out of it" is the rallying cry of the legalization advocates. After reviewing the larger history of narcotic, alcohol, and tobacco use and regulation, it appears that this debate should be recast. It would be more accurate to ask whether society should risk an unknown but possibly substantial increase in drug abuse and addiction in order to bring about an unknown *reduction* in illicit trafficking and other costs of drug prohibition. Controlled legalization would take some, but by no means all, of the crime out of it. Just how much and what sort of crime would be eliminated would depend upon which groups were to be denied which drugs, the overall level of taxation, and differences in state tax and legalization policies. If the excluded groups were few *and* all states legalized all drugs *and* all governments taxed at uniformly low levels, then the black market would be largely eliminated. But these are precisely the conditions that would be most likely to bring about an unacceptably high level of drug abuse. The same variables that would determine how successful the controlled-legalization policy would be in eliminating the black market would also largely determine how unsuccessful it was in containing drug addiction.

POSTSCRIPT

Should Drugs Be Legalized?

Boaz states that governmental efforts to control drug use will create serious social problems, and in the end fail to keep the forbidden substances out of the hands of people who want to use them. A strong governmental effort—like the current war on drugs—threatens people's civil liberties and provides criminals with incentive to engage in illegal drug trafficking. Boaz asserts that the tendency of the government to attempt to control its citizens' lives is wrong. An individual should be able to take personal responsibility for his or her actions and choose what substances he or she consumes.

Courtwright counters that talk of personal responsibility applies only in an abstract world. In the real world, where "crack babies" never have a choice about what substances to consume and where many adults suffer from drug addiction, the idea of assuming "personal responsibility" may be of limited application. Furthermore, Courtwright asserts that many of the benefits predicted by proponents of drug legalization will not come to pass. Tight controls will not guarantee that drugs will only be available under "appropriate" circumstances. Drug smuggling, black market sales, violence, and crime will continue to exist. Also, the extent of drug use and addiction will mostly likely rise if drugs are legalized even if it is in the form of controlled legislation.

Further readings on the legalization of drugs include Steve Otto, *War on Drugs or War on People? A Resource Book for the Debate* (Ide House, 1996); Paul B. Stares, *Global Habit: The Drug Problem in a Borderless World* (Brookings Institution, 1996); Thomas W. Clark, "Keep Marijuana Illegal—for Teens," *The Humanist* (May/June 1997); Robert H. Dowd, *The Enemy Is Us: How to Defeat Drug Abuse and End the "War on Drugs"* (Hefty Press, 1997); Eric Goode, *Drug Legalization Debate* (St. Martin's Press, 1997); Jennifer Croft, *Drugs and the Legalization Debate* (Rosen Publishing Group, 1997); Charles P. Cozic, ed., *Illegal Drugs* (Greenhaven Press, 1998); Stephen P. Thompson, ed., *The War on Drugs: Opposing Viewpoints* (Greenhaven Press, 1998); Jeffrey A. Schaler, ed., *Drugs: Should We Legalize, Decriminalize or Deregulate?* (Prometheus Books, 1998); Dirk Chase Eldredge, *Ending the War on Drugs: A Solution for America* (Bridge Works Publishing, 1998); Robert J. MacCoun and Peter Reuter, *Drug War Heresies: Learning From Other Vices, Times, and Places* (Cambridge University Press, 2001); Douglas N. Husak, *Drugs and Rights* (Cambridge University Press, 2002); and Larry K. Gaines and Peter B. Kraska, *Drugs, Crime, and Justice: Contemporary Perspectives,* 2d ed. (Waveland Press, 2002).

ISSUE 12

Is It Morally Permissible to Eat Meat?

YES: Holmes Rolston III, from *Environmental Ethics: Duties to and Values in the Natural World* (Temple University Press, 1988)

NO: John Mizzoni, from "Against Rolston's Defense of Eating Animals: Reckoning With the Nutritional Factor in the Argument for Vegetarianism," *International Journal of Applied Philosophy* (Spring 2002)

ISSUE SUMMARY

YES: Environmental thinker Holmes Rolston III maintains that meat eating by humans is a natural part of the ecosystem. He states that it is important that animals do not suffer needlessly, but it would be a mistake to think that animals, like humans, are members of a culture. Rolston concludes that people too readily project human nature on animal nature.

NO: Philosopher John Mizzoni counters that eating meat is not a nutritional requirement for humans and that by eating meat we are following a cultural practice—one that causes unnecessary suffering. Mizzoni agrees with Rolston that there is an important distinction between culture and nature but asserts that Rolston misapplies this distinction.

This issue comes about because humans are rational beings and, at least to some extent, we are able to control our actions. Many other living things eat meat but are not rational beings. Lions, for example, eat meat—but a male lion will often kill all the lion cubs of his new mate, which would certainly seem by human standards to be an irrational act. The idea that we are just following nature when we eat meat may not exactly be true, say many who recognize that some animal behaviors are not to be used as models by people. Instead we must pick and choose the behaviors that we model.

Moreover, unlike lions, most people do not *have* to eat meat in order to survive. Indeed, some entire cultures are vegetarian. Individual vegetarians can be found in other cultures as well, for example, in American culture. On the other hand, in American culture the practice of meat eating is the norm and is quite widespread—just look at all the McDonald's and Burger Kings!

As a justification for eating meat, some conclude that it is not quite right to say that we are just doing what the other living things do—for we do not follow animal behavior if we think it would be wrong to do so. But if meat eating is a cultural practice, then, like any other cultural practice, it is subject to rational judgment and moral critique. We know that in the past, many socially accepted practices have been condoned at the time they were practiced but later found to be morally wanting. We can look back now in amazement at the practice of slavery in the South in the early part of the 1800s or the way great poverty was ignored in Victorian England while some people lived lives of luxury. One wonders, "How could people *do* that?" Could it be that future generations will look back at the Americans who thought nothing of consuming Big Macs and likewise wonder, "How could people *do* that?"

Many find the basic problem with meat eating to be the conditions under which animals who are raised for food live. The people who eat meat bring about these deplorable conditions, some argue, because high consumer demand dictates that the supermarkets are well stocked with meat, that fast food outlets sell meat, and therefore make it easier to obtain a meal with meat than one without. Animal husbandry is big business, and it is big business because the customers demand the product. Because of this huge demand, it can be said that many people look the other way when farmers raise animals under conditions that many vegetarians find appalling.

In the following selections, Holmes Rolston III maintains that the human consumption of meat is part of our human interaction with the natural (as opposed to the cultural) environment. He asserts that it is important that animals do not suffer needlessly, of course, but it would be a mistake to think that animals are members of a culture in the same way that humans belong to a culture. People too readily project human nature on animal nature, he contends. John Mizzoni argues specifically against Rolston. He stresses in particular that eating meat is not a nutritional requirement for humans. By eating meat we are following a cultural practice that causes unnecessary suffering, says Mizzoni.

Higher Animals: Duties to Sentient Life

Domestic and Hunted Animals

Domestic Food Animals

Animal agriculture is tangential to an environmental ethic, yet there is a carry-over connecting the one to the other. Domestic animals are breeds, no longer natural kinds. They are "living artifacts,"[1] kept in culture for so long that it is often not known precisely what their natural progenitors were. They fit no environmental niche; the breeding of them for traits that humans desire has removed them from the forces of natural selection. Without human interest in these animals they would soon cease to exist. Most domestic breeds would go extinct; a few might revert to feral conditions; fewer still might resettle homeostatically into environmental niches. Most feral forms, unchecked by predators, competitors, and diseases, are misfits that cause heavy environmental degradation.

But domestic animals cannot enter the culture that maintains them. By all behavioral evidence, sheep, cows, and pigs are oblivious to the economy for which they are reared, much less to the cultural context of the persons who care for them. They cannot live in the world ethically, cognitively, and critically in those superior human ways. Pet dogs may join the life of the family, enthusiastically eating hot dogs at a picnic; nevertheless, pets are not in culture. Although food animals are taken out of nature and transformed by culture, they remain uncultured in their sentient life, cultural objects that cannot become cultural subjects. They live neither in nature nor in culture but in the peripheral rural world. Meanwhile, they can suffer.

This *is* the case, descriptive of their condition. What *ought* to be? . . . [W]e recognize the wild condition from which such animals were once taken and recognize also that they can neither return to the wild nor enter cultural subjectivity. Although tamed, they can have horizons, interests, goods no higher than those of wild subjectivity, natural sentience. They ought to be treated, by the homologous, baseline principle, with no more suffering than might have been their lot in the wild, on average, adjusting for their modified capacities to care for themselves. In taking an interest in them, humans have assumed a responsibility for them. (Whether modern industrial farming introduces suffering in excess of ecological norms will have to be investigated elsewhere.)

By a weaker (but significant) hedonist principle, domestic animals ought to be spared pointless suffering, but they have no claim to be spared innocent suffering. The killing and the eating of animals, when they occur in culture, are still events in nature; they are ecological events, no matter how superimposed by culture. Humans are claiming no superiority or privilege exotic to nature. Analogous to predation, human consumption of animals is to be judged by the principles of environmental ethics, not those of interhuman ethics. We step back from culture into agriculture, toward the wild, and fit the ecological pattern. What *is* in nature may not always imply *ought* (and it may seldom do so in inter-human ethics), but *ought* in environmental ethics seldom negates what *is* in wild nature. Humans eat meat, and meat-eating is a natural component of ecosystems, one to which we do not object in nature nor try to eliminate from our cultural interactions with nature.

A troop of half a dozen chimpanzees, our nearest relatives, will kill and eat about a hundred medium-sized animals a year. Hunter-gatherer cultures are the earliest known, and when agricultural cultures replace them, humans have no duty to cease to be omnivores and become herbivores. They might elect to become vegetarians, perhaps on grounds of more efficient food production or better nutrition, but they have no duty to sentient life to do so.

A characteristic argument for vegetarianism runs as follows:

1. Pain is a bad thing, whether in humans or in animals.
2. Humans (at least most of them) can live nutritiously without causing animal pain.
3. It is immoral for humans to kill and eat humans, causing them pain.
4. Food animals suffer pain, similarly to the way humans do, if killed and eaten.
5. There are no morally relevant differences between humans and food animals.
6. It is immoral for humans to kill and eat animals, causing them pain.

Appealing to sentiment and logically attractive in its charitable egalitarianism, such argument fails to distinguish between nature and culture, between environmental ethics and interhuman ethics. We simply see ourselves in fur. But there are morally relevant differences that distinguish persons in culture from food animals in agriculture, where quasi-ecosystemic processes remain. Whether or not there are differences in pain thresholds between sheep and humans, the value destruction when a sheep is eaten is far less, especially since the sheep have been bred for this purpose and would not otherwise exist. Because animals cannot enter culture, they do not suffer the *affliction* (a heightened, cognitively based pain, distinct from physical pain) that humans would if bred to be eaten.

Chickens can live in ignorant bliss of their forthcoming slaughter (until the moment of execution); persons in such a position could not, because they are in the world culturally and critically. Even if such a fate could be kept secret from persons, the value destruction in their killing would still be greater. The fact that there are twilight zones (humans who are pre-persons or failed persons) does not challenge the existence of morally relevant class differences. In recognizing the human superiority, nothing should be subtracted from the natural condition of animals. But we have no strong duty to deny their original ecology, and only a weaker duty to make their lot better by avoiding pointless pain.

It is not "unfair" or "unjust" to eat a pig. Even an alligator that eats humans is not being unfair or unjust (although humans will be reprehensible if they do not try to prevent it). Humans in their eating habits follow nature; they can and ought to do so. But humans do not eat other humans because such events interrupt culture; they destroy those superior ways in which humans live in the world. The eating of other humans, even if this were shown to be an event in nature, would be overridden by its cultural destructiveness. Cannibalism destroys interpersonal relations. But in nature no such relations obtain, or can obtain. (Human cannibalism has been rare and virtually always a cultural event with religious overtones, not a natural event.)

It may be objected that the differences in rules for those with superior gifts means here that the only moral animals should refuse to participate in the meat-eating phase of their ecology, just as they refuse to play the game merely by the rules of natural selection. Humans do not look to the behavior of wild animals as an ethical guide in other matters (marriage, truth-telling, promise-keeping, justice, charity). Why should they justify their dietary habits by watching what animals do? But these other matters are affairs of culture. Marriage, truth-telling, promise-keeping, justice, charity—these are not events at all in spontaneous nature. They are person-to-person events. By contrast, eating is omnipresent in spontaneous nature; humans eat because they are in nature, not because they are in culture. Eating animals is not an event between persons but a human-to-animal event, and the rules for it come from the ecosystems in which humans evolved and which they have no duty to remake. Humans, then, can model their dietary habits on their ecosystems, but they cannot and should not model their interpersonal justice or charity on ecosystems.

It may seem that while animals are not to be treated like persons in all respects, both they and persons have about equally the capacity to feel pain, and so both ought to be treated equally in this relevant respect involving the pain-pleasure scale. But this is not the only relevant scale, because it does not catch the full scale of value destructions at stake. The eating of persons would destroy cultural values, which the eating of animals does not. The eating of animals, though it does destroy values, reallocates such values when humans gain nutrition and pleasure at the sacrifice of animal lives in a manner wholly consistent with the operation of the natural ecosystem in which such animals were once emplaced and are still quasi-placed in their agricultural stations. Different rules do apply to persons, to persons in exchange with persons, and even to persons in exchange with nature. These rules do require that animals lives count morally, but they do not require humans to deny their ecology and replace it with a charity or justice appropriate to culture.

Sentience in nature and sentience in culture are not really the same thing, despite their common physiology and origin. Sentience in nature belongs with food chains and natural selection; sentience in culture has been transformed into another gestalt, that of self-reflective personality and moral agency. Eating an animal implies no disrespect for animal life . . . ; to the contrary, it respects that ecology. Eating a person would disrupt personal life as set in a cultural pattern; it would reduce personal life to the level of animal life in an ecology. It insults persons to treat them as food objects by the criteria of animal ecology; persons may and must treat nonhuman lives as food objects, but it respects animals to treat them so.

Pain is a bad thing in humans or in animals. But this fools us until we distinguish between intrinsic and instrumental pain. Instrumental pain has contributory reference to further goods; intrinsic pain has no such reference. Intrinsic pain is a bad thing, absolutely; but only instrumental pain is characteristic of nature, where intrinsic pain is a nonfunctional anomaly. Pain is routinely instrumental in ecological defenses, captures, and transfers of goods, and the pains imposed in agriculture are homologous. They are not intrinsic pains; they must be judged in their instrumentality and with no presumption against innocent suffering.

Enjoying pleasure and escaping pain are of value, and evolutionary ecosystems are full of devices for accomplishing both. But much pain remains, and much thwarted pleasure. In nature, the pain-pleasure axis is not the only spectrum of value; indeed, it is not the highest value in either human or nonhuman life. It might be said, for instance, that knowing the meaning of life is more important for humans than leading a painless life, that a life with courage and sacrificial charity in it, which requires the presence of some pain, is a richer life than one without it. Similarly, the evolution of a world with carnivorous mammals, primates, humans, and culture is a richer world than one without them, and the presence of pain seems to have been necessary for such evolution. In that sense, advanced values are frequently built on suffering.

Perhaps it is not merely the pain but the indignity of domestication that is deplorable. A gazelle is pure wild grace, but a cow is a meat factory, pure and simple; a cow might even suffer less than a gazelle but be greatly disgraced. Cows cannot know they are disgraced, of course, and the capture of values in nature is not undignified. A lioness destroys a gazelle, and there is nothing unworthy here. Likewise, in domestication, humans parallel ecosystems and capture agriculturally the values in a cow. There is nothing undignified in this event, even though the once-natural values in the cow, like those in the gazelle, have to be destroyed by the predator.

Although we have defended eating animals as a primary, natural event, we have also said, secondarily, that there is an obligation to avoid pointless pain. Consider, for instance, the following case. There are more than 2,000,000 Muslims in Britain; the Jewish community numbers nearly 400,000. Muslims still practice animal sacrifice; a sheep or goat is sacrificed during a feast concluding a month of fasting, and often at the birth of a child. The animal is sacrificed to Allah, and the meat is eaten and enjoyed. Though Jews no longer practice animal sacrifice as they did in former times, they require their meat to be kosher, slaughtered according to religious ritual. Modern secular abattoirs stun animals with a massive blow or an electric shock before butchering them, and this is thought to be more humane. But it makes the animal unacceptable to Jews and Muslims, who must sever the major blood vessels of an unblemished animal. About 1,500,000 sheep and goats and 100,000 cattle are slaughtered by Jews and Muslims each year.

Animal rights activists have pressed to require stunning, and a government report finds that religious methods of slaughter result in a degree of suffering and distress that does not occur in a properly stunned animal. Muslims and Jews have joined forces to defend their practices.[2] But the additional pain that their methods impose, no longer necessary, cannot be interpreted in the context of ecology; it is pain inflicted for culture-based reasons. Unblemished animals make better sacrifices to God; they enhance religious cleanliness. This pain is ecologically pointless; it has point only culturally and, by the account given here, is not justified. This pain is not homologous; it is superfluous. Perhaps both Jews and Muslims can reach reformed religious convictions, in which respect for animal life overrides their previous concepts of cleanliness, or where the mercy of God prohibits pointless suffering.

Notes

1.   J. Baird Callicott, "Animal Liberation: A Triangular Affair," *Environmental Ethics* 2, 1980, p. 330.

2.   Karen DeYoung, "Ritual Slaughter Sparks Debate," *Washington Post,* 27 December 1985, pp. A19–20.

NO

John Mizzoni

Against Rolston's Defense of Eating Animals: Reckoning With the Nutritional Factor in the Argument for Vegetarianism

The practical objection to animal food in my case was its uncleanness; and, besides, when I had caught and cleaned and cooked and eaten my fish, they seemed not to have fed me essentially. It was insignificant and unnecessary, and cost more than it came to.

—H. D. Thoreau[1]

In his book, *Environmental Ethics: Duties to and Values in the Natural World,* the internationally acclaimed environmental ethicist, Holmes Rolston III, defends the view that nature and animals have values in and of themselves apart from the value they have *for* humans.[2] But when it comes to our duties to animals Rolston claims that humans have no duty to sentient life to become vegetarians.[3] Thus, in chapter 2, he defends the eating of animals. For Rolston, when human beings eat animals they are doing nothing more than following the ways of nature, in which pain, killing, and eating are natural and necessary elements of ecology.

In what follows, I examine the argument for vegetarianism that Rolston considers and summarily dismisses. It is the nutritional factor in the argument for vegetarianism, I will argue, that Rolston does not sufficiently address. By the nutritional factor I mean the fact that the eating of animals is not nutritionally required to sustain human life. In addition, although Rolston's criterion for distinguishing when to model human conduct on animal conduct is defensible, he applies it inconsistently. One reason for this is that Rolston misplaces the line he attempts to draw between culture and nature. Although he makes a distinction himself between culture and nature, Rolston fails to recognize that the nutritional "need" to eat meat is a cultural creation, not a natural event. For these reasons, Rolston's defense of eating animals is severely impaired.

From John Mizzoni, "Against Rolston's Defense of Eating Animals: Reckoning With the Nutritional Factor in the Argument for Vegetarianism," *International Journal of Applied Philosophy,* vol. 16 (Spring 2002), pp. 125–131. Copyright © 2002 by *International Journal of Applied Philosophy.* Reprinted by permission of the editor.

Rolston notes,

[a] characteristic argument for vegetarianism runs as follows:

1. Pain is a bad thing, whether in humans or in animals.

2. Humans (at least most of them) can live nutritiously without causing animal pain.

3. It is immoral for humans to kill and eat humans, causing them pain.

4. Food animals suffer pain, similarly to the way humans do, if killed and eaten.

5. There are no morally relevant differences between humans and food animals, [therefore]

6. It is immoral for humans to kill and eat animals, causing them pain.[4]

Rolston claims that the argument fails to distinguish between nature and culture. He says we should judge events in nature with an environmental ethic and events in culture with an interhuman ethic. This argument, says Rolston, misses the important "morally relevant differences that distinguish persons in culture from food animals in agriculture, where quasi-ecosystemic processes remain."[5] Apparently, Rolston does not think that premise two—the nutritional factor—pulls much weight in this argument, for he never mentions it again for the rest of the chapter. If we focus on the relevance of the nutritional factor, however, I think we will see what Rolston does not see, namely, that there is a disanalogy between animals eating animals in an ecosystem, and humans eating animals in a culture.

I will not try to prove the truth of the nutritional factor. Since Rolston does not dispute its truth we can only assume that he takes it as unproblematic. More and more, though, we are hearing from diverse sources that a vegetarian diet supplies sufficient human nutrition.[6]

With regard to vegetarianism, Rolston sets the boundaries of the issue as follows. On the one hand, he maintains that

(P) [H]uman conduct is not to be modeled on animal conduct.[7]

That we should not merely follow the example of "beasts" in the wild is, I think, uncontroversial. But on the other hand, he also argues that

(Q) [Animals] ought to be treated, by the homologous baseline principle, with no more suffering than might have been their lot in the wild, on average, adjusting for their modified capacities to care for themselves.[8]

This is where we should draw the line between inflicting pain that is "instrumental" to the natural functioning of an ecosystem and inflicting "pointless pain."[9]

Something like principle Q is commonly mentioned in environmental ethics. Paul Taylor's "Principle of Proportionality" (PP), for instance, captures the same idea. For Taylor, it is a principle to use when judging the effect of human conduct on animals:

> (PP) Actions that pursue nonbasic human interests are prohibited when they aggress against the basic interests of (wild) animals and plants and are incompatible with the attitude of respect for nature.[10]

James Sterba's "Principle of Disproportionality" (PD) is very similar:

> (PD) Actions that meet nonbasic or luxury needs of humans are prohibited when they aggress against the basic needs of individual animals and plants, or of whole species or ecosystems.[11]

Rolston's Principle Q, Taylor's (PP), and Sterba's (PD) are plausible initial principles for working out an ethic for animals and the environment. The difficulty that arises for Rolston maintaining his position is that P and Q are inconsistent demands. If P is true, then Q must be false, and when Q is true, then P must be false. When we say that we do not want to inflict more suffering on animals than they would suffer in the wild, in some sense we *are* modeling our conduct on animal conduct! The relevant criterion, or the "functional baseline," as Rolston calls it, is clearly derived from nature's ways. Is he not saying, with Q, that we should look at the amount of suffering the animal experiences in the wild and then model our conduct by inflicting no more suffering than they experience there?

The larger problem here is that Rolston wants to decide the morality of vegetarianism by looking at the facts about animals in the wild (i.e., the amount of suffering they experience). My point is that if we believe that we ought not to model our conduct on animals then we shouldn't focus on the facts about animals in the wild, but we should focus on the facts about us (i.e., the nutritional factor).

Rolston's inconsistency is most conspicuous when he says that "Humans in their eating habits follow nature; they can and ought to do so," and "Humans . . . can model their dietary habits on their ecosystems, but they cannot and should not model their interpersonal justice or charity on ecosystems."[12] Why is it that Rolston maintains that we *ought to* model our eating habits on the ecosystem, but not our interpersonal justice? It must be because Rolston really is asserting

> (P') It is impermissible to model interhuman conduct on animal conduct but permissible (and obligatory) to model human-to-animal conduct on animal conduct.

As we clarify Rolston's position to this point we can see the emphasis he places on the difference between interhuman conduct and human-to-animal conduct. What it comes down to for him is a difference between culture and nature. As he says, "The killing and eating of animals, when they occur in culture, are still events in nature; they are ecological events, no matter how superimposed by culture."[13] But, when these events are occurring within culture, how can one know if the events are simply culture-generated or genuinely natural events? It appears that Rolston has a rather generous test to check to see if certain human-to-animal actions are acceptable. But I will mention four cultural reasons for eating animals that have nothing to do with natural events. As this list grows longer, then, the less plausible it is to think that eating animals is simply a natural event.

One reason for eating animals is that it carries with it a certain status. Frances Moore Lappe calls it the "meat mystique." Meat, especially beef, she says, is a status symbol.[14] As Jeremy Rifkin describes it,

> [t]he identification of raw meat with power, male dominance, and privilege is among the oldest and most archaic cultural symbols still visible in contemporary civilization. The fact that meat, and especially beef, is still widely used as a tool of gender discrimination is a testimonial to the tenacity of prehistoric dietary practices and myths and the influence that food and diet have on the politics of society.[15]

There is much to be said about the psychological associations between meat, strength, masculinity, power, and prestige.

We may add to this a second reason: to most people, meat tastes good. We must wonder about this. Is meat-eating an acquired taste that is all the more palatable because of psychological associations like those already mentioned? If we say that it is not an acquired taste because there are biological urges for meat caused by our physiological make-up, that only pushes the question back in time. At that point, we could argue that the taste was acquired a very long time ago, but the fact would remain that it is still an acquired taste.

A third reason for eating animals might be what Lappe calls the "protein myth."[16] This ties into the nutritional factor. If many people still believe that they must eat animals in order to get the proper amount of protein for good nutrition, when that fact has been shown to be false by the nutritional factor, then we have a purely cultural reason for eating animals.

The last reason I will mention (I am sure there are many more) is pure convenience. The fact that animal food products are all around us, and the fact that so many people come from a tradition of meat-based diets, adds up to a very strong cultural reason for eating animals.

If that is what we know, and that is what we are familiar with, and what is most readily available to us are animal-based foods, then the view that cultural reasons explain the eating of animals is more feasible than Rolston's interpretation that the eating of animals is merely an event occurring in an ecosystemic context. According to Mary Midgley, in our culture today "There is . . . now a much greater gap between the way in which most of us will let a particular animal be treated if we can see it in front of us and the way in which we let masses of animals be treated out of our sight than has arisen in any previous state of culture."[17] This kind of phenomenon is possible precisely because of the cocoon-like feature of culture. Culture shields us in so many untold ways that things become excessively cloudy when we try to make decisions about human-to-animal conduct. Amidst the pressures of culture, however, and specifically compared to the cultural reasons of status, taste, protein, and convenience, the nutritional factor stands out as a steadier benchmark for deciding on our diet.

Although Rolston himself puts no emphasis whatsoever on the nutritional factor, as we have seen, he does embrace Principle Q, which is very much like Taylor's PP and Sterba's PD. I will next argue that, when Rolston wields Q, this will only breed inconsistencies for his stance on eating animals.

The benchmark for eating animals basically has two components: the precedent set in nature for eating meat and the fact that the pain inflicted on animals when humans kill them and eat them is not pointless, but rather instrumental to legitimate human ends. As an example of when pointless pain in inflicted on animals, Rolston cites the practice of severing the major blood vessels of animals, which is performed by the Muslim community in Britain for the purpose of animal sacrifice, and performed by the Jewish community for the purpose of kosher slaughtering. This is a case where Rolston claims the additional pain their methods impose cannot be interpreted in the context of ecology because it is pain inflicted for purely cultural reasons.[18]

Another similar case is the intense demand for feathers among ladies in London in 1914. After 20,000 birds of paradise, 40,000 hummingbirds, and 30,000 birds of other species were slaughtered for their feathers, the trade was judged unconscionable and greatly reduced.[19] In the same vein Rolston discusses fur worn solely for status, and also sport hunting.

These four cases, (1) religious ritual killing, (2) stylish feathers, (3) status symbol fur, and (4) sport hunting to satisfy male vanity, are cases that, for Rolston, are at odds with principle Q, which observes a difference between suffering that is instrumental to an ecosystem and suffering that is pointless. All four are morally unjustified and are supported only by rationalizing illusion. Rather than call cases (1) through (4) "pointless," though, it would be better to say (as an application of PP) that these actions are morally prohibited because they are pursuits of nonbasic human interests that are aggressing against the basic interests of animals, or (as an application of PD) that these actions are morally prohibited because they are meeting luxury needs of humans while aggressing against the basic needs of animals.

Given the way Rolston reasons about these four cases, and given the truth of the nutritional factor, why wouldn't an application of principle Q tell us that eating animals is also unjustified? Since eating animals is not required for nutrition, then it would count as a luxury, a non-basic need. Animals are being sacrificed for only culture-based reasons.

Rolston's first response to this would be that ritual throat cutting, killing for feathers, killing for status symbols, and killing for sport do not occur in nature, whereas eating meat does. But this response would assume that because a process is natural, it is right. As a counterexample to this assumption Peter Singer states that "It is, no doubt, 'natural' for women to produce an infant every year or two from puberty to menopause, but this does not mean that it is wrong to interfere with this process."[20] So, although meat eating occurs in the wild and is thus a candidate for us to consider, this alone does not make it acceptable.

Also, just as there are omnivores and carnivores in nature, there are also herbivores. In this case, then, even if we were to follow nature, it would not yield one obvious response. We have choices. When we look a little deeper than the appearance of meat eating occurring in nature and meat eating occurring in culture, and we confront the nutritional factor, then we are faced with the fact that eating animals is a luxury in which our non-basic needs are prioritized over the basic needs of animals. The nutritional factor seems to me to be very important in making a choice about including animals in our diet.

If we look at Rolston's principle Q and ask how, according to Rolston, sport hunting runs afoul of animal and environmental ethics, we will see an interesting parallel to be drawn about vegetarianism. Hunting, as Rolston admits, is an ecological event that occurs in nature. But unlike therapeutic hunting, which is done to manage certain species that will overpopulate and degrade their environment, and subsistence hunting, which is done in places where other adequate nutrition is unavailable, sport hunting crosses a line. (The distinctions between therapeutic hunting, subsistence hunting, and sport hunting are not Rolston's, but Varner's).[21] As Rolston sees it, "not one hunter in several hundred needs the game in his diet. They eat what they kill; they do not hunt to eat."[22] Although hunting, then, is an ecological event (like meat-eating), when it occurs for unnecessary reasons such as "flattering male vanities" (or satisfying desires of taste, status, or convenience), then it becomes ethically suspect. So shouldn't it follow that, although meat eating is an ecological event, when it occurs for unnecessary reasons, then *it* becomes ethically suspect?

It seems to me that, when Rolston uses principle Q to show that sport hunting is wrong, that commits him to the conclusion that meat eating is wrong (if, of course, the nutritional factor is true). If sport hunting can be seen as a cultural event, then meat eating can also be seen as a cultural event. And, in fact, it is more plausible (in the light of the four reasons I've given above) to see meat eating as a cultural, rather than a merely ecological, event.

We can accept Rolston's principles P' and Q as consistent. When we use principle Q to decide how to treat animals by seeking to create no more suffering than they might experience in the wild, then we are also using principle P' because, by measuring the pain of the animals, we are, in a sense, modeling human-to-animal conduct on animal conduct.

Does eating animals, then, respect the ecology as Rolston alleges? Even if the evolution of a world with mammals, primates, humans, and culture is a richer world than one without them, and the presence of pain was necessary, it does not follow, by Rolston's own principles, that we should inflict more pain than that which is necessary. And if the nutritional factor is true then we *are* inflicting more pain than is necessary when we eat animals. We can, most easily, in the manner of Henry David Thoreau, respect the ecology without eating animals.[23]

Notes

1.   H. D. Thoreau, *Walden; or, Life in the Woods* (New York: Dover Publications, 1854 [1995]): 139.

2. H. Rolston III, *Environmental Ethics: Duties to and Values in the Natural World,* (Philadelphia: Temple University Press, 1988).

3. Ibid., 80.

4. Ibid.

5. Ibid.

6. F. M. Lappe, *Diet for a Small Planet* (New York: Ballantine Books, 20th Anniversary Edition, 1991); W. Aiken, "Ethical Issues in Agriculture," *Earthbound: Introductory Essays in Environmental Ethics,* ed. T. Regan (Prospect Heights, Ill.: Waveland Press, 1990 [reissue of 1984 volume]): 247–288; P. Singer, *Practical Ethics* (New York: Cambridge University Press, 2nd ed., 1993); S. K. Yntema, *Vegetarian Children* (Ithaca, N.Y.: McBooks Press, 1995).

7. H. Rolston, *Environmental Ethics,* 77.

8. Ibid., 79.

9. Ibid., 60, 82.

10. P. W. Taylor, *Respect for Nature: A Theory of Environmental Ethics* (Princeton, N.J.: Princeton University Press, 1986): 263.

11. J. P. Sterba, "Reconciling Anthropocentric and Nonanthropocentric Environmental Ethics," *Environmental Values* 3 (1994): 229–244, esp. 232; J. P. Sterba, "From Biocentric Individualism to Biocentric Pluralism," *Environmental Ethics* 17 (1995): 191–207, esp. 199.

12. H. Rolston, *Environmental Ethics,* 81.

13. Ibid., 79.

14. F. M. Lappe, *Diet for a Small Planet,* 90.

15. J. Rifkin, *Beyond Beef: The Rise and Fall of the Cattle Culture* (New York: Penguin Books, 1992): 244.

16. F. M. Lappe, *Diet for a Small Planet,* 158.

17. M. Midgley, "Towards a More Humane View of the Beasts?" *The Environment in Question: Ethics and Global Issues,* ed. D. E. Cooper and J. A. Palmer (New York: Routledge, 1992): 28–36, esp. 29.

18. H. Rolston, *Environmental Ethics,* 83–84.

19. Ibid., 84.

20. P. Singer, *Practical Ethics,* 71.

21. G. E. Varner, "Can Animal Rights Activists Be Environmentalists?" *Environmental Philosophy and Environmental Activism,* ed. D. E. Marietta, Jr. and L. Embree (Lanham, Md.: Rowman & Littlefield, 1995): 169–201, esp. 174.

22. H. Rolston, *Environmental Ethics,* 90.

23. This paper was presented to the Society for the Study of Ethics and Animals at the December 1997 meeting of the American Philosophical Association, which was held in Philadelphia.

POSTSCRIPT

Is It Morally Permissible to Eat Meat?

Traditionally, there has been no question with regard to the moral question of eating meat. There is no law against it; it is widely practiced; and it is supported by the biblical idea that God gave people animals to eat. So it is to some extent a great change in the moral climate that this question is even being raised at all.

It is partly due to the views of environmental thinkers such as Rolston that people have begun to think seriously about the place of human beings within the larger biological environment. This naturally leads to questions about animals and human beings and their relationship.

The most significant fact that unites all people and animals (except for very primitive animals) is that all can suffer. All can feel pain. Once this is acknowledged, the question is whether or not the animals raised for food are made to suffer pain needlessly.

A classic work in this field is Peter Singer, *Animal Liberation* (New York Review of Books, 1990). Bernard E. Rollin, in *Farm Animal Welfare: Social, Bioethical, and Research Issues* (Iowa State University Press, 1995), and Howard F. Lyman, in *Mad Cowboy: Plain Truth From the Cattle Rancher Who Won't Eat Meat* (Scribner, 1998), address the conditions under which animals are raised for food, and Lyman in particular is critical of the negative impact that this has on human beings. Carol J. Adams, in *The Sexual Politics of Meat: A Feminist-Vegetarian Critical Theory,* 10th anniversary ed. (Continuum Pub Group, 1999), argues that meat eating is connected with male dominance. Also relevant are Craig B. Stanford et al., eds., *Meat-Eating and Human Evolution* (Oxford University Press, 2001); Eric Schlosser, *Fast Food Nation: The Dark Side of the All-American Meal* (Harper-Collins, 2002); Matthew Scully, *Dominion: The Power of Man, the Suffering of Animals, and the Call to Mercy* (St. Martin's Press, 2002); and Charles Patterson, *Eternal Treblinka: Our Treatment of Animals and the Holocaust* (Lantern Books, 2002).

ISSUE 13

Is Affirmative Action Fair?

YES: Albert G. Mosley, from "Affirmative Action: Pro," in Albert G. Mosley and Nicholas Capaldi, *Affirmative Action: Social Justice or Unfair Preference?* (Rowman & Littlefield, 1996)

NO: Louis P. Pojman, from "The Case Against Affirmative Action," *International Journal of Applied Philosophy* (Spring 1998)

ISSUE SUMMARY

YES: Professor of philosophy Albert G. Mosley argues that affirmative action is a continuation of the history of black progress since the *Brown v. Board of Education* desegregation decision of 1954 and the Civil Rights Act of 1964. He defends affirmative action as a "benign use of race."

NO: Professor of philosophy Louis P. Pojman contends that affirmative action violates the moral principle that maintains that each person is to be treated as an individual, not as representative of a group. He stresses that individual merit needs to be appreciated and that respect should be given to each person on an individual basis.

T hroughout history, women and minority groups have been discriminated against in the United States. However, it might be difficult for many of us today to appreciate the extent of past discrimination and the ways in which social, legal, and political institutions were discriminatory.

Slavery is probably the most blatant form of past racism. We know that people were bought and sold, but the words are so familiar that the realities they stand for may never rise to consciousness. Many particular events and experiences lie behind a simple word like *slavery*. For example, the importation of slaves to this country was illegal before slaveholding itself became so. When ships at sea bringing African slaves to America found themselves in danger of being confronted by the law, it was easy to do what smugglers on the high seas always do with their contraband: the blacks, chained together and weighted down, were dropped overboard. Even after the Civil War, blacks were denied the right to vote, to testify in court, to own land, or to make contracts. In many states, laws restricted blacks in every conceivable aspect of their lives, including education, employment, and housing.

With respect to discrimination against women, consider the following, written by U.S. Supreme Court justice Joseph Bradley in concurring with the Court's decision in *Bradwell v. Illinois* (1873) that the state of Illinois was justified in denying Myra Bradwell a license to practice law on the grounds that she was a woman:

> [T]he civil law, as well as nature herself, has always recognized a wide difference in the respective spheres and destinies of man and woman. Man is, or should be, woman's protector and defender. The natural and proper timidity and delicacy which belongs to the female sex evidently unfits it for many of the occupations of civil life. The constitution of the family organization, which is founded in the divine ordinance, as well as in the nature of things, indicates the domestic sphere as that which properly belongs to the domain and functions of womanhood. The harmony . . . of interests and views which belong . . . to the family institution is repugnant to the idea of a woman adopting a distinct and independent career from that of her husband. . . . The paramount destiny and mission of woman are to fulfill the noble and benign offices of wife and mother.

Such thoughts are rarely openly expressed these days, and segregation and discrimination do not have legal support. One wonders, though, how much attitudes have actually changed. The law can change, but old attitudes can persist, and they can even be preserved and passed down from generation to generation. Moreover, the results of past social injustices are with us today.

Some of the consequences of past discrimination are systemic rather than individual-based. However much *individuals* might reject certain attitudes and practices of the past, there will usually be some *systemic* problems that are not so easily eliminated. There are systemic consequences of racist and sexist practices in the professions, in housing, in education, in the distribution of wealth, etc. For example, even if previously "white only" schools take down their "white only" signs, and the individuals involved agree to accept applicants of any race, the school system itself would be left virtually unchanged from its segregationist days. The situation of white-only schools would systematically perpetuate itself. This is where many feel that affirmative action can step in and change the system.

Albert G. Mosley places controversies surrounding affirmative action in a historical context and considers the justification of affirmative action both from the "backward-looking" perspective of corrective justice and from the "forward-looking" perspective of the social distribution of harms and benefits. Louis P. Pojman explains what he means by the term *affirmative action*. He maintains that affirmative action requires us to practice *reverse discrimination*, to fail to treat people as individuals, and to undervalue merit.

Albert G. Mosley  **YES**

Affirmative Action: Pro

Legislative and Judicial Background

In 1941, Franklin Roosevelt issued Executive Order 8802 banning discrimination in employment by the federal government and defense contractors. Subsequently, many bills were introduced in Congress mandating equal employment opportunity but none were passed until the Civil Rights Act of 1964. The penalty for discrimination in Executive Order 8802 and the bills subsequently proposed was that the specific victim of discrimination be "made whole," that is, put in the position he or she would have held were it not for the discriminatory act, including damages for lost pay and legal expenses.

The contemporary debate concerning affirmative action can be traced to the landmark decision of *Brown v. Board of Education* (1954), whereby local, state, and federal ordinances enforcing segregation by race were ruled unconstitutional. In subsequent opinions, the Court ruled that state-mandated segregation in libraries, swimming pools, and other publicly funded facilities was also unconstitutional. In *Swann v. Charlotte-Mecklenburg* (1971), the Court declared that "in order to prepare students to live in a pluralistic society" school authorities might implement their desegregation order by deciding that "each school should have a prescribed ratio of Negro to White students reflecting the proportion for the district as a whole."[1] The ratio was not to be an inflexible one, but should reflect local variations in the ratio of Whites to Blacks. But any predominantly one-race school in a district with a mixed population and a history of segregation was subject to "close scrutiny." This requirement was attacked by conservatives as imposing a "racial quota," a charge that reverberates in the contemporary debate concerning affirmative action.

With the Montgomery bus boycotts of the mid-1950s, Blacks initiated an era of nonviolent direct action to publicly protest unjust laws and practices that supported racial discrimination. The graphic portrayals of repression and violence produced by the civil rights movement precipitated a national revulsion against the unequal treatment of African Americans. Blacks demanded their constitutional right to participate in the political process and share equal access to public accommodations, government-supported programs, and employment opportunities. But as John F. Kennedy stated in an address to Congress:

"There is little value in a Negro's obtaining the right to be admitted to hotels and restaurants if he has no cash in his pocket and no job."[2]

Kennedy stressed that the issue was not merely eliminating discrimination, but eliminating as well the oppressive economic and social burdens imposed on Blacks by racial discrimination.[3] To this end, he advocated a weak form of affirmative action, involving eliminating discrimination and expanding educational and employment opportunities (including apprenticeships and on-the-job training). The liberal vision was that, given such opportunities, Blacks would move up the economic ladder to a degree relative to their own merit. Thus, a principal aim of the Civil Rights Act of 1964 was to effect a redistribution of social, political, and economic benefits and to provide legal remedies for the denial of individual rights.

The Civil Rights Act of 1964

The first use of the phrase "affirmative action" is found in Executive Order 10952, issued by President John F. Kennedy in 1961. This order established the Equal Employment Opportunity Commission (EEOC) and directed that contractors on projects funded, in whole or in part, with federal funds "take affirmative action to ensure that applicants are employed, and employees are treated during their employment, without regard to the race, creed, color, or national origin."

As a result of continuing public outrage at the level of violence and animosity shown toward Blacks, a stronger version of the Civil Rights Bill was presented to the Congress than Kennedy had originally recommended. Advocates pointed out that Blacks suffered an unemployment rate that was twice that of Whites and that Black employment was concentrated in semiskilled and unskilled jobs. They emphasized that national prosperity would be improved by eliminating discrimination and integrating Black talent into its skilled and professional workforce.[4]

Fewer Blacks were employed in professional positions than had the requisite skills, and those Blacks who did occupy positions commensurate with their skill level had half the lifetime earnings of Whites. Such facts were introduced during legislative hearings to show the need to more fully utilize and reward qualified Blacks throughout the labor force, and not merely in the unskilled and semiskilled sectors. . . .

Conceptual Issues

There are many interests that governments pursue—maximization of social production; equitable distribution of rights, opportunities, and services; social safety and cohesion; restitution—and those interests may conflict in various situations. In particular, governments as well as their constituents have a prima facie obligation to satisfy the liabilities they incur. One such liability derives from past and present unjust exclusionary acts depriving minorities and women of opportunities and amenities made available to other groups.

"Backward looking" arguments defend affirmative action as a matter of *corrective justice,* where paradigmatically the harmdoer is to make restitution to the harmed so as to put the harmed in the position the harmed most likely would have occupied had the harm not occurred. An important part of making restitution is the acknowledgment it provides that the actions causing injury were unjust and such actions will be curtailed and corrected. In this regard Bernard Boxill writes:

> Without the acknowledgement of error, the injurer implies that the injured has been treated in a manner that befits him. . . . In such a case, even if the unjust party repairs the damage he has caused . . . nothing can be demanded on legal or moral grounds, and the repairs made are gratuitous. . . . justice requires that we acknowledge that this treatment of others can be required of us; thus, where an unjust injury has occurred, the injurer reaffirms his belief in the other's equality by conceding that repair can be demanded of him, and the injured rejects the allegation of his inferiority . . . by demanding reparation.[5]

This view is based on the idea that restitution is a basic moral principle that creates obligations that are just as strong as the obligations to maximize wealth and distribute it fairly.[6] If x has deprived y of opportunities y had a right not to be deprived of in this manner, then x is obligated to return y to the position y would have occupied had x not intervened; x has this obligation irrespective of other obligations x may have. . . .

[An] application of this principle involves the case where x is not a person but an entity, like a government or a business. If y was unjustly deprived of employment when firm F hired z instead of y because z was White and y Black, then y has a right to be made whole, that is, brought to the position he/she would have achieved had that deprivation not occurred. Typically, this involves giving y a position at least as good as the one he/she would have acquired originally and issuing back pay in the amount that y would have received had he/she been hired at the time of the initial attempt.

Most critics of preferential treatment acknowledge the applicability of principles of restitution to individuals in specific instances of discrimination. The strongest case is where y was as or more qualified than z in the initial competition, but the position was given to z because y was Black and z was White.[7] Subsequently, y may not be as qualified for an equivalent position as some new candidate z', but is given preference because of the past act of discrimination by F that deprived y of the position he or she otherwise would have received.

Some critics have suggested that, in such cases, z' is being treated unfairly. For z', as the most qualified applicant, has a right not to be excluded from the position in question purely on the basis of race; and y has a right to restitution for having unjustly been denied the position in the past. But the dilemma is one in appearance only. For having unjustly excluded y in the past, the current position that z' has applied for is not one that F is free to offer to the public. It is a position that is already owed to y, and is not available for open competition. Judith Jarvis Thomson makes a similar point:

> suppose two candidates [A and B] for a civil service job have equally good test scores, but there is only one job available. We could decide between them by coin-tossing. But in fact we do allow for declaring for A straightway, where A is a veteran, and B is not. It may be that B is a non-veteran through no fault of his own . . . Yet the fact is that B is not a veteran and A is. On the assumption that the veteran has served his country, the country owes him something. And it is plain that giving him preference is not an unjust way in which part of that debt of gratitude can be paid.[8]

In a similar way, individual Blacks who have suffered from acts of unjust discrimination are owed something by the perpetrator(s) of such acts, and this debt takes precedence over the perpetrator's right to use his or her options to hire the most qualified person for the position in question.

Many White males have developed expectations about the likelihood of their being selected for educational, employment, and entrepreneurial opportunities that are realistic only because of the general exclusion of women and non-Whites as competitors for such positions. Individuals enjoying inflated odds of obtaining such opportunities because of racist and sexist practices are recipients of an "unjust enrichment."

Redistributing opportunities would clearly curtail benefits that many have come to expect. And given the frustration of their traditional expectations, it is understandable that they would feel resentment. But blocking traditional expectations is not unjust if those expectations conflict with the equally important moral duties of restitution and just distribution. It is a question, not of "is," but of "ought": not "Do those with decreased opportunities as a result of affirmative action feel resentment?" but "Should those with decreased opportunities as a result of affirmative action feel resentment?" . . .

Since Title VII [of the Civil Rights Act of 1964] protects bona fide seniority plans, it forces the burden of rectification to be borne by Whites who are entering the labor force rather than Whites who are the direct beneficiaries of past discriminatory practices. Given this limitation placed on affirmative action remedies, the burden of social restitution may, in many cases, be borne by those who were not directly involved in past discriminatory practices. But it is generally not true that those burdened have not benefited at all from past discriminatory practices. For the latent effects of acts of invidious racial discrimination have plausibly bolstered and encouraged the efforts of Whites in roughly the same proportion as it inhibited and discouraged the efforts of Blacks. Such considerations are also applicable to cases where F discriminated against y in favor of z, but the make-whole remedy involves providing compensation to y' rather than y. This suggests that y' is an *undeserving beneficiary* of the preferential treatment meant to compensate for the unjust discrimination against y, just as z' above appeared to be the innocent victim forced to bear the burden that z benefited from. Many critics have argued that this misappropriation of benefits and burdens demonstrates the unfairness of compensation to groups rather than individuals. But it is important that the context and rationale for such remedies be appreciated.

In cases of "egregious" racial discrimination, not only is it true that F discriminated against a particular Black person y, but F's discrimination advertised a general disposition to discriminate against any other Black person who might seek such positions. The specific effect of F's unjust discrimination was that y was refused a position he or she would otherwise have received. The latent (or dispositional) effect of F's unjust discrimination was that many Blacks who otherwise would have sought such positions were discouraged from doing so. Thus, even if the specific y actually discriminated against can no longer be compensated, F has an obligation to take affirmative action to communicate to Blacks as a group that such positions are indeed open to them. After being found in violation of laws prohibiting racial discrimination, many agencies have disclaimed further discrimination while in fact continuing to do so.[9] In such cases, the courts have required the discriminating agencies to actually hire and/or promote Blacks who may not be as qualified as some current White applicants until Blacks approach the proportion in F's labor force they in all likelihood would have achieved had F's unjust discriminatory acts not deterred them.

Of course, what this proportion would have been is a matter of speculation. It may have been less than the proportion of Blacks available in the relevant labor pool from which applicants are drawn if factors other than racial discrimination act to depress the merit of such applicants. This point is made again and again by critics. Some, such as Thomas Sowell, argue that cultural factors often mitigate against Blacks meriting representation in a particular labor force in proportion to their presence in the pool of candidates looking for jobs or seeking promotions.[10] Others, such as Michael Levin, argue that cognitive deficits limit Blacks from being hired and promoted at a rate proportionate to their presence in the relevant labor pool.[11] What such critics reject is the assumption that, were it not for pervasive discrimination and overexploitation, Blacks would be equally represented in the positions in question. What is scarcely considered is the possibility that, were it not for racist exclusions, Blacks might be over rather than under represented in competitive positions.

Establishing Blacks' presence at a level commensurate with their proportion in the relevant labor market need not be seen as an attempt to actualize some valid prediction. Rather, given the impossibility of determining what level of representation Blacks would have achieved were it not for racist discrimination, the assumption of proportional representation is the only *fair* assumption to make. This is not to argue that Blacks should be maintained in such positions, but their contrived exclusion merits an equally contrived rectification.[12]

Racist acts excluding Blacks affected particular individuals, but were directed at affecting the behavior of the group of all those similar to the victim. Likewise, the benefits of affirmative action policies should not be conceived as limited in their effects to the specific individuals receiving them. Rather, those benefits should be conceived as extending to all those identified with the recipient, sending the message that opportunities are indeed available to qualified Black candidates who would have been excluded in the past. . . .

Forward-Looking Justifications of Affirmative Action

. . . [Some] have defended preferential treatment but denied that it should be viewed as a form of reparation. This latter group rejects "backward looking" justifications of affirmative action and defends it instead on "forward-looking" grounds that include distributive justice, minimizing subordination, and maximizing social utility.

Thus, Ronald Fiscus argues that backward-looking arguments have distorted the proper justification for affirmative action policies.[13] Backward-looking arguments depend on the paradigm of traditional tort cases, where a specific individual x has deprived another individual y of a specific good t through an identifiable act a, and x is required to restore y to the position y would have had, had a not occurred. But typically, preferential treatment requires that x' (rather than x) restore y' (instead of y) with a good t' that y' supposedly would have achieved had y not been deprived of t by x. The displacement of perpetrator (x' for x) and victim (y' for y) gives rise to the problem of (1) White males who are innocent of acts having caused harm nonetheless being forced to provide restitution for such acts; and (2) Blacks who were not directly harmed by those acts nonetheless becoming the principal beneficiaries of restitution for those acts. . . .

Fiscus argues that the backward-looking argument reinforces the perception that preferential treatment is unfair to innocent White males, and so long as this is the case, both the courts and the public are likely to oppose strong affirmative action policies such as quotas, set-asides, and other preferential treatment policies.

In contrast, Fiscus recommends that preferential treatment be justified in terms of distributive justice, which as a matter of equal protection, "requires that individuals be awarded the positions, advantages, or benefits they would have been awarded under fair conditions," that is, conditions under which racist exclusion would not have precluded Blacks from attaining "their deserved proportion of the society's important benefits." Conversely, "distributive justice also holds that individuals or groups may not claim positions, advantages, or benefits that they would not have been awarded under fair conditions."[14] These conditions jointly prohibit White males from claiming an unreasonable share of social benefits and protects White males from having to bear an unreasonable share of the redistributive burden.

Fiscus takes the position that any deviation between Blacks and Whites from strict proportionality in the distribution of current goods is evidence of racism. Thus, if Blacks were 20 percent of a particular population but held no positions in the police or fire departments, that is indicative of past and present racial discrimination. . . .

Because the Equal Protection Clause of the Fourteenth Amendment protects citizens from statistical discrimination on the basis of race, the use of race as the principal reason for excluding certain citizens from benefits made available to other citizens is a violation of that person's constitutional rights. This was one basis for [Alan] Bakke's suit against the UC-Davis medical school's 16 percent minority set-aside for medical school admission. There were eighty-four seats out of the one hundred admission slots that he was eligible to fill, and he was excluded from competing for the other sixteen slots because of his race. On the basis of the standard criteria (GPA, MCAT scores, etc.), Bakke argued that he would have been admitted before any of the Black applicants admitted under the minority set-aside. He therefore claimed that he was being excluded from the additional places available because he was White.

Currently, Blacks have approximately 3.25 times fewer physicians than would be expected given their numbers in the population. Native Americans have 7 times fewer physicians than what would have been expected if intelligent, well-trained, and motivated Native Americans had tried to become physicians at the same rate as did European Americans.

For Fiscus, the underrepresentation of African and Native Americans among physicians and the maldistribution of medical resources to minority communities is clearly the effect of generations of racist exclusions. . . . Not only are qualified members of the oppressed group harmed by . . . prejudice, but even more harmed are the many who would have been qualified but for injuries induced by racial prejudice.

For Fiscus, individuals of different races would have been as equally distributed in the social body as the molecules of a gas in a container and he identifies the belief in the inherent equality of races with the Equal Protection Clause of the Fourteenth Amendment.[15] In a world without racism, minorities would be represented among the top one hundred medical school applicants at UC-Davis in the same proportion as they were in the general population. Accordingly, because Bakke did not score among the top eighty-four Whites, he would not have qualified for admission. Thus, he had no right to the position he was contesting, and indeed if he were given such a position in lieu of awarding it to a minority, Bakke would be much like a person who had received stolen goods. "Individuals who have not personally harmed minorities may nevertheless be prevented from reaping the benefits of the harm inflicted by the society at large."[16]

Justice O'Connor has voiced skepticism toward the assumption that members of different races would "gravitate with mathematical exactitude to each employer or union absent unlawful discrimination."[17] She considers it sheer speculation as to "how many minority students would have been admitted to the medical school at Davis absent past discrimination in educational opportunities."[18] I likewise consider it speculative to assume that races would be represented in every area in proportion to their proportion of the general population. But because it is impossible to reasonably predict what that distribution would have been absent racial discrimination, it is not mere speculation but morally fair practice to assume that it would have been the same as the proportion in the general population. Given the fact of legally sanctioned invidious racism against Blacks in U.S. history, the burden of proof should not be on the oppressed group to prove that it would be represented at a level proportionate to its presence in the general population. Rather, the burden of proof should be on the majority to show why its overrepresentation among the most well off is not the result of unfair competition imposed by racism. We are morally obligated to assume proportional representation until there are more plausible reasons than racism for assuming otherwise. . . .

Thus, it should be the responsibility of the Alabama Department of Public Safety to show why no Blacks were members of its highway patrol as of 1970, even though Blacks were 25 percent of the relevant workforce in Alabama. It should be the responsibility of the company and the union to explain why there were no Blacks with seniority in the union at the Kaiser plant in Louisiana, although Blacks made up 39 percent of the surrounding population. Likewise, it should be the responsibility of the union to explain why no Blacks had been admitted to the Sheet Metal Workers' Union in New York City although minorities were 29 percent of the available workforce. If no alternative explanations are more plausible, then the assumption that the disparity in representation is the result of racism should stand.

The question should not be whether White males are innocent or guilty of racism or sexism, but whether they have a right to inflated odds of obtaining benefits relative to minorities and women. A White male is innocent only up to the point where he takes advantage of "a benefit he would not qualify for without the accumulated effects of racism. At that point he becomes an accomplice in, and a beneficiary of, society's racism. He becomes the recipient of stolen goods."[19] . . .

Cass Sunstein also argues that the traditional compensation model based on the model of a discrete injury caused by one individual (the tort-feasor or defendant) and suffered by another individual (the plaintiff) is inadequate to capture the situation arising from racial and sexual discrimination.[20] With the traditional tortlike model, the situation existing prior to the injury is assumed to be noncontestable, and the purpose of restitution is to restore the injured party to the position that party would have occupied if the injury had not occurred. But in cases where the injury is not well defined, where neither defendant nor plaintiff are individuals connected by a discrete event, and where the position the injured party would have occupied but for the injury is unspecifiable, then in such cases dependence on the traditional model of compensatory justice is questionable.[21]

In contrast to the position taken by Fiscus, Sunstein argues that the claim that affirmative action and preferential treatment is meant to put individuals in the position they would have occupied had their groups not been subject to racial and sexual discrimination is nonsensical: "What would the world look like if it had been unaffected by past discrimination on the basis of race and sex? . . . the question is unanswerable, not because of the absence of good social science, but because of the obscure epistemological status of the question itself."[22]

Affirmative action must be justified in terms of alternative conceptions of the purpose of legal intervention, and Sunstein recommends instead the notion of "risk management" (intended to offset increased risks faced by a group rather than compensate the injuries suffered by a particular individual) and the "principle of nonsubordination" (whereby measures are taken to reverse a situation in which an irrelevant difference has been transformed by legally sanctioned acts of the state into a social disadvantage). The notion of risk management is meant to apply to cases where injuries are "individually small but collectively large" so that pursuing each case individually would be too costly both in terms of time and effort.[23] In such cases, those harmed may be unable to establish a direct causal link between their injuries and the plaintiff's actions. Thus, a person who develops a certain type of cancer associated with a toxin produced by a particular company might have developed that condition even in the absence of the company's negligent behavior. At most, they can argue that the company's actions caused an increased risk of injury, rather than any specific instance of that injury.

Harms suffered in this way systematically affect certain groups with higher frequency than other groups, without it being possible to establish causal links between the injuries of specific plaintiffs and the actions of the defendant. Regulatory agencies should be designed to address harms that are the result of increased risks rather than of a discrete action.[24] One of their principle aims should be not to compensate each injured party (and only injured parties), "but instead to deter and punish the risk-creating behavior" by redistributing social goods.[25] . . .

The principle of nonsubordination is meant to apply to cases where the existing distribution of wealth and opportunities between groups are the result of law rather than natural attributes.[26] The purpose of affirmative action from a forward-looking perspective should be to end social subordination and reverse the situation in which irrelevant differences have been, through social and legal structures, turned into systematic disadvantages operative in multiple spheres that diminish participation in democratic forms of life.[27] . . .

> affirmative action does not appear an impermissible 'taking' of an antecedent entitlement. Because the existing distribution of benefits and burdens between Blacks and Whites and men and women is not natural . . . and because it is in part a product of current laws and practices having discriminatory effects, it is not decisive if some Whites and men are disadvantaged as a result.[28]

A central question in the debate over affirmative action is the extent to which racial classifications are important in accomplishing the goal of relieving the subordinate status of minorities and women. Given the aim of improving safety in transportation, classifying people in terms of their race is rationally irrelevant, while classifying them in terms of their driving competency, visual acuity, and maturity is essential. On the other hand, given the aim of improving health care in Black neighborhoods, classifying applicants for medical school in terms of their race is, in addition to their academic and clinical abilities, a very relevant factor.

To illustrate, African Americans, Hispanics, and Native Americans make up 22 percent of the population but represent only 10 percent of entering medical students and 7 percent of practicing physicians. A number of studies have shown that underrepresented minority physicians are more likely than their majority counterparts to care for poor patients and patients of similar ethnicity. Indeed, "each ethnic group of patients was more likely to be cared for by a physician of their own ethnic background than by a physician of another ethnic background."[29] This suggests that sociocultural factors such as language, physical identity, personal background, and experiences are relevant factors in determining the kinds of communities in which a physician will establish a practice. If this is the case, then the race of a medical school applicant would be an important factor in providing medical services to certain underrepresented communities. Thus, while there might be some purposes for which race is irrelevant, there might be other purposes in which race is important (though perhaps not necessary) for achieving the end in view.[30] The remedy targets Blacks as a group because racially discriminatory practices were directed against Blacks as a group.[31]

. . . Preferential treatment programs are meant to offset the disadvantages imposed by racism so that Blacks are not forced to bear the principal costs of that error.

. . . To condemn polices meant to correct for racial barriers as themselves erecting barriers is to ignore the difference between action and reaction, cause and effect, aggression and self-defense. . . .

Conclusion

Racism was directed against Blacks whether they were talented, average, or mediocre, and attenuating the effects of racism requires distributing remedies similarly. Affirmative action policies compensate for the harms of racism (overt and institutional) through antidiscrimination laws and preferential policies. Prohibiting the benign use of race as a factor in the award of educational, employment and business opportunities would eliminate compensation for past and present racism and reinforce the moral validity of the status quo, with Blacks overrepresented among the least well off and underrepresented among the most well off.

It has become popular to use affirmative action as a scapegoat for the increased vulnerability of the White working class. But it should be recognized that the civil rights revolution (in general) and affirmative action (in particular) has been beneficial, not just to Blacks, but also to Whites (e.g., women, the disabled, the elderly) who otherwise would be substantially more vulnerable than they are now.

Affirmative action is directed toward empowering those groups that have been adversely affected by past and present exclusionary practices. Initiatives to abolish preferential treatment would inflict a grave injustice on African Americans, for they signal a reluctance to acknowledge that the plight of African Americans is the result of institutional practices that require institutional responses.

Notes

1. Kent Greenawalt, *Discrimination and Reverse Discrimination* (New York: Alfred A. Knopf, 1983), 129 ff.

2. Kathanne W. Greene, *Affirmative Action and Principles of Justice* (New York: Greenwood Press, 1989), 22.

3. Kennedy stated: "Even the complete elimination of racial discrimination in employment—a goal toward which this nation must strive—will not put a single unemployed Negro to work unless he has the skills required." Greene, *Affirmative Action,* 23.

4. Greene, *Affirmative Action,* 31.

5. Bernard Boxill, "The Morality of Reparation" in *Social Theory and Practice,* 2, no. 1, Spring 1972: 118–119. It is for such reasons that welfare programs are not sufficient to satisfy the claims of Blacks for restitution. Welfare programs contain no admission of the unjust violation of rights and seek merely to provide the basic means for all to pursue opportunities in the future.

6. I am presuming that most of us would recognize certain primae facie duties such as truth telling, promise keeping, restitution, benevolence, justice, nonmalficience as generally obligatory. See W. D. Ross, *The Right and the Good* (Oxford: Clarendon Press, 1930).

7. Even in the case where y was only as qualified as z, a fair method of choice between candidates should produce an equitable distribution of such positions between Blacks and Whites in the long run if not in the short.

8. Judith Jarvis Thompson, *Philosophy and Public Affairs* 2 (Summer 1973): 379–380.

9. *Sheet Metal Workers v. EEOC* (1986); *United States v. Paradise* (1987).

10. Thomas Sowell, *Ethnic America* (New York: Basic Books, 1981); *Preferential Policies: An International Perspective* (New York: William Morrow, 1990); For a recent critique of Sowell's position, see Christopher Jencks, *Rethinking Social Policy: Race, Poverty, and the Underclass* (New York: Harper, 1993) chap. 1.

11. Michael Levin, "Race, Biology, and Justice" in *Public Affairs Quarterly,* 8, no. 3 (July 1994). There are many good reasons for skepticism regarding the validity of using IQ as a measure of cognitive ability. See *The Bell Curve Wars* ed. Steven Fraser (New York: Basic Books, 1995); *The Bell Curve Debate* ed. by Russell Jacoby and Naomi Glauberman (New York: Times Books, 1995); Allan Chase, *The Legacy of Malthus* (Urbana: University of Illinois Press, 1980); Steven J. Gould, *The Mismeasure of Man* (New York: Norton, 1981); R. C. Lewontin, S. Rose, L. J. Kamin, *Not In Our Genes* (New York: Pantheon Books, 1984).

12. See Robert Fullinwider, *The Reverse Discrimination Controversy: A Moral and Legal Analysis* (Totowa, N.J.: Rowman & Littlefield, 1980), 117. Ronald Fiscus, *The Constitutional Logic of Affirmative Action* (Durham, N.C.: Duke University Press, 1992).

13. Ronald J. Fiscus, *The Constitutional Logic of Affirmative Action* (Durham, N.C.: Duke University Press, 1992).

14. Fiscus, *Constitutional Logic,* 13.

15. Fiscus, *Constitutional Logic,* 20–26.

16. Fiscus, *Constitutional Logic,* 38.

17. *Sheet Metal Workers v. EEOC,* 478 US 421, 494 (1986); Fiscus, *Constitutional Logic,* 42.

18. *City of Richmond v. J. A. Croson Co.,* 109 S.Ct. at 724 (1989); Fiscus, *Constitutional Logic,* 42.

19. Fiscus, *Constitutional Logic,* 47. With regard to the problem of so-called "undeserving beneficiaries" of affirmative action Fiscus writes: "When the rightful owner of stolen goods cannot be found, the law . . . may or may not award possession to the original but wrongful claimant; but if it does not, if it awards pos-

session to a third party whose claim is arguable, the original claimant cannot justifiably feel morally harmed. And the government's action cannot be said to be arbitrary unless it awards the goods to an individual whose claim is even less plausible than that of the original claimant." (49).

20. Cass Sunstein, "Limits of Compensatory Justice" in *Nomos* 33, *Compensatory Justice,* ed. John Chapman (New York: New York University Press, 1991), 281–310.

21. "It is not controlling and perhaps not even relevant that the harms that affirmative action attempts to redress cannot be understood in the usual compensatory terms. . . . the nature of the problem guarantees that the legal response cannot take the form of discrete remedies for discrete harms" (Sunstein, "Limits," 297).

22. Sunstein, "Limits," 303.

23. The orientation of the EEOC toward investigating individual cases of alleged discrimination is one explanation of its extraordinary backlog of over 80,000 cases. This orientation precludes it from focusing on systemic practices that affect many individuals, and instead forces it to expend resources dealing with particular instances. See "The EEOC: Pattern and Practice Imperfect" by Maurice Munroe in *Yale Law and Policy Review,* 13, no. 2, (1995):219–80.

24. Sunstein, "Limits," 292.

25. Sunstein, "Limits," 289.

26. "The current distribution of benefits and burdens as between blacks and whites and women and men is not part of the state of nature but a consequence of past and present social practices" (Sunstein, "Limits," 294).

27. See also Thomas H. Simon, *Democracy and Social Justice* (Lanham, Md.: Rowman & Littlefield, 1995), chap. 5.

28. Sunstein, "Limits," 306.

29. Gang Xu, Sylvia Fields, et al., "The Relationship between the Ethnicity of Generalist Physicians and Their Care for Underserved Populations," Ohio University College of Osteopathic Medicine, Athens, Ohio, 10.

30. Of course, we may ask whether the use of race is necessary for the achievement of the end in view or whether it is one among alternative ways of achieving that end. For instance, it might be possible to induce doctors to practice in Black neighborhoods by providing doctors, irrespective of their race, with suitable monetary incentives. But given the importance of nonmonetary factors in physician-patient relationships, it is doubtful that purely monetary rewards would be sufficient to meet the needs of underserved populations.

31. Remedial action based on the imbalance between blacks in the available work force and their presence in skilled jobs categories presumes that imbalance is caused by racial discrimination. This assumption has been challenged by many who cite cultural and cognitive factors that might equally be the cause of such imbalances. See Thomas Sowell, *Markets and Minorities* (New York: Basic Books, 1981); Richard Herrenstein and Charles Murray, *The Bell Curve* (New York: The Free Press, 1994). This literature has itself been subject to critique: for Sowell, see Christopher Jencks, *Rethinking Social Policy* (New York: Harper, 1993); for Herrenstein and Murray, see *The Bell Curve Wars,* ed. Steven Fraser (New York: Basic Books, 1995).

Louis P. Pojman

 **NO**

The Case Against Affirmative Action

Let us agree that despite the evidences of a booming economy, the poor are suffering grievously, with children being born into desperate material and psychological poverty; for them the ideal of "equal opportunity for all" is a cruel joke. Many feel that the federal government has abandoned its guarantee to provide the minimum necessities for each American, so that the pace of this tragedy seems to be worsening daily. In addition to this, African-Americans have a legacy of slavery and unjust discrimination to contend with, and other minorities have also suffered from injustice. Women have their own peculiar history of being treated unequally in relevant ways. What is the answer to this national problem? Is it increased welfare? More job training? More support for education? Required licensing of parents to have children? Negative income tax? More support for families or for mothers with small children? All of these have merit and should be part of the national debate. But, my thesis is, however tragic the situation may be (and we may disagree on just how tragic it is), one policy is *not* a legitimate part of the solution and that is *reverse, unjust discrimination* against young white males. Strong Affirmative Action, which implicitly advocates reverse discrimination, while no doubt well intentioned, is morally heinous, asserting, by implication, that *two wrongs make a right*.

The *Two Wrongs Make a Right* Thesis goes like this: Because *some* Whites once enslaved some Blacks, the descendants of those slaves (some of whom now may enjoy high incomes and social status) have a right to opportunities and offices over better qualified Whites who had nothing to do with either slavery or the oppression of Blacks (and who may even have suffered hardship comparable to that of poor Blacks). In addition, Strong Affirmative Action creates a new Hierarchy of the Oppressed: Blacks get primary preferential treatment, women second, Native Americans third, Hispanics fourth, Handicapped fifth, and Asians sixth and so on until White males, no matter how needy or well qualified, must accept the leftovers. . . .

Before analyzing arguments concerning Affirmative Action, I must define my terms.

By *Weak Affirmative Action* I mean policies that will increase the opportunities of disadvantaged people to attain social goods and offices. It includes such things as dismantling of segregated institutions, widespread advertise-

From Louis P. Pojman, "The Case Against Affirmative Action," *International Journal of Applied Philosophy*, vol. 12 (Spring 1998). Copyright © 1998 by *International Journal of Applied Philosophy*. Reprinted by permission of the editor.

ment to groups not previously represented in certain privileged positions, special scholarships for the disadvantaged classes (e.g., the poor, regardless of race or gender), and even using diversity or under-representation of groups with a history of past discrimination as a tie breaker when candidates for these goods and offices are relatively equal. The goal of *Weak Affirmative Action* is equal opportunity to compete, not equal results. We seek to provide each citizen regardless of race or gender a fair chance to the most favored positions in society. . . .

By *Strong Affirmative Action* I mean preferential treatment on the basis of race, ethnicity or gender (or some other morally irrelevant criterion), discriminating in favor of underrepresented groups against overrepresented groups, aiming at roughly equal results. *Strong Affirmative Action* is *reverse discrimination.* It says it is right to do wrong to correct a wrong. This is the policy currently being promoted under the name of *Affirmative Action,* so I will use that term or "AA" for short throughout this essay to stand for this version of affirmative action. I will not argue for or against the principle of *Weak Affirmative Action.* Indeed, I think it has some moral weight. *Strong Affirmative Action* has none, or so I will argue.

This essay concentrates on AA policies with regard to race, but the arguments can be extended to cover ethnicity and gender. I think that if a case for Affirmative Action can be made it will be as a corrective to racial oppression. I will examine eight arguments regarding AA. The first six will be *negative,* attempting to show that the best arguments for Affirmative Action fail. The last [two] will be *positive* arguments for policies opposing Affirmative Action:

A Critique of Arguments for Affirmative Action

The Need for Role Models

This argument is straightforward. We all have need of role models, and it helps to know that others like us can be successful. We learn and are encouraged to strive for excellence by emulating our heroes and "our kind of people" who have succeeded.

In the first place it's not clear that role models of one's own racial or sexual type are necessary (let alone sufficient) for success. One of my heroes was Gandhi, an Indian Hindu, another was my grade school science teacher, Miss DeVoe, and another Martin Luther King, behind whom I marched in Civil Rights demonstrations. More important than having role models of one's "own type" is having genuinely good people, of whatever race or gender, to emulate. Our common humanity should be a sufficient basis for us to see the possibility of success in people of virtue and merit. To yield to the demand, however tempting it may be, for "role-models-just-like-us" is to treat people like means not ends. . . .

The Compensation Argument

The argument goes like this: blacks have been wronged and severely harmed by whites. Therefore white society should compensate blacks for the injury caused them. Reverse discrimination in terms of preferential hiring, contracts, and scholarships is a fitting way to compensate for the past wrongs.[1]

This argument actually involves a distorted notion of compensation. Normally, we think of compensation as owed by a specific person A to another person B whom A has wronged in a specific way C. For Example, if I have stolen your car and used it for a period of time to make business profits that would have gone to you, it is not enough that I return your car. I must pay you an amount reflecting your loss and my ability to pay. If I have made $5,000 and only have $10,000 in assets, it would not be possible for you to collect $20,000 in damages—even though that is the amount of loss you have incurred. . . .

On the face of it, demands by blacks for compensation do not fit the usual pattern. Southern States with Jim Crow laws could be accused of unjustly harming blacks, but it is hard to see that the United States government was involved in doing so. Much of the harm done to blacks was the result of private discrimination, not state action. . . . Furthermore, it is not clear that all blacks were harmed in the same way or whether some were *unjustly* harmed or harmed more than poor whites and others (e.g., short people). Finally, even if identifiable blacks were harmed by identifiable social practices, it is not clear that most forms of Affirmative Action are appropriate to restore the situation. The usual practice of a financial payment seems more appropriate than giving a high level job to someone unqualified or only minimally qualified. . . .

Still, there may be something intuitively compelling about compensating members of an oppressed group who are minimally qualified. Suppose that the Hatfields and the McCoys are enemy clans and some youths from the Hatfields go over and steal diamonds and gold from the McCoys, distributing it within the Hatfield economy. Even though we do not know which Hatfield youths did the stealing, we would want to restore the wealth, as far as possible, to the McCoys. One way might be to tax the Hatfields, but another might be to give preferential treatment in terms of scholarships and training programs and hiring to the McCoys.

This is perhaps the strongest argument for Affirmative Action, and it may well justify some weaker versions of AA, but it is doubtful whether it is sufficient to justify strong versions with quotas and goals and time tables in skilled positions. There are at least two reasons for this. First, we have no way of knowing how many people of any given group would have achieved some given level of competence had the world been different. . . . Secondly, the normal criterion of competence is a strong prima facie consideration when the most important positions are at stake. There are three reasons for this: (1) treating people according to their merits respects them as persons, as ends in themselves, rather than as means to social ends (if we believe that individuals possess a dignity which deserves to be respected, then we ought to treat that individual on the basis of his or her merits, not as a mere instrument for social policy); (2) society has given people expectations that if they attain certain levels of excellence they will be awarded appropriately and (3) filling the most important positions with the best qualified is the best way to ensure efficiency in job-related areas and in society in general. These reasons are not absolutes. They can be overridden.[2]

But there is a strong presumption in their favor, so that a burden of proof rests with those who would overrride them. . . .

The Argument for Compensation From Those Who Innocently Benefitted From Past Injustice

Young White males as innocent beneficiaries of unjust discrimination against blacks and women have no grounds for complaint when society seeks to level the tilted field. They may be innocent of oppressing blacks, other minorities, and women, but they have unjustly benefitted from that oppression or discrimination. So it is perfectly proper that less qualified women and blacks be hired before them.

The operative principle is: He who knowingly and willingly benefits from a wrong must help pay for the wrong. Judith Jarvis Thomson puts it this way. "Many [white males] have been direct beneficiaries of policies which have downgraded blacks and women . . . and even those who did not directly benefit . . . had, at any rate, the advantage in the competition which comes of the confidence in one's full membership [in the community] and of one's right being recognized as a matter of course."[3] That is, white males obtain advantages in self respect and self-confidence deriving from a racist/sexist system which denies these to blacks and women.

Here is my response to this argument: As I noted in the previous section, compensation is normally individual and specific. If A harms B regarding x, B has a right to compensation from A in regards to x. If A steals B's car and wrecks it, A has an obligation to compensate B for the stolen car, but A's son has no obligation to compensate B. Furthermore, if A dies or disappears, B has no moral right to claim that society compensate him for the stolen car—though if he has insurance, he can make such a claim to the insurance company. Sometimes a wrong cannot be compensated, and we just have to make the best of an imperfect world. . . .

The Diversity Argument

It is important that we learn to live in a pluralistic world, learning to get along with those of other races, conditions, and cultures, so we should have schools and employment situations as fully integrated as possible. . . . Diversity is an important symbol and educative device. Thus, proponents of AA argue, preferential treatment is warranted to perform this role in society.

Once again, there is some truth in these concerns. Diversity of ideas challenges us to scrutinize our own values and beliefs. . . . Diversity may expand our moral horizons. But, again, while we can admit the value of diversity, it hardly seems adequate to override the moral requirement to treat each person with equal respect. *Diversity for diversity's sake is moral promiscuity,* since it obfuscates rational distinctions, undermines treating individuals as ends, treating them, instead as mere means (to the goals of social engineering), and, furthermore, unless those hired are highly qualified, the diversity factor threatens to become a fetish. . . .

There may be times when diversity may seem to be "crucial" to the well-being of a diverse community, such as for a police force. Suppose that White policemen tend to overreact to young Black males and the latter group distrusts White policemen. Hiring more less qualified Black policemen, who would relate better to these youth, may have overall utilitarian value. But such a move, while we might make it as a lesser evil, could have serious consequences in allowing the demographic prejudices to dictate social policy. A better strategy would be to hire the best police, that is, those who can perform in [a] disciplined, intelligent manner, regardless of their race. A White policeman must be able to arrest a Black burglar, even as a Black policeman must be able to arrest a White rapist. The quality of the police man or woman, not their race or gender, is what counts.

On the other hand, if a Black policeman, though lacking some of the formal skills of the White policeman, really is able to do a better job in the Black community, this might constitute a case of merit, not Affirmative Action. As Stephen Kershnar points out, this is similar to the legitimacy of hiring Chinese men to act as undercover agents in Chinatown.[4]

The Equal Results Argument

Some philosophers and social scientists hold that human nature is roughly identical, so that on a fair playing field the same proportion from every race and ethnic group and both genders would attain to the highest positions in every area of endeavor. It would follow that any inequality of results itself is evidence for inequality of opportunity.

> History is important when considering governmental rules like Test 21 because low scores by blacks can be traced in large measure to the legacy of slavery and racism: segregation, poor schooling, exclusion from trade unions, malnutrition, and poverty have all played their roles. Unless one assumes that blacks are naturally less able to pass the test, the conclusion must be that the results are themselves socially and legally constructed, not a mere given for which law and society can claim no responsibility.
>
> The conclusion seems to be that genuine equality eventually requires equal results. Obviously blacks have been treated unequally throughout U.S. history, and just as obviously the economic and psychological effects of that inequality linger to this day, showing up in lower income and poorer performance in school and on tests than whites achieve. Since we have no reason to believe that differences in performance can be explained by factors other than history, equal results are a good benchmark by which to measure progress made toward genuine equality. (John Arthur, *The Unfinished Constitution* [Belmont, CA: Wadsworth Publishing Co, 1990], p. 238)

. . . Albert G. Mosley develops a similar argument. "Establishing Blacks' presence at a level commensurate with their proportion in the relevant labor market need not be seen as an attempt to actualize some valid prediction. Rather, given the impossibility of determining what level of representation Blacks would have achieved were it not for racial discrimination, the assumption of proportional representation is the only *fair* assumption to make. This is not to argue that Blacks should be maintained in such positions, but their contrived exclusion merits equally contrived rectification."[5] . . . However, Arthur [and] Mosley . . . fail even to consider studies that suggest that there are innate differences between races, sexes, and groups. If there are genetic differences in intelligence, temperament, and other qualities within families, why should we not expect such differences between racial groups and the two genders? Why should the evidence for this be completely discounted?

Mosley's reasoning is as follows: Since we don't know for certain whether groups proportionately differ in talent, we should presume that they are equal in every respect. So we should presume that if we were living in a just society, there would be roughly proportionate representation in every field (e.g., equal representation of doctors, lawyers, professors, carpenters, airplane pilots, basketball players, and criminals). Hence, it is only fair—productive of justice—to aim at proportionate representation in these fields.

But the logic is flawed. Under a situation of ignorance we should not presume equality or inequality of representation—but conclude that we *don't know* what the results would be in a just society. Ignorance doesn't favor equal group representation any more than it favors unequal group representation. It is neutral between them . . .

The "No One Deserves His Talents" Argument Against Meritocracy

According to this argument, the competent do not deserve their intelligence, their superior character, their industriousness, or their discipline; therefore they have no right to the best positions in society; therefore it is not unjust to give these positions to less (but still minimally) qualified blacks and women. In one form this argument holds that since no one deserves anything, society may use any criteria it pleases to distribute goods. The criterion most often designated is social utility. Versions of this argument are found in the writings of John Arthur, John Rawls, Bernard Boxill, Michael Kinsley, Ronald Dworkin, and Richard Wasserstrom. Rawls writes, "No one deserves his place in the distribution of native endowments, any more than one deserves one's initial starting place in society. The assertion that a man deserves the superior character that enables him to make the effort to cultivate his abilities is equally problematic; for his character depends in large part upon fortunate family and social circumstances for which he can claim no credit. The notion of desert seems not to apply to these cases."[6] Michael Kinsley is even more adamant:

> Opponents of affirmative action are hung up on a distinction that seems more profoundly irrelevant: treating individuals versus treating groups. What is the moral difference between dispensing favors to people on their "merits" as individuals and passing out society's benefits on the basis of group identification?
>
> Group identifications like race and sex are, of course, immutable. They have nothing to do with a person's moral worth. But the same is true of most of what comes under the label "merit." The tools you need for getting ahead in a meritocratic society—not all of them but most: talent, education,

instilled cultural values such as ambition—are distributed just as arbitrarily as skin color. They are fate. The notion that people somehow "deserve" the advantages of these characteristics in a way they don't "deserve" the advantage of their race is powerful, but illogical.[7]

It will help to put the argument in outline form.

1. Society may award jobs and positions as it sees fit as long as individuals have no claim to these positions.
2. To have a claim to something means that one has earned it or deserves it.
3. But no one has earned or deserves his intelligence, talent, education or cultural values which produce superior qualifications.
4. If a person does not deserve what produces something, he does not deserve its products.
5. Therefore better qualified people do not deserve their qualifications.
6. Therefore, society may override their qualifications in awarding jobs and positions as it sees fit (for social utility or to compensate for previous wrongs).

So it is permissible if a minimally qualified black or woman is admitted to law or medical school ahead of a white male with excellent credentials or if a less qualified person from an "underutilized" group gets a professorship ahead of an eminently better qualified white male. Sufficiency and underutilization together outweigh excellence.

My response: Premise 4 is false. To see this, reflect that just because I do not deserve the money that I have been given as a gift (for instance) does not mean that I am not entitled to what I get with that money. If you and I both get a gift of $100 and I bury mine in the sand for 5 years while you invest yours wisely and double its value at the end of five years, I cannot complain that you should split the increase 50/50 since neither of us deserved the original gift. . . .

But there is no good reason to accept the argument against [moral] desert. We do act freely and, as such, we are responsible for our actions. We deserve the fruits of our labor, reward for our noble feats and punishment for our misbehavior.[8]

We have considered six arguments for Affirmative Action and have found no compelling case for Strong AA and only one plausible argument (a version of the compensation argument) for Weak AA. We must now turn to the arguments against Affirmative Action to see whether they fare any better.

Arguments Against Affirmative Action

Affirmative Action Requires Discrimination Against a Different Group

Weak AA weakly discriminates against new minorities, mostly innocent young white males, and Strong Affirmative Action strongly discriminates against these new minorities. . . . [T]his discrimination is unwarranted, since, even if some compensation to blacks were indicated, it would be unfair to make innocent white males bear the whole brunt of the payments. . . . [I]t is poor white youth who become the new pariahs on the job market. The children of the wealthy have little trouble getting into the best private grammar schools and, on the basis of superior early education, into the best universities, graduate schools, managerial and professional positions. Affirmative Action simply shifts injustice, setting Blacks, Hispanics, Native Americans, Asians and women against young white males, especially ethnic and poor white males. It makes no more sense to discriminate in favor of a rich Black or female who had the opportunity of the best family and education available against a poor White, than it does to discriminate in favor of White males against Blacks or women. It does little to rectify the goal of providing equal opportunity to all. . . .

Respect for persons entails that we treat each person as an end in him or herself, not simply as a means to be used for social purposes. What is wrong about discrimination against Blacks is that it fails to treat Black people as individuals, judging them instead by their skin color not their merit. What is wrong about discrimination against women is that it fails to treat them as individuals, judging them by their gender, not their merit. What is equally wrong about *Affirmative Action* is that it fails to treat White males with dignity as individuals, judging them by *both their race and gender,* instead of their merit. *Current Strong Affirmative Action* is both racist and sexist. . . .

An Argument From the Principle of Merit

Traditionally, we have believed that the highest positions in society should be awarded to those who are best qualified. Rewarding excellence both seems just to the individuals in the competition and makes for efficiency. Note that one of the most successful acts of racial integration, the Brooklyn Dodgers's recruitment of Jackie Robinson in the late 40s, was done in just this way, according to merit. If Robinson had been brought into the major league as a mediocre player or had batted .200 he would have been scorned and sent back to the minors where he belonged.

As mentioned earlier, merit is not an absolute value, but there are strong *prima facie* reasons for awarding positions on that basis, and it should enjoy a weighty presumption in our social practices.

. . . We generally want the best to have the best positions. . . . Only when little is at stake do we weaken the standards and content ourselves with sufficiency (rather than excellence)—there are plenty of jobs where "sufficiency" rather than excellence is required. Perhaps we have even come to feel that medicine or law or university professorships are so routine that they can be performed by minimally qualified people—in which case AA has a place.

Note! no one is calling for quotas or proportional representation of *underutilized* groups in the National Basketball Association where blacks make up 80% of the players. But, surely, if merit and merit alone reigns in sports, should it not be valued at least as much in education and industry?

The case for meritocracy has two pillars. One pillar is a deontological argument which holds that we ought to treat people as ends and not merely means.

By giving people what they deserve as *individuals,* rather than as members of *groups*, we show respect for their inherent worth. . . .

The second pillar for meritocracy is utilitarian. In the end, we will be better off by honoring excellence. We want the best leaders, teachers, policemen, physicians, generals, lawyers, and airplane pilots that we can possibly produce in society. So our program should be to promote equal opportunity, as much as is feasible in a free market economy, and reward people according to their individual merit.[9]

Conclusion

Let me sum up my discussion. The goal of the Civil Rights movement and of moral people everywhere has been justice for all, including equal opportunity. The question is: how best to get there. Civil Rights legislation removed the unjust legal barriers, opening the way towards equal opportunity, but it did not tackle the deeper causes that produce differential result. Weak Affirmative Action aims at encouraging minorities to strive for excellence in all areas of life, without unduly jeopardizing the rights of majorities. The problem of Weak Affirmative Action is that it easily slides into Strong Affirmative Action where quotas, "goals and timetables," "equal results"—in a word—*reverse discrimination*—prevail and are forced onto groups, thus promoting mediocrity, inefficiency, and resentment. Furthermore, AA aims at the higher levels of society-universities and skilled jobs, but if we want to improve our society, the best way to do it is to concentrate on families, children, early education, and the like, so all are prepared to avail themselves of opportunity. Affirmative Action, on the one hand, is too much, too soon and on the other hand, too little, too late. . . .

Martin Luther said that humanity is like a man mounting a horse who always tends to fall off on the other side of the horse. This seems to be the case with Affirmative Action. Attempting to redress the discriminatory iniquities of our history, our well-intentioned social engineers now engage in new forms of discriminatory iniquity and thereby think that they have successfully mounted the horse of racial harmony. They have only fallen off on the other side of the issue.[10]

1. For a good discussion of this argument see B. Boxill, "The Morality of Reparation," in *Social Theory and Practice* 2:1 (1972) and Albert G. Mosley in his and Nicholas Capaldi, *Affirmative Action; Social Justice or Unfair Preference?* (Rowman and Littlefield, 1996), p. 23–27.
2. Merit sometimes may be justifiably overridden by need, as when parents choose to spend extra earnings on special education for their disabled child rather than for their gifted child. Sometimes we may override merit for utilitarian purposes. E.g., suppose you are the best shortstop on a baseball team but are also the best catcher. You'd rather play shortstop, but the manager decides to put you at catcher because, while your friend can do an adequate job at short, no one else is adequate at catcher. It's permissible for you to be assigned the job of catcher. Probably, some expression of appreciation would be due you.

3. Judith Jarvis Thomson, "Preferential Hiring," in Marshall Cohen, Thomas Nagel and Thomas Scanlon, eds., *Equality and Preferential Treatment* (Princeton: Princeton University Press, 1977).
4. Stephen Kershnar pointed this out in written comments (December 22, 1997).
5. See Mosley, op cit., p. 28, and Bernard Boxill, *Blacks and Social Justice* (Rowman & Littlefield, 1984), whom Mosley quotes in his article, also defends this position.
6. John Rawls, *A Theory of Justice* (Harvard University Press, 1971), p. 104. See Bernard Boxill, "The Morality of Preferential Hiring," *Philosophy and Public Affairs* 7:3 (1983).
7. Michael Kinsley, "Equal Lack of Opportunity," *Harper's* (June 1983).
8. My point does not depend on any particular theory of free will. One is reminded of Nozick's point that Rawls' professed aim of articulating the enormous worth of each individual seems contrary to the reductive determinism in his natural lottery argument.
9. For further discussion of this point see my "Equality and Desert," *Philosophy* 72 (1997).
10. Some of the material in this essay appeared in "The Moral Status of Affirmative Action," *Public Affairs Quarterly* 6:2 (1992). I have not had space to consider all the objections to my position or discuss the issue of freedom of association which, I think, should be given much scope in private but not in public institutions. Barbara Bergmann (*In Defense of Affirmative Action* [New York: Basic Books, 1996], pp. 122–25) and others argue that we already offer preferential treatment for athletes and veterans, especially in university admissions, so being consistent, we should provide it for women and minorities. My answer is that I am against giving athletic scholarships, and I regard scholarships to veterans as a part of a contractual relationship, a reward for service to one's country. But I distinguish entrance programs from actual employment. I don't think that veterans should be afforded special privilege in hiring practice, unless it be as a tie breaker.

I should also mention that my arguments from merit and respect apply more specifically to public institutions than private ones, where issues of property rights and freedom of association carry more weight.

POSTSCRIPT

Is Affirmative Action Fair?

That racial discrimination and sexual discrimination have existed in the United States is a matter of historical record and beyond dispute. But the question remains, What follows for us here and now?

Opponents of affirmative action say that nothing at all follows, except perhaps that we might be more careful and vigilant about allowing any form of discrimination, including modern forms of reverse discrimination.

Proponents of strong affirmative action say that although these views might *look* fair and aim to *be* fair, they are not fair. Just preventing discrimination without taking positive action to improve minorities' positions in society would simply freeze an unfairly established status quo. As American society is now, blacks are not represented in professions, in graduate schools, in business boardrooms, or in positions of social and political leadership in a way that is consistent with their numbers in the population. This is not for lack of interest or ability; it is a legacy of social injustice. To insist that we now freeze this status quo and proceed "fairly," on a case-by-case basis, will guarantee that the white-biased social momentum will continue for at least the foreseeable future. Advocates of affirmative action want to eradicate the effects of past discrimination and to put an end to the bias in momentum as soon as possible. They call for active measures to achieve this.

Sources that are relevant to this issue include Gertrude Ezorsky, *Racism and Justice: The Case for Affirmative Action* (Cornell University Press, 1991); Andrew Kull, *The Colorblind Constitution* (Harvard University Press, 1992); Bernard R. Boxhill, *Blacks and Social Justice*, rev. ed. (Rowman & Littlefield, 1992); Andrew Hacker, *Two Nations: Black and White, Separate, Hostile, Unequal* (Scribner, 1992); Stanley Fish, "Reverse Racism, or How the Pot Got to Call the Kettle Black," *The Atlantic Monthly* (November 1993); Steven M. Cahn, ed., *Affirmative Action and the University* (Temple University Press, 1993); Carl Cohen, *Naked Racial Preference: The Case Against Affirmative Action* (Madison Books, 1995); Ralph R. Reiland, "Affirmative Action or Equal Opportunity?" *Regulation* (vol. 18, 1995), pp. 19–23; and Steven M. Cahn, ed., *The Affirmative Action Debates*, 2d ed. (Routledge, 2002).

Other sources on this controversial policy are George E. Curry, ed., *The Affirmative Action Debate* (Addison-Wesley, 1996); Richard F. Thomasson, Faye J. Crosby, and Sharon D. Herzberger, *Affirmative Action: The Pros and Cons of Policy and Practice* (University Press of America, 1996); John David Skrentny, *The Ironies of Affirmative Action: Politics, Culture, and Justice in America* (University of Chicago Press, 1996); Robert Emmett Long, ed., *Affirmative Action* (H. W. Wilson, 1996); Barbara Bergmann, *In Defense of Affirmative Action* (Basic Books,

1996); Terry Eastland, *Ending Affirmative Action: The Case for Colorblind Justice* (Basic Books, 1996); Jewelle Taylor Gibbs, *Color of Justice: Rodney King, O. J. Simpson, and Race in America* (Jossey-Bass, 1996); K. Anthony Appiah and Amy Gutmann, *Color Conscious: The Political Morality of Race* (Princeton University Press, 1996); David Theo Goldberg, *Racial Subjects: Writing on Race in America* (Routledge, 1997); Michael Levin, *Why Race Matters: Race Differences and What They Mean* (Greenwood Publishing Group, 1997); Abigail Thernstrom and Stephen Thernstrom, *America in Black and White: One Nation, Indivisible* (Simon & Schuster, 1997); Peter Skerry, "The Strange Politics of Affirmative Action," *Wilson Quarterly* (Winter 1997); Francis J. Beckwith, Todd E. Jones, eds., *Affirmative Action: Social Justice or Reverse Discrimination?* (Prometheus Books, 1997); Glenn C. Loury, "How to Mend Affirmative Action," *The Public Interest* (Spring 1997); Charles R. Lawrence III and Mari Matsuda, *We Won't Go Back: Making the Case for Affirmative Action* (Houghton Mifflin, 1997); David K. Shipler, *A Country of Strangers: Blacks and Whites in America* (Alfred A. Knopf, 1997); Lincoln Caplan, *Up Against the Law: Affirmative Action and the Supreme Court* (Century Foundation, 1997); Jim Sleeper, *Liberal Racism* (Viking Penguin, 1997); "Racism and the Law: The Legacy and Lessons of Plessy," a special issue of *Law and Philosophy* (May 1997); "The Affirmative Action Debate," a special issue of *Report From the Institute for Philosophy and Public Policy* (Winter–Spring 1997); Bryan K. Fair, *Notes of a Racial Caste Baby: Color Blindness and the End of Affirmative Action* (New York University Press, 1997); John Davis Skrentny, "Affirmative Action: Some Advice for the Pundits," *American Behavioral Scientist* (April 1998); *Focus on Law Studies* (Spring 1998) (this entire issue concerns affirmative action); Matt Cavanagh, *Against Equality of Opportunity* (Clarendon Press, 2002); Samuel Leiter and William M. Leiter, *Affirmative Action in Antidiscrimination Law and Policy: An Overview and Synthesis* (State University of New York Press, 2002); Charles V. Dale, *Affirmative Action Revisited* (Nova Science Publishers, 2002); and Fred L. Pincus, *Reverse Discrimination: Dismantling the Myth* (Lynne Rienner Publishers, 2003).

A concise account of civil rights history (including the birth of the phrase "affirmative action") is Hugh Davis Graham, *Civil Rights and the Presidency: Race and Gender in American Politics, 1960–1972* (Oxford University Press, 1992). Another useful historical account is Paul D. Moreno, *From Direct Action to Affirmative Action: Fair Employment Law and Policy in America, 1933–1972* (Louisiana State University Press, 1999). The position that affirmative action policies are necessary for women is defended by Susan D. Clayton and Faye J. Crosby, *Justice, Gender and Affirmative Action* (University of Michigan Press, 1992).

ISSUE 14

Should the Supreme Court Prohibit Racial Preferences in College Admissions?

YES: Deroy Murdock, from "Should the Supreme Court Prohibit Racial Preferences in College Admissions? Yes," *Insight on the News* (February 18–March 3, 2003)

NO: Jamin B. Raskin, from "Should the Supreme Court Prohibit Racial Preferences in College Admissions? No," *Insight on the News* (February 18–March 3, 2003)

ISSUE SUMMARY

YES: Columnist Deroy Murdock contends that programs of preferential treatment that award special bonus points to applicants of certain racial or ethnic backgrounds are no more than academic racial profiling. These programs assume that certain people need the bonus points. Murdock reasons that this shows that people from certain racial or ethnic groups are thought to be intellectually inferior.

NO: Professor of constitutional law and local-government law Jamin B. Raskin states that programs of affirmative action in college admissions do not violate the Constitution. If equality of opportunity is the goal, then there are many steps—not immediately involving the abolition of affirmative action—that could be taken in order to work toward that goal in a meaningful way.

In some ways, racial preference in college admissions contains some of the most positive aspects of affirmative action. It is mainly at places like colleges, medical schools, etc. that students earn the credentials and qualifications that will enable them to enjoy successful careers. Whereas many programs of preferential treatment are criticized for not paying close enough attention to *qualifications*, college admissions do not seem to have the same problem. Not surprisingly, the brightest students coming out of high school, those with the strongest amount of extracurricular activities and the highest grade point averages, will tend to be the students that college faculty find easiest to teach.

Note that this issue addresses college admission only. Few could argue that actual grades or college credits should be distributed in racially preferential ways. Thus, for example, a medical student who has been admitted to medical school under an affirmative action program will be confronted with the same educational demands, degree requirements, etc. as all other students.

But opponents find this problematic. Against a historical background in which race was used as part of injustice and widespread social discrimination, opponents can contend that *any* appeal to racial classification is unjust. They say that we must not engage in any sort of racial preference at all, that we must be "color blind." Where once the Supreme Court ruled in favor of racial classification and the provision of facilities that were "separate but equal," it is now generally agreed that this was a serious mistake. But in the wake of the dismantling of segregation, the question arises as to what our current view should be. We know that "separate but equal" is out—separate is inherently unequal. But what should take its place? One response is that we should be very wary about the whole idea of classifying people racially. The point, many agree, is to leave all that behind us.

One of the key considerations with regard to this issue is the Constitution. But that document is subject to interpretation. (Indeed, the Justices of the Supreme Court generally disagree with each other's interpretations, and most decisions are split decisions.)

In the following selections, Deroy Murdock argues that programs of preferential treatment that award special bonus points to applicants of certain racial or ethnic backgrounds are no more than academic racial profiling. These programs assume that these applicants—classified into racial or ethnic groups— need the bonus points. Apparently, Murdock reasons, they are perceived as intellectually inferior. Jamin B. Raskin maintains that programs of affirmative action in college admissions do not violate the Constitution. He argues that if equality of opportunity is the goal, then there are many steps—not immediately involving the abolition of affirmative action—that could be taken in order to work toward that goal in a meaningful way.

Deroy Murdock

 **YES**

Racial Profiling to Favor Black Students Hurts Them in the Long Run

President George W. Bush's opposition to Michigan's racial-preference scheme could not have been more perfectly timed. On what would have been Dr. Martin Luther King Jr.'s 74th birthday, Bush announced plans to file an amicus curiae brief asking the Supreme Court to overturn Michigan's admissions system. Bush's decision recalled Dr. King's dream that his children would "live one day in a nation where they will not be judged by the color of their skin but by the content of their character."

While Bush applauds Michigan's desire to attract an integrated student body, he believes it should not racially discriminate in doing so. As the president explained in his Jan. 15 [2003] speech: "A college education should teach respect and understanding and good will. And these values are strengthened when students live and learn with people from many backgrounds. Yet quota systems that use race to include or exclude people from higher education and the opportunities it offers are divisive, unfair and impossible to square with the Constitution."

Michigan currently gives each undergraduate black, Hispanic and American Indian applicant 20 bonus points (out of 150) just for having the correct complexion. Interestingly enough, Asians and Americans of Oriental extraction need not apply for this bonus. Apparently, some minorities are more minor than others.

Michigan exemplifies what Bush calls "the soft bigotry of low expectations." Its admissions officers do not practice the nasty, snarling bigotry born of hatred, but instead the polite, smiling bigotry born of pity. Yet it is bigotry nonetheless.

Black, brown and red candidates enjoy a 13.3 percent boost over those with white or yellow flesh equally eager to learn in Ann Arbor. How dare Michigan's administrators automatically assume that minority applicants are disadvantaged and downtrodden?

This is academic racial profiling. If—as civil-rights activists scream until they swoon—it is wrong for cops to see a black man and prejudge that he is a

From Deroy Murdock, "Racial Profiling to Favor Black Students Hurts Them in the Long Run," *Insight on the News* (February 18–March 3, 2003). Copyright © 2003 by News World Communications, Inc. Reprinted by permission.

criminal, why is it right for Michigan to see someone and prejudge that he needs special help simply for applying while black?

Those 20 extra points that Michigan gives "underrepresented" minority contenders resemble wheelchair ramps. In some cases, they might reward applicants who have performed well in school through years of diligent work against long odds. But white and yellow students overcome personal hardship, too. Why no bonus for them? And does a minority applicant who is an honor student, varsity athlete and student-body president really deserve those 20 points when her existing credentials would win her an acceptance letter anyway?

Admissions officers should evaluate applicants as individuals rather than as ethnic inputs. Today they treat some minorities as proxies for benighted communities of color. Meanwhile, they regard whites as, ipso facto, privileged. Some of them, indeed, may have spent their formative years bobbing about in America's yacht basins. But other Caucasians have excelled within this country's chicken farms, trailer parks and coal-mining regions.

It's amazing how far the civil-rights community has traveled to embrace such racial preferences. It was not always this way. Consider the words of the late U.S. Supreme Court justice and liberal deity, Thurgood Marshall. While acting as lead plaintiff's attorney in the landmark 1954 *Brown v. Board of Education* desegregation case, Marshall wrote this in his brief to the high court: "Distinctions by race are so evil, so arbitrary and so insidious that a state bound to defend the equal protection of the laws must not allow them in any public sphere. . . . Classifications and distinctions based upon race or color have no moral or legal validity in our society."

During the next five decades, Marshall's words became a long-forgotten speed bump on the road to reverse discrimination. In 1995, the liberal president of New Jersey's public Rutgers University discussed plans to lower the SAT scores expected of black applicants. Why? Blacks, Francis Lawrence explained, constitute "a disadvantaged population that doesn't have the genetic hereditary background to have a higher average" on the SAT.

Until three years ago, the entrance procedures at one Bay Area campus were more offensive than Michigan's. San Francisco required a test for admission to Lowell Academy, a selective government high school. Students of Chinese descent needed at least 62 points (out of 69) to pass. Whites and "other Asians" required 58 points for admission, while blacks and Hispanics could enter with just 53.

How degrading. Who were San Francisco's educrats to deem blacks and Hispanics intellectually inferior to other students? And were these Chinese kids uniformly brilliant? Surely, a few of them were dim bulbs. Some of them even might have been less bright than "other Asian" students with roots in Japan and Korea.

This unconstitutional abomination was scrapped in the 2000–2001 academic year after Chinese students won a lawsuit that claimed that their 14th Amendment equal-protection rights were violated.

The Michigan case raises a difficult question no one wants to ask: Why are students of Asian heritage so well-represented in Ann Arbor that they are refused that 20-point minority bonus? Do they have blond hair and blue eyes? No. Do white admissions officers look at them and think, "They're just like us!" Unlikely. Have students of Asian stock benefited from centuries of privilege in America? The families of these young people might beg to differ:

- The great-grandparents of Chinese kids could explain how their relatives helped build America's railroads—often in harrowing conditions and for little money—and sometimes were abandoned in the mountains.
- The grandmas and grandpas of students of Japanese extraction could describe Manzanar, Gila River and other camps in which President Franklin Delano Roosevelt imprisoned them during World War II.
- The parents of Vietnamese pupils could share still-vivid memories of fleeing the Viet Cong in leaky boats just 28 years ago.
- And the moms and dads of Cambodian children could weep as they recall aunts, uncles and cousins whose bones still fertilize the Khmer Rouge's tropical killing fields.

Or is there something about the homes of Asians and Americans of Asian descent that engenders such academic excellence that Michigan essentially believes that too many yellow students have earned their way in?

Rather than presume that all black, brown and red applicants need special help to enter Michigan and other public colleges, America must strive to see that such students do not need these academic crutches in the first place. In this connection, President Bush and other leaders should replace the soft bigotry of low expectations with the tough love of high expectations. They can do this most effectively by relentlessly pursuing school choice and ever-higher academic standards.

They should fight the teachers' unions and educrats whose social-promotion schemes let students advance from one grade to the next despite their failure to read, write and calculate at grade level. They should challenge parents to tell their kids to put down their Playstations and pick up their composition books and geometry proofs. They should foil ethnic activists who, by turns, consider standard English inauthentically black and counsel Hispanic parents to keep their children in Spanish-language classrooms long after they have been exposed to basic English and can advance to mainstream settings.

They also should detonate the "acting-white" syndrome under which promising black students who participate in class and speak proper English are thought to do the "white thing." Though rarely mentioned outside black circles, this self-administered poison holds blacks down more effectively than anything "The Man" ever concocted.

Yes, it will be tough to change attitudes within and around too many minority communities where merit and achievement have yielded to grievance and slipping standards, even as self-esteem climbs meaninglessly into the heavens. Fortunately, there are glowing examples of places where changed attitudes are making changes.

As Chicago's Marva Collins Preparatory School (MCPS) demonstrates, kids exposed to highly challenging material can go from the ghetto to the university to further greatness. A few years ago, CBS' *60 Minutes* introduced viewers to Erika McCoy Pace, a resident of one of the Windy City's poorest neighborhoods. When she was just 6, the local government school gave up on Erika, declaring her "borderline retarded."

Nonetheless, she entered Westside Prep, as MCPS was known back then. At this rigorous, private institution, a visionary teacher named Marva Collins insisted that Erika and her colleagues perform at the highest standard imaginable: Shakespeare; Milton; Dostoyevsky. Erika and other kids from the 'hood read them all. After leaving Westside Prep, Erika reached Virginia's Norfolk State University. The little girl whom the experts dismissed as "borderline retarded" graduated summa cum laude.

Consider, also, the Harlem Educational Activities Fund (www.heaf.org). Since 1989, it has offered Harlem's boys and girls—from kindergarten through college—the skills and virtues to excel. Its $2 million annual budget is 100 percent private. "We're not interested in excuses," HEAF Chairman Dan Rose tells me. "Environment is not destiny. All children can learn."

HEAF's students often are severely disadvantaged; most qualify for federal school-lunch subsidies. Nonetheless, through coaching and mentoring, HEAF's pupils at Mott Hall Middle School have earned six national chess championships since 1993. The team, called the Dark Knights, works closely with Friends of Education, a HEAF spin-off.

HEAF's high-school students receive tutoring, learn test-preparation skills and get other hands-on assistance. Its alumni have graduated from Bryn Mawr, Columbia and Yale, among other universities.

"Most people believe there is a quick fix," Rose says. "Our goal is to inculcate high levels of aspiration and high levels of personal confidence based on positive achievement, positive peer pressure and the continuing interest and support of encouraging adults. The results have been extraordinarily successful."

As Marva Collins and HEAF already have done, the Supreme Court should lift the bar for minority students. Rather than patronize pupils of color, the justices should follow President Bush's lead and inspire these young Americans to dream, strive and succeed. After all, to demand less of minority children than of their white counterparts simply is racism, no matter how elegantly it may be decorated.

Jamin B. Raskin

Wise or Unwise, Affirmative Action Clearly Is Constitutional

Whether you like affirmative action or despise it, all Americans ought to agree that the Supreme Court should only prohibit affirmative action in college admissions if the U.S. Constitution itself forbids it. After all, to strike down affirmative action in state-university admissions would constitute extraordinary interference by the high court with the rights of states to conduct their own affairs. The high court should undertake this sweeping activism against federalism only if the Constitution itself makes affirmative action unlawful.

This is an elementary point that, curiously, most "states'-rights" conservatives, in their rush to denounce the intolerable unfairness of "racial preferences," merrily skip over.

The Constitution, of course, says nothing about racial preferences, much less does it explicitly ban them. Thus, self-proclaimed "strict constructionists" on the high court must conclude that nothing in the letter of the Constitution compels the court to order the state of Michigan to alter its chosen college- and law-school admissions processes. The University of Michigan uses weighted preferences for racial minorities to undo the horrendous effects of its decades of exclusion and segregation, which amounted to nothing less than continuous affirmative action and racial quotas for white students.

Yet, the white plaintiffs today say Michigan's efforts to diversify its universities violate the equal-protection clause of the 14th Amendment. But any justice who truly believes in "original intent" must reject this argument. Equal protection was added to the Constitution in 1868 by Radical Republicans to "secure 'to a race recently emancipated, a race that through many generations has been held in slavery, all the civil rights that the superior race enjoys,'" as Justice John M. Harlan argued in dissent in *Plessy v. Ferguson* (1896).

The Congress that voted on equal protection wanted to topple the stubborn reign of white supremacy, not pretend it was not there. Congress designed Reconstruction in a specifically race-conscious way to uplift blacks and block the restoration of the slave masters. The so-called "Freedmen's Bureau" was set up to distribute free food and clothing not to all citizens but to blacks, and was authorized to sell 40-acre lots of confiscated land to them. The Radical Republican Congress also passed appropriations specifically to aid "destitute colored women and children." Thus, the members of Congress who wrote equal protection into the Constitution (and gave themselves power to enforce it) saw affirmative, race-conscious legislation as serving the 14th Amendment, not violating it.

In his famous dissent in *Plessy*, Harlan originated the "color-blindness" metaphor that now is the cri de coeur of conservatives who have been anything but color-blind for most of American history. But Harlan used that phrase to attack American apartheid and never once cast doubt on the validity of policies designed explicitly to benefit the black population. Moreover, in *Plessy* he repeatedly invoked the 13th Amendment ban on slavery to explain why racial segregation was unlawful: "[T]he arbitrary separation of citizens on the basis of race while they are on a public highway is a badge of servitude wholly inconsistent with the civil freedom and the equality before the law established by the Constitution."

Is affirmative action today a "badge of servitude" and slavery worn by whites? I know that it's not always easy being a white male but, come on guys, let's be serious. Guaranteeing a racially diverse freshmen class does not make us an oppressed minority.

Furthermore, even if you want to conscript Justice Harlan to the anti-affirmative-action cause a century later, his words only illuminate the severe moral limitations of the jurisprudence of color-blindness. For he saw color-blindness as perfectly compatible with the continuation of white supremacy. Consider the almost-always redacted words that precede his famous dictum: "The white race deems itself to be the dominant race in this country. And so it is in prestige, in achievements, in education, in wealth and in power. So I doubt not, it will continue to be for all time, if it remains true to its great heritage and holds fast to the principles of constitutional liberty. But in view of the Constitution, in the eye of the law, there is in this country no superior, dominant, ruling class of citizens. There is no caste here. Our Constitution is color-blind."

Thus, even if we (quite unreasonably) assume that Harlan's vision of color-blindness was intended to stop positive efforts such as affirmative action, such a vision is untenable because it only marries the pretense of legal neutrality with the reality of perpetual white supremacy. One might forgive Harlan—a former slave-owner and Know-Nothing crusader struggling to articulate racial liberalism—for the horrors of such a vision. As for his modern-day conservative enthusiasts, their polemical conversion to color-blindness seems too little, too late and all too convenient.

There may be good policy arguments against affirmative action, and conservatives certainly have been free to bring them before the Michigan Legislature. Some states, such as California, have debated affirmative action at state universities and dropped the policy. There is nothing compulsory about affirmative action, and its defenders certainly are not trying to use the courts to impose one admissions policy on all America. But there also is nothing forbidden about affirmative action. Yet, conservatives do want to use their 5-4 majority on the high court to clinch an issue judicially they cannot win democratically. With the Rehnquist court's invalidation of the Violence Against Women Act, the Gun-Free

School Zones Act, the Religious Freedom Restoration Act, the Brady Handgun Control Act, parts of the Americans with Disabilities Act, majority-minority congressional districts and dozens of other federal and state laws, we clearly have entered an age of dangerous judicial activism and supremacy.

Just because you feel affirmative action stigmatizes minorities or is unfair to whites or has outlived its social utility—all plausible but deeply controversial claims—simply does not make it unconstitutional. Today's conservatives are trying to inscribe their political preferences into constitutional law in a madcap way that is totally at odds with the text and original understanding of the Constitution, as well as settled law in the *Bakke* decision (1976).

Some policy arguments against affirmative action warrant consideration, especially the claim that it benefits only more-affluent minority students and distracts us from making much more sweeping change in our economically segregated education system. But, as a professor, I not only cherish but depend upon the intellectual, political, social, class and racial diversity of my classroom to teach effectively. I would not want to see any teacher or student have to give up that diversity. At the very least, there is a host of other changes that I would want to see implemented first to convince me that the critics of affirmative action áre really seeking perfect meritocracy and not simply the destruction of the civil-rights movement.

First, we should abolish all alumni "legacy" preferences in public and private universities. These preferences, along with "donor" preferences, not only undermine the merit process but systematically favor whites, who are much more likely to have family ties at these schools. Second, we should abolish all geographic-distribution preferences. Like racial preferences, this factor advances only the much reviled "diversity" and does not reflect individual "merit." Third, all public and private universities that discriminated against blacks and other minorities in the past—which is to say almost all of them—should pay a huge one-time fee into a minority-student college tuition fund. Fourth, we should abolish property-tax-based systems of school funding and equalize public-school expenditures across rich and poor counties in America. Finally, we should make a massive social investment in rebuilding public schools across the nation and create world-class, preschool-education programs nationally.

These steps properly would show that the people campaigning against affirmative action truly believe in "equality of opportunity" and deeply despise all special preferences for undeserving applicants. I quickly would drop my support for affirmative action if we took these measures. But, with all due respect, can we really expect President George W. Bush—the self-proclaimed "C" student and legacy admittee to Yale College and Harvard Business School—to attack alumni preferences? Can we expect the conservatives who would divert untold billions of dollars from public schools to voucher programs suddenly to reinvest in our urban public schools? Can we expect a commitment to equal educational opportunity from conservatives such as Justice Clarence Thomas, whose career has embodied— shall we say, delicately—a paradoxical relationship to affirmative action?

In any event, these policy hypotheticals lead us far astray. The issue at hand simply is whether the Constitution itself bans affirmative action. Any serious reading of the Constitution tells us no. Conservatives used to know the difference between a constitutional question and a policy question. But that was long ago. The Rehnquist court, drunk on its own power, sorely will be tempted now to force all 50 states to drop any use of racial and ethnic diversity as a factor in higher-education admissions. The justices think they will be striking a blow for color-blindness, but they really will be striking a blow for Constitution-blindness.

Sen. Trent Lott (R-Miss.) finally has come around on the affirmative-action issue. When will the rest of America's conservatives catch up to him?

POSTSCRIPT

Should the Supreme Court Prohibit Racial Preferences in College Admissions?

This issue is part of a general question having to do with the acceptability of race-conscious affirmative action. Murdock argues that such programs of preferential treatment actually hurt those that they are intended to help. Moreover, they are insulting to those who—in Murdock's understanding—are deemed too intellectually inferior to compete without the preference. Raskin counters that even if the preferential programs of college admissions are not the best policy, they are indeed constitutional and ought to be allowed.

Murdock wants preferential programs immediately scrapped, but Raskin can agree that if other steps are also undertaken to help in the development of competitive minority students, to do away with "legacy" college admissions, etc., then the programs could be scrapped.

As these words are being written, the Supreme Court has not yet rendered an opinion about the Michigan case—which will be of great legal importance to this issue. But even after the decision is settled by the Court—the law of the land—a moral question could still remain about whether or not the decision that was reached was right. For example, many look back at the Court's 1896 *Plessy v. Ferguson* decision, which legalized the practice of "separate but equal," and see that it was not right. (In this case the Court upheld the doctrine of "separate but equal" by a vote of eight to one. The only Supreme Court justice to disagree spoke of the law needing to be "color blind.") It is also possible to take a critical stance toward any decision that the Supreme Court makes, even a contemporary decision. But just as the Court backs up and supports its findings with arguments and explanations, so, too, any contemporary disagreement with the Court's findings must also employ arguments and explanations.

Informed opinion on these matters can be well served by familiarity with William G. Bowen and Derek Bok, *The Shape of the River* (Princeton University Press, 2000), which is a classic in the field. Other relevant publications include Gary Orfield and Edward Miller, eds., *Chilling Admissions: The Affirmative Action Crisis and the Search for Alternatives* (Harvard Education Publishing Group, 1998); Faye J. Crosby and Cheryl Vandeveer, eds., *Sex, Race, and Merit: Debating Affirmative Action in Education and Employment* (University of Michigan Press, 2000); Gary Orfield and Mindy Kornhaber, eds., *Raising Standards or Raising Barriers? Inequality and High Stakes Testing in Public Education* (Century Foundation Press, 2001); Lani Guinier and Susan Sturm, *Who's Qualified?* (Beacon Press, 2001); Jacques Steinberg, *The Gatekeepers: Inside the Admissions Process of a Pre-*

mier College (Viking Press, 2002); Douglas S. Massey et al., *Source of the River: The Social Origin of Freshmen at America's Selective Colleges and Universities* (Princeton University Press, 2003); and Mitchell J. Chang et al., eds., *Compelling Interest: Examining the Evidence on Racial Dynamics in Colleges and Universities* (Stanford University Press, 2003).

ISSUE 15

Are African Americans Owed Reparations for Slavery?

YES: Ronald Walters, from "Let's Resolve the Inequity," *The World & I* (April 2000)

NO: Jay Parker, from "Don't Perpetuate Division," *The World & I* (April 2000)

ISSUE SUMMARY

YES: Distinguished Leadership Scholar Ronald Walters states that much of the wealth of America was created with unpaid slave labor, while many of the social problems that plague African Americans today are grounded in the "pauperization" of African Americans as they were systematically deprived of the wealth they helped to create. Paying reparations is paying an unpaid bill, concludes Walters.

NO: Jay Parker, president of the Lincoln Institute for Research and Education, argues that African Americans have made great strides in recent years and that to support the idea of reparations is to perpetuate racial division and strife. He maintains that this is not good for African Americans, and it is not good for American society.

Virtually everyone these days agrees that slavery was a terrible thing, a great injustice, and a great blot on American history. But disputes arise when we ask what we are to do now with respect to that injustice.

One idea is that of paying *reparations* to the descendants of slaves. Although this might seem to incorporate some of the most criticized features of affirmative action (e.g., that it benefits people who did not suffer the original harm and that it creates a burden for present-day people—none of whom owned slaves), there are also some fundamental differences. One difference, for example, is that the idea of reparations for slavery involves both a symbolic meaning as well as an actual financial payment. Part of reparation is to express regret and remorse—to recognize that what was done was in fact an injustice and not to pretend that it never happened. It makes an important public statement. Secondly, the problem that is acknowledged is the wrongfulness of slavery (and its aftermath) as social practices. There is no effort to identify details about harms to specific individuals or to measure the amount of harm they suffered. The harm is considered part of the injustice and the wrongfulness of the social practices itself.

This is an issue that cuts across color lines. It is not the case that whites are on one side and African Americans are on the other. When we contemplate some great injustice like American slavery, there are contrary reactions, and these reactions occur across the races. One reaction is to acknowledge the wrong, own up to it, and (in the present case) pay reparations. But the second response, although it too can acknowledge the wrong, does so only briefly, and then attempts to move on—to put it behind us. In this view, there is no good to be gotten from lingering over unjust social practices or focusing our attention on them. In the present case, this response leads to the conclusion that reparations should not be painful. In fact, in this view, what should be acknowledged and celebrated are the great advances that African Americans have made in recent times. Opponents of reparations say that America is already moving toward justice for all, and to focus on injustice is to turn back the clock.

History presents us with a permanent problem. The historical record is already set. It shows, among other things, that Americans of white European descent have treated others—Native Americans, African Americans, Asian Americans, etc.—unjustly. We know, for example, that Native American lands were taken and that treaties were broken. In the case of Americans of Japanese descent, we know that they were held behind barbed wire in internment camps during World War II. But at least some of the wrongfulness of these cases has been addressed. Native Americans have their own tribal reservations, and to some extent, their own traditional culture. The Japanese victims of the internment camps have been paid reparations. But slavery and the mistreatment of African Americans also looms large in American history, and the question of reparations has therefore been raised.

In the following selections, Ronald Walters supports the idea of reparations, arguing that unpaid slave labor lay behind much of what has made America the wealthiest nation in the world. Jay Parker contends that the real contemporary problems that face African Americans have to do with inner-city poverty, the breakdown of the family, and other social ills that are not at all addressed by the idea of reparations.

Let's Resolve the Inequity

W̲e are in a period of history where morality and ethics are emphasized as the primary ingredients of civil virtue. However, one of the most immoral acts in the development of the United States was the enslavement of Africans, compounded by (1) failure to acknowledge that the grandeur of this country was based, in substantial part, upon the monumental resources made possible by unpaid slave labor, and (2) refusal to make reparations for this crime. Most Americans have rejected the strength of America's slave heritage, and in so doing they devalue its contribution to the country's economic strength.

For example, the factory system emerged as an outgrowth of slavery when in 1790 Samuel Slater, an English immigrant who knew the secrets of English textile machinery, built a cotton-spinning mill at Pawtucket, Rhode Island, for a merchant named Moses Brown. This mill, with 72 spindles, became the first successful American factory. By the end of the War of 1812, hundreds of factories, with an estimated 130,000 spindles, were in operation, and by 1840 the number of spindles reached 2 million. Enslaved Africans in the South picked the cotton that fed these spindles and fueled the growth of the textile industry in New England.

This led to larger and more sophisticated manufacturing institutions known as corporations, until in 1865, at the end of the Civil War, a group of businessmen—including Frances Cabot Lowell, Nathan Appleton, and Patrick Tracy Jackson—formed the Boston Manufacturing Company, which later came to be known as the Boston Associates, in Waltham, Massachusetts. This was the first integrated factory in textiles; in other words, it performed every operation. In 1920 the company shifted operations to Lowell, Massachusetts, and became the Merrick Manufacturing Company, and in the 1920s and '30s it bought companies in Massachusetts and New Hampshire, making the manufacturing corporation an entrenched institution in America.

This failure to acknowledge the contribution of African Americans to the country's development fosters such cynicism and alienation that it prevents full faith in the institutionalized version of the American dream. Moreover, it contributes to the differential perceptions and interpretations of American life by blacks and whites, such as the O. J. murder verdict, the Los Angeles rebellions after the Rodney King verdict, and other racially charged incidents.

In 1998, we completed a cycle of national discussions on race known as "The Race Initiative," sponsored by President Clinton. However, this project failed to capture the imagination of the American people, partially because of the desperate attempt of conservatives to deny and suppress a discussion of the importance of the slave origins of American wealth and the country's debt to African Americans. Contrast this modern flight from responsibility to the words of William Pitt the Younger, head of state in 1807 when the English Parliament was passing legislation prohibiting the slave trade:

> I therefore congratulate this House, the country and the world that this great point is gained: that we may now consider this trade as having received its condemnation; that its sentence is sealed; that this curse of mankind is seen by the House in its true light; and that the greatest stigma on our national character which ever yet existed is about to be removed. And sir, (which is still more important) that mankind, I trust, in general, are now likely to be delivered from the greatest practical evil that ever has afflicted the human race—from the severest and most extensive calamity recorded in the history of the world!

Pitt did not temporize about the depth of the crime of slavery, as is generally the case in so many quarters today. Thus, when President Clinton, while traveling in Africa in March 1998, used language that appeared to broach an apology for slavery, by admitting that America had not always done the right thing by Africa, members of the Republican Party in Congress rose to denounce him immediately.

The distinguished black American intellectual W.E.B. DuBois noted in his study *The Philadelphia Negro* (1897) that "everywhere slavery was accompanied by pauperization" and that this condition of poverty prevented blacks from establishing a black middle class when wave upon wave of poor migrants from the South overwhelmed the fledgling black elite and defined poverty as the basic condition of the black urban ghetto.

DuBois, Professors Kenneth Clark and William Wilson, and others have established a clear link between the "pauperization" of blacks and such social conditions as high crime rates, poor health, educational gaps, family social disorganization, high unemployment rates, poor neighborhoods, and substandard housing and other structures.

The reasons for these conditions, which characterize the black urban ghetto and the institutions within it even today, have been mystified, but slavery is responsible for having robbed black people of the economic resources necessary to acquire the cultural tools and institutions of the dominant group.

These economic resources would have made possible the construction of schools and colleges that would have long ago closed any cultural gap in test scores and produced a large middle class of blacks that would have developed companies the equal of AT&T, IBM, or Morgan Stanley. This would have institutionalized a private economy that would have provided a substantial foundation for financial independence within the black community. The dimensions of this debt have attracted individuals such as Nobel Prize–winning Yale economist Boris Bittker, who analyzed this problem in his book *The Case for Black Reparations* as early as 1973.

The Longevity of Slavery

One reason given for denying reparations to African Americans and according them to Asian Americans is that the events that constituted a basis for the latter group occurred more recently, during World War II. However, it is one of the myths of American history and its historians that slavery ended in 1865. In fact, although legal slavery ended, in many places, especially in the South, the practice continued well into the twentieth century.

The National Archives contains files of letters written in the 1920s, '30s, and '40s and sent to the NAACP by blacks who were still being held in slavery conditions on plantations in the South, still being forced to work without pay or to receive only symbolic wages, and still being brutalized. Then, debt slavery—where the sharecropping system held many former slaves in legal bondage, forcing them to work to pay mythical debts to landowners, was common.

Finally, the prison system was expanded in the South and utilized to administer the convict-lease system, where blacks were convicted on petty or nonexistent crimes and leased out to work for merchants and plantation owners in slavery conditions. These situations were in many cases merely other forms of slavery, often worse than the original kind.

This system carried well into the twentieth century, as records of the Justice Department show. In a 1996 *Washington Post* article titled "Slavery Did Not End With the Civil War; One Man's Odyssey Into a Nation's Secret Shame," Len Cooper cites a newspaper story that described a Justice Department prosecution of the Dial brothers in Sumpter County, Alabama, in 1954 because they had held blacks in involuntary servitude. This means that the civil rights movement was the force that broke the final link to slavery.

The fact that some blacks were held in slavery until after World War II and that cases of lynching also extended to that period refutes any proposition that slavery ended in 1865. This establishes a modern basis for reparations for the descendants of slaves as legitimate as that of any other group.

We also live in an era when there is much public dialogue about "individual responsibility," rather than the responsibility of government. Yet, in this case, there is both a rejection of individual responsibility for slavery—on the basis of longevity, recency of immigration, or other factors—and a reluctance to acknowledge the culpability of the state in administering the past slave status of African Americans. These have combined into the feeling that since neither individual nor government responsibility was possible, the pursuit of such a public policy was "unrealistic" and used ultimately, by both blacks and whites, to successfully evade an American dialogue about this issue.

Real reparations, however, have been given to other groups. Slavery and the extermination of the Native American are the only truly American holocausts, but whereas the Native Americans have been given land and a system of government, however flawed, black Americans have not been compensated for slavery and certainly have not enjoyed benefits beyond those available to other American citizens. And while reparations have been informally refused blacks, Japanese-American internees during World War II received them.

In fact, it is possible to argue that past attempts made to make amelioration for slavery have been dismantled before they could be implemented, or changed to advantage the majority, whether in the case of Reconstruction, civil rights, or even affirmative action.

I refer to the responsibility of government as the main authority figure in arranging recompense for slavery because at every stage individual Americans were permitted to practice slavery by writ of law, by each of the colonial territories even before there was a United States of America, certainly by the Constitutional Congress, and by successive acts of the Supreme Court, the Congress, and the state governments.

There is a deep sensitivity among the descendants of slaves in America today that a substantial part of the social distance between them and white America was created by the process of enslavement. Despite the rampant economic growth, the structural distance in economic resources has been maintained in that blacks still have only one-tenth the wealth, more than twice the poverty rate, and double the unemployment rate of whites.

This means that the failure to replace appropriated black economic resources as an "unrealistic" public policy is one of the powerful factors that results in the inability of both blacks and whites to "get beyond race," because the reluctant pace of resolving the inequality continues to place an emphasis on the fact that blacks in America are the only group expected to come all the way up the rough side of the mountain—in the most economically competitive society in the world—without the requisite resources to do so.

At the height of the attempt to pass civil rights laws in the 1960s, those opposed argued that the key to full black participation in American life is not the passage of laws but social acceptance. The other side of this equation is that acceptance must also come from blacks, and its foundation begins with acknowledging the role of the dominant culture in (1) the crime of slavery, (2) the equal crime of pretending that the gap between Africans and others is a natural condition rather than a product of enslavement, and (3) the need to make material recompense for the unpaid labor of those enslaved.

In the famous picture of Washington crossing the Delaware River, there is a black man in the boat at the oars. His name was Prince Whipple, the son of a king in West Africa. He was sent to America for education but was instead enslaved by William Whipple, one of the signatories to the Declaration of Independence. Whipple seconded Prince to be Washington's aide when Whipple went to war.

As Whipple was leaving to join the fight for American independence as an officer, Prince Whipple was recorded to have said: "You are going to fight for your liberty, but I have none to fight for." Resolving the debt of slavery through reparations will help to combine what has been two different historical struggles for "freedom" into one.

NO

Don't Perpetuate Division

In year 2000 campaign interviews and during debates in Iowa and New Hampshire, both Vice President Al Gore and former Sen. Bill Bradley again flirted with the notion of calling for a "national dialogue on race." It sounded a bit like a broken record. The suggestion, for many of us, elicits groans.

We cannot help recalling that in mid-June 1997, President Clinton launched what he said would be a "great and unprecedented conversation about race" that would "transform the problem of prejudice into the promise of unity." The would-be "conversation" became such a slanted forum for black grievances that many of its early advocates found the dialogues to be considerably less than memorable. However, in the fall of 1997 and the beginning of '98, three successive issues of the *Lincoln Review Letter* addressed the subject. Portions of that series, with some updating, are presented here as a refresher course on the subject.

At the same time in 1997, it should be recalled, several members of Congress wanted the United States to issue an official apology for slavery. A number of black organizations and leaders called for the federal government to pay "reparations" to the descendants of slaves. Apologizing, it seemed then and seems still, was and is very much in vogue—and not only in America.

The then new British prime minister, Tony Blair, apologized for the treatment of the Irish during the potato famine in the nineteenth century. Pope John Paul II apologized for the Roman Catholic Church's treatment of "heretics" and others during the Inquisition and Counter-Reformation. Australia continues to apologize for its treatment of the aborigines.

Here at home, President Clinton has already apologized to Hawaiians for the overthrow of Queen Liliuokalani a century ago, as well as to the victims of the Tuskegee syphilis experiments in World War II. Apologies and reparations were paid 20 years ago to the still-living Japanese-Americans who were incarcerated in detention camps after Pearl Harbor. It is quite different, however, when it comes to apologizing to black slaves, long dead, for deeds committed by white slave masters, also long dead.

The debate over an apology for slavery, needless to say, does not involve anyone who argues that slavery was, in any way, a worthy or defensible institution. There has long been a consensus in the Western world that slavery is an abomination. It was an abomination to many slave owners, but sad to say, economically it was deemed too important to relinquish. "If slavery is not wrong, nothing is wrong," Abraham Lincoln wrote in a letter to A. C. Hodges in 1864.

Those who advocate a formal apology believe that such a step would have an ameliorating effect upon race relations, but many others sharply disagree.

Professor Thomas Sowell calls an apology for slavery "mindless mush." He writes: "First of all, slavery is not something like stepping on someone's toe accidentally, where you can say excuse me. If the people who actually enslaved their fellow human beings were alive today, hanging would be too good for them. If an apology would make no sense coming from those who were personally guilty, what sense does it make for someone else to apologize . . . today?

"A national apology," writes Sowell, "also betrays a gross ignorance of history. Slavery existed all over the planet, among people of every color, religion and nationality. Why then a national apology for a worldwide evil? Is a national apology for murder next?"

Underlying many race-based programs in recent years has been the notion that all living white Americans are somehow beneficiaries of centuries of discrimination against blacks. Conversely, we are led to believe, all contemporary blacks are its continuing victims. In this formulation, white Americans whose ancestors arrived on these shores after the Civil War and Emancipation remain beneficiaries of slavery, and black Americans born more than a century after slavery's end are still being victimized by it. Columnist Mona Charen asks, "What about immigrants, like Koreans or Vietnamese, who only just arrived? They did not participate in discrimination against blacks, nor did their ancestors."

Then Charen adds: "So many blacks in Africa have suffered starvation and massacres in the 130 years since slavery was abolished that at least one black writer has expressed his gratitude that his ancestors were taken as slaves to America. History is not simple."

What many black activists want, of course, is not an official apology for slavery but the payment of massive reparations to today's black community. In the 1950s and '60s, the reparations movement was manifested as the Republic of New Africa and led by the likes of Audley "Queen Mother" Moore and the former fugitive Robert Williams.

In 1969, James Forman, director of international affairs with the Student Non-Violent Coordinating Committee, interrupted a service at New York City's Riverside Church to deliver his "Black Manifesto" demanding $500 million in reparations from white synagogues and churches. At the 1995 National African-American Leadership Summit—billed as a follow-up to the massive District of Columbia rally sponsored by Rev. Louis Farrakhan and the Nation of Islam—the call for reparations drew a quick consensus. Even such so-called moderates as Hugh Price, president of the National Urban League, and offbeat Harvard Professor Cornel West, who shared the stage with radical ministers Farrakhan and Ben Chavis, expressed no disagreement.

In 1994 a summit was held in Detroit by the National Coalition of Blacks for Reparations in America. The group called for, among other things, the creation of an independent state exclusively for blacks and $23,000—as well as access to land, money, technology, and tax deductions—for any black citizen descended from slaves. Among those attending were Rev. Jesse Jackson, Rosa Parks, and Nation of Islam leaders, and demands varied from speaker to speaker.

Many black voices have risen in opposition to the very idea of reparations for slavery. Walter Williams, chairman of the Department of Economics at George Mason University, describes the call for reparations as "just another scam" and argues that at this point in history, "slave owners cannot be punished and slaves cannot be rewarded. Black people in our country have gone further than any other race of people. You cannot portray blacks as victims. It's an insult to their progress and success. Most of [today's] problems have nothing to do with race; they're social and economic."

The call for reparations, states Michael Meyer, executive director of the New York Civil Rights Coalition, "is an embarrassment of muddled thinking—but then, foolishness and pie-in-the-sky sounding off are par for those who believe the world owes them. . . . However one defines it, 'reparations' is just another word for the old racial hustle." But columnist Charles Krauthammer proposed "a historic compromise, a monetary reparation to blacks for centuries of oppression in return for the total abolition of all programs of racial preference; a one-time cash payment in return for a new era of irrevocable color blindness." Is he serious? How much cash is enough to "settle the score"—$15 per black? Sounds uncomfortably like the old slave auction, but look who's holding the gavel this time.

The fact is that the problem facing black Americans has nothing to do with a legacy of slavery and, as a result, can hardly be ameliorated by "reparations." The problem is that many black leaders and groups have a vested interest in proclaiming that things are bad and getting worse. Yet, while black leaders persist in this direction, the facts vitiate their claims.

The main story with regard to black Americans since the 1960s is "black progress," argues Abigail Thernstrom, coauthor with her husband of the widely praised study in book form *Americans in Black and White.* "No group in American history ever improved its position so dramatically in so short a time," notes Thernstrom.

In the 1950s, barely 1 in 10 blacks were in white-collar occupations. By the 1990s, 4 in 10 held such positions, compared with 1 in 5 whites. In 1990, the median income of black married couples was a little under $40,000, which was 84 percent of the income of white married couples. In 1967 the comparable figure was 60 percent.

The real problems, which do exist, relate in large measure to the black underclass in the nation's inner cities who suffer not from "white racism" or the "legacy of slavery" but from an internal breakdown of the family structure. In the 1960s, the overall family structure of black Americans began to crumble.

In 1950, some 78 percent of black households featured a married couple, comparing loosely with 88 percent of white households. The proportion of black children born in female-headed households was 23 percent in 1960 and 62 percent by the end of the 1980s. In 1988, some 56 percent of single-parent black households with children were living in poverty, compared with 12.5 percent of two-parent families with children.

No serious problem facing society will ever be resolved unless it is diagnosed properly. Our inner-city problems will not be solved by "apologies" and "reparations." Liberal Professor Henry Louis "Skip" Gates Jr. of Harvard tells his fellow black scholars that they must learn to speak about black poverty in a way that "doesn't falsify the reality of black achievement." *Washington Post* columnist William Raspberry says that the civil rights movement was a largely successful battle against the "external enemies of black progress." It is now time, he insists, "for a full-scale movement against the internal enemies of our progress."

The Civil Rights Act of 1964, we often forget, specifically states that discrimination based on race, religion, sex, and age is to come to an end. In the year 2000, much of it has. Let's continue to move forward to a society in which individuals are judged on their personal merits, not their race or color. Let's not perpetuate division by harkening back to a society in which Americans of different races were at war.

POSTSCRIPT

Are African Americans Owed Reparations for Slavery?

Slavery and the Jim Crow laws—which established "separate but equal" facilities for blacks and whites—and socially widespread discrimination that continued the unjust treatment of African Americans after slavery are of course a great stain on America's history. But now the question of reparations is raised. In other cases where reparations have been paid, e.g., to the Japanese Americans who were confined in internment camps in World War II, payment was made not just to any Japanese Americans but to those particular individuals, if they were still alive, who lived in the camps. So one immediate problem is that there are no living slaves to whom to pay reparations. But this is only a preliminary point. A case could be made that the injustice done to African Americans was far more thorough than that inflicted upon Japanese Americans in World War II. After all, the Japanese Americans were free before the war and free again after it. They did face the continued second-class citizenship that attended African Americans; however, African Americans served in segregated units in World War II and came home to an America that was still practicing segregation. Moreover, as Walters argues, much of the wealth of the country—and the United States is the wealthiest nation in history—was built upon slave labor. Slavery is over, but proponents of reparations can argue that African Americans are owed far more than the Japanese Americans of World War II because the injustice against them was far more devastating. Generations of African Americans, although they had worked to build the nation, were prevented from sharing in the wealth. If slavery is over, perhaps now, proponents argue, is the time that the wealth can finally be shared.

Parker mocks the idea that cash will "settle the score." He argues that blacks are doing fine without these measures. And for many, the idea of "doing fine" is the bottom line. For Parker and for many opponents, to raise issues about slavery and reparations now is to hold on to the racial divides that should be disappearing.

One of the more notorious books in this area is David Horowitz, *Uncivil Wars: The Controversy Over Reparations for Slavery* (Encounter Books, 2002). Another important source is Randall N. Robinson, *The Debt: What America Owes to Blacks* (Plume, 2001). Further sources include Roy L. Brooks, ed., *When Sorry Isn't Enough: The Controversy Over Apologies and Reparations for Human Injustice* (New York University Press, 2000). See Thomas Sowell's online article at http://

www.jewishworldreview.com/cols/sowell071700.asp. Other online articles and links can be found at http://www.claremont.org/writings/020505erler.html, http://www.hrw.org/press/2001/07/reparations-0719.htm, http://www.hrw.org/campaigns/race/reparations.htm, http://www.cnn.com/2002/LAW/03/26/slavery.reparations, and http://slaveryreparations.newstrove.com.

ISSUE 16

Should Hate-Crime Laws Explicitly Protect Sexual Orientation?

YES: Elizabeth Birch, from "Should Hate-Crime Laws Explicitly Protect 'Sexual Orientation'? Yes," *Insight on the News* (July 24, 2000)

NO: Paul M. Weyrich, from "Should Hate-Crime Laws Explicitly Protect 'Sexual Orientation'? No," *Insight on the News* (July 24, 2000)

ISSUE SUMMARY

YES: Elizabeth Birch, executive director of the Human Rights Campaign, reviews data on the prevalence and seriousness of hate crimes, including crimes against gay males and lesbians. She favors a federal law that addresses these matters because the federal government is traditionally responsible for the prosecution of civil rights violations and because the federal government can aid state and local police in law enforcement efforts.

NO: Paul M. Weyrich, president of the Free Congress Foundation, argues that the inclusion of sexual orientation as a protected category is part of a gay agenda that seeks the mainstreaming of homosexuality.

It is not difficult to see that historically there have been problems between people of different ethnicities, religions, etc., and some people have been unjustly treated for being a member of a despised group. Nowadays, hate-crime laws are particularly aimed at the protection of individuals who are members of a group that might otherwise suffer.

Right away, it is important to understand what hate crimes are—and what they are not. Some people believe that hate crimes are ideas in the head, beliefs, or hateful attitudes. But it is erroneous to think that a hate crime is the criminal hating of someone and that those who enforce hate-crime laws are "thought police." Suppose some neo-Nazis go out one night and victimize a member of a minority group because they hate that group. (If the neo-Nazis had just stayed home that night, there would have been no hate crime—but plenty of hate.)

The crime occurs when they beat the person up. The hate was *why* they picked that person—he's one of *them*, and *they hate them*. Hate-crime laws recognize this fact. They recognize that the victim was not chosen at random (for example, that he or she did not just happen to be working at the 7-Eleven when some people came in to rob it). The victim was chosen for attack precisely because he or she was a member of the hated group.

So we might feel it reasonable to have hate-crime laws that are specifically focused on the vulnerability of some despised ethnic or religious group. After all, America is diverse and accepts diversity. But what about sexual orientation? Some say that this is a different matter, that it is a matter of choice. Many counter that the choice model works better for religion, for one can choose to convert or otherwise choose one's religion. On the other hand, it is not easy to imagine choosing your own sexual orientation. (Choice *might* come into play for someone who is somewhat undecided between males and females as a focus of his or her sexual orientation. But for most people, there is no choice about the gender that attracts them.)

What many opponents say is really going on with this issue is that homosexuality and heterosexuality are being put on a par. Both are now called "sexual orientations." A person's sexual orientation—like his or her race or religion—becomes a protected category. Yet, opponents say, they are not actually on a par at all. In fact, some contend, according to some of the same religious beliefs that are supposed to be protected, one of these orientations is a sin. It is one thing to say that America is a nation in which people are guaranteed their freedoms regardless of sex, race, religion, etc., but it may be another thing altogether to say that America is a nation in which everyone is equally free to have one sexual orientation or the other.

In the following selections, Elizabeth Birch argues in the affirmative and discusses the prevalence and seriousness of hate crimes. She states that the three most common forms of hate crime are those that are directed against victims on account of race, religion, and sexual orientation. She favors a federal law that addresses these matters because the federal government is traditionally responsible for the prosecution of civil rights violations and because the federal government can aid state and local police in law enforcement efforts. Paul M. Weyrich argues that the inclusion of sexual orientation as a protected category is part of a gay agenda that seeks to have homosexuality count on a par with heterosexuality, so that no criticism of the former will be allowed. This is, he asserts, part of the mainstreaming of homosexuality.

Elizabeth Birch

YES

Crimes Against Gays and Lesbians Are Widespread and Need Special Treatment

Although they never met each other and lived more than 1,000 miles apart, University of Wyoming student Matthew Shepard and Alabama textile worker Billy Jack Gaither had one ritual in common. On weekends, they both often would drive several hours to find refuge in big-city gay bars to escape momentarily the stifling, antigay attitudes in the small towns where they resided. Like many gay and lesbian Americans, Shepard and Gaither took these long treks because they understood the potentially dangerous ramifications of getting identified as gay in places where the label makes one a target for violence. Sadly, their suspicions proved to be correct, as they both were murdered in grisly fashion when they failed to take their true identities out of town.

Across America more gay and lesbian people are refusing to live their lives in the shadows. But the increased honesty and visibility that has led to more fulfilling and productive lives for millions of people has been accompanied by a backlash. Most striking about hate crimes is the ferocity and ruthlessness involved in the assaults. A survey by the National Coalition of Anti-Violence Programs reports that in antigay hate crimes in 1998, guns used during assaults grew 71 percent; ropes and restraints, 133 percent; vehicles, 150 percent; and blunt objects, clubs and bats, 47 percent.

These alarming statistics show that the intent of perpetrators is not simply to kill their victims, but to destroy and punish what their victims represent. In a sense, the victims are not the real targets but convenient outlets for those who hate and wish to unleash their bigoted rage and fury against an entire group. In a multicultural country such as America, hate crimes are a form of domestic terrorism and threaten the very fabric of our nation. These crimes are unique in the way they divide society and serve as atomic bombs to national unity. The Hate Crimes Prevention Act, or HCPA, which passed by the Senate 57-42 on June 20, is a common-sense measure to address these crimes which have a corrosive effect on society. Unfortunately, extreme groups that oppose its passage in the House are waging an orchestrated campaign of misinformation.

Opponents to hate-crime legislation argue that HCPA is not needed because current laws already exist to punish those who commit hate crimes. But

Congress has before recognized that crimes motivated by hate have broad social implications and therefore need to be treated differently. In 1996, Congress passed the Church Arson Protection Act in response to a national outbreak of church burnings. Arson laws already were on the books, but legislators recognized a difference between targeting a church to send a message to parishioners and randomly torching a 7-Eleven. If members of Congress can recognize that the desecration of buildings can be used to intimidate entire communities, they ought to be just as vigilant when the symbol chosen to send a hateful message to a community is a person. Furthermore, if these opponents truly believed their own rhetoric about "all crimes being hate crimes," they would try in earnest to repeal the existing federal hate-crime law that covers race, religion, color and national origin. But it is clear their only interest lies in making sure sexual orientation isn't covered. Unfortunately, this sends a message that the lives of gay men and women are worth less than those who already are covered. This attitude is inexplicable considering that in 1998, the latest year for which the FBI has statistics, sexual orientation represented the third-highest category of all hate crime victims (16 percent), behind race (56 percent), and religion (18 percent).

Some people have "moral" objections to sexual orientation being added to federal hate-crime laws. HCPA cosponsor Sen. Gordon Smith, an Oregon Republican, astutely countered this argument in a recent *Washington Post* op-ed. According to Smith, "I often have told those who attempt to wield the sword of morality against others that if they want to talk about sin, go with me to church, but if they want to talk about policy, go with me to the Senate. That is the separation of church and state."

Perhaps the biggest fallacy perpetuated by those on the extreme right is that the HCPA treats some victims more equally than others. The truth is, all people are covered under this inclusive legislation. Those who misleadingly say that this legislation elevates some victims over others must somehow be under the impression that they do not belong to a race, have a religion or a sexual orientation. They can rest easy that if they do, they too will be covered.

Opponents of hate-crime legislation like to obfuscate the issue by saying that hate-crime laws punish thought. However, the HCPA does not apply to hateful thoughts, just violent actions that cause bodily injuries or death. Last year, at a recent Senate Judiciary Committee hearing on hate crimes, Judy Shepard, Matthew's mother, best articulated why this argument is false. According to Shepard, "I can assure opponents of this legislation firsthand, it was not words or thoughts, but violent actions that killed my son."

Interestingly, in the 22 states that have hate-crime laws that include sexual orientation, all the dire predictions of the far right have not come to pass. The world has not ended and thoughts or free speech have not been limited.

In fact, the Supreme Court squarely addressed the constitutionality of hate-crime laws in the early 1990s in two cases: *R.A.V. v. City of St. Paul* and *Wisconsin v. Mitchell*. These cases clearly demonstrate that a hate-crime statute may consider bias motivation when that motivation is directly connected to a defendant's criminal conduct. By requiring this connection to criminal activity, these statutes do not chill protected speech and do not violate the First Amendment.

In *Wisconsin v. Mitchell,* the Supreme Court made clear that "the First Amendment . . . does not prohibit the evidentiary use of speech to establish the elements of a crime or to prove motive or intent." The HCPA actually would promote free speech by protecting entire groups from being silenced through fear and threats of violence. The right to free speech belongs to all Americans, not just to those who wish to spread hate.

The focus by some critics on penalties intentionally misses the point of this legislation. The HCPA does not increase penalties for hate crimes. Its purpose is to help law enforcement by allowing federal assistance, when necessary, in the investigation and prosecution of hate crimes. It would do this by providing them with the latest in technical and forensic technology. It also could provide grants of as much as $100,000 to state, local and American Indian law-enforcement officials who have incurred extraordinary expenses associated with investigating and prosecuting hate crimes.

A perfect example of where the HCPA could have been useful was in the Matthew Shepard case. During the investigation, the Albany County [Wyoming] Sheriff's office had to furlough five investigators because of soaring costs. If HCPA were passed, this never would have happened. According to Cmdr. David O'Malley of the Laramie, Wyo., Police Department, who worked on the investigation, "I call on Congress to give local law-enforcement agencies the tools they need properly to investigate and prosecute hate crimes."

HCPA has broad support from notable law-enforcement agencies and state and local leaders—including 22 state attorneys general, the National Sheriffs Association, the Police Foundation, the International Association of Chiefs of Police and the U.S. Conference of Mayors.

Opponents who say passing hate-crime legislation will unnecessarily federalize crime not only miss the point that it is supported by law enforcement but that this measure has a precedent. The federal government historically has played a significant role in the prosecution and punishment of civil-rights violations. Although criminal law is traditionally the domain of the states, Congress regularly has criminalized behavior in areas with broad national implications, including organized crime, terrorism, corporate fraud transcending state lines and civil rights. In fact, the federal government has enacted more than 3,000 criminal statutes since 1866—a great many of which have concerned civil rights.

Indeed, while arguing that criminal law is solely an area of state interest, the Republican-controlled Congress has enacted at least 14 laws that create new federal crimes or impose new federal criminal penalties for conduct that is or may also be criminal under state law. These laws address a broad range of issues—from punishing "deadbeat dads" to protecting veterans' cemeteries.

The most insidious argument from those on the extreme right is that gay advocates are using these laws to "legitimize" gay rights. Ironically, these opponents are the only people talking about homosexuality in this debate. They are so obsessed with gay people that they are willing to buck the wishes of law enforcement and deny them the tools they need to solve crimes. They inexplicably believe that in order for their families to succeed and prosper, they must deny justice to the families of hate-crime victims. Fortunately, in their zeal to attack gay people and their families, the true colors of the extreme right have come into clear focus and this is why most Americans support federal crime legislation.

Gay and lesbian Americans who live in hostile environments don't need to see the latest statistics to know that hate crimes are an ever-present threat. In news reports, it was estimated that nearly 100 gay people live in Sylacauga, Ala., the town of 13,000 where Gaither grew up and was killed. Not one of them is openly gay. Like Gaither and Shepard, these people clearly understand the deadly consequences they may face if their neighbors discover their sexual orientation. Members of Congress should recognize that this palpable climate of fear may exist in their districts. A vote for the Hate Crimes Prevention Act is a vote to correct this grave injustice and protect all citizens fairly and equally.

 **NO**

Stop the Drive to Mainstream Homosexuality and to Silence Critics of the Gay Agenda

Sometimes I wonder whether there really is a Republican majority in Congress. Some Republicans supposedly oppose judicial activism, yet they confirm even the most controversial and activist nominees without batting an eyelid. They sing the praises of limited government, yet cannot find the will to eliminate funding for the National Endowment for the Arts. It seems they never can quite stand up for the things they claim to stand for. The U.S. Senate's recent vote on hate-crime legislation was no exception.

The Senate voted June 20 [2000] to expand federal hate-crime laws to include crimes committed because of the victim's sex, disability or sexual orientation. The legislation—sponsored by Democratic Sen. Edward Kennedy of Massachusetts and presented as an amendment to the defense authorization bill—also allows the federal government to intervene in cases where no federally protected activity, such as voting, is involved. Thirteen Republicans supported the amendment, which passed by a vote of 57-42.

In addition to approving Kennedy's amendment, the Senate also passed a hate-crime amendment sponsored by Senate Judiciary Committee Chairman Orrin Hatch of Utah. His proposal, approved 50-49, did not add sexual orientation to the list of hate-crime protected classes, and instead authorized a study of state prosecutions of hate crimes.

Part of the problem with both amendments is that Congress continues to federalize crimes traditionally prosecuted by the states—crimes such as the violent ones covered by this legislation. Members of the majority party blithely ignore warnings from the likes of Chief Justice William Rehnquist, who wrote in his 1998 year-end report on the federal judiciary that this is a trend that threatens to change entirely the nature of our federal system. They seem indifferent. Why?

Well, according to Sen. Larry Craig, an Idaho Republican who opposed the Kennedy amendment, some senators were afraid to vote against the legislation for fear of being labeled "homophobic." Apparently, more than half of the Republicans who voted for it were up for reelection, several of them running in tight races. I suppose that "homophobic" is one of those magic words that melts all resistance—you know, the sort of accusation that cannot be fought or defended against.

The fact is that violent crimes such as murder and battery are illegal under state laws, regardless of the criminal's motive. Those who commit a violent crime should be prosecuted vigorously and held accountable under the law; no reasonable person argues otherwise. When one maintains that the federal government should not continue federalizing crimes, it's not a sexist argument. It's not antidisabled. And it is not "homophobic," in either the literal or commonly used sense of the word.

But the reliance on the "homophobe" label does reveal what adding the sexual-orientation category is really about: mainstreaming homosexuality. The mainstreaming movement preaches a sort of moral equivalency between homosexuality and heterosexuality, either subtly or overtly. Every choreographed step is taken with that agenda in mind. It's a movement that has borne fruit in shaping public opinion in nearly every way possible: it has made inroads into education; it sets the spin in the news media; it has taken root in some religious denominations; it permeates the writing for TV shows and motion pictures. Almost everywhere you turn, you're told that homosexuality really is an acceptable alternative lifestyle and anyone who disagrees is hopelessly mired in the past. And now the mainstreaming efforts have moved on to the next battleground—federal legislation.

Mainstreaming homosexuality through legislation has been a three-step process. To begin, homosexuality had to become a protected class under federal law and, to accomplish that, homosexual activists needed a crisis, something to goad Congress into action. They couldn't find one, so they manufactured a crisis instead.

Homosexual-advocacy groups adamantly have maintained that there is an epidemic of hate crimes in the United States, even when their own statistics have shown that violence against homosexuals is on the decline. The news media—and even some scholarly commentators—take these assertions at face value, accepting them almost without question.

The facts, however, tell a different story. In 1998, for example, of the 16,914 murders committed in the United States, 13 were classified as hate crimes. Of every 20,000 robberies that year, five (0.026 percent) were hate crimes. For every 20,000 aggravated assaults in 1998, 22 (0.11 percent) were hate crimes. Keep in mind that these are the statistics for all hate crimes, not merely those committed against homosexuals. While murder, robbery and aggravated assault are wrong, these numbers simply do not backup the claim of an "epidemic."

But who cares about facts? The homosexual activists count on their willing accomplices in the media to let their statements go unverified. They know that no one will call their bluff. And, for the most part, no one has.

Their insistence that there is an epidemic of violence against homosexuals received more acceptance after the publicity surrounding a few heinous crimes, such as the murder of Matthew Shepard two years ago. In truth, Shepard's death was a catalyst for the addition of sexual orientation to the hate-crime statute. It affixed the idea of a crisis in the minds of many people and created the perfect opportunity to pressure Congress for action on the homosexual agenda. And with that came the second mainstreaming step: gaining legitimacy.

Enter the politicians. Legislators usually say hate-crime laws are necessary to send a message that "hate" and prejudice are not acceptable in our enlightened society. The perpetrator of a hate crime is dealt with differently than other criminals who commit the same violent crime, and others who might follow in his footsteps are deterred from doing so, they claim.

That always has seemed a bit incredible to me. Would criminals, who regularly ignore all the threats, punishments and deterrents for violent crime, be any less likely to act because of hate-crime legislation? If they were going to do something that falls within the usual definition of a hate crime—targeting someone for a violent crime because they fit within a protected class—would they really hold their desire to act in abeyance because society condemns their motivation? After all, society has a much more longstanding condemnation of the violent crime itself and, if that doesn't sway them, a protected classification probably won't either. Declaring homosexuality to be a protected class is a purely political act. It tells the homosexual activists that senators support them, identify with their cause, care about them and want their vote. But more significantly in the long run, it grants an aura of legitimacy to the people who engage in the behavior that has been given protected status.

The next and final step in the mainstreaming process is the silencing of any and all criticism of homosexual behavior. Again, the goal of criminalizing certain motives for violent crime is to modify societal attitudes about the protected class. And one way to shape public opinion about a certain type of behavior—one long regarded as immoral—is to muzzle all criticism. By adding the homosexual element to hate-crime legislation, homosexual activists are trying to create a sort of guilt by association. In commentaries and news reports, those who disapprove of homosexuality on moral grounds are linked with the people who commit so-called "hate crimes." After all, isn't it true that neither group likes homosexuals? And isn't moral disapproval just a right-wing code word for "hate?"

Take the controversy surrounding Dr. Laura Schlessinger's forthcoming TV show, for example. Schlessinger's unabashed disapproval of homosexual behavior has brought her a lot of criticism, including the suggestion that her "hateful rhetoric" will foster a "climate of hate" that will encourage . . . "hate crimes." Of course, she does not advocate criminal activity, violent or otherwise, and probably condemns it as forcefully as anyone. But that little point gets lost amid the loud and endless repetition of the word "hate."

As you might expect, this type of criticism has put plans for her show in peril. The company that had planned to produce the program wavered before finally resolving to go ahead, and several big-name advertisers, such as Procter & Gamble, publicly have announced that they will not purchase time on the show. The people waging the campaign against Schlessinger have been quite open about what they want: no public forum at all for a person who has dared to say that homosexual behavior isn't right.

Don't think that this tactic will not become more widespread in the days to come. In the aftermath of the Oklahoma City bombing, President Clinton and the liberals did not hesitate to blame talk radio for fostering a climate of antigovernment sentiment that led to the tragedy. Law-abiding people who condemned the big-government policies of the liberals suddenly were being told they bore responsibility for something they had absolutely nothing to do with.

It's no stretch to picture that tactic being used against average people, not just talk show hosts such as Dr. Laura, who express their opinion about homosexuality. The threat is very real, and the voice of reason is completely ignored.

In the debate on the Senate floor, as Kennedy called for passage of his amendment, he said "[We] are not going to say we have equal protection under the law only if you are 'straight.'" Well, no reasonable person is arguing that homosexuals should not have equal protection under the law. Hate-crime legislation does not suddenly grant equal protection; homosexuals already have it. What the homosexual activists do not have is complete public acceptance—at least, not yet. But with the Senate's vote, they are just one more step closer to their goal.

POSTSCRIPT

Should Hate-Crime Laws Explicitly Protect Sexual Orientation?

Birch argues that there is a need for hate-crime laws protecting sexual orientation, that the federal government is the logical place for such laws, that the "moral" objection is a red herring, and that opposition to these hate-crime laws leaves some people and their families without recourse for justice. Opposition is itself, she implies, part of the hate to which gay males and lesbians who live in hostile environments are subject.

Weyrich has argued both that federal hate-crime legislation is a case of the expansion of the federal government and that the inclusion of sexual orientation is a case of going along with the gay agenda to mainstream homosexuality and to gain the support of law. These are two importantly different kinds of objection. The first has to do with the proper relationship between the state and the federal government. The second has to do more specifically with the inclusion of sexual orientation as a protected category. Some opponents object to federal hate-crime legislation because the acts in question (acts of violence, for example) are already against the law. So, they assert, it is useless (or needlessly redundant) for the federal government to make a crime out of what the state government already outlaws. This kind of objection is rather like Weyrich's first objection. However, some opponents specifically object to the inclusion of sexual orientation as a protected category because part of what is being protected is immoral. This kind of objection is like Weyrich's second one about the mainstreaming of homosexuality.

For many people, it is somewhat difficult to understand the mind of the hate-crime perpetrator. The following publications may be useful. See Gregory M. Herek and Kevin T. Berrill, eds., *Hate Crimes: Confronting Violence Against Lesbians and Gay Men* (Sage Publications, 1992); Valerie Jenness and Kendal Broad, *Hate Crimes: New Social Movements and the Politics of Violence* (Aldine de Gruyter, 1997); Mary E. Swigonski et al., eds., *From Hate Crimes to Human Rights: A Tribute to Matthew Shepard* (Haworth Press, 2001); Barbara Perry, *In the Name of Hate: Understanding Hate Crimes* (Routledge, 2001); Jack Levin and Jack McDevitt, *Hate Crimes Revisited: America's War on Those Who Are Different* (Westview Press, 2002); and Jeannine Bell, *Policing Hatred: Law Enforcement, Civil Rights, and Hate Crime* (New York University Press, 2002).

ISSUE 17

Should Handguns Be Banned?

YES: Nicholas Dixon, from "Why We Should Ban Handguns in the United States," *Public Law Review* (1993)

NO: Daniel D. Polsby, from "The False Promise of Gun Control," *The Atlantic Monthly* (March 1994)

ISSUE SUMMARY

YES: Philosopher Nicholas Dixon examines the contrast between gun ownership and murders in foreign countries and gun ownership and murders in the United States. He argues that there is a causal relationship between gun ownership and murder and that a ban on handguns would bring more benefit than harm.

NO: Professor of law Daniel D. Polsby asserts that gun control legislation is misguided. He maintains that if there was a ban on handguns, criminals would still arm themselves, but law-abiding citizens would not, resulting in more crime and more innocent victims.

Murder and violence are serious problems in the United States and guns play a significant role. In the wake of recent tragedies such as the Littleton, Colorado, high school killings and the mass murders in Atlanta we are especially conscious of the role guns play. But beyond these striking events is the more routine, day-to-day violence that involves guns and killing.

The resulting question is: What should be done to prevent further killing?

One suggestion is to regulate the traffic in guns, in particular, handguns. It is thought by some that this would have a favorable impact by eliminating some of the violence and killing associated with the possession of guns. It would lessen the ability of career criminals to obtain weapons and use them to commit crimes and it would prevent situations in which noncriminals might cause damage through the use of guns that they later regret but which cannot be undone. Ideally, the number of guns in circulation would be so limited that it would be difficult (or impossible) for a criminal to obtain a gun even through the black market.

Some would argue that these positive results are seriously overestimated. They counter that regulating the traffic in guns does not reduce the number of guns in circulation. Instead, regulations reduce the number of guns that are sold on open markets, where people follow restrictions, while there is little or no impact on the number of guns sold through the black market, where people do not follow restrictions. As a result, law-abiding citizens would not have guns—but criminals would. In this case, with law-abiding people at the mercy of criminals, the situation would be far worse, not better.

Gun control is one of those topics that generally separate political conservatives from political liberals. Conservatives tend to stand by the right of citizens to possess guns, while liberals tend to stand by the right of society to outlaw guns (or to restrict their sale or use). Conservatives tend to think that gun restrictions will have a larger impact on law-abiding citizens (who will follow restrictions) than on criminals (who will not); liberals tend to think that bringing the overall number of guns down will definitely have a beneficial impact on a society that is prone to use guns for the wrong reasons. Conservatives sometimes point out that guns don't kill people: people kill people. They often believe that what is required is personal responsibility and self-control, not gun control. Some liberals state that ideas of "personal responsibility" apply in an ideal world, but not in the real world, which contains excessive violence in the media and inner-city poverty.

In the selections that follow, Nicholas Dixon defends the view that handguns should be banned. He argues that the positive effects will outweigh the negative effects. Daniel D. Polsby counters that gun control will not deliver the positive effects that its proponents hope for.

Nicholas Dixon

Why We Should Ban Handguns in the United States

Readers of this review are likely to be familiar with the controversy over whether restrictions on gun ownership are compatible with the Second Amendment's guarantee of "the right to bear arms." There would be little point in discussing the complex question of the constitutionality of gun restrictions, however, unless there were good reasons for implementing them in the first place. The purpose of this paper, which will be confined to *handguns,* is to argue that there *are* good reasons for the most stringent restriction—an outright handgun ban. . . .

My argument for banning handguns is utilitarian: the likely good consequences of my proposal, I argue, far outweigh the possible bad consequences. . . .

Introduction

In 1990 there were 23,438 homicides in the United States, 9,923 of which are known to have been committed with handguns. Of the 639,271 robberies in the United States in 1990, 36.6% involved firearms, while 23.1% of the 1,054,863 aggravated assaults were made with guns.

THESIS   There are strong reasons for believing that one of the major causes of these 9,923 murders is the extremely high rate of private ownership of handguns in the United States. Similarly, this high rate is also a major cause of the 233,973 firearms robberies and 243,673 firearms assaults. Reducing the handgun ownership rate will reduce handgun violence, and hence the overall number of violent crimes. The most effective way to achieve such a reduction is a ban on the private ownership of handguns, with exceptions narrowly confined to the armed forces, the police, private security guards, and licensed gun collectors.

A ban on the private ownership of handguns will restrict the freedom of United States citizens and require an adjustment in the way that some of them spend their leisure time. . . . My argument is primarily a utilitarian discussion of the beneficial consequences of a handgun ban (a reduction in the murder rate and a general decrease in violent crime, especially robbery and aggravated assault). The pleasure and additional self-defense which is alleged to result from owning and using handguns is trivial compared to the death and misery that is caused by their misuse. However, my thesis could be equally well expressed in terms of rights (the right to life, freedom from assault, and property of victims of handgun crimes). The restriction of the alleged right to bear arms is minor compared to the violations of the rights of the victims of handgun crimes that occur every day. I have focused on a handgun ban primarily because handguns are the weapon of choice of violent criminals. In 1990 handguns were used in 77.2% of murders involving firearms and 49.5% of all murders in the United States. More recent figures are not available, but in 1967 96% of firearms used in robberies and 86% of those used in aggravated assaults were handguns. These numbers are almost certainly attributable to their relative cheapness, their small size (and hence greater concealability), and the fact that they are easy to use. At the same time, long guns (shot guns and rifles) are used more than handguns in recreational pursuits, which, *ceteris paribus* [other things being equal], it would be desirable to allow to go unhindered. Consequently, and in view of their minimal criminal use, I see no pressing need for a ban on long guns. Because of the high percentage of violent crimes that are committed with handguns, and because they are uniquely suited to such use, a handgun ban will result in a reduction in *overall* rates of violent crime.

Many recreational uses of handguns are compatible with a ban on private ownership. For instance, target shooting can still be enjoyed at licensed facilities. Shooters would be allowed to own or rent handguns that would be permanently stored at the shooting ranges.[1] . . .

An International Comparison

In 1988 Interpol reported the . . . number of handgun homicides for the . . . countries [shown in Table 1].

It was this astounding disparity between the United States and other developed countries which first drew my attention to the issue of handgun control.

My contention is that a major cause of this disparity is the much higher rate of handgun ownership among private citizens in the United States compared to other countries. More generally, I argue that any country's handgun ownership rate is a major determinant of its handgun homicide rate. [T]able 2 is based on information from government agencies, including police departments, in the respective countries. . . . The numbers refer to estimates of the total number of handguns owned by civilians in each country, both legally and illegally.

The close coincidence between the rank ordering of handgun ownership and handgun homicide rates in these six diverse countries is most plausibly explained by the causal connection I assert. The multiplicity of causes of handgun homicide which opponents of handgun control are eager to assert, and which I accept, make a perfect correlation most unlikely. The one anomaly is the relative position of Australia and Canada; but the actual handgun homicide numbers

Table 1

	Handgun Homicides	Population	Rate per 100,000
Australia	13	16,538,000 (1988)	0.07
Canada	8	25,857,000 (1987)	0.031
Great Britain	7	57,376,000 (1990)	0.012
Israel	25	4,614,000 (1990)	0.542
Sweden	19	8,332,000 (1984)	0.228
Switzerland	53	6,473,000 (1985)	0.819
United States	8,915	250,410,000 (1990)	3.560

Table 2

	Handguns	Handguns per 100,000	Handgun Homicides per 100,000
United States	56,833,000	22,696	3.56
Israel	171,448	3,716	0.542
Sweden	308,261	3,700	0.228
Canada	595,000	2,301	0.031
Australia	263,000	1,596	0.07
Great Britain	480,000	837	0.012

(The Swiss government was unable to provide any handgun ownership estimates.)

(13 and 8, respectively) are so small as to make the difference in homicide rate of little importance.

Of more interest than the rank ordering of individual nations, . . . is the emergence of three clear categories in which handgun owners and handgun homicide rates coincide: low (Canada, Australia, and Great Britain), moderate (Israel and Sweden), and high (United States). The most significant fact of all is the vast disparity between the United States and all the comparison countries in both the handgun ownership and handgun homicide rates. I conclude that a dramatic reduction in the handgun ownership rate in this country would substantially reduce handgun homicide rates.

I am assuming that the number of handguns in a country depends on (1) the permissiveness of its handgun laws, and (2) the demand for handguns.

Handgun laws in the United States are far more permissive than in any of the comparison countries. Since the law is much more easily controlled than the people's wishes, by far the easiest way to reduce handgun ownership is to pass more restrictive laws. My proposal, then, is that the best way to reduce handgun homicides is to pass maximally restrictive laws—a handgun ban.

Two interesting points concerning the demand for handguns are worth noting. First, it is probable that, doubtless due in part to the long history of private gun ownership in this country, there is more demand for them in the United States than in the other countries. In order to achieve the same levels of gun ownership in the United States as in other countries, therefore, it is likely that even more restrictive handgun laws will be required. Second, a reduction in the number of handguns in this country (by means of a handgun ban) can reasonably be expected to result in a reduction in demand, which will in turn cause a further reduction in ownership levels. This result is because a major reason for handgun ownership at present is to defend oneself against the huge number of people who already have handguns. . . . I propose stemming this spiral of gun ownership at its source rather than simply acquiescing in the unlimited proliferation of handguns.

Two important clarifications need to be made at this point. First, it is not being claimed that the high rate of gun ownership in the United States is the *only,* or even the main, cause of its exceptionally high handgun homicide rate. What is being claimed is that its handgun ownership rate is *one* of the causes. Furthermore, it is the easiest to control of all of the probable causes. Consequently, reducing ownership of handguns is the most realistic way to start reducing murder and handgun-related crime in the United States. Second, I am fully cognizant of the error of assuming that a correlation implies a causal connection. In order to avoid this error, anyone who posits a causal connection based on a correlation must do at least two things. One must first show that there are no other variables which correlate better with the effect, and which would account for the effect better than, or in place of, the posited cause. . . .

Since I do not claim that handguns are the only cause of murder, I do not need to rule out the existence of other causes. Consequently, to try to refute my position by pointing out these other causes is to commit a straw man fallacy. All I need to show is that there is no other cause that correlates so well with handgun murder as to rule out my own causal hypothesis. . . . While the evidence does indeed suggest a *prima facie* case for several other causal factors, none of them is nearly strong enough to be considered as the *only* cause, and hence, to disprove my hypothesis. [Secondly, a]s for a theoretical explanation of why high rates of handgun ownership correlate with high rates of handgun related murder, one need not go beyond common sense. Assuming human nature to be relatively similar in different developed democratic countries (i.e. those represented in the Interpol statistics quoted [in Tables 1 and 2]), one would expect people to be subject to roughly similar amounts of stress, provocation, jealousy, anger, desperation, resentment of other people's affluence, and whatever other factors are liable to lead some people to violence. If one of these nations has a vastly higher rate of private ownership of handguns, one would expect that the similar provocations to violence would spill over into handgun murder far more often than in the other nations. . . .

The Burden of Proof

I have presented evidence of a striking correlation between the rate of private ownership of handguns and the rate of handgun murder in six different countries. I have given a theoretical account of why this correlation is a causal one. . . . [N]one of the other alleged causes of the high homicide rate in the United States comes even close to disproving my hypothesis that the high ownership rate of handguns is one of its significant causes. . . .

I now wish to go on the offensive and suggest that I have already written enough to issue a . . . burden of proof challenge to opponents of a ban on handguns, in light of the strong *prima facie* case I have made for my causal hypothesis. In the case of my comparative international homicide statistics, and of the other satistics that I will adduce throughout my paper, it is incumbent on them to produce an alternative causal account proving that the United States' high handgun murder rate is caused by factors unrelated to its high rate of handgun ownership. They must specify what these causes are, quantify their relative presence in the United States as compared to the countries with lower homicide rates, demonstrate that variations in these factors correlate with variations in the murder rate, and provide a plausible theory explaining the causal mechanisms at work. I contend that they have utterly failed to even approach a satisfactory response to this burden of proof. . . .

To be fair to opponents of gun control, there is a substantial literature addressing the burden of proof challenge that I have issued. Defenders of private handgun ownership have written extensively on why, appearances notwithstanding, a ban on handguns will not reduce the homicide rate in the United States. This section will be devoted to the analysis of such defenses.

Comparisons With Other Countries

Since comparisons with the far lower murder rates in countries that have stricter handgun control were the main impetus for gun control, it is wise to start with this issue. The overall strategy of handgun supporters is to argue that the higher murder rate in the United States compared to other developed countries is attributable to factors other than the higher prevalence of handguns in the United States. For example, Don Kates, one of the most prolific and articulate opponents of banning handguns, argues: "The determinants of violence are . . . fundamental economic, sociocultural, and institutional differences. . . . Since gun laws, by definition, do not focus on these kinds of fundamental determinants, their potential benefits can be no more than marginal.[2] . . .

Other opponents of gun control try to show that international comparisons actually *weaken* the case for gun control. Though I could not obtain any handgun ownership statistics from the Swiss government, it is often claimed that the rate of gun ownership in Switzerland is higher than that in the United States. This is alleged to disprove any causal connection between firearm ownership and homicide rates. However, there are two crucial differences between this country and the United States. First, the guns owned in Switzerland are primarily long guns. Long guns are not the issue in this paper, which advocates a ban on handguns only. Second, all male citizens in Switzerland are required to retain the gun that they were given during their military service. The context of their gun ownership is, then, mandatory service in a citizens' militia, with its attendant training and discipline, which bears no comparison with the minimally controlled private handgun ownership in the United States. In fact, this comparison was most ill-advised on the part of handgun supporters. The handgun homicide rate in Switzerland, though less than that in the United States, is almost four times higher than that in Sweden and is on average over ten times higher than that in other countries with restrictive handgun laws (Australia, Canada, and Britain). The factors to which opponents of gun control appeal in order to explain the high rate of handgun homicide in the United States—e.g. extensive poverty, high unemployment, a minimal welfare system, and racial tension—cannot plausibly be asserted of Switzerland. The United States' alleged high rate of firearms ownership remains the most plausible explanation of its comparatively high handgun homicide rate.

More importantly, it is not necessary for me to respond to these and other attempts to discredit my international comparison by reference to causes of crime that are unrelated to gun laws. I have already made clear that I do not deny that factors other than the prevalence of handguns may influence the rate of violent crime. It should be no surprise that these factors prevent a uniform correspondence in all countries between levels of gun ownership and violent crime. Advocating a ban on handguns is perfectly compatible with recognizing that a concerted attack on unemployment, homelessness, huge disparities in wealth and real opportunity, racial inequality, and other sources of injustice are of much greater importance in the attempt to reduce homicide and violence.

My central thesis is that a major cause of the high handgun homicide rate in the United States is its huge arsenal of privately owned guns, and a handgun ban would be the best way to reduce this arsenal. I have presented striking empirical data to support my causal hypothesis. The burden of proof that I have charged to opponents of gun control is certainly not met by pointing out the existence of some causes of murder and violent crime that are not addressed by gun control. In view of the fact that the deeper socio-economic causes of violent crime are very difficult to control, we need to address other causes that *are* amenable to control. The availability of firearms is one such factor that can be controlled by legislation. It is ironic that opponents of a handgun ban point out these deeper, more institutional causes of violence in the United States, as if they somehow show the pointlessness of remedial measures. On the contrary, they only serve to underline the need for strict handgun control measures.

Scepticism as to the value of international comparisons concerning gun control and gun related crime is even less plausible in light of a study done in 1988.[3] In order to isolate the key variable—the impact of gun control on violent crime in general and on firearm violence in particular—the authors studied two cities that are very similar in most other respects: Seattle and Vancouver, Canada.[4] The two cities have a similar population, geography, climate, level of schooling, unemployment rate, median annual household income, and cultural values. Of particular interest, however, is the great similarity in their overall crime statistics. Vancouver had a very slightly higher burglary rate, and in other types of crime, Seattle had a slightly higher relative risk: robbery (1.09:1), simple assault (1.18:1), and aggravated assault (1.16:1). With regard to the weapons used in aggravated assaults, both cities reported almost identical rates of assaults with knives, other dangerous weapons, and hands and feet. These similarities are in precisely the same factors to which gun control opponents usually appeal in order to account for the higher rate of gun violence in the United States. At this point the similarities in crime patterns end. In the period studied, Seattle had 11.3 homicides per 100,000 person-years, whereas Vancouver had 6.9 per 100,000 person-years. Consequently, the relative risk of being murdered in Seattle as compared to Vancouver was 1.63:1. The relative risk of homicide excluding those committed with firearms was very similar (1.08:1), but the risk of being murdered with a firearm in Seattle as compared to Vancouver was 4.8:1. Eighty-five percent of the firearms homicides in both cities were committed with handguns. It will be difficult to deny that the almost fivefold difference in the frequency of homicides committed with firearms is responsible for the substantially higher homicide rate in Seattle.

One marked difference between the two cities is that Vancouver, like all of Canada, has significantly stricter gun control laws. The most important difference is that Vancouver does not allow concealed weapons and grants handgun permits for sporting and collecting purposes only. Handguns may be transported by car only if they are stored in the trunk in a locked box. In Seattle, concealed weapons are allowed with a permit. This has resulted in a disparity in the rates of gun ownership in the two cities. In the 1984–88 period, the total number of handgun permits issued in Vancouver was 4137. In the same time span, Seattle issued 15,289 concealed weapons permits; in addition, no permit at all was needed for handguns kept at home. An independent measure of gun ownership is provided by "Cook's gun prevalence index," which is based on surveys and the number of suicides, assaults, and homicides involving firearms in forty-nine cities in the United States. The index assigns a 41% gun ownership rate to Seattle, and only 12% to Vancouver. To summarize, we have two cities which closely resemble each other in terms of sociology, population, economics, culture, and overall crime patterns, including nonhomicidal violent crime. However, there is a noticeable disparity in their rates of homicide and a huge difference in their rates of gun-related homicide. The city with the lower homicide rates has far stricter gun control laws (especially for handguns, which are responsible for 85% of the firearms-related murders in both cities), and, not surprisingly, a far lower rate of gun ownership. The burden is on opponents of gun control to show why this study does not demonstrate the link between rates of gun ownership and homicide rates. . . .

Handguns, Criminals, and Law-Abiding Citizens

A . . . troubling argument, however, concerns the different impact that a handgun ban is likely to have on criminal and law-abiding citizens. It seems plausible to suggest that law-abiding citizens are more likely than criminals to voluntarily comply with gun control laws, including outright bans on handguns, which will require owners to turn in their guns to the police. Criminal gunowners have already committed felonies or intend to use their guns for the commission of felonies in the future, and the fact that they are committing a further felony by keeping their guns will not force compliance with handgun control laws. Indeed, the penalty for possessing an illegal gun is likely to be minimal compared to penalties that criminals face should they be apprehended for the more serious crimes that they intend to commit with the help of their guns. The very fact that they have bought guns for this purpose indicates that they are not deterred by the heavier penalties for the felonies that they plan to commit. Furthermore, drying up legal access to handguns will effectively prevent normally law-abiding citizens from becoming new handgun owners. In contrast, criminals are likely to have access to illegal black market guns and will not hesitate to avail themselves of it. The very success of a handgun ban in reducing the existing "pool" of handguns will thus result in a higher percentage of them being owned by criminals. The likely result of gun control, then, especially an outright ban on handguns, is to disarm the general population, while criminals remain just as heavily armed as they are today. No matter how effective a gun ban is in reducing the number of handguns in circulation, "the number of potential misusers is so small that the number of firearms legally or illegally available to its members will always be ample for their needs, regardless of how restrictive gun laws are or how strenuously they are enforced."[5] In the light of these plausible projections, some people who oppose a handgun ban do support measures which are targeted at precisely those criminal elements who will be most resistant to bans on guns and are most likely to abuse their guns.... [F]or instance, . . . a ban on gun ownership for those with prior criminal convictions, which would leave the law-abiding gun owner undisturbed.

Underlying the effort to target gun control at those who have prior convictions is the belief that it is these people who are most likely to misuse firearms in the future, especially in the case of homicide. However, in the case of homicides, this belief is vigorously challenged by advocates of gun control. Murder, the argument goes, is not confined to the ranks of those with criminal records. It is an act of terrible violence of which we are all capable if sufficiently provoked. Only 21% of murders occur during the commission of another felony. In at least 48.8% of 1990 homicides, the victim was either a relative or an acquaintance of the murderer. In 1990, 34.5% of all murders resulted from domestic or other kinds of argument. Since we are all capable of heated arguments, we are all, in the wrong circumstances, capable of losing control and killing our opponent. There, but for the grace of God, we all go. Given the ease with which homicide can be committed with a handgun as opposed to other more primitive methods (e.g. clubs or knives), the ease of availability of handguns may well be the factor which transforms a heated argument into a lethal attack. The simple option of running away—which is very seldom mentioned in the anti-gun control literature—will be available far more often in the case of these other kinds of attacks than in the case of a handgun attack. Gun control measures that are targeted solely at those with criminal records fail to protect us from the most likely source of handgun murder: ordinary citizens.

. . . [One] reason why a general ban is preferable to a targeted restriction is that, by virtue of reducing the overall "pool" of guns, it will reduce the real number of guns in the hands of criminals, even if it does increase the percentage of gun owners who are felons. The illegal means by which criminals would have to obtain guns—for instance buying them from unlicensed pawnbrokers, illegal transfers, buying them from friends who originally bought them legally, and outright theft—are all dependent on the presence of a substantial supply of legally purchased handguns on the market. My proposal would shrink this supply, and hence make it increasingly difficult for criminals to obtain handguns. It would also help to keep guns out of the hands of lawbreakers who have so far eluded conviction, and would hence qualify for gun ownership under a "targeted" ban. The "cost" of my proposal is that it does restrict many gun owners who never would have used their guns to commit homicide or any other crime. However, this price is more than justified by its far greater effectiveness than felons-only bans in reducing the number of murders, as it gradually and over the years reduces the number of handguns in circulation in the United States and chips away at the "gun culture" that encourages their use. . . .

Conclusion

. . . I have established a strong *prima facie* case for my hypothesis, justifying at least an *experimental* handgun ban, for, say, twenty-five years.[6]

If my hypothesis is wrong, a minor restriction on people's behavior will have been needlessly imposed, and whatever self-defense handguns may have provided will have been lost. This loss is minimal in comparison with the many *harmful* uses of handguns which, if I am correct, would be prevented by a handgun ban. Consequently, even assuming that there is only a 50% chance that my hypothesis is true (though I have argued that the probability is far higher), a handgun ban is justified on the ground of its greater expected utility.

I have not addressed what may be considered the strongest objection to a handgun ban: the Second Amendment, and its guarantee of the right to bear arms. What I *have* shown is that there is a strong utilitarian case for banning handguns, and that the constitutionality of such a ban therefore merits careful consideration.

Notes

1. In Canada, handgun owners are allowed to keep their weapons at home, and then transport them to shooting ranges only in a locked box. Because of the far greater rate of handgun violence in the United States . . . target shooters must not be allowed to keep handguns at home in this country.

2. FIREARMS AND VIOLENCE: ISSUES OF PUBLIC POLICY 529 (Don B. Kates, Jr., ed., 1984).

3. John Henry Sloan, Arthur L. Kellermann, Donald T. Reay, James A. Ferris, Thomas Koepsell, Frederick P. Rivara, Charles Rice, Laurel Gray, and James LoGerfo, *Handgun Regulations, Crime, Assaults, and Homicide: A Tale of Two Cities* 319 NEW ENG. J. MED. 1256–62 (1988).

4. These two cities are particularly well chosen to eliminate any bias due to the generally higher level of violence, especially homicide, in the United States as compared with Canada. Seattle's homicide rate is only 50–70% that of other major United States cities, while Vancouver's homicide rate is two to three times higher than that of Ottawa, Toronto, and Calgary. *Id.* at 1259.

5. KATES, [op. cit.,] 528.

6. Such a lengthy trial period is necessary in order for a gradual decrease in the vast number of handguns *already* in circulation to take effect. To this end, I support the "buyback" schemes currently operated by some police departments.

Daniel D. Polsby  **NO**

The False Promise of Gun Control

During the 1960s and 1970s the robbery rate in the United States increased sixfold, and the murder rate doubled; the rate of handgun ownership nearly doubled in that period as well. Handguns and criminal violence grew together apace, and national opinion leaders did not fail to remark on the coincidence.

It has become a bipartisan article of faith that more handguns cause more violence. Such was the unequivocal conclusion of the National Commission on the Causes and Prevention of Violence in 1969, and such is now the editorial opinion of virtually every influential newspaper and magazine, from *The Washington Post* to *The Economist* to the *Chicago Tribune.* Members of the House and Senate who have not dared to confront the gun lobby concede the connection privately. Even if the National Rifle Association can produce blizzards of angry calls and letters to the Capitol virtually overnight, House members one by one have been going public, often after some new firearms atrocity at a fast-food restaurant or the like. And [in] November [1993] they passed the Brady bill.

Alas, however well accepted, the conventional wisdom about guns and violence is mistaken. Guns don't increase national rates of crime and violence—but the continued proliferation of gun-control laws almost certainly does. Current rates of crime and violence are a bit below the peaks of the late 1970s. . . . The rising generation of criminals will have no more difficulty than their elders did in obtaining the tools of their trade. Growing violence will lead to calls for laws still more severe. Each fresh round of legislation will be followed by renewed frustration.

Gun-control laws don't work. What is worse, they act perversely. While legitimate users of firearms encounter intense regulation, scrutiny, and bureaucratic control, illicit markets easily adapt to whatever difficulties a free society throws in their way. Also, efforts to curtail the supply of firearms inflict collateral damage on freedom and privacy interests that have long been considered central to American public life. Thanks to the seemingly never-ending war on drugs and long experience attempting to suppress prostitution and pornography, we know a great deal about how illicit markets function and how costly to the public attempts to control them can be. It is essential that we make use of this experience in coming to grips with gun control.

From Daniel D. Polsby, "The False Promise of Gun Control," *The Atlantic Monthly,* vol. 273, no. 3 (March 1994). Copyright © 1994 by Daniel D. Polsby. Reprinted by permission of the author.

The thousands of gun-control laws in the United States are of two general types. The older kind sought to regulate how, where, and by whom firearms could be carried. More recent laws have sought to make it more costly to buy, sell, or use firearms (or certain classes of firearms, such as assault rifles, Saturday-night specials, and so on) by imposing fees, special taxes, or surtaxes on them. The Brady bill is of both types: it has a background-check provision, and its five-day waiting period amounts to a "time tax" on acquiring handguns. All such laws can be called scarcity-inducing, because they seek to raise the cost of buying firearms, as figured in terms of money, time, nuisance, or stigmatization.

Despite the mounting number of scarcity-inducing laws, no one is very satisfied with them. Hobbyists want to get rid of them, and gun-control proponents don't think they go nearly far enough. Everyone seems to agree that gun-control laws have some effect on the distribution of firearms. But it has not been the dramatic and measurable effect their proponents desired.

Opponents of gun control have traditionally wrapped their arguments in the Second Amendment to the Constitution. Indeed, most modern scholarship affirms that so far as the drafters of the Bill of Rights were concerned, the right to bear arms was to be enjoyed by everyone, not just a militia, and that one of the principal justifications for an armed populace was to secure the tranquillity and good order of the community. But most people are not dedicated antiquitarians, and would not be impressed by the argument "I admit that my behavior is very dangerous to public safety, but the Second Amendment says I have a right to do it anyway." That would be a case for repealing the Second Amendment, not respecting it.

Fighting the Demand Curve

Everyone knows that possessing a handgun makes it easier to intimidate, wound, or kill someone. But the implication of this point for social policy has not been so well understood. It is easy to count the bodies of those who have been killed or wounded with guns, but not easy to count the people who have avoided harm because they had access to weapons. Think about uniformed police officers, who carry handguns in plain view not in order to kill people but simply to daunt potential attackers. And it works. Criminals generally do not single out police officers for opportunistic attack. Though officers can expect to draw their guns from time to time, few even in big-city departments will actually fire a shot (except in target practice) in the course of a year. This observation points to an important truth: people who are armed make comparatively unattractive victims. A criminal might not know if any one civilian is armed, but if it becomes known that a large number of civilians do carry weapons, criminals will become warier.

Which weapons laws are the right kinds can be decided only after considering two related questions. First, what is the connection between civilian possession of firearms and social violence? Second, how can we expect gun-control laws to alter people's behavior? Most recent scholarship raises serious questions about the "weapons increase violence" hypothesis. The second question is emphasized here, because it is routinely overlooked and often mocked when noticed; yet it is crucial. Rational gun control requires understanding not only the relationship between weapons and violence but also the relationship between laws and people's behavior. Some things are very hard to accomplish with laws. The purpose of a law and its likely effects are not always the same thing. Many statutes are notorious for the way in which their unintended effects have swamped their intended ones.

In order to predict who will comply with gun-control laws, we should remember that guns are economic goods that are traded in markets. Consumers' interest in them varies. For religious, moral, aesthetic, or practical reasons, some people would refuse to buy firearms at any price. Other people willingly pay very high prices for them.

Handguns, so often the subject of gun-control laws, are desirable for one purpose—to allow a person tactically to dominate a hostile transaction with another person. The value of a weapon to a given person is a function of two factors: how much he or she wants to dominate a confrontation if one occurs, and how likely it is that he or she will actually be in a situation calling for a gun.

Dominating a transaction simply means getting what one wants without being hurt. Where people differ is in how likely it is that they will be involved in a situation in which a gun will be valuable. Someone who *intends* to engage in a transaction involving a gun—a criminal, for example—is obviously in the best possible position to predict that likelihood. Criminals should therefore be willing to pay more for a weapon than most other people would. Professors, politicians, and newspaper editors are, as a group, at very low risk of being involved in such transactions, and they thus systematically underrate the value of defensive handguns. (Correlative, perhaps, is their uncritical readiness to accept studies that debunk the utility of firearms for self-defense.) The class of people we wish to deprive of guns, then, is the very class with the most inelastic demand for them—criminals—whereas the people most likely to comply with gun-control laws don't value guns in the first place.

Do Guns Drive Up Crime Rates?

Which premise is true—that guns increase crime or that the fear of crime causes people to obtain guns? . . .

If firearms increased violence and crime, then rates of spousal homicide would have skyrocketed, because the stock of privately owned handguns has increased rapidly since the mid-1960s. But according to an authoritative study of spousal homicide in the *American Journal of Public Health*, by James Mercy and Linda Saltzman, rates of spousal homicide in the years 1976 to 1985 fell. If firearms increased violence and crime, the crime rate should have increased throughout the 1980s, while the national stock of privately owned handguns increased by more than a million units in every year of the decade. It did not. Nor should the rates of violence and crime in Switzerland, New Zealand, and Israel be as low as they are, since the number of firearms per civilian household is comparable to that in the United States. Conversely, gun-controlled Mexico and South Africa should be islands of peace instead of having murder rates more than twice as high as those here. The determinants of crime and law-abidingness are, of course, complex matters, which are not fully understood and certainly not explicable in terms of a country's laws. But gun-control enthusiasts, who have made capital out of the low murder rate in England, which is largely disarmed, simply ignore the counterexamples that don't fit their theory.

If firearms increased violence and crime, Florida's murder rate should not have been falling since the introduction . . . of a law that makes it easier for ordinary citizens to get permits to carry concealed handguns. Yet the murder rate has remained the same or fallen every year since the law was enacted, and it is now lower than the national murder rate (which has been rising). As of November [1993] 183,561 permits had been issued, and only seventeen of the permits had been revoked because the holder was involved in a firearms offense. It would be precipitate to claim that the new law has "caused" the murder rate to subside. Yet here is a situation that doesn't fit the hypothesis that weapons increase violence.

If firearms increased violence and crime, programs of induced scarcity would suppress violence and crime. But—another anomaly—they don't. Why not? A theorem, which we could call the futility theorem, explains why gun-control laws must either be ineffectual or in the long term actually provoke more violence and crime. Any theorem depends on both observable fact and assumption. An assumption that can be made with confidence is that the higher the number of victims a criminal assumes to be armed, the higher will be the risk—the price—of assaulting them. By definition, gun-control laws should make weapons scarcer and thus more expensive. By our prior reasoning about demand among various types of consumers, after the laws are enacted criminals should be better armed, compared with noncriminals, than they were before. Of course, plenty of noncriminals will remain armed. But even if many noncriminals will pay as high a price as criminals will to obtain firearms, a larger number will not.

Criminals will thus still take the same gamble they already take in assaulting a victim who might or might not be armed. But they may appreciate that the laws have given them a freer field, and that crime still pays—pays even better, in fact, than before. What will happen to the rate of violence? Only a relatively few gun-mediated transactions—currently, five percent of armed robberies committed with firearms—result in someone's actually being shot (the statistics are not broken down into encounters between armed assailants and unarmed victims, and encounters in which both parties are armed). It seems reasonable to fear that if the number of such transactions were to increase because criminals thought they faced fewer deterrents, there would be a corresponding increase in shootings. Conversely, if gun-mediated transactions declined—if criminals initiated fewer of them because they feared encountering an armed victim or an armed good Samaritan—the number of shootings would go down. The magnitude of these effects is, admittedly, uncertain. Yet it is hard to doubt the general tendency of a change in the law that imposes legal burdens on buying guns. The futility theorem suggests that gun-control laws, if effective at all, would unfavorably affect the rate of violent crime. . . .

Are there empirical studies that can serve to help us choose between the futility theorem and the hypothesis that guns increase violence? Unfortunately, no: the best studies of the effects of gun-control laws are quite inconclusive. Our statistical tools are too weak to allow us to identify an effect clearly enough to persuade an open-minded skeptic. But it is precisely when we are dealing with undetectable statistical effects that we have to be certain we are using the best models available of human behavior.

Sealing the Border

Handguns are not legally for sale in the city of Chicago, and have not been since April of 1982. Rifles, shotguns, and ammunition are available, but only to people who possess an Illinois Firearm Owner's Identification [FOID] card. It takes up to a month to get this card, which involves a background check. Even if one has a FOID card there is a waiting period for the delivery of a gun. In few places in America is it as difficult to get a firearm legally as in the city of Chicago.

Yet there are hundreds of thousands of unregistered guns in the city, and new ones arriving all the time. It is not difficult to get handguns—even legally. Chicago residents with FOID cards merely go to gun shops in the suburbs. Trying to establish a city as an island of prohibition in a sea of legal firearms seems an impossible project.

Is a state large enough to be an effective island, then? Suppose Illinois adopted Chicago's handgun ban. Same problem again. Some people could just get guns elsewhere: Indiana actually borders the city, and Wisconsin is only forty miles away. Though federal law prohibits the sale of handguns in one state to residents of another, thousands of Chicagoans with summer homes in other states could buy handguns there. And, of course, a black market would serve the needs of other customers.

When would the island be large enough to sustain a weapons-free environment? In the United States people and cargoes move across state lines without supervision or hindrance. Local shortages of goods are always transient, no matter whether the shortage is induced by natural disasters, prohibitory laws, or something else.

Even if many states outlawed sales of handguns, then, they would continue to be available, albeit at a somewhat higher price, reflecting the increased legal risk of selling them. Mindful of the way markets work to undermine their efforts, gun-control proponents press for federal regulation of firearms, because they believe that only Congress wields the authority to frustrate the interstate movement of firearms.

Why, though, would one think that federal policing of illegal firearms would be better than local policing? The logic of that argument is far from clear. Cities, after all, are comparatively small places. Washington, D.C., for example, has an area of less than 45,000 acres. Yet local officers have had little luck repressing the illegal firearms trade there. Why should federal officers do any better watching the United States' 12,000 miles of coastline and millions of square miles of interior? Criminals should be able to frustrate federal police forces just as well as they can local ones. Ten years of increasingly stringent federal efforts to abate cocaine trafficking, for example, have not succeeded in raising the street price of the drug. . . .

In firearms regulation, translating theory into practice will continue to be difficult, at least if the objective is to lessen the practical availability of firearms to people who might abuse them. On the demand side, for defending oneself against predation there is no substitute for a firearm. Criminals, at least, can switch to varieties of law-breaking in which a gun confers little or no advantage (burglary, smash-and-grab), but people who are afraid of confrontations with criminals, whether rationally or (as an accountant might reckon it) irrationally, will be very highly motivated to acquire firearms. . . . [P]eople's demand for personal security and for the tools they believe provide it will remain strong.

On the supply side, firearms transactions can be consummated behind closed doors. Firearms buyers, unlike those who use drugs, pornography, or prostitution, need not recurrently expose themselves to legal jeopardy. One trip to the marketplace is enough to arm oneself for life. This could justify a consumer's taking even greater precautions to avoid apprehension, which would translate into even steeper enforcement costs for the police. . . .

Administering Prohibition

. . . Unless people are prepared to surrender their guns voluntarily, how can the U.S. government confiscate an appreciable fraction of our country's nearly 200 million privately owned firearms? We know that it is possible to set up weapons-free zones in certain locations—commercial airports and many courthouses and, lately, some troubled big city high schools and housing projects. The sacrifices of privacy and convenience, and the costs of paying guards, have been thought worth the (perceived) gain in security. No doubt it would be possible, though it would probably not be easy, to make weapons-free zones of shopping centers, department stores, movie theaters, ball parks. But it is not obvious how one would cordon off the whole of an open society.

Voluntary programs have been ineffectual. From time to time community-action groups or police departments have sponsored "turn in your gun" days, which are nearly always disappointing. Sometimes the government offers to buy guns at some price. . . . If the price offered exceeds that at which a gun can be bought on the street, one can expect to see plans of this kind yield some sort of harvest—as indeed they have. But it is implausible that these schemes will actually result in a less-dangerous population. Government programs to buy up surplus cheese cause more cheese to be produced without affecting the availability of cheese to people who want to buy it. So it is with guns.

One could extend the concept of intermittent roadblocks of the sort approved by the Supreme Court for discouraging drunk driving. Metal detectors could be positioned on every street corner, or ambulatory metal-detector squads could check people randomly, or hidden magnetometers could be installed around towns, to detect concealed weapons. As for firearms kept in homes (about half of American households), warrantless searches might be rationalized on the well-established theory that probable cause is not required when authorities are trying to correct dangers to public safety rather than searching for evidence of a crime. . . .

Ignoring the Ultimate Sources of Crime and Violence

The American experience with prohibition has been that black marketeers—often professional criminals—move in to profit when legal markets are closed down or disturbed. In order to combat them, new laws and law-enforcement techniques are developed, which are circumvented almost as soon as they are put in place. New and yet more stringent laws are enacted, and greater sacrifices of civil liberties and privacy demanded and submitted to. But in this case the problem, crime and violence, will not go away, because guns and ammunition (which, of course, won't go away either) do not cause it. One cannot expect people to quit seeking new weapons as long as the tactical advantages of weapons are seen to outweigh the costs imposed by prohibition. Nor can one expect large numbers of people to surrender firearms they already own. The only way to make people give up their guns is to create a world in which guns are perceived as having little value. This world will come into being when criminals choose not to use guns because the penalties for being caught with them are too great, and when ordinary citizens don't think they need firearms because they aren't afraid of criminals anymore.

Neither of these eventualities seems very likely without substantial departures in law-enforcement policy. Politicians' nostrums—increasing the punishment for crime, slapping a few more death-penalty provisions into the code—are taken seriously by few students of the crime problem. The existing penalties for predatory crimes are quite severe enough. The problem is that they are rarely meted out in the real world. The penalties formally published by the code are in practice steeply discounted, and criminals recognize that the judicial and penal systems cannot function without bargaining in the vast majority of cases. This problem is not obviously one that legislation could solve. . . .

The problem is not simply that criminals pay little attention to the punishments in the books. Nor is it even that they also know that for the majority of crimes, their chances of being arrested are small. The most important reason for criminal behavior is this: the income that offenders can earn in the world of crime, as compared with the world of work, all too often makes crime appear to be the better choice.

. . . More prisons means that fewer violent offenders will have to be released early in order to make space for new arrivals; perhaps fewer plea bargains will have to be struck—all to the good. Yet a moment's reflection should make clear that one more criminal locked up does not necessarily mean one less criminal on the street. The situation is very like one that conservationists and hunters have always understood. Populations of game animals readily recover from hunting seasons but not from loss of habitat. Mean streets, when there are few legitimate entry level opportunities for young men, are a criminal habitat, so to speak, in the social ecology of modern American cities. Cull however much one will, the habitat will be reoccupied promptly after its previous occupant is sent away. So social science has found.

Similarly, whereas increasing the number of police officers cannot hurt, and may well increase people's subjective feelings of security, there is little evidence to suggest that doing so will diminish the rate of crime. Police forces are basically reactive institutions. . . .

There is a challenge here that is quite beyond being met with tough talk. Most public officials can see the mismatch between their tax base and the social entropies they are being asked to repair. There simply isn't enough money; existing public resources, as they are now employed, cannot possibly solve the crime problem. But mayors and senators and police chiefs must not say so out loud: too-disquieting implications would follow. For if the authorities are incapable of restoring public safety and personal security under the existing ground rules, then obviously the ground rules must change. . . .

Communities must, in short, organize more effectively to protect themselves against predators. No doubt this means encouraging properly qualified private citizens to possess and carry firearms legally. It is not morally tenable— nor, for that matter, is it even practical—to insist that police officers, few of whom are at a risk remotely as great as are the residents of many city neighborhoods, retain a monopoly on legal firearms. It is needless to fear giving honest men and women the training and equipment to make it possible for them to take back their own streets.

Over the long run, however, there is no substitute for addressing the root causes of crime—bad education and lack of job opportunities and the disintegration of families. Root causes are much out of fashion nowadays as explanations of criminal behavior, but fashionable or not, they are fundamental. *The root cause of crime is that for certain people, predation is a rational occupational choice.* Conventional crime-control measures, which by stiffening punishments or raising the probability of arrest aim to make crime pay less, cannot consistently affect the behavior of people who believe that their alternatives to crime will pay virtually nothing. Young men who did not learn basic literacy and numeracy skills before dropping out of their wretched public schools may not [be] worth hiring at the minimum wage. . . . Their legitimate opportunities, always precarious in a society where race and class still matter, often diminish to the point of being for all intents and purposes absent. . . .

The solution to the problem of crime lies in improving the chances of young men. Easier said than done, to be sure. No one has yet proposed a convincing program for checking all the dislocating forces that government assistance can set in motion. One relatively straightforward change would be reform of the educational system. Nothing guarantees prudent behavior like a sense of the future, and with average skills in reading, writing, and math, young people can realistically look forward to constructive employment and the straight life that steady work makes possible.

But firearms are nowhere near the root of the problem of violence. As long as people come in unlike sizes, shapes, ages, and temperaments, as long as they diverge in their taste for risk and their willingness and capacity to prey on other people or to defend themselves from predation, and above all as long as some people have little or nothing to lose by spending their lives in crime, dispositions to violence will persist.

This is what makes the case for the right to bear arms, not the Second Amendment. It is foolish to let anything ride on hopes for effective gun control. As long as crime pays as well as it does, we will have plenty of it, and honest folk must choose between being victims and defending themselves.

POSTSCRIPT

Should Handguns Be Banned?

Dixon asserts that there are good reasons to ban handguns. What is also important to consider is whether there are equally good reasons *not* to ban handguns.

If Dixon is correct that there is a "gun culture" in the United States (but not in other countries), then the problem that he and Polsby address is far greater than Dixon lets on. If, indeed, guns are intertwined with other aspects of American life, then their presence is not just some isolated fact that can simply be changed. Think about ecology, where things are interconnected with one another; to change one thing may seem simple but may have unanticipated impacts elsewhere in the system. This fact may support Polsby's point that life will not continue much as it did before only without the crime and violence that is associated with guns simply by removing guns. According to Polsby, by removing legal handguns, incentives for criminals to obtain guns through other channels—or even to engage in the manufacturing, smuggling, or sales of guns themselves—are created.

However, one must also consider whether banning handguns has the support of *reason*. All things considered, is the banning of handguns simply the reasonable thing to do?

Relevant literature includes Tamara L. Roleff, ed., *Gun Control: Opposing Viewpoints* (Greenhaven Press, 1997); Benedict D. Larosa, *Gun Control,* 3rd ed. (Candlestick Publishing, 1997); Gary Kleck, *Targeting Guns: Firearms and Their Control* (Aldine De Gruyter, 1997); Gregg Lee Carter, *The Gun Control Movement* (Twayne Publishing, 1997); Marjolijn Bijlefeld, ed., *The Gun Control Debate* (Greenwood Publishing Group, 1997); Suzanne Squyres, Jacquelyn Quiram, and Nancy R. Jacobs, ed., *Gun Control: Restricting Rights or Protecting People?* (Information Plus, 1997); Jacob G. Hornberger and Richard M. Ebeling, eds., *The Tyranny of Gun Control* (Future of Freedom Foundation, 1998); John R. Lott, Jr., *More Guns, Less Crime: Understanding Crime and Gun-Control Laws* (University of Chicago Press, 1998); Jan E. Dizard, Robert Merrill Muth, and Stephen P. Andrews, eds., *Guns in America: A Reader* (New York University Press, 1999); and Glenn H. Utter, *Encyclopedia of Gun Control & Gun Rights* (Oryx Press, 1999).

Recent publications include Richard Poe, *The Seven Myths of Gun Control: Reclaiming the Truth About Guns, Crime, and the Second Amendment* (Prima Publishing, 2001); James B. Jacobs, *Can Gun Control Work?* (Oxford University Press, 2002); John R. Lott, Jr., *The Bias Against Guns: Why Almost Everything You've Heard About Gun Control Is Wrong* (Regnery Publishing, 2003); and Angela Valdez and Alan Marzilli, *Gun Control* (Chelsea House Publishers, 2003).

ISSUE 18

Should the Death Penalty Be Retained?

YES: Ernest van den Haag, from "The Death Penalty Once More,"
U.C. Davis Law Review (Summer 1985)

NO: Mark Costanzo, from *Just Revenge: Costs and Consequences of the Death Penalty* (St. Martin's Press, 1997)

ISSUE SUMMARY

YES: Professor of law Ernest van den Haag argues that the death penalty is entirely in line with the U.S. Constitution and that although studies of its deterrent effect are inconclusive, the death penalty is morally justified and should be retained.

NO: Psychologist Mark Costanzo denies that the death penalty has the positive practical effects that retentionists often attribute to it and states that religious and moral arguments go against the death penalty.

Since punishment involves the intentional infliction of harm upon another person, and since the intentional infliction of harm is generally wrong, the idea of punishment itself is somewhat problematic. Punishment requires some strong rationale if it is not to be just another form of wrongdoing; capital punishment requires an especially strong rationale.

Consider some actual cases of capital punishment: Socrates was tried in ancient Athens and condemned to die (by drinking poison) for not believing in the gods of the state and for corrupting young people. In 1977 a princess and her lover were executed (by firing squad and beheading, respectively) in Saudi Arabia for adultery. Also in 1977 Gary Gilmore insisted that he receive the death penalty and was executed by a firing squad in Utah for murder.

Justification for capital punishment usually comes down to one of two different lines of reasoning. One is based on the idea of justice, the other on the idea of deterrence.

Justice, it is said, demands that certain criminal acts be paid for by death. The idea is that some people deserve death and have to pay for their criminal acts with their lives.

There are several objections to this view. One of the most important of these focuses on the idea of a person "paying" for a crime by death (or even in some other way). What concept of "paying" is being used here? It does not seem like an ordinary case of paying a debt. It seems to be a kind of vengeance, as when one person says to another "I'll make you pay for that," meaning "I'll make you suffer for that." Yet one of the ideas behind state-inflicted punishment is that it is supposed to be very official, even bureaucratic, and it is designed to eliminate private vendettas and personal vindictiveness. The state, in a civilized society, is not supposed to be motivated by revenge or vindictiveness. The state's only intent is to support law and order and to protect its citizens from coming to harm at the hands of wrongdoers.

The other major line of reasoning in support of capital punishment is based on the idea of deterrence. According to this view, capital punishment must be retained in order to deter criminals and potential criminals from committing capital crimes. An old joke reflects this view: A Texan tells a visitor that in the old days the local punishment for horse-stealing was hanging. The visitor is shocked. "You used to hang people just for taking horses?" "Nope," says the Texan, "horses never got stolen."

Unlike the argument about "paying," the logic behind deterrence is supposed to be intuitively easy to understand. However, assertions concerning deterrence do not seem to be clearly borne out by actual statistics and empirical evidence.

Your intuition may support the judgment that the death penalty deters crime, but the empirical evidence is not similarly uniform and clear, and in some cases the evidence even points to the opposite conclusion. (For example, some people may be more likely to murder an innocent victim if they are reasonably certain of achieving their own death and perhaps some notoriety.) Or consider the example of the failure of deterrence that occurred in England when public hanging was the punishment for the crime of pickpocketing. Professional pickpockets, undeterred by the activity on the gallows, circulated among the crowd of spectators, aware that a good time to pick pockets was when everyone's attention was focused on something else—in this case, when the rope tightened around the neck of the convicted pickpocket.

Further thought about this matter of deterrence raises more questions. Consider this scenario: Two men get into an argument while drinking, and one pulls a gun and shoots the other, who dies. Do we suppose that this killer is even aware of the punishment for murder when he acts? Would he be deterred by the prospect of capital punishment but be willing to shoot if the punishment were only 20 years or life in prison?

In the following selections, Ernest van den Haag makes the case for the retention of capital punishment, while Mark Costanzo argues for its abolition. Both authors discuss practical matters associated with the death penalty (e.g., its value as a deterrent) but they consider the question of its moral acceptability to be paramount.

Ernest van den Haag  **YES**

The Death Penalty Once More

P eople concerned with capital punishment disagree on essentially three questions: (1) Is it constitutional? (2) Does the death penalty deter crime more than life imprisonment? (3) Is the death penalty morally justifiable?

Is the Death Penalty Constitutional?

The fifth amendment, passed in 1791, states that "no person shall be deprived of life, liberty, or property, without due process of law." Thus, with "due process of law," the Constitution authorizes depriving persons "of life, liberty or property." The fourteenth amendment, passed in 1868, applies an identical provision to the states. The Constitution, then, authorizes the death penalty. It is left to elected bodies to decide whether or not to retain it.

The eighth amendment, reproducing almost verbatim a passage from the English Bill of Rights of 1689, prohibits "cruel and unusual punishments." This prohibition was not meant to repeal the fifth amendment since the amendments were passed simultaneously. "Cruel" punishment is not prohibited unless "unusual" as well, that is, new, rare, not legislated, or disproportionate to the crime punished. Neither the English Bill of Rights, nor the eighth amendment, hitherto has been found inconsistent with capital punishment.

Evolving Standards

Some commentators argue that, in *Trop v. Dulles,* the Supreme Court indicated that "evolving standards of decency that mark the progress of a maturing society" allow courts to declare "cruel and unusual," punishments authorized by the Constitution. However, *Trop* was concerned with expatriation, a punishment that is not specifically authorized by the Constitution. The death penalty is. *Trop* did not suggest that "evolving standards" could de-authorize what the Constitution repeatedly authorizes. Indeed, Chief Justice Warren, writing for the majority in *Trop,* declared that "the death penalty . . . cannot be said to violate the constitutional concept of cruelty."[1] Furthermore, the argument based on "evolving standards" is paradoxical: the Constitution would be redundant if current views, enacted by judicial fiat, could supersede what it plainly says. If

From Ernest van den Haag, "The Death Penalty Once More," *U.C. Davis Law Review,* vol. 18, no. 4 (Summer 1985). Copyright © 1985 by The Regents of the University of California. Reprinted by permission. Some notes omitted.

"standards of decency" currently invented or evolved could, without formal amendment, replace or repeal the standards authorized by the Constitution, the Constitution would be superfluous.

It must be remembered that the Constitution does not force capital punishment on the population but merely authorizes it. Elected bodies are left to decide whether to use the authorization. As for "evolving standards," how could courts detect them without popular consensus as a guide? Moral revelations accepted by judges, religious leaders, sociologists, or academic elites, but not by the majority of voters, cannot suffice. The opinions of the most organized, most articulate, or most vocal might receive unjustified deference. Surely the eighth amendment was meant to limit, but was not meant to replace, decisions by the legislative branch, or to enable the judiciary [to] do what the voters won't do.[2] The general consensus on which the courts would have to rely could be registered only by elected bodies. They favor capital punishment. Indeed, at present, more than seventy percent of the voters approve of the death penalty. The state legislatures reflect as much. Wherefore, the Supreme Court, albeit reluctantly, rejected abolition of the death penalty by judicial *fiat*. This decision was subsequently qualified by a finding that the death penalty for rape is disproportionate to the crime,[3] and by rejecting all mandatory capital punishment.

Caprice

Laws that allowed courts too much latitude to decide, perhaps capriciously, whether to actually impose the death penalty in capital cases also were found unconstitutional. In response, more than two-thirds of the states have modified their death penalty statutes, listing aggravating and mitigating factors, and imposing capital punishment only when the former outweigh the latter. The Supreme Court is satisfied that this procedure meets the constitutional requirements of non-capriciousness. However, abolitionists are not.

In *Capital Punishment: The Inevitability of Caprice and Mistake*,[4] Professor Charles Black contends that the death penalty is necessarily imposed capriciously, for irremediable reasons. If he is right, he has proved too much, unless capital punishment is imposed more capriciously now than it was in 1791 or 1868, when the fifth and fourteenth amendments were enacted. He does not contend that it is. Professor Black also stresses that the elements of chance, unavoidable in all penalizations, are least tolerable when capital punishment is involved. But the irreducible chanciness inherent in human efforts does not constitutionally require the abolition of capital punishment, unless the framers were less aware of chance and human frailty than Professor Black is. (I shall turn to the moral as distinguished from the legal bearing of chanciness anon.)

Discrimination

Sociologists have demonstrated that the death penalty has been distributed in a discriminatory pattern in the past: black or poor defendants were more likely to be executed than equally guilty others. This argues for correction of the distributive process, but not for abolition of the penalty it distributes, unless constitutionally excessive maldistribution ineluctably inheres in the penalty. There is no evidence to that effect. Actually, although we cannot be sure that it has disappeared altogether, discrimination has greatly decreased compared to the past.[5]

However, recently the debate on discrimination has taken a new turn. Statistical studies have found that, *ceteris paribus,* a black man who murders a white has a much greater chance to be executed than he would have had, had his victim been black.[6] This discriminates against black *victims* of murder: they are not as fully, or as often, vindicated as are white victims. However, although unjustified per se, discrimination against a class of victims need not, and here does not, amount to discrimination against their victimizers. The pattern discriminates *against* black murderers of whites and *for* black murderers of blacks. One may describe it as discrimination for, or discrimination against, just as one may describe a glass of water as half full or half empty. Discrimination against one group (here, blacks who kill whites) is necessarily discrimination in favor of another (here, blacks who kill blacks).

Most black victims are killed by black murderers, and a disproportionate number of murder victims is black. Wherefore the discrimination in favor of murderers of black victims more than offsets, numerically, any remaining discrimination against other black murderers.[7]

Comparative Excessiveness

Recently lawyers have argued that the death penalty is unconstitutionally disproportionate if defendants, elsewhere in the state, received lesser sentences for comparable crimes. But the Constitution only requires that penalties be appropriate to the gravity of the crime, not that they cannot exceed penalties imposed elsewhere. Although some states have adopted "comparative excessiveness" reviews, there is no constitutional requirement to do so.

Unavoidably, different courts, prosecutors, defense lawyers, judges and juries produce different penalties even when crimes seem comparable. Chance plays a great role in human affairs. Some offenders are never caught or convicted, while others are executed; some are punished more than others guilty of worse crimes. Thus, a guilty person, or group of persons, may get away with no punishment, or with a light punishment, while others receive the punishment they deserve. Should we let these others go too, or punish them less severely? Should we abolish the penalty applied unequally or discriminatorily?[8]

The late Justice Douglas suggested an answer to these questions:

> A law that . . . said that blacks, those who never went beyond the fifth grade in school, those who made less than $3,000 a year, or those who were unpopular or unstable should be the only people executed [would be wrong]. A law which in the overall view reaches that result in practice has no more sanctity than a law which in terms provides the same.[9]

Justice Douglas' answer here conflates an imagined discriminatory law with the discriminatory application of a non-discriminatory law. His imagined law would be inconsistent with the "equal protection of the laws" demanded by the fourteenth amendment, and the Court would have to invalidate it *ipso facto.* But discrimination caused by uneven application of non-discriminatory death penalty laws may be remedied by means other than abolition, as long as the discrimination is not intrinsic to the laws.

Consider now, albeit fleetingly, the moral as distinguished from the constitutional bearing of discrimination. Suppose guilty defendants are justly executed, but only if poor, or black and not otherwise. This unequal justice would be morally offensive for what may be called tautological reasons:[10] if any punishment for a given crime is just, then a greater or lesser punishment is not. Only one punishment can be just for all persons equally guilty of the same crime.[11] Therefore, different punishments for equally guilty persons or group members are unjust: some offenders are punished more than they deserve, or others less.

Still, equality and justice are not the same. "Equal justice" is not a redundant phrase. Rather, we strive for two distinct ideals, justice and equality. Neither can replace the other. We want to have justice and, having it, we want to extend it equally to all. We would not want equal injustice. Yet, sometimes, we must choose between equal injustice and unequal justice. What should we prefer? Unequal justice is justice still, even if only for some, whereas equal injustice is injustice for all. If not every equally guilty person is punished equally, we have unequal justice. It seems preferable to equal injustice—having no guilty person punished as deserved.[12] Since it is never possible to punish equally all equally guilty murderers, we should punish, as they deserve, as many of those we apprehend and convict as possible. Thus, even if the death penalty were inherently discriminatory—which is not the case—but deserved by those who receive it, it would be morally just to impose it on them. If, as I contend, capital punishment is just and not inherently discriminatory, it remains desirable to eliminate inequality in distribution, to apply the penalty to all who deserve it, sparing no racial or economic class. But if a guilty person or group escaped the penalty through our porous system, wherein is this an argument for sparing others?

If one does not believe capital punishment can be just, discrimination becomes a subordinate argument, since one would object to capital punishment even if it were distributed equally to all the guilty. If one does believe that capital punishment for murderers is deserved, discrimination against guilty black murderers and in favor of equally guilty white murderers is wrong, not because blacks receive the deserved punishment, but because whites escape it.

Consider a less emotionally charged analogy. Suppose traffic police ticketed all drivers who violated the rules, except drivers of luxury cars. Should we abolish tickets? Should we decide that the ticketed drivers of nonluxury cars were unjustly punished and ought not to pay their fines? Would they become innocent of the violation they are guilty of because others have not been ticketed? Surely the drivers of luxury cars should not be exempted. But the fact that they were is no reason to exempt drivers of nonluxury cars as well. Laws could never be applied if the escape of one person, or group, were accepted as ground for not punishing another. To do justice is primarily to punish as deserved, and only secondarily to punish equally.

Guilt is personal. No one becomes less guilty or less deserving of punishment because another was punished leniently or not at all. That justice does not catch up with all guilty persons understandably is resented by those caught. But it does not affect their guilt. If some, or all, white and rich murderers escape the death penalty, how does that reduce the guilt of black or poor murderers, or make them less deserving of punishment, or deserving of a lesser punishment?

Some lawyers have insisted that the death penalty is distributed among those guilty of murder as though by a lottery and that the worst may escape it.[13] They exaggerate, but suppose one grants the point. How do those among the guilty selected for execution by lottery become less deserving of punishment because others escaped it? What is wrong is that these others escaped, not that those among the guilty who were selected by the lottery did not.

Those among the guilty actually punished by a criminal justice system unavoidably are selected by chance, not because we want to so select them, but because the outcome of our efforts largely depends on chance. No murderer is punished unless he is unlucky enough both to be caught and to have convinced a court of his guilt. And courts consider evidence not truth. They find truth only when the evidence establishes it. Thus they may have reasonable doubts about the guilt of an actually guilty person. Although we may strive to make justice as equal as possible, unequal justice will remain our lot in this world. We should not give up justice, or the death penalty, because we cannot extend it as equally to all the guilty as we wish. If we were not to punish one offender because another got away because of caprice or discrimination, we would give up justice for the sake of equality. We would reverse the proper order of priorities.

Is the Death Penalty More Deterrent Than Other Punishments?

Whether or not the death penalty deters the crimes it punishes more than alternative penalties—in this case life imprisonment with or without parole—has been widely debated since Isaac Ehrlich broke the abolitionist ranks by finding that from 1933–65 "an additional execution per year . . . may have resulted on the average in seven or eight fewer murders."[14] Since his article appeared, a whole cottage industry devoted to refuting his findings has arisen.[15] Ehrlich, no slouch, has been refuting those who refuted him.[16] The result seems inconclusive.[17] Statistics have not proved conclusively that the death penalty does or does not deter murder more than other penalties.[18] Still, Ehrlich has the merit of being the first to use a sophisticated statistical analysis to tackle the problem, and of defending his analysis, although it showed deterrence. (Ehrlich started as an abolitionist.) His predecessors cannot be accused of mathematical sophistication. Yet the academic community uncritically accepted their abolitionist results. I myself have no contribution to make to the mathematical analyses of deterrent effects. Perhaps this is why I have come to believe that they may becloud the issue, leading us to rely on demonstrable deterrence as though decisive.

Most abolitionists believe that the death penalty does not deter more than other penalties. But most abolitionists would abolish it, even if it did.[19] I have discussed this matter with prominent abolitionists such as Charles Black, Henry Schwarzchild, Hugo Adam Bedau, Ramsey Clark, and many others. Each told me that, even if every execution were to deter a hundred murders, he would oppose it. I infer that, to these abolitionist leaders, the life of every murderer is more valuable than the lives of a hundred prospective victims, for these abolitionists would spare the murderer, even if doing so would cost a hundred future victims their lives.

Obviously, deterrence cannot be the decisive issue for these abolitionists. It is not necessarily for me either, since I would be for capital punishment on grounds of justice alone. On the other hand, I should favor the death penalty for murderers, if probably deterrent, or even just possibly deterrent. To me, the life of any innocent victim who might be spared has great value; the life of a convicted murderer does not. This is why I would not take the risk of sacrificing innocents by not executing murderers.

Even though statistical demonstrations are not conclusive, and perhaps cannot be, I believe that capital punishment is likely to deter more than anything else. They fear most death deliberately inflicted by law and scheduled by the courts. Whatever people fear most is likely to deter most. Hence, I believe that the threat of the death penalty may deter some murderers who otherwise might not have been deterred. And surely the death penalty is the only penalty that could deter prisoners already serving a life sentence and tempted to kill a guard, or offenders about to be arrested and facing a life sentence. Perhaps they will not be deterred. But they would certainly not be deterred by anything else. We owe all the protection we can give to law enforcers exposed to special risks.

Many murders are "crimes of passion" that, perhaps, cannot be deterred by any threat. Whether or not they can be would depend on the degree of passion; it is unlikely to be always so extreme as to make the person seized by it totally undeterrable. At any rate, offenders sentenced to death ordinarily are guilty of premediated murder, felony murder, or multiple murders. Some are rape murderers, or hit men, but, to my knowledge, no one convicted of a "crime of passion" is on death row. Whatever the motive, some prospective offenders are not deterrable at all, others are easily deterred, and most are in between. Even if only some murders were, or could be, deterred by capital punishment, it would be worthwhile. . . .

Almost all convicted murderers try to avoid the death penalty by appeals for commutation to life imprisonment. However, a minuscule proportion of convicted murderers prefer execution. It is sometimes argued that they murdered for the sake of being executed, of committing suicide via execution. More likely, they prefer execution to life imprisonment. Although shared by few, this preference is not irrational per se. It is also possible that these convicts accept the verdict of the court, and feel that they deserve the death penalty for the crimes they committed, although the modern mind finds it hard to imagine such feelings. But not all murderers are ACLU humanists. . . .

Is the Death Penalty Moral?

Miscarriages

Miscarriages of justice are rare, but do occur. Over a long enough time they lead to the execution of some innocents.[20] Does this make irrevocable punishments morally wrong? Hardly. Our government employs trucks. They run over innocent bystanders more frequently than courts sentence innocents to death. We do not give up trucks because the benefits they produce outweigh the harm, including the death of innocents. Many human activities, even quite trivial ones, forseeably cause wrongful deaths. Courts may cause fewer wrongful deaths than golf. Whether one sees the benefit of doing justice by imposing capital punishment as moral, or as material, or both, it outweighs the loss of innocent lives through miscarriages, which are as unintended as traffic accidents.

Vengeance

Some abolitionists feel that the motive for the death penalty is an un-Christian and unacceptable desire for vengeance. But though vengeance be the motive, it is not the purpose of the death penalty. Doing justice and deterring crime are the purposes, whatever the motive. Purpose (let alone effect) and motive are not the same.

The Lord is often quoted as saying "Vengeance is mine." He did not condemn vengeance. He merely reserved it to Himself—and to the government. For, in the same epistle He is also quoted as saying that the ruler is "the minister of God, a revenger, to execute wrath upon him that doeth evil." The religious notion of hell indicates that the biblical God favored harsh and everlasting punishment for some. However, particularly in a secular society, we cannot wait for the day of judgment to see murderers consigned to hell. Our courts must "execute wrath upon him that doeth evil" here and now.

Charity and Justice

Today many religious leaders oppose capital punishment. This is surprising, because there is no biblical warrant for their opposition. The Roman Catholic Church and most Protestant denominations traditionally have supported capital punishment. Why have their moral views changed? When sharing secular power, the churches clearly distinguished between justice, including penalization as deserved, a function of the secular power, and charity, which, according to religious doctrine, we should feel for all those who suffer for whatever reasons. Currently, religious leaders seem to conflate justice and charity, to conclude that the death penalty and, perhaps, all punishment, is wrong because uncharitable. Churches no longer share secular power. Perhaps bystanders are more ready to replace justice with charity than are those responsible for governing.

Human Dignity

Let me return to the morality of execution. Many abolitionists believe that capital punishment is "degrading to human dignity" and inconsistent with the "sanctity of life." Justice Brennan, concurring in *Furnam,* stressed these phrases repeatedly. [21] He did not explain what he meant.

Why would execution degrade human dignity more than life imprisonment? One may prefer the latter; but it seems at least as degrading as execution. Philosophers, such as Immanuel Kant and G. F. W. Hegel, thought capital punishment indispensable to redeem, or restore, the human dignity of the executed. Perhaps they were wrong. But they argued their case, whereas no one has explained why capital punishment degrades. Apparently those who argue that it does degrade dignity simply define the death penalty as degrading. If so, degradation (or dehumanization) merely is a disguised synonym for their disapproval. Assertion, reassertion, or definition, do not constitute evidence or argument, nor do they otherwise justify, or even explain, disapproval of capital punishment.

Writers, such as Albert Camus, have suggested that murderers have a miserable time waiting for execution and anticipating it.[22] I do not doubt that. But punishments are not meant to be pleasant. Other people suffer greatly waiting for the end, in hospitals, under circumstances that, I am afraid, are at least as degrading to their dignity as execution. These sufferers have not deserved their suffering by committing crimes, whereas murderers have. Yet, murderers suffer less on death row, unless their consciences bother them.

Lex Talionis

Some writers insist that the suffering the death penalty imposes on murderers exceeds the suffering of their victims. This is hard to determine, but probably true in some cases and not in other cases. However, the comparison is irrelevant. Murderers are punished, as are all offenders, not just for the suffering they caused their victims, but for the harm they do to society by making life insecure, by threatening everyone, and by requiring protective measures. Punishment, ultimately, is a vindication of the moral and legal order of society and not limited by the *Lex Talionis*, meant to limit private retaliation for harms originally regarded as private.

Sanctity of Life

We are enjoined by the Declaration of Independence to secure life. How can this best be achieved? The Constitution authorizes us to secure innocent life by taking the life of murderers, so that any one who deliberately wants to take an innocent life will know that he risks forfeiting his own. The framers did not think that taking the life of a murderer is inconsistent with the "sanctity of life" which Justice Brennan champions. He has not indicated why they were wrong.[23]

Legalized Murder?

Ever since Cesare Bonesana, Marchese di Beccaria, wrote *Dei Delitti e Delle Pene*, abolitionists have contended that executing murderers legitimizes murder by doing to the murderer what he did to his victim. Indeed, capital punishment retributes, or pays back the offender. Occasionally we do punish offenders by doing to them what they did to their victims. We may lock away a kidnapper who wrongfully locked away his victim, and we may kill the murderer who wrongfully killed his victim. To lawfully do to the offender what he unlawfully did to his victim in no way legitimizes his crime. It legitimizes (some) killing, and not murder. An act does not become a crime because of its physical character, which, indeed, it may share with the legal punishment, but because of its social, or, better, antisocial, character—because it is an unlawful act.

Severity

Is the death penalty too severe? It stands in a class by itself. But so does murder. Execution is irreparable. So is murder. In contrast, all other crimes and punishments are, at least partly or potentially, reparable. The death penalty thus is congruous with the moral and material gravity of the crime it punishes.[24]

Still, is it repulsive? Torture, however well deserved, now is repulsive to us. But torture is an artifact. Death is not, since nature has placed us all under sentence of death. Capital punishment, in John Stuart Mills' phrase, only "hastens death"—which is what the murderer did to his victim. I find nothing repulsive in hastening the murderer's death, provided it be done in a nontorturous manner. Had he wished to be secure in his life, he could have avoided murder.

To believe that capital punishment is too severe for any act, one must believe that there can be no act horrible enough to deserve death.[25] I find this belief difficult to understand. I should readily impose the death penalty on a Hitler or a Stalin, or on anyone who does what they did, albeit on a smaller scale.

Conclusion

The death penalty has become a major issue in public debate. This is somewhat puzzling, because quantitatively it is insignificant. Still, capital punishment has separated the voters as a whole from a small, but influential, abolitionist elite. There are, I believe, two reasons that explain the prominence of the issue.

First, I think, there is a genuine ethical issue. Some philosophers believe that the right to life is equally imprescriptible for all, that the murderer has as much right to live as his victim. Others do not push egalitarianism that far. They believe that there is a vital difference, that one's right to live is lost when one intentionally takes an innocent life, that everyone has just the right to one life, his own. If he unlawfully takes that of another he, *eo ipso*, loses his own right to life.

Second, and perhaps as important, the death penalty has symbolic significance. Those who favor it believe that the major remedy for crime is punishment. Those who do not, in the main, believe that the remedy is anything but punishment. They look at the causes of crime and conflate them with compulsions, or with excuses, and refuse to blame. The majority of the people are less sophisticated, but perhaps they have better judgment. They believe that everyone who can understand the nature and effects of his acts is responsible for them, and should be blamed and punished, if he could know that what he did was wrong. Human beings are human because they can be held responsible, as animals cannot be. In that Kantian sense the death penalty is a symbolic affirmation of the humanity of both victim and murderer.

Notes

1. 356 U.S. 99 (1958).

2. The courts have sometimes confirmed the obsolescence of non-repealed laws or punishments. But here they are asked to invent it.

3. In Coker v. Georgia, 433 U.S. 584, 592 (1977), the Court concluded that the eighth amendment prohibits punishments that are "'excessive' in relation to the crime committed." I am not sure about this disproportion. However, threatening execution would tempt rapists to murder their victims who, after all, are potential witnesses. By murdering their victims, rapists would increase their chances of escaping execution without adding to their risk. Therefore, I agree with the court's conclusion, though not with its argument.

4. C. Black, Capital Punishment: The Inevitability of Caprice and Mistake (2d ed. 1981).

5. Most discrimination occurred in rape cases and was eliminated when the death penalty for rape was declared unconstitutional.

6. For a survey of the statistical literature, see, e.g., Bowers, *The Pervasiveness of Arbitrariness and Discrimination under Post-Furman Capital Statutes,* 74 J. Crim. L. & Criminology 1067 (1983). His article is part of a "Symposium on Current Death Penalty Issues" compiled by death penalty opponents.

7. Those who demonstrated the pattern seem to have been under the impression that they had shown discrimination against black murderers. They were wrong. However, the discrimination against black victims is invidious and should be corrected.

8. The capriciousness argument is undermined when capriciousness is conceded to be unavoidable. But even when capriciousness is thought reducible, one wonders whether releasing or retrying one guilty defendant, because another equally guilty defendant was not punished as much, would help reduce capriciousness. It does not seem a logical remedy.

9. Furman v. Georgia, 408 U.S. 238, 256 (1971) (Douglas, J., concurring).

10. I shall not consider here the actual psychological motives that power our unending thirst for equality.

11. If courts impose different punishments on different persons, we may not be able to establish in all cases whether the punishment is just, or (it amounts to the same) whether the different persons were equally guilty of the same crime, or whether their crimes were identical in all relevant respects. Thus, we may not be able to tell which of two unequal punishments is just. Both may be, or neither may be. Inequality may not entail more injustice than equality, and equality would entail justice only if we were sure that the punishment meted out was the just punishment.

12. Similarly, it is better that only some innocents suffer undeserved punishment than that all suffer it equally.

13. It would be desirable that all of the worst murderers be sentenced to death. However, since murderers are tried in different courts, this is unlikely. Further, sometimes the testimony of one murderer is needed to convict another, and cannot be obtained except by leniency. Morally, and legally it is enough that those sentenced to death deserve the penalty for their crimes, even if others, who may deserve it as much, or more, were not sentenced to death.

14. Ehrlich, *The Deterrent Effect of Capital Punishment: A Question of Life or Death,* 65 Am. Econ. Rev. 397, 414 (1975).

15. *See, e.g.,* Baldus & Cole, *A Comparison of the Work of Thorsten Sellin and Isaac Ehrlich on the Deterrent Effect of Capital Punishment,* 85 YALE L.J. 170 (1975); Bowers & Pierce, *Deterrence or Brutalization: What is the Effect of Executions?,* 26 CRIME & DELINQ. 453 (1980); Bowers & Pierce, *The Illusion of Deterrence in Isaac Ehrlich's Research on Capital Punishment,* 85 YALE L.J. 187 (1975).

16. Ehrlich, *Fear of Deterrence,* 6 J. LEGAL STUD. 293 (1977); Ehrlich & Gibbons, *On the Measurement of the Deterrent Effect of Capital Punishment and the Theory of Deterrence,* 6 J. LEGAL STUD. 35 (1977).

17. At present there is no agreement even on whether the short run effects of executions delay or accelerate homicides. *See* Phillips, *The Deterrent Effect of Capital Punishment: New Evidence on an Old Controversy,* 86, AM. J. SOC. 139 (1980).

18. As stated in Gregg v. Georgia, 428 U.S. 153, 185 (1976), "Although some of the studies suggest that the death penalty may not function as a significantly greater deterrent than lesser penalties, there is no convincing empirical evidence either supporting or refuting this view."

19. Jeffrey Reiman is an honorable exception. *See* Reiman, *Justice, Civilization, and the Death Penalty: Answering van den Haag,* 14 PHIL. & PUB. AFF. 115 (1985).

20. Life imprisonment avoids the problem of executing innocent persons to some extent. It can be revoked. But the convict also may die in prison before his innocence is discovered.

21. "[T]he Cruel and Unusual Punishments Clause prohibits the infliction of uncivilized and inhuman punishments. The State, even as it punishes, must treat its members with respect for their intrinsic worth as human beings." Furman v. Georgia, 408 U.S. 238, 270 (1972) (Brennan, J., concurring). "When we consider why [certain punishments] have been condemned, . . . we realize that the pain involved is not the only reason. The true significance of these punishments [that have been condemned] is that they treat members of the human race as nonhumans, as objects to be toyed with and discarded." *Id.* at 272–73.

> In determining whether a punishment comports with human dignity, we are aided also by a second principle inherent in the Clause— that the State must not arbitrarily inflict a severe punishment. This principle derives from the notion that the State does not respect human dignity when, without reason, it inflicts upon some people a severe punishment that it does not inflict upon others.

Id. at 274. "Death is truly an awesome punishment. The calculated killing of a human being by the State involves, by its very nature, a denial of the executed person's humanity." *Id.* at 290. "In comparison to all other punishments today, then, the deliberate extinguishment of human life by the State is uniquely degrading to human dignity." *Id.* at 291.

22. In *Reflections on the Guillotine,* Camus stated that "[t]he parcel [the condemned person] is no longer subject to the laws of chance that hang over the living creature but to mechanical laws that allow him to foresee accurately the day of his beheading. . . . The Greeks, after all, were more humane with their hemlock." A. CAMUS, RESISTANCE, REBELLION AND DEATH 175, 202 (1960).

23. "Sanctity of life" may mean that we should not take, and should punish taking innocent life: "*homo homini res sacra.*" In the past this meant that we should take the life of a murderer to secure innocent life, and stress its sacredness. Justice Brennan seems to mean that the life of the murderer should be sacred too—but no argument is given for this premise.

24. Capital punishment is not inconsistent with Weems v. United States, 217 U.S. 349 (1910), which merely held that punishment cannot be excessive, that is, out of proportion to the gravity of the crime. Indeed, if life imprisonment suffices for anything else, it cannot be appropriate for murder.

25. The notion of deserving is strictly moral, depending exclusively on our sense of justice, unlike the notion of deterrence, which depends on the expected factual consequences of punishment. Whilst deterrence alone would justify most of the punishments we should impose, it may not suffice to justify all those punishments that our sense of justice demands. Wherefore criminal justice must rest on desert as well as deterrence, to be seen as morally justified.

Mark Costanzo

 **NO**

Is Killing Murderers Morally Justified?

With every cell in my being, and with every fibre of my memory, I oppose the death penalty in all forms.

—Elie Wiesel

I do not know whether capital punishment should or should not be abolished: for neither the natural light, nor Scripture, nor ecclesiastical authority seems to tell me.

—C. S. Lewis

When faced with compelling evidence that the death penalty is costly, arbitrary, discriminatory, prone to error, and without deterrent value, retentionists often retreat into the murky waters of moral philosophy. They argue that capital punishment is not only morally legitimate, but also morally necessary. Although we can decide questions of fact—questions about cost, deterrence, fairness, and public opinion—by analyzing the relevant data, the question of whether the death penalty is ethically justified cannot be answered by any amount of data. It is a matter of faith and argument. And that is precisely why many supporters of the death penalty would prefer to debate philosophy instead of effectiveness. If we are morally compelled to kill those who kill, further discussion of troublesome facts is irrelevant and unnecessary. Questions about how the death penalty is administered, about the cost or the consequences of the penalty may be interesting, but they do not have the power to refute a moral imperative.

The philosophical arguments surrounding punishment are based on religious authority, moral philosophy [and] criminal responsibility. . . .

The Bible Tells Me So

In their final appeals to jurors, prosecutors in capital murder trials are fond of quoting Scripture to lend authority to their arguments. And there are many verses to choose from. In particular, the Old Testament seems to suggest killing as a response to a variety of crimes. The most popular quotation is from

From Mark Costanzo, *Just Revenge: Costs and Consequences of the Death Penalty* (St. Martin's Press, 1997). Copyright © 1997 by Mark Costanzo. Reprinted by permission of St. Martin's Press, LLC.

Deuteronomy (19:21): "Life for life, eye for eye, tooth for tooth, hand for hand, foot for foot." Moreover, the Old Testament recommends death for an assortment of crimes, including murder, contempt for parental authority, defiling sacred places or objects, kidnapping for ransom, sorcery, bestiality, worshiping false gods, profaning the Sabbath, adultery, incest, homosexuality, blasphemy, bearing false witness in court, harlotry, negligence that results in a death, and false prophesy.[1]

Yet, despite the apparent biblical endorsement of executions, there is much even in the Old Testament to suggest that killing may not be the appropriate penalty for murder. God did not kill Cain for the murder of Abel, and several cities of refuge were established so that wrongdoers could escape vengeance at the hands of the victims' families. The idea that "vengeance belongs to the Lord" and that we should "love our neighbor as ourselves" are major themes of the Old Testament. Even the often misinterpreted "eye for an eye" passage was meant to *restrain* rather than to *require* vengeance. Religious scholars point out that, taken in context, the passage does not tell us that we must exact proportional revenge, but that we may not take from others more than has been taken from us, that we must resist the urge to retaliate with ever greater violence.[2] *Lex talionis,* the doctrine of legal retaliation, represented an advance, a movement away from unrestrained retaliation.

Though the Old Testament authorizes executions in principle, in practice "there were such extensive procedural requirements for the imposition of the death penalty that, by design, it was nearly impossible to secure a death verdict."[3] Mosaic law and, later, the Rabbinic tradition established a nearly unreachable standard of proof. In the Talmudic courts (called Sanhedrins) two witnesses judged to be competent had to testify that they saw the accused commit the crime after being forewarned that the act was illegal and punishable by death. Confessions were inadmissible. So was testimony against the defendant by family members of the victim or persons with a preexisting grievance against the defendant. If any aspect of the evidence or testimony was found to be unreliable, the defendant could not be killed. Such restrictions served to make capital punishment extremely rare under Talmudic law.[4]

For Christians, the Old Testament must be interpreted in light of the New Testament, which goes much farther in repudiating revenge: "You have heard that it was said, 'An eye for an eye and a tooth for a tooth.' But I say to you, do not resist one who is evil. But if any one strikes you on the right cheek, turn to him the other also" (Matthew 5:38–41). The New Testament emphasizes love, compassion, mercy, charity, forgiveness. And, if we are to follow the example of Christ, forgiveness and compassion are especially important when dealing with criminals and outcasts. When Christ was confronted with a woman convicted of adultery (a capital crime at the time), the crowd who had assembled to stone her asked, "Teacher, this woman hath been taken in adultery, in the very act. Now the law of Moses commanded us to stone such: What then sayest thou of her?" In response, Jesus "lifted up himself and said unto them, 'He that is without sin among you, let him cast the first stone' (John 8:3–11). The same message can be found in Luke: "Judge not and you will not be judged; condemn not, and you will not be condemned; forgive, and you will be forgiven" (6:37).

The entire life and teachings of Jesus argue against killing as a form of punishment. Though not a theologian, Charles Dickens made the point well:

> Though every other man who wields a pen should turn himself into a commentator on the scriptures—not all their united efforts could persuade me that executions are a Christian law. . . . If any text appeared to justify the claim, I would reject that limited appeal, and rest upon the character of the Redeemer and the great scheme of His religion.[5]

Although the Bible can be read to support the death penalty, this support is subject to severe restrictions. Specifically, guilt must be certain and execution must be necessary to serve the interests of justice (e.g., to protect others or to instill respect for moral authority).[6] Indeed, no less an authority than Pope John Paul II has observed that the necessary requirements for the death penalty are seldom, if ever, met. In "Evangelium Vitae" (The Gospel of Life) the pope argues that "as explicitly formulated, the precept 'You shall not kill' is strongly negative: it indicates the extreme limit which can never be exceeded."[7] John Paul II goes on to note that punishment

> ought not go to the extreme of executing the offender except in cases of absolute necessity: in other words, when it would not be possible otherwise to defend society. Today, however, as a result of steady improvements in the organization of the penal system, such cases are very rare, if not practically nonexistent. . . . If bloodless means are sufficient to defend human lives against an aggressor and to protect public order and the safety of persons, public authority must limit itself to such means.[8]

The pope is not a lone voice among religious leaders. Religious organizations are nearly unanimous in their condemnation of capital punishment. More than forty such organizations (including American Baptists, Catholics, Episcopalians, Jews, Lutherans, Mennonites, Methodists, Presbyterians, Quakers, and Unitarians) have issued statements calling for the abolition of capital punishment.

Moral Philosophy and the Functions of Punishment

When measured against the usual standards for evaluating punishment, the death penalty doesn't make much sense. Obviously, killing a prisoner eliminates the possiblity of rehabilitation; a corpse cannot go on to lead a more virtuous life. The goal of incapacitation is not advanced: the condemned man is already safely behind prison walls, unable to commit further crimes in free society. The supposed deterrent effect is illusory: . . . executions appear actually to increase the level of violence in society. And since incapacitation and protection of society are just as effectively—and more cheaply—achieved through life imprisonment, killing the prisoner is simply unnecessary.

Moreover, how does the notion of killing murderers square with the cherished principle of "the sanctity of human life"? This idea is central to the world's great religions as well as the ancient Greek, Egyptian, Persian, and Babylonian moral philosophers. If life is sacred, it means that every person has the right to live simply by virtue of the fact that he or she is a living, breathing human being. This right is unearned and inalienable, in part because we are created "in the image of God." This basic principle certainly implies that the death penalty is morally wrong. However, three centuries ago, John Locke offered a classic defense of the death penalty on moral grounds. He argued that although the right to life is inherent and absolute, it is possible to "forfeit" one's right to life by committing a crime that "deserves death." His arguments have provided ammunition for supporters of capital punishment ever since. Locke also argued for severe punishment on the grounds of deterrence. He believed that we should punish "to the degree and with as much severity, as will suffice to make it an ill bargain to the offender, give him cause to repent, and terrify others from doing the like."[9]

Another influential moral argument is usually traced to Immanuel Kant. He believed that murderers must be killed based on the principle of "equal" or "just" retribution:

> What kind and what degree of punishment does public legal justice adopt as its principle and standard? None other than the principle of equality . . . any undeserved evil that you inflict on someone else among the people is one that you do to yourself. . . . Only the law of retribution can determine exactly the kind and degree of punishment.[10]

This idea has an elegant and appealing simplicity. It is an elaboration of the idea of *lex talionis* and is similar to the argument that murderers must be "paid back" in kind for their crimes. The principle of equality introduced by Kant seems to provide a standard that is independent of religious or political authority. And whereas Locke linked his notion of retribution to deterrence, Kant apparently felt that such practical considerations were not important enough to discuss.

Another argument offered in defense of the idea that justice requires the killing of murderers might be called the "moral solidarity" argument. If societies are held together, in part, by a shared consensus of what constitutes immoral behavior, then those who violate the moral order must be punished to restore moral balance in society. Further, for murderers, any punishment less than death is too weak to convey the strong sense of outrage and condemnation felt by the community. Only by killing the murderer can we repair the moral integrity of the larger community. In his book *For Capital Punishment*, Walter Berns puts it like this:

> [The death penalty] serves to remind us of the majesty of the moral order that is embodied in our law and of the terrible consequences of its breach. . . . The criminal law must be made awful, by which I mean awe-inspiring, or commanding "profound respect or reverential fear." It must remind us of the moral order by which alone we can live as human beings.[11]

These arguments raise several questions. If by killing, murderers forfeit their right to live, does that mean that we are, in turn, *obliged* to kill them? Or will other forms of severe punishment suffice? If someone *deserves* to die, does it mean that we have the right to kill him? Should we try to induce in prisoners the equivalent amount of suffering they induced in their victims? Do executions really strengthen the moral solidarity of the community, or do they demean and corrupt the collective morality? Should executions be bloody, excruciating, and public to fully inspire awe and "reverential fear"? Is it necessary to kill in order to show that killing is wrong? And given the varied backgrounds and capacities of defendants, the diverse types of murder, and the limits of human understanding, is it even possible to decide fairly which murderers deserve to die?

The simplest counterargument is that, if killing is morally wrong, it is wrong for both the individual and the state. To be sure, there are circumstances where killing may be necessary, for example, when a police officer shoots a robber who is about to kill a clerk, when a soldier kills an enemy soldier during a time of war, when a woman shoots a violently abusive husband who is coming toward her brandishing a knife. These situations involve imminent danger, split-second decisions, and self-defense or defense of innocent others. Unlike police officers, who occasionally kill to protect their own lives or the lives of innocent people, the executioner performs an unnecessary killing, a killing that has nothing to do with self-defense, imminent danger, or the protection of society. The murderer has already been captured and waits in a prison cell safely isolated from the community.

The law of equal retribution proposed by Kant and others cannot be a literal prescription for how to punish violent criminals. We would find it morally repugnant to torture torturers, rape rapists, or terrorize terrorists. We do not try to kill murderers using the same method they used to kill their victims. Instead, we imprison them. Our efforts to mitigate punishments arise out of the recognition that we must not sink to the level of the criminal; raping a rapist would debase us, weaken our moral solidarity, and undermine the moral authority of the state. We cannot simply respond to cruelty with our own acts of cruelty. Acts of brutality committed by the state in the name of justice never ennoble us. There must be severe punishment for horrible crimes, but that does not oblige us to kill those who have killed.

⚬⟨☉⟩⚬

Try as we might, we can never sever the ties between moral concerns and practical realities. *Morality can only be assessed in practice.* Even if we accept the morality of the death penalty in the abstract, we must always look at how it is administered in the real world. Is the death penalty still moral if innocent people are sometimes convicted or executed? Is it still moral if the race of the murderer or the victim play a substantial role in determining which defendants will be sentenced to die? Is it still moral if the ultimate penalty squanders money that could be more productively spent on preventing crime? Is it still moral if executions provoke, rather than deter, violent criminals? These questions must be answered before any final judgment can be made about the morality of the death penalty. Moral theory must give way to moral practice, and abstract benefits must be balanced against tangible costs. Defenders of capital punishment must defend this punishment *as it exists* in the real world.

Moral Responsibility and Free Will

. . . Imagine that you are a juror in a capital case. You have already decided that the defendant is guilty, and now you must decide whether he should be killed or sent to prison for the rest of his life. To decide whether to show mercy, you must make a full and fair assessment of the multitude of factors that led to the murder. To make this assessment, it is first necessary to have the defendant's important life events and experiences laid out before you: his upbringing, family environment, education, formative experiences, the things that shaped his character and behavior. You would also need to know something of his innate, inherited talents, abilities, and predilections. You would also need to have some understanding of how he responded to the events in his life, the impact of his experiences. Of course, it is impossible to know all of this. It is difficult enough to understand the behavior of people we have known for years. Even if we could manage to shut off our feelings of rage and revulsion, it would still be exceedingly difficult to find and consider enough information to allow us to fathom the reasons for a brutal murder. And, as a practical matter, no defendant or public defender can afford to present all the necessary information, and no set of jury instructions can adequately guide jurors in making this morally profound decision. Few defense attorneys even attempt to present sufficient information to make such an assessment.

Despite scientific advances in behavioral genetics and psychology, we are still a very long way from completely mapping out the motives, intentions, habits, interpretations, and situational pressures that propel a particular act of violence. The process is still mysterious. Perhaps if we had complete information and a year or two to sift through the information, we could arrive at a definitive answer to the question, Why did this person commit this terrible crime? But a thorough evaluation of moral culpability is clearly impossible within the constraints of the American courtroom. Some defenders present little information to help the jurors, and even the most careful defenders and prosecutors cannot uncover and present all of the reasons for the violent act. It is simply beyond human understanding. To believe that we can make such judgments is misguided hubris.

At the heart of the matter is an ancient and unresolvable philosophical debate: Free will versus determinism. Without at least an assumption of free will there can be no discussion of ethical behavior or criminal responsibility. Nearly all of us believe in some measure of free will, but we are all partly determinists too. Do you or do you not believe that you are a product of your genetic endowment and your life experiences? If you believe that your behavior is a function of inheritance and experience, you are, at least, a limited determinist, what William James, the great philosopher and psychologist, might have called a "soft determinist." Whereas the "hard determinist" insists that our actions are entirely determined, that no one is free to act differently from the way he or she does act, the soft determinist believes that we possess free will within the constraints imposed by heredity and environment. That, although our actions are not fully determined, our actions are strongly influenced by our conditioning, our values and habits, and the situations we find ourselves in.

In discussing the reasons behind criminal behavior, Stephen Nathanson argues that we must take into account the effort required by a criminal to resist criminal actions and the obstacles to moral behavior encountered by the criminal:

> A person's degree of moral desert is determined by considerations of what could reasonably be expected of him. If a person faces such powerful obstacles to moral behavior that it would require extraordinary amounts of effort to act well, then, though he acts badly, he is not morally to blame . . . different behavior could not reasonably be expected. The causes of difficulty need not be environmental. They could be physical, psychological, or of any sort, but if they make alternative actions extremely difficult or impossible, a person is not fully blameworthy for his deeds, even if they were wrong acts triggered by bad motives.[12]

The philosopher Jeffrey Reiman takes an even broader view suggesting that the larger society must bear some responsibility for the actions of murderers.[13] America spawns more vicious murderers than any other "civilized" country on earth. The social conditions that predictably produce violent offenders (e.g., poverty, routine exposure to violence as a child, access to lethal weapons) are at least partly to blame. It has been said that each nation gets the criminals it deserves. Put differently, a society bears responsibility for violent criminals to the extent that it tolerates social conditions that predictably lead to violence. Until these conditions are remediated, some of the blame rests with the larger community.

Let me be clear: The argument is not that murderers should be excused for their crimes. They must be held accountable and punished severely. The argument is that we cannot possibly fathom the multiple and subtle influences that cause a particular behavior. Instead of pretending omniscience, we should be more humble about our capacity to understand fully why someone commits a horrible crime. We can and should send a dangerous criminal to prison for the rest of his or her life, but we should not presume to judge which people deserve to live and which deserve to die. Our judgments are bound to be faulty.

Just Revenge

Beneath the usual justifications for punishing criminals lurks a more visceral and potent motive for the death penalty: revenge. The desire to lash back at those who have harmed us has deep roots in our evolutionary past. It is a powerful human motive that must be taken seriously, but it is not a sufficient justification for killing. Although individually we all feel the primitive urge to exact revenge against those who harm us, collectively we must strive to be more rational, fair, moral, and humane than the criminals who commit the acts of violence or cruelty that we condemn. We all sympathize with a bereaved father who attempts to kill the man who murdered his child. But a group's craving for revenge is far less innocent and immediate, and far less justifiable. A victim's relative who attempts to kill a murderer commits a crime of passion motivated by rage and grief. In contrast, the process leading up to a state-sponsored killing is slow, deliberate, methodical, and largely stripped of human emotion. The anger of families of victims is understandable, but anger should not be the basis of social policy. A community's angry cry for killing a murderer is far uglier than the anger felt by an individual who has been wronged by another.

We have all felt wronged and we have all experienced the powerful emotions that drive the hunger for revenge. The urge to see a murderer killed is rooted in the rage and revulsion that most Americans feel when they hear about a horrible, inexplicable murder. We empathize with the victim and the family of the victim, and we want to see the murderer pay dearly for his or her crime. In movies, operas, plays, and novels, exacting revenge on those who offend us is often portrayed as emotionally satisfying. But just because the appetite for revenge is real and powerful, that does not mean we should indulge our appetite or build it into our legal system. Justice must take precedence over revenge. Arthur Koestler made this point vividly: "Deep inside every civilized being there lurks a tiny Stone Age man, dangling a club to rob and rape, and screaming 'an eye for an eye.' But we would rather not have that little fur-clad figure dictate the law of the land."[14] Feelings of anger and revulsion at a horrible crime are understandably human and maybe even a healthy indication of concern for the welfare of others. However, even if we accept the legitimacy of anger, anger does not outweigh all other considerations. Feelings of outrage and the quest for revenge do not guarantee that punishments will be fairly or rationally imposed. Anger does not ensure justice; it is an obstacle to justice.

It would be immoral to execute everyone who kills another human being. Every legal system on earth recognizes this. Consequently, every nation with capital punishment must create some method of selecting out those killers who truly "deserve" to die. Because no selection process is perfect, bias, prejudice, and error creep into every system of capital punishment. If the morality of revenge and the morality of the death penalty are to be defended, the defense must be of the death penalty as it is administered in the real world. Too often, defenders of the death penalty argue for its morality in a theoretical, idealized world. The claim that killing is morally justified must be reconciled with disquieting facts: the inevitability of wrongful convictions, the reality of discrimination on the basis of wealth and race, the likelihood that executions increase the murder rate, the reality that millions of dollars must be squandered to bring about a single execution.

Killing is a morally acceptable penalty only if it is essential, and only if it provides substantial benefits that cannot be gained by any other means. Capital punishment is not just a moral abstraction. It is a reality that must be evaluated on the basis of benefits and costs.

References

1 Bailey, L. R. (1987). *Capital Punishment: What the Bible Says*. Nashville: Abingdon Press, pp. 19–22; Melton, G. (1989). *Capital Punishment: Official Statements from Religious Bodies and Ecumenical Organizations*. Detroit: Gale Research, Inc.

2. Cohn, H. (1970). "The Penology of the Talmud." *Israel Law Review,* vol. 5, pp. 451–463.

3. Tabak, R. J., and Lane, M. (1989). "The Execution of Justice: A Cost and Lack-of-Benefit Analysis of the Death Penalty." *Loyola of Los Angeles Law Review,* vol. 23 (2), p. 142.

4. Erez, M. (1981). "Thou Shalt Not Execute: Hebrew Law Perspective on Capital Punishment." *Criminology,* vol. 19.

5. Quoted in Koestler, A. (1957). *Reflections on Hanging.* New York: Macmillan. p. 99.

6. Bailey, L. R. (1987). *Capital Punishment: What the Bible Says.* Nashville: Abingdon Press.

7. Pope John Paul II (1995). *The Gospel of Life: On the Value and Inviolability of Human Life.* Washington, D.C.: United States Catholic Conference, p. 96.

8. Ibid, p. 100.

9. Locke, J. (1690). *Two Treatises of Government.* Cambridge University Press (1963).

10. Kant, I. (1797). *The Metaphysical Elements of Justice.* Indianapolis: Bobbs-Merrill (1965), p. 101.

11. Berns, W. (1979). *For Capital Punishment.* New York: Basic Books, p. 194.

12. Nathanson, S. (1987). *An Eye for an Eye?* Totowa, New Jersey: Roman and Littlefield, p. 89.

13. Reiman, J. (1988). "The Justice of the Death Penalty in an Unjust World." In K. C. Haas and J. A. Inciardi (eds.), *Challenging Capital Punishment* (pp. 29–48). Newbury Park, Cal.: Sage.

14. Koestler, A. (1957). *Reflections on Hanging.* New York: Macmillan, p. 101.

POSTSCRIPT

Should the Death Penalty Be Retained?

The argument is sometimes made that even if capital punishment is not a deterrent (or, more radically, even if capital punishment actually encourages crime), justice demands that certain criminals be executed. For example, former Nazis who killed many innocent people are today tracked down and brought to trial. Usually, these are elderly men who have lived many years without killing anyone. If the death penalty is demanded for these people, would this demand receive support from the deterrence line of reasoning? Probably not. First, these people have already stopped killing and so do not need to be deterred. Second, should we suppose that executing them will deter potential future Nazis, Aryan supremacists, and other racists from murder? More likely, in these cases, the argument is that these former Nazis should die for what they have done as a matter of justice.

A special issue for Americans is whether or not the death penalty is constitutional—in particular, whether or not it is cruel and unusual punishment. In a series of important legal cases (including *Furman v. Georgia,* 1972, and *Gregg v. Georgia,* 1976), the U.S. Supreme Court found that capital punishment *as then applied* was indeed unconstitutional. The main problem was that a lack of explicit standards in applying the death penalty gave much room for discretion, which in turn allowed prejudice and racism to hide behind legality. But the Court allowed the development of procedures of administering capital punishment that did not violate the Constitution.

Relevant literature includes Hugo Adam Bedau, *The Death Penalty in America: Current Controversies* (Oxford University Press, 1997); Paul A. Winters, ed., *Death Penalty,* 3rd ed. (Greenhaven Press, 1997); *Capital Punishment in the United States* (Greenwood Press, 1997); James R. Acker, Robert M. Bohm, and Charles S. Lanier, eds., *America's Experiment With Capital Punishment: Reflections on the Past, Present, and Future of the Ultimate Penal Sanction* (Carolina Academic Press, 1998); Mark Grossman, *Encyclopedia of Capital Punishment* (ABC-CLIO, 1998); Austin Sarat, ed., *The Killing State: Capital Punishment in Law, Politics, and Culture* (Oxford University Press, 1998); Glen H. Stassen, ed., *Capital Punishment: A Reader* (Pilgrim Press, 1998); Stuart Banner, *The Death Penalty: An American History* (Harvard University Press, 2002); and Stephen P. Garvey, ed., *Beyond Repair? America's Death Penalty* (Duke University Press, 2003).

ISSUE 19

Should Physician-Assisted Suicide Be Legalized by the States?

YES: Faye Girsh, from "Should Physician-Assisted Suicide Be Legalized by the States? Yes," *Insight on the News* (March 8, 1999)

NO: Rita L. Marker, from "Should Physician-Assisted Suicide Be Legalized by the States? No," *Insight on the News* (March 8, 1999)

ISSUE SUMMARY

YES: Faye Girsh, executive director of the Hemlock Society, maintains that patients have a right to physician-assisted suicide, that physicians themselves should not be regarded as criminals since they are complying with their patients' wishes, and that a public policy of physician-assisted suicide will not have the dire consequences that some opponents anticipate.

NO: Attorney Rita L. Marker argues that a policy that would permit physician-assisted suicide is best examined in the real-world context in which it would be implemented. Here, there is cost-consciousness in medical care, which brings about strong constraints on the amount of time physicians can spend with patients and encourages physicians to seek lower-priced alternatives whenever possible. Therefore, the relatively lower monetary cost of physician-assisted suicide makes it a desirable alternative for the wrong reasons.

Suicide has generally been regarded in Western history as wrong and even evil. In fact, it has traditionally been regarded as a serious sin by the Roman Catholic Church and by most of the Protestant denominations that have arisen since the Reformation. Other cultures have not always branded it as evil, however. In Japan, for example, there is a long history of what is known as "honorable suicide." The view concerning honorable suicide is that in some cases it is more honorable to commit suicide than it would be to live on in shame. Even in Western culture, if we examine the beliefs of ancient Greece, we will encounter the Stoic school of philosophy that expounds the view that inner tranquility is the most important thing in life. Consequently, the Stoics taught that although a wise person will aim to maintain inner peace—even in the face of external adversity—the rational thing to do, in some severe cases, is to end one's life. The door, they believed, was always open.

We face a dilemma today that is related to the Stoics' ideas. On the one hand, physicians and medical personnel want to maintain a patient's health and inner tranquility. They want to relieve pain and suffering as much as possible. But with advances in medical knowledge and the ever-increasing use of technology, it is now possible to keep a patient alive for months and sometimes years in situations where, in the past, the patient would have died. In one sense, this is a great success story for medicine. But in another sense, one may wonder how much of a success it is. It is currently possible for patients to be kept alive on machines for longer than the time after which they would have naturally died. And during this additional time, the patient does not have a strong quality of life; on the contrary, the patient ends up deteriorating more and more, until finally medical science can do no more and the patient dies.

Many people are in denial about dying. Even physicians sometimes seem to be in denial. If a physician always counts the death of a patient as a "failure," there is denial. Physicians might feel that it is their job to "save life." But another way of looking at the situation is to say that it is the physician's job to help us into the world, through it, and out of it.

Patients themselves are wary of the treatments that they might receive at the end of life. There comes a point, some would say, when the imposition of medical technology—which is *supposed* to help promote "inner tranquility," is actually disruptive of inner tranquility. They might maintain—along with the Stoics—that at some point positively choosing death is the rational thing to do. And if that is indeed their choice, then they may well be in need of medical assistance in actually bringing it about.

In the following selections, Faye Girsh argues for the legal provision of physician-assisted suicide due to the contention that patients should have the right to choose this course of action. Rita L. Marker asserts that the combination of cost-consciousness (which is generally present in medical treatment situations) and physician-assisted suicide is extremely dangerous; it will *always* be cheaper to buy lethal pills than it will be to keep the patient in the hospital for one more day.

Faye Girsh

Don't Make Doctors Criminals for Helping People Escape Painful Terminal Illnesses

Many people agree that there are horrifying situations at the end of life which cry out for the help of a doctor to end the suffering by providing a peaceful, wished-for death. But, opponents argue, that does not mean that the practice should be legalized. They contend that these are the exceptional cases from which bad law would result.

I disagree. It is precisely these kinds of hard deaths that people fear and that happen to 7 to 10 percent of those who are dying that convince them to support the right to choose a hastened death with medical assistance. The reason that polls in this country—and in Canada, Australia, Great Britain and other parts of Europe—show 60 to 80 percent support for legalization of assisted suicide is that people want to know they will have a way out if their suffering becomes too great. They dread losing control not only of their bodies but of what will happen to them in the medical system. As a multiple-sclerosis patient wrote to the Hemlock Society: "I feel like I am just rotting away. . . . If there is something that gives life meaning and purpose it is this: a peaceful end to a good life before the last part of it becomes even more hellish."

Even with the best of hospice care people want to know that there can be some way to shorten a tortured dying process. A man whose wife was dying from cancer wrote, "For us, hospice care was our choice. We, however, still had 'our way,' also our choice, as 'our alternative.' We were prepared. And the 'choice' should be that of the patient and family."

It is not pain that causes people to ask for a hastened death but the indignities and suffering accompanying some terminal disorders such as cancer, stroke and AIDS. A survey in the Netherlands found that the primary reason to choose help in dying was to avoid "senseless suffering."

Hospice can make people more comfortable, can bring spiritual solace and can work with the family, but—as long as hospice is sworn neither to prolong nor hasten death—it will not be the whole answer for everyone. People should not have to make a choice between seeking hospice care and choosing to hasten the dying process. The best hospice care should be available to everyone, as should the option of a quick, gentle, certain death with loved ones around when the suffering has become unbearable. Both should be part of the continuum of care at the end of life.

We have the right to commit suicide and the right to refuse unwanted medical treatment, including food and water. But what we don't have—unless we live in Oregon—is the right to get help from a doctor to achieve a peaceful death. As the trial judge in the Florida case of *Kirscher vs McIver,* an AIDS patient who wanted his doctor's help in dying, said in his decision: "Physicians are permitted to assist their terminal patients by disconnecting life support or by prescribing medication to ease their starvation. Yet medications to produce a quick death, free of pain and protracted agony, are prohibited. This is a difference without distinction."

The Oregon example has shown us that, although a large number of people want to know the choice is there, only a small number will take advantage of it. During the first eight months of the Oregon "Death with Dignity" law, only 10 people took the opportunity to obtain the medications and eight used them to end their lives. In the Netherlands it consistently has been less than 5 percent of the total number of people who die every year who choose to get help in doing so from their doctor.

In Switzerland, where physician-assisted death also is legal, about 120 people die annually with the help of medical assistance. There is no deluge of people wanting to put themselves out of their misery nor of greedy doctors and hospitals encouraging that alternative. People want to live as long as possible. There are repeated testimonials to the fact that people can live longer and with less anguish once they know that help will be available if they want to end it. Even Jack Kevorkian, who says he helped 130 people die since 1990, has averaged only 14 deaths a year.

To the credit of the right-to-die movement, end-of-life care has improved because of the push for assisted dying. In Oregon, end-of-life care is the best in the country: Oregon is No. 1 in morphine use, twice as many people there use hospice as the national average and more people die at home than in the hospital. In Maine there will be an initiative on the ballot in 2000 to legalize physician aid in dying, and in Arizona a physician-assisted-dying bill has been introduced.* In both states the Robert Woods Johnson Foundation has awarded sizable grants to expand hospice care and to improve end-of-life care.

It is gratifying that the specter of assisted dying has spurred such concern for care at the end of life. Clearly, if we take the pressure off, the issue will disappear back into the closet. No matter how good the care gets, there still will be a need to have an assisted death as one choice. The better the care gets, the less that need will exist.

The pope and his minions in the Catholic Church, as well as the religious right, announce that assisted dying is part of the "culture of death." Murder,

---

* [The initiative to legalize physician aid in dying was narrowly defeated in a voter referendum in 2000.—Ed.]

lawlessness, suicide, the cheapening of life with killing in the media, the accessibility of guns, war—those create a culture of death, not providing help to a dying person who repeatedly requests an end to his or her suffering by a day or a week. Not all religious people believe that. The Rev. Bishop Spong of the Episcopal Diocese of Newark, N.J., said: "My personal creed asserts that every person is sacred. I see the holiness of life enhanced, not diminished, by letting people have a say in how they choose to die. Many of us want the moral and legal right to choose to die with our faculties intact, surrounded by those we love before we are reduced to breathing cadavers with no human dignity attached to our final days. Life must not be identified with the extension of biological existence. [Assisted suicide] is a life-affirming moral choice."

The Catholic belief that suicide is a sin which will cause a person to burn in hell is at the root of the well-financed, virulent opposition to physician aid in dying. This has resulted in expenditures of more than $10 million in losing efforts to defeat the two Oregon initiatives and a successful campaign to defeat the recent Michigan measure. And $6 million was spent in Michigan, most of which came from Catholic donors, to show four TV ads six weeks before voters saw the issue on the 1998 ballot. The ads never attacked the concept of physician aid in dying, but hammered on the well-crafted Proposal B. Surely that money could have been spent to protect life in better ways than to frustrate people who have come to terms with their deaths and want to move on. The arguments that life is sacred and that it is a gift from God rarely are heard now from the opposition. Most Americans do not want to be governed by religious beliefs they don't share, so the argument has shifted to "protection of the vulnerable and the slippery slope." Note, however, that the proposed death-with-dignity laws carefully are written to protect the vulnerable. The request for physician-assisted death must be voluntary, must be from a competent adult and must be documented and repeated during a waiting period. Two doctors must examine the patient and, if there is any question of depression or incompetence or coercion, a mental-health professional can be consulted. After that it must be up to the requester to mix and swallow the lethal medication. No one forces anyone to do anything!

The same arguments were raised in 1976 when the first "living-will" law was passed in California. It again was raised in 1990 when the Supreme Court ruled that every American has the right to refuse medical treatment, including food and hydration, and to designate a proxy to make those decisions if they cannot. This has not been a downhill slope in the last 22 years but an expansion of rights and choices. It has not led to abuse but rather to more freedom. Those who raise the specter of the Nazis must remember that we are in greater danger of having our freedoms limited by religious dogma than of having them expanded so that more choices are available. When the state dictates how the most intimate and personal choices will be made, based on how some religious groups think it should be, then we as individuals and as a country are in serious trouble.

One observer said about the Oregon Death With Dignity law: "This is a permissive law. It allows something. It requires nothing. It forbids nothing and taxes no one. It enhances freedom. It lets people do a little more of what they want without hurting anyone else. It removes a slight bit of the weight of government regulation and threat of punishment that hangs over all of us all the time if we step out of line."

Making physician aid in dying legal as a matter of public policy will accomplish several objectives. Right now we have a model of prohibition. There is an underground cadre of doctors—of whom Kevorkian is the tip of the iceberg—who are helping people die. The number varies, according to survey, from 6 to 16 percent to 20 to 53 percent. The 53 percent is for doctors in San Francisco who work with people with AIDS where networks for assisted dying have existed for many years. This practice is not regulated or reported; the criteria and methods used are unknown. There is some information that the majority of these deaths are done by lethal injection. Millions of viewers witnessed on *60 Minutes* the videotape of Kevorkian using this method to assist in the death of Thomas Youk. If the practice is regulated, there will be more uniformity, doctors will be able to and will have to obtain a second opinion and will have the option of having a mental-health professional consult on the case. Most importantly for patients, they will be able to talk about all their options openly with their health-care providers and their loved ones.

Another consequence is that desperately ill people will not have to resort to dying in a Michigan motel with Kevorkian's assistance, with a plastic bag on their heads, with a gun in their mouth or, worse, botching the job and winding up in worse shape and traumatizing their families. They won't have to die the way someone else wants them to die, rather than the way they choose. As Ronald Dworkin said in *Life's Dominion:* "Making someone die in a way others approve, but he believes a horrifying contradiction of his life, is a devastating, odious form of tyranny."

Rita L. Marker

 **NO**

Accepting Physician-Assisted Suicide Would Lead America Down a Cold, Cruel Path

Of all public controversies in recent years, assisted suicide perhaps is the one surrounded by the greatest degree of misunderstanding. For example, one often hears it referred to as the "right to die." Yes assisted suicide has nothing to do with letting someone die. Neither the law nor medical ethics requires that a person be kept alive by being subjected to unwanted medical treatment.

Furthermore, the debate isn't about the tragic, personal act of suicide, nor is it about attempted suicide. Neither suicide nor attempted suicide is considered a criminal act. Instead, the current debate is about whether public policy should be changed in a way that will transform prescriptions for poison into "medical treatment."

Oregon is the only place in the world with a specific law permitting assisted suicide. (Although widely practiced in the Netherlands, euthanasia and assisted suicide remain technically illegal in that country.) Unfortunately, there is no way to know of abuses, or even the number of deaths, occurring under the Oregon law, since failure to adhere to its reporting requirements is not penalized.

But we do know that in Oregon a doctor can write a prescription for drugs that are intended to kill the patient. When the prescription is filled, the pharmacist doesn't give the usual instructions about how to take it safely. Instead, a patient is more likely to hear, "Be sure to take all of these pills at one time—with a light snack or alcohol—to induce death." Directions center around making certain that the patient dies after taking the prescription.

The lethal drugs are covered by some Oregon health-insurance plans. They are paid for by the state Medicaid program under a funding category called "comfort care." (This certainly gives meaning to the statement, "All social engineering is preceded by verbal engineering.") Even though Oregon stands alone in approving such so-called comfort care, there is a full-court press to expand its legalization to every state. Already Hawaii's governor has vowed to propose legalization of both euthanasia as well as assisted suicide. A court challenge to Alaska's law prohibiting assisted suicide has been filed. Attempts to place the issue on the ballot have begun in several states. And, in virtually every state, there is a lawmaker who is drafting an assisted-suicide proposal.

Assisted-suicide activists expect many of these efforts to fail initially but count on their providing the opportunity for publicity. This publicity follows a rarely altered pattern. First, a "hard case" is spotlighted. This is accompanied by the assertion that assisted suicide was a necessary last resort. Assurances are made that the method and timing of death were freely chosen by the person (who is, conveniently, dead and thus unable to refute these claims). Finally, accusations are made that anyone who dares raise questions about such a demise lacks compassion and merely wants to force others to suffer.

It should be noted that many advocates of assisted suicide seriously believe that what they're proposing is a compassionate choice that should be available. However, despite their sincerity and good intent, it is the content, not the intent, of the policies and laws they espouse that ultimately will affect each and every person.

Whether other states embrace Oregon-style "comfort care" will depend upon a willingness to carefully examine what truly is at stake in this debate. This is, above all, a debate about public policy.

No matter what one's views may be about the concept of assisted suicide, it's necessary to reflect on the context in which it would be carried out. This reflection necessarily includes consideration of contemporary economic forces affecting health care. As acting solicitor general Walter Dellinger said during his 1997 argument against assisted suicide before the U.S. Supreme Court, "The least costly treatment for any illness is lethal medication." He was, of course, correct. A prescription for a deadly overdose runs about $35. Once taken, the patient won't consume any more health-care dollars.

Cost containment well could become the engine that pulls the legislative train along the track to death on demand. Those who advocate dismantling the barriers that now protect patients from assisted suicide recognize the power of cost containment. For example, Hemlock Society cofounder Derek Humphry recently explained his belief that, in the final analysis, economics will drive assisted suicide to the plateau of acceptable practice.

There's no question that economic considerations always have played a role in decisions about health care. Most of us can recall a time not long ago when patients routinely were subjected to unneeded tests and treatments. And we know now that money fueled these abuses. Then, health providers were reimbursed for everything they did to or for a patient.

Fortunately, patients and families became more aware of their rights to reject unwanted and unnecessary interventions. But the end to overtreatment didn't stem primarily from a respect for patients' rights. Instead, it grew out of changes in the way health care is reimbursed.

No longer do doctors and hospitals get paid for all they do. Instead, their incomes often depend upon how little they provide. And now, not surprisingly, the pendulum has swung to the other extreme, where more and more people (insured and uninsured alike) find it difficult, if not impossible, to get needed and wanted health care. Again, the fuel for change is money. The catalyst has been managed care.

Managed care has dominated health-care delivery in recent years. A significant number of health-maintenance organizations, or HMOs, are "for-profit" enterprises where stockholder benefit, not patient well-being, is the bottom line. Gatekeepers operate to protect resources by delaying or denying authorization for services.

Some programs have what are called "gag rules," which prohibit doctors from telling patients the whole truth about interventions that might be helpful. The stark words, "There's nothing that can be done" may really mean, "There's nothing more we'll pay for." But patients may not know that.

Imagine the patient who is in pain and is given the "nothing can be done" routine. Pain control definitely is given short shrift by many health plans. Some plans don't provide coverage for chronic pain except in very limited circumstances. Others put an unreasonably low cap on the amount paid for hospice care. (One Oregon insurer limits payment for hospice care to a $1,000 maximum.)

Navigating the murky health-insurance waters of services not covered, services not approved and the complex methods of copayments is particularly difficult for patients who are seriously ill and/or in pain. They have precious little energy to deal with a system that seems impenetrable.

Few people pay much attention to the particulars of their health-insurance coverage until they are ill. By then it may be too late. Assisted-suicide advocates assure us that a physician only would prescribe the lethal overdose after careful discussion with the patient.

To make this assertion represents the height of naïveté, if not disingenuousness. It's a presumption made by those relatively few people who have the luxury of a personal family physician who also may be a golfing or bridge partner. Having a physician friend who would talk over a planned assisted suicide before prescribing a lethal dose is nothing more than a fantasy for the vast majority of Americans.

Today most people are fortunate if they see the same doctor from visit to visit and, even when they do, time constraints exist. For example, some managed-care programs expect physicians to limit new-patient visits to 20 minutes and are told to devote no more than 10 minutes to a returning patient. Do we really believe that health plans that limit doctors' time in this manner would let doctors spend hours discussing the pros and cons of assisted suicide before prescribing the fatal dose?

Conflicts of interest also should be recognized. An obvious concern is the possibility that a physician could persuasively "offer" the option of assisted suicide to a patient whom the physician knows may pose the threat of a malpractice case. But there are more subtle, more likely, types of competing interests between physicians and patients. For instance, some health programs provide financial bonuses to doctors who conserve economic resources by withholding time or care from patients. It's reasonable to point out that this has the potential for conflicts of interest between patients and physicians.

Add to this the results of a survey published in 1998 in the *Archives of Internal Medicine*. It found that doctors who are the most thrifty when it comes to medical expenses would be six times more likely than their counterparts to provide a lethal prescription. These same doctors would be diagnosing, screening and counseling patients—and prescribing lethal drugs for assisted suicide.

Even in light of such concerns, activists favoring assisted suicide contend that the choice of assisted suicide should be available. Choice is meaningless, however, if there is only one affordable option. True, advocates of assisted suicide insist that every person, prior to receiving assisted suicide, would be offered all options. This appears protective. But there is a vast difference between an offer of something and the ability to accept that offer. This difference was acknowledged at a conference in which assisted-suicide guidelines, drafted by a San Francisco ethics committee, were under discussion. The guidelines stated that physicians had to offer palliative care (pain and symptom management) to patients before providing assisted suicide. However, when asked if there was also a mandate that patients have actual access to this care before being given a lethal prescription, the ethics-committee spokesperson replied that there was no such requirement.

Thus, the offer of all options is grossly misleading. It creates the illusion that all options would be available to people when, in fact, they would not. In theory, offering the choices between unaffordable palliative care and an affordable drug overdose is one thing. In practice, it takes little imagination to figure out which "choice" is really available. As attorney and consumer advocate Wesley Smith has said, "The last people to receive medical care will be the first to receive assisted suicide." If we embrace assisted suicide as medical treatment, it will return our embrace with a death grip that is cold, cruel and anything but compassionate.

POSTSCRIPT

Should Physician-Assisted Suicide Be Legalized by the States?

Even if we prove that there are particular cases in which it is true that physician-assisted suicide is appropriate for the situation, Marker is correct to remind us that a policy permitting physician-assisted suicide has to work in the real world (and not only in some idealized cases). In the real world there are financial constraints everywhere surrounding death. Physicians are under pressure to keep medical costs low, but, in addition, there is another, more subtle type of social influence operating here. Often, older people feel that they do not want to be a "burden" (their word) on their families. And the family members too may stand to inherit more money if the older one dies before incurring the cost of long-term medical treatment. Both of these (often unspoken) ideas may work together to encourage the "choice" of euthanasia. This is an issue where many find it difficult to distinguish what is in the best interests of both the patients and their families.

Relevant readings include Gerald Dworkin, R. G. Frey, and Sissela Bok, *Euthanasia and Physician-Assisted Suicide* (Cambridge University Press, 1998), which contains essays on both sides of the debate; Sheila McLean and Alison Britton, *The Case for Physician Assisted Suicide* (New York University Press, 1998); Linda L. Emanuel, ed., *Regulating How We Die: The Ethical, Medical, and Legal Issues Surrounding Physician-Assisted Suicide* (Harvard University Press, 1998); Lisa Yount, *Physician-Assisted Suicide and Euthanasia* (Facts on File, 2000); Margaret P. Battin, David Mayo, and Susan M. Wolf, eds., *Physician-Assisted Suicide: Pro and Con* (Rowman & Littlefield, 2001); Margaret A. Somerville, *Death Talk: The Case Against Euthanasia and Physician-Assisted Suicide* (McGill-Queen's University Press, 2001); Arthur J. Dyck, *When Killing Is Wrong: Physician-Assisted Suicide and the Courts* (Pilgrim Press, 2001); Raphael Cohen-Almagor, *The Right to Die With Dignity: An Argument in Ethics, Medicine, and Law* (Rutgers University Press, 2002); and Loretta M. Kopelman and Kenneth A. de Ville, eds., *Physician-Assisted Suicide* (Kluwer Academic Publishers, 2002).

Contributors to This Volume

EDITOR

STEPHEN SATRIS was born in New York City. He received a B.A. in philosophy from the University of California, Los Angeles, an M.A. in philosophy from the University of Hawaii at Manoa, and a Ph.D. in philosophy from Cambridge University, England. He has written on moral and philosophical issues for professional journals, and he is the author of *Ethical Emotivism* (Martinus Nijhoff, 1987). He has taught at several American universities, and he currently teaches philosophy at Clemson University in Clemson, South Carolina. Professor Satris is a former president of the South Carolina Society for Philosophy.

STAFF

Jeffrey L. Hahn   Vice President/Publisher
Theodore Knight   Managing Editor
David Brackley   Senior Developmental Editor
Juliana Gribbins   Developmental Editor
Rose Gleich   Permissions Assistant
Brenda S. Filley   Director of Production/Manufacturing
Julie Marsh   Project Editor
Juliana Arbo   Typesetting Supervisor
Richard Tietjen   Publishing Systems Manager
Charles Vitelli   Designer

AUTHORS

GEORGE J. ANNAS is the Edward R. Utley Professor of Law and Medicine at Boston University's Schools of Medicine and Public Health in Boston, Massachusetts. He is also director of Boston University's Law, Medicine, and Ethics Program and chair of the Department of Health Law. His publications include *Some Choice: Law, Medicine, and the Market* (Oxford University Press, 1998). He is the author of the forthcoming third edition of *The Rights of Patients* (Southern Illinois University Press, 2004).

JOHN ARTHUR is a philosopher at the State University of New York at Binghamton. He has published works on social, political, and legal philosophy.

ELIZABETH BIRCH is the executive director of the Human Rights Campaign, the nation's largest lesbian and gay political, social, and educational organization.

DAVID BOAZ is executive vice president of the Cato Institute. An expert on such issues as the failure of big government, the politics of the baby-boom generation, drug prohibition, and educational choice, he writes widely on these subjects and others for such publications as the *New York Times*, the *Washington Post*, and the *Wall Street Journal*. He is the author of *The Libertarian Reader: Classic and Contemporary Writings From Lao-Tzu to Milton Friedman* (Simon & Schuster Trade, 1998). His latest publication is *Toward Liberty* (Cato Institute, 2002).

MARK COSTANZO is a psychologist at Clarement McKenna College and serves on the editorial board of *Law and Human Behavior*. He is the author of *Just Revenge* (St. Martin's Press, 1997) and coauthor, with Stuart Oskamp, of *Violence and the Law* (Sage Publications, 1994).

DAVID T. COURTWRIGHT is a professor of history at the University of North Florida in Jacksonville, Florida. A member of the American Historical Association, his research focuses on drug use and American social history. His most recent publications are *Dark Paradise: A History of Opiate Addiction in America*, exp. ed. (Harvard University Press, 2001) and *Forces of Habit: Drugs and the Making of the Modern World* (Harvard University Press, 2001).

NICHOLAS DIXON is an associate professor of philosophy at Alma College in Alma, Michigan.

JANE ENGLISH (1947–1978) was a philosopher whose published work was primarily on feminism and social philosophy.

MICHAEL B. GILL is an assistant professor in the Department of Philosophy at the College of Charleston in South Carolina.

FAYE GIRSH is the senior vice president (and past president) of Hemlock Society USA, the nation's oldest and largest right-to-die society. She is a clinical and forensic psychologist and has published extensively in legal and psychological journals. Girsh has lectured and debated on various college and university campuses and has been interviewed on numerous television programs.

ALAN H. GOLDMAN is a professor of philosophy at the University of Miami in Coral Gables, Florida. He has published in the areas of epistemology, ethics, and aesthetics. Goldman is the author of *Aesthetic Value* (Westview Press, 1995), and his most recent book is *Practical Rules: When We Need Them and When We Don't* (Cambridge University Press, 2001).

MELVILLE J. HERSKOVITS (1895–1963) was a prominent American anthropologist who conducted field research in West Africa, sub-Saharan Africa, the Caribbean, and South America. He was the founding president of the African Studies Association.

RAE LANGTON is a philosopher at the University of Edinburgh in Scotland. She has taught at several universities, including Monash University in Australia and Sheffield University in England. Langton has lectured in several countries, including the United States, New Zealand, and Switzerland. She specializes in moral philosophy, the history of philosophy (especially Kant), and feminist philosophy. She is the author of *Kantian Humility: Our Ignorance of Things in Themselves* (Oxford University Press, 1998).

C. STEPHEN LAYMAN is a professor of the philosophy of religion and ethics in the Department of Philosophy at Seattle Pacific University in Seattle, Washington. He is the author of *The Shape of the Good: Christian Reflections on the Foundations of Ethics* (University of Notre Dame Press, 1991).

RITA L. MARKER is an attorney and the executive director of the International Anti-Euthanasia Task Force based in Steubenville, Ohio. She is the author of *Euthanasia: Killing or Caring* (Life Cycle Books, 1992) and *Deadly Compassion* (Morrow/Avon, 1995).

DON MARQUIS is a professor of philosophy at the University of Kansas in Lawrence, Kansas. He has written on issues in medical ethics.

JOE S. McILHANEY is an obstetrician/gynecologist. He is also president of the Medical Institute for Sexual Health, a nonprofit medical and educational research organization that he established in 1992 in Austin, Texas.

JOHN MIZZONI is a philosopher at Neumann College in Pennsylvania. His research focuses on environmental ethics and moral realism.

ALBERT G. MOSLEY, philosopher and musician, is currently at Smith College in Massachusetts. He is the editor of *African Philosophy: Selected Readings* (Pearson Education, 1995) and coauthor, with Nicholas Capaldi, of *Affirmative Action* (Rowman & Littlefied, 1996).

DEROY MURDOCK is a New York City–based columnist with Scripps Howard News Service, a senior fellow at the Atlas Economic Research Foundation in Fairfax, Virginia, and a television commentator.

JAY PARKER is president of the Lincoln Institute for Research and Education, a nonpartisan public policy organization in Washington, D.C. He is the editor of the *Lincoln Review* and president of the Abraham Lincoln Foundation for Public Policy Research.

LOUIS P. POJMAN is a professor of philosophy at the United States Military Academy. He is the author or editor of more than 20 books, including *What Can We Know?* (Wadsworth, 1995). He earned his Ph.D. from Oxford University, and he has been a Fulbright Fellow to the University of Copenhagen.

DANIEL D. POLSBY is associate dean for academic affairs and professor of law at George Mason University's School of Law. Polsby was on the faculty of Northwestern Law School for over 20 years, and for over 10 of those years he was the Kirkland & Ellis Professor of Law. In addition, he has held visiting appointments at the University of Southern California, the University of Michigan, and Cornell University. He has published widely in many areas of law, including voting rights, family law, employment rights, and gun control.

ELIZABETH POWERS is a writer living in New York City. She is coeditor of *Pilgrim Souls: An Anthology of Spiritual Autobiography* (Simon & Schuster, 1998).

VINCENT C. PUNZO is a professor in the Department of Philosophy at Saint Louis University in Saint Louis, Missouri. His specialties are ethics and political philosophy.

JAMIN B. RASKIN is a professor of constitutional law at American University in Washington, D.C. His books include *We the Students: Supreme Court Cases for and About Students* (CQ Press, 2000) and *Overruling Democracy: The Supreme Court Versus the American People* (Routledge, 2003).

JOHN A. ROBERTSON holds the Vinson and Elkins Chair at the University of Texas School of Law at Austin. He has written and lectured widely on law and bioethical issues. He is the author of *The Rights of the Critically Ill* (Ballinger Publishing Company, 1983) and *Children of Choice: Freedom and the New Reproductive Technologies* (Princeton University Press, 1994). He is also the author of numerous articles on reproductive rights, genetics, organ transplantation, and human experimentation. Robertson has served on or has been a consultant to many national bioethics advisory bodies and is currently chair of the Ethics Committee of the American Society for Reproductive Medicine.

MELISSA ROGERS, an attorney, is executive director of the Pew Forum on Religion and Public Life. She has written about religious liberty and has played an active role in legal matters that have an impact on religious freedom.

HOLMES ROLSTON III is an internationally known philosopher of the environment. He is University Distinguished Professor at Colorado State University in Fort Collins, Colorado. He has written extensively and lectured widely on the environment, science, and religion. His works have been translated into many languages.

DAVID J. ROTHMAN is Bernard Schoenberg Professor of Social Medicine, director of the Center for the Study of Society and Medicine at the Columbia College of Physicians and Surgeons, and a professor of history at Columbia

University. His publications include *Strangers at the Bedside: A History of How Law and Bioethics Transformed Medical Decision-Making* (Basic Books, 1991). Rothman holds particular interest in ethics, human rights, and medicine.

ROBERT M. SADE is a professor of surgery at the Medical University of South Carolina in Charleston.

RUTH SIDEL is a professor of sociology at Hunter College in New York City. She received an M.S.W. at the Boston University School of Social Work and a Ph.D. at Union Graduate School. Her publications include *Women and Children Last: The Plight of Poor Women in Affluent America* (Viking Penguin, 1987) and *On Her Own: Growing Up in the Shadow of the American Dream* (Viking, 1990). Her most recent book, *Keeping Women and Children Last: America's War on the Poor,* was published by Penguin Books in 1996. (A revised edition was printed in 1998).

RONALD J. SIDER is professor of theology at Eastern Baptist Theological Seminary in Pennsylvania. He is president of Evangelicals for Social Action and the author of over 20 books. Perhaps his most well-known work, now in its 4th edition, is *Rich Christians in an Age of Hunger* (Word Publishing, 1997).

NADINE STROSSEN has been president of the American Civil Liberties Union since 1991. She is also professor of law at New York University Law School. She has written hundreds of articles, lectured at college campuses throughout the United States, and has appeared on radio and television programs. Strossen is the author of *Defending Pornography: Free Speech, Sex, and the Fight for Women's Rights* (Scribner, 1995).

HEIDI ROLLAND UNRUH is a project analyst with Evangelicals for Social Action. She is coauthor of *Churches That Make a Difference: Reaching Your Community With Good News and Good Works* (Baker Book House, 2002).

ERNEST VAN DEN HAAG (1914–2002) was a distinguished lecturer at Columbia University, Yale University, and Harvard University. For many years he was John M. Olin Professor of Jurisprudence at Fordham University and also a scholar at the Heritage Foundation. Van den Haag was both a psychoanalyst and a criminologist. He is coauthor, with John P. Conrad, of *The Death Penalty: A Debate* (Plenum, 1983).

JAMES WAGONER is president of Advocates for Youth, a nonprofit organization promoting programs and policies that help young people make informed decisions about reproductive and sexual health.

RONALD WALTERS is a member of the faculty of the Department of Government and Politics and the Afro-American Studies Program at the University of Maryland in College Park. Additionally, he is a senior fellow and director of the African American Leadership Program at the University of Maryland's Academy of Leadership. He is the author of *Black Presidential Politics in America: A Strategic Approach* (State University of New York Press, 1988). He is coauthor of *Beyond the Boundaries: Reverend Jesse Jackson in Inter-*

national Affairs (State University of New York Press, 1997) and *African American Leadership* (State University of New York Press, 1999). He has appeared on numerous radio and television programs.

PAUL M. WEYRICH is president of the Washington-based Free Congress Foundation, a television talk-show host, a long-time conservative activist, and a cofounder of the Heritage Foundation.

Index

374